Wakefield Press

RED PROFESSOR

THE COLD WAR LIFE OF FRED ROSE

Peter Monteath teaches History in the School of International Studies at Flinders University in Adelaide, Australia. He is also a Fellow of the Alexander von Humboldt Foundation. He is the author of *POW: Australian Prisoners of War in Hitler's Reich* (PanMacmillan 2011). His most recent book with Wakefield Press is *Interned: Torrens Island 1914–1915* (2014).

Valerie Munt is an Adjunct Lecturer in History in the School of International Studies at Flinders University. She was born and educated in Adelaide, graduating with an Honours Degree in History and a PhD from Flinders University and a Masters degree in Education from the University of South Australia. She was tutor in Modern European History at Flinders University from 2005 to 2010. Her current research interests are in the history of Anthropology and the history of ideas.

RED PROFESSOR

THE COLD WAR LIFE OF FRED ROSE

PETER MONTEATH AND VALERIE MUNT

Wakefield
Press

Wakefield Press
16 Rose Street
Mile End
South Australia 5031
www.wakefieldpress.com.au

First published 2015

Edited by Julia Beaven, Wakefield Press
Text designed and typeset by Wakefield Press

National Library of Australia Cataloguing-in-Publication entry

Creator: Monteath, Peter, author.
Title: Red professor: the cold war life of Fred Rose /
                Peter Monteath and Valerie Munt.
ISBN: 978 1 74305 372 0 (paperback).
Notes: Includes bibliographical references and index.
Subjects: Rose, Frederick G.G. (Frederick George Godfrey),
                    1915–1991.
                Communists – Australia – Biography.
                Communists – Germany – Biography.
                Anthropologists – Australia – Biography.
                Anthropologists – Germany – Biography.
Other Creators/
Contributors: Munt, Valerie, author.
Dewey Number: 335.43092

Australian Government

Publication of this book was assisted by the Commonwealth Government through the Australia Council, its arts funding and advisory body.

Contents

Acknowledgements

This book has had a long gestation, longer than most. There were very many who gave advice along the way, and many attentive midwives present as the contractions intensified.

First and foremost we are deeply indebted to surviving members of Fred Rose's family, and in particular his daughters Sonja, Ruth and Nita, who have suffered our meddling in their family's history with exemplary forbearance. Without their support this biography would have suffered a still-birth. Above all we note the generosity of Ruth Struwe and her husband Rainer, who not only opened the doors of their home to strangers but facilitated access to a collection of words and images that helped us gain a much firmer grasp of Fred Rose's life than would otherwise have been conceivable.

As Fred Rose was long dead before we had even heard of him, we have relied hugely on the memories and the generosity of many who came to know Fred and who played greater or lesser roles in his life, whether in Australia, Germany or Rose's native England. For their generosity in recalling the life and times of Fred Rose we extend our sincerest thanks to Eric Aarons, Hans-Horst Bethge, Cathy Bloch, Eric Bogle, Anke Bornschein, Gordon Briscoe, Neville Cunningham, Ted Egan, Salomea Genin, Elena Govor, Günter Guhr, Ann Ikoku, Erika Karasek, Walter Kaufmann, Stefan Kurella, Esther Linde, Judy Maclean, Hannah Middleton, Ute Mohrmann, John Mulvaney, Nicolas Peterson, Lee Rhiannon, Deborah Bird Rose, Kathrin Rose-Dabrunz, Lothar Stein, Harald Struwe, Ursula Thiemer-Sachse, Bob Tonkinson, Mirna Tonkinson, David Turner, Victor Williams, Monika Wolf, Julia Worsley and Alan Wright.

When we began our research there was not so much as a Wikipedia article on Fred Rose, at least not on *our* Fred Rose. In hauling him from near-oblivion we were aided by the staff of numerous archives in libraries in Australia and Germany. Our thanks go to all of them. We would like to express our particular gratitude to Jim Andrighetti and Sarah Morley at the State Library of New South Wales, Marion Kretzschmar and Gerlinde Schade at the archive of the Agency of the Federal Commissioner for the Stasi Records in Berlin, Sylvia Gräfe at the Bundesarchiv in Berlin-Lichterfelde, Françoise Barr at the Northern Territory Archives Service, Dagmar Seemel at the Humboldt University Archive, Barry Cundy, Polly Mailau, Kylie Simpson and Russell Taylor at AIATSIS, and both Craig Brittain and Sita Austin at the Flinders University Library. Pamela Lynch in Canberra helped fill gaps in our records of the collection of the National Archives in Canberra. Keith Lambert, accompanied by Robert and Kenny, excelled in introducing us to the 'living archive' of today's Umbakumba and what remains of the flying boat base on Groote Eylandt. Last but by no means least, special thanks go to Martina Voigt of the Museum of German Resistance in Berlin, who not only helped us navigate our way through Stasi records but also helped piece together the remarkable history of the Linde family.

Not all were as helpful as they might have been. The relative transparency of records of espionage in Germany and Australia contrasted strikingly with the murky world of the CIA and the British Secret Service. Following their policy of 'neither confirm nor deny', representatives of both organisations consigned our queries to the Rumsfeldian domain of unknown unknowns.

As the life of Fred Rose at times took us outside our own intellectual comfort zones, we solicited advice from many scholars who helped us to understand, even if all too imperfectly, the worlds of twentieth century anthropology, espionage and politics. We are especially grateful to Des Ball, Lachlan Clohesy, Woodrow Denham, Brian Dickey, John Docker, Bill Edwards, Geoff Gray, Ben Hall, Philip Jones, Beate Kosmala, David McKnight, Humphrey McQueen, Ursula Rack, Tom Sheridan, Evan Smith, Peter Sutton, Martin Thomas, James Urry and Christine Winter.

Sadly not all who helped us have lived long enough to see the fruits of their labours. We hope we have done justice to their contributions. Before he died in 2009, Vladimir Kabo shared with us some of his recollections of Fred Rose. The late Arthur Easton introduced us to the vast, uncatalogued collection of Rose's papers in the State Library of New South Wales, while Coral Bell, who knew

Rose in Canberra in the late 1940s, shared her recollections of a fellow-public servant shortly before her death in 2012. The redoubtable Peter Worsley, who probably knew Fred Rose as a man and a scholar as well as anyone, died in 2013, having lavished us with practical advice and gratefully received moral support. Last but no means least, the late Geoff Curthoys shared with us his memories of Fred and the Australia they both knew so well.

Work on this book would not have been possible without financial support from Flinders University and the Alexander von Humboldt Foundation. It would not have become a book at all if not for Wakefield Press; in particular we would like to thank Michael Bollen for agreeing to publish the book, as well as Julia Beaven and Michael Deves for their labours in knocking it into shape.

Though their names are for the most part unknown, it would be remiss of us not to mention the contribution of the countless individuals who, in a professional capacity or otherwise, engaged in the dark art of passing on secrets. In the favoured expression of Fred Rose, who knew a thing or two about this topic from personal experience, these were the people who 'ratted'. We owe so much of our knowledge of Fred Rose to their unstinting, nefarious labours. Indeed, without them the history of the twentieth century would have been very different.

Last but not least, we thank our respective partners, Catherine Amis and Peter Munt, whose delight at the appearance of this book will be exceeded only by the relief that at last we need no longer discuss how it is coming along.

Peter Monteath and Valerie Munt

Prologue

A Night at the Opera

On a mid-summer's evening in East Berlin, a crowd began to gather at the state opera house in the city's showcase boulevard, Unter den Linden. *The Marriage of Figaro*, a tale of lustful scheming and marital infidelity, was on the bill. In the foyer an expectant and unusually cosmopolitan party of enthusiasts performed a round of introductions – in English, and with Australian accents.

The tallest member of the group needed no introduction, at least not to the eleven others around him. It was Gough Whitlam, and as this was the year 1976, he was leader of the opposition in Australia. For now, though, he was on the other side of the world, visiting the German Democratic Republic with his wife Margaret, and the evening was to be devoted to culture, not work. Both were avid opera goers.

If he was not reminding his interlocutors at the time, Whitlam was well aware that the person they all had to thank most for their presence in East Berlin and for the delights of the evening ahead was – him. Just three-and-a-half years earlier, when he was the freshly elected Prime Minister of Australia, one of his first and boldest acts of international diplomacy was to extend to the German Democratic Republic the diplomatic recognition he believed it deserved.

To add some local flavour to the evening, the Australian Ambassador Malcolm Morris had invited along the Roses, German-born Edith and English-born Fred. Both had lived for many years in Australia, but by now they had been residents of the GDR for over two decades. It was politics that had taken them there – both were communists. The Cambridge graduate Fred Rose had held a chair in anthropology at Berlin's Humboldt University for many years; in East Germany he was *the* expert on Australia.

An extraordinary coincidence connected the Roses and the Morrises. When Malcolm Morris as a fledgling diplomat served a stint in postwar Canberra, he and his family lived in a modest red-brick bungalow in the suburb of Turner. A daughter was born there. Not much later, with Morris beginning the series of postings which would eventually bring him via war-torn Saigon, Kabul and Vienna to East Berlin, the Roses moved into the very same house. To mark the coincidence, Rose presented the Morrises with a couple of photos of their former residence.

Whitlam knew enough of Fred Rose to greet him good-humouredly with *Genosse* – comrade – a common salutation in the GDR. He then joked that the seating arrangements from left to right reflected the full political spectrum. As the members of the party assumed their places in the auditorium's front row, it was Fred Rose who took the seat on the far left.

Erudite, energetic and witty, Rose was a fine choice of company for the Whitlams. He and Gough were of the same generation, born just a year apart during World War I; they had a host of shared interests, including Australian politics and Aboriginal land rights. There was much to discuss before the opera and in the interval as well. With more ground still to cover, the party adjourned to a café down the road in the *Palast der Republik*, the GDR's newly constructed, multi-function parliament house, for some *après-opera* refreshments and further conversation.

One of the topics of discussion that evening was Whitlam's dismissal as Prime Minister just a few months earlier. In cheerful deference to the German setting, Whitlam used a German word to describe his unseating – it had been a *Putsch*. Rose thought no differently, indeed he wondered why Whitlam had appointed John Kerr to the office of Governor-General in the first place. Depicted by the cartoonists of his day as a top-hatted flunkey to royalty, Kerr's role in Whitlam's demise had contained all the ingredients of a comic opera. Back as far as the 1950s, when Rose was on the payroll of the Waterside Workers Federation, he had known Kerr as a barrister working for the other side – the stevedores.

The conversation might well have led one member of the party, the junior diplomat Roger Pescott, to prick up his ears. Literally and metaphorically Pescott – later a Kennett government minister in Victoria – was placed well to the right of Rose, and he, too, knew Kerr. Had he not already committed himself to the East Berlin posting, he could have accepted Kerr's offer to join the Governor-General's personal staff just a year earlier. In the month after Labor's fall, as Pescott took an antipodean break from the unremitting bleakness of an East Berlin winter, he was summoned to Yarralumla. For some two hours Kerr held forth on why there had been no choice but to sack Whitlam.[1]

Fred Rose, too, had suffered grave misfortune at the hands of his political opponents in Australia. And although those events lay more than twenty years in the past, they still stuck in his craw and demanded a delayed debriefing in the presence of Whitlam. Over a period of several years before their departure from Australia, the Roses were held under surveillance by ASIO. Fred was accused of spying for the Soviets, his Froggatt Street home considered a hive of seditious communist activity. These were suspicions that first cost him his public service job, then led to him being hauled – twice – before Menzies' Royal Commission into Espionage. Rose believed himself hard done by, and he told Whitlam so.

The conversation turned in due course to other figures. There was Bob Hawke, president not just of the ACTU but also of the ALP at that time, and still, as was noted, 'on his Zionist line'. That was certainly not Rose's line, and Whitlam too wondered whether Hawke was backing the wrong horse as Australia's Arab population grew. Gordon Bryant was another who was well known to both men. Indeed he had led a parliamentary delegation to East Germany just the previous year. Rose knew him as a fervent advocate of Aboriginal land rights, and indeed his sympathy with indigenous Australians had helped land him the job of Minister for Aboriginal Affairs – until Whitlam sacked him just ten months into his tenure.

And there was another former Cabinet colleague of Whitlam in Kim Beazley Senior. Rose knew him from as far back as 1942, when Rose had joined the Communist Party of Australia. Whitlam was surprised to learn that Beazley had been a member of the same suburban branch in Perth as Rose. It did not sit easily with Beazley's post-war drift to the right-wing of

Labor politics – passing Whitlam on the way. It was, Whitlam thought, an interesting piece of information he might store for future use.

Not until after midnight did the group finally exit the *Palast* and disband. The diplomats returned to their residences, the Whitlams to their hotel, and the Roses to their apartment. It had been an altogether pleasant evening.

The Roses, it seems, never saw the Whitlams again. And yet the evening had a sequel of sorts. As he had already been doing for many years, Rose met with his Stasi handler a few days later.[2] He told him about everything of note that had been happening in his life since their last meeting, including that enjoyable – and informative – night at the opera. What kind of man would do that?

1. War Child

Around the time Fred Rose was conceived – in all likelihood in the bedroom of his parents' modest dwelling in south-west London – Europe teetered unwittingly on the brink of calamity. In a distant outpost of the Austro-Hungarian Empire, the Archduke Franz Ferdinand was assassinated by the Serb terrorist Gavrilo Princip. That single act of violence sparked a series of events which, weeks later, would lead to the outbreak of a war no-one wanted. A world was coming to an end, just as at 142 Strathyre Avenue Norbury a new life was being formed.

It would be a life lived in the shadow of the Chinese curse. The century of 'interesting times', heralded by those fateful gunshots ringing out through Sarajevo and then around the world, began with four years of bloodshed. Fred Rose was born with these cursed times, and he would die with them as well.

When he first glimpsed the light of day, on 22 March 1915, the full horror of the new age was dawning. Zeppelins were bombing Paris, and the *London Daily Mail* reported the disturbing news that SS *Batavier V* of the London to Rotterdam passenger line had been seized by a German submarine. Rumours of espionage and spy stories were daily fare in the press. By now Ottoman Turkey, too, had entered the fray, extending it beyond Europe. As the newborn drew his first breaths, British imperial forces were gathering for an ill-advised assault on their newest foe. When old enough to commit his first impression of the disintegrating world around him to memory, Rose recalled huddling beneath a solid dining room table, his back 'supported by one of its stalwart legs, sheltering from a German Zeppelin raid'.[1]

The war hit the Roses hard. Fred's mother Frances Isabel Godfrey was the eldest child of a close-knit family from Kennington, just south of the river Thames. Two of Frances Godfrey's brothers, Edward and Fred, were killed in the trenches. A third brother Henry (Harry) managed to survive the war and to migrate to Australia under the *War Service Settlement Scheme*. His news from Queensland was discussed eagerly in London and perhaps planted a seed in young Fred Rose's mind that he might one day follow in his uncle's wake.[2]

Fred's mother Frances was musically gifted, and her theatrical ambitions led to voice training in her youth. Her dreams of a stage career were dashed, however, on engagement to George Rose, who regarded the stage in the same light as prostitution. Undaunted, Frances maintained her interest in the theatre, and young Fred and his older sister Dora later took full advantage of her connections to get regular seats at operas, plays and concerts at London's Old Vic.[3] In keeping with the social traditions of London's 'East-enders', once married, Frances had almost nothing to do with her parents-in-law but regularly boarded the tram with her children to visit her own mother, unmarried sisters Edith, Dora and Dobbie and bachelor brother Fitzpatrick (Fitz), who lived together in cheerful domesticity on Kennington Park Road. Although baby Dobbie had been born well after her father's death, she was fully accepted by the family except her new brother-in law George, who took a dim view of her illegitimacy. Musical afternoons around the piano or cello were the usual order of the day when the Godfreys entertained.[4]

Fred Rose's father George was born in St Pancras, a notorious slum district north of the River Thames, but he was living in the suburb of Walworth when he met his wife-to-be. George Rose's father, also named George, had begun his working life as a humble labourer but soon pulled himself up by his bootstraps. Showing tenacity in evening class studies, he rapidly achieved the level then designated as 'engineer' and became a permanent worker on the Tower Bridge. He and Jessie shared a house in Henshaw Street with his brother William and unmarried sister Ethel. Fred's memories of his paternal grandparents were shadowy, and he did not recall them ever visiting their son's family home. A suggestion that

Fred's grandfather was something of a heavy drinker and domestic tyrant was perhaps reason enough for his daughter-in-law to keep her distance. Fred did, however, recall one visit from his father's cousin, an 'unkempt bus conductor'. The Roses considered this a most 'plebeian' occupation, with the result that he found no place in the bosom of the family.[5]

George Rose junior pursued the modest career of rate collector for the Town Hall in Walworth Road. Perhaps Fred's formidable maternal grandmother Caroline (Carrie) felt that her daughter Frances had 'married down', a suggestion painfully revealed by a retort that Frances made to her husband (in young Fred's hearing) that 'Carrie's relatives go back generations while yours disappear into the gutter after only two'. George seemed somewhat of an 'outsider' in his wife's family and perhaps almost envied the way his precocious young son shone in their domestic circle. Fred Rose's only clue to the allegedly 'superior' Godfrey genealogy lay in the antique family portraits that had been inherited by his mother on grandmother Carrie's demise. However, when he visited London several decades later – by now as an anthropologist with an abiding interest in kinship – no trace of them remained.[6]

If his parents were conventionally aspirational members of the lower middle class, Fred Rose later in life was more inclined to emphasise his family's social and geographical proximity to the working class. Perhaps this was the nostalgia of the mature Marxist searching for the source of his proletarian empathies. He came to regard the working-class London suburbs of Kennington and Walworth as his proverbial 'roots'. In reality, within five years of their marriage his parents were living in an outer suburb on the margin of middle-class metropolitan society, and they had few doubts as to where their next steps would lead. George Rose joined the Ebury Freemason's Lodge and Frances that bastion of the Conservative Party, the Primrose League.[7]

By 1925 the Roses' social ascent became even more conspicuous with the purchase of a new home. Only a street south of Strathyre Avenue, their new residence was a double-fronted detached house occupying two housing blocks, no longer in London but in Warwick Road, Thornton

Heath. Boasting an indoor and outdoor toilet, it had five bedrooms and large kitchen with separate scullery, pantry and washroom. It was an ideal setting for Frances to entertain her new friends at 'Mothers' Meetings', presided over by the vicar of St Stephen's. While tea, cakes and gossip were consumed in the parlour, the children were relegated to the kitchen. Young Fred would not be left out of the limelight for long. He duly shocked the Anglican ladies with a freshly caught mouse from the cupboard.[8]

After completing his primary education at Winterbourne Road Primary School, in 1926 Fred Rose began seven years of secondary schooling at Whitgift Middle School in Croydon. The most prestigious of the schools he might have attended with the aid of a scholarship was Whitgift Grammar, which would have gratified his father's ambitions, however this distinction fell to younger brother Don, much to his father's satisfaction. Fred's examination performance sufficed only for Whitgift Middle School.

At Whitgift Fred came to realise both his academic strengths and weaknesses. Chief among the latter was Latin, which, as with the learning of other languages, he regarded as a 'necessary evil'.[9] His strengths in mathematics and the natural sciences enabled him to pass the required public examinations with distinctions or honours. So at only fifteen he gained exemption from matriculation and could have commenced studies at the University of London. Although strong pressure was exerted by his father to become a secondary school teacher – a profession which required a university degree – Fred had no desire to teach; the very thought of remaining in 'the smug oppressive atmosphere of middle class life in the outer suburbs of London' filled him with dread.[10] If there was already a wedge between Fred and his father, the burning issue of Fred's chosen path in life drove it deeper. His mother, by contrast, remained close, the person to whom he could always turn to 'weep my sad bosom empty' after conflicts with his controlling father.[11]

Fred may have disappointed his father, but his schoolmasters knew they were dealing with a youth of considerable intellect, unafraid to speak his mind. An early incident at Whitgift Middle School illustrated these qualities. A hapless school inspector, presiding over a history lesson on the subject of Anglo-French rivalry in North America, mistakenly lauded the cooperation between General Wolfe and Admiral Nelson, when young Rose boldly informed him that he must be mistaken; Wolfe had been killed in action in 1759 and Nelson at the Battle of Trafalgar in 1805. Both the class and unfortunate inspector were shocked by Rose's temerity. Nevertheless he was handsomely rewarded by a public acknowledgement from the inspector at the following school assembly and the unexpected presentation of a book aptly dedicated with a cricket metaphor: 'Middle-stump, 11//3/1926, F.O. Mann, Inspector of Schools.'[12]

Rose privately concluded that he was 'more or less predestined to go to university studies in sciences'.[13] It was a view shared by his teachers, one of whom enthusiastically extolled his qualities as 'a keen student and an exceptionally hard worker' with 'an attractive personality and a pleasant carriage and appearance'. In Rose he detected 'great keenness and powers of leadership, with which he combines tact and sound judgment'.[14] London University was certainly an option, since his deficiencies in Latin were no obstacle to taking a science course there. Brighter possibilities were Oxford and Cambridge, which did, however, present impediments. One was financial – to study away from home at either institution meant expenses far beyond the family's means. Moreover, he could commence such studies only after reaching the age of eighteen. Additionally, there was the obstacle of Latin, a compulsory subject for matriculation at both of those august institutions.

In 1932, when Rose first sat for a prized state scholarship – his only chance of gaining the necessary funds for studies at Oxbridge – he was unsuccessful, despite three distinctions in science subjects. He chose to sit again the following year. Having finished school he prepared himself not in class but under the general supervision of his science masters, with the result that he read much further than the syllabus into chemistry, physics and mathematics. This time he passed with flying colours, earning the coveted scholarship that would cover the costs of study.[15] He was granted an Open Exhibition in sciences at St Catharine's College, and when he miraculously fluked a pass in Latin on his fifth attempt, his last hurdle on the road to Cambridge was cleared.[16]

Rose's parents had every reason to be proud as their son prepared to take his place among England's budding elite. Yet the timing coincided with a rupture in the relationship between Fred and his father George which would never be repaired. While Fred was away from London sitting an exam, his brother Don fell ill and died of typhoid fever, as Fred discovered to his horror on his return. His father, who adored Don, was 'absolutely distraught'. When Fred confessed some misgivings about his exam performance, his grief-stricken father 'launched into a tirade of abuse telling me that I had deliberately done badly to spite him and then incredibly accused me of killing my brother'. George Rose openly mourned the loss of his 'better son', the exemplary student who had been dux of his class, and whose athletic prowess had earned him a place in his school's Second XV rugby team at the age of just thirteen.[17]

With Don's early death, his image could never be tarnished. Fred, already convinced when Don was alive that his younger brother was the favoured son, could never compete with a memory frozen in time. The prospect of moving to Cambridge was now much more than an opportunity for Fred to develop a keen intellect. It was a release from the 'oppressive domination' of his father and a welcome escape from the cheerlessness of suburban London.[18]

2. Red Cambridge

In October 1933 Frederick Rose entered the ancient bastion of learning, Cambridge University, to read natural science and mathematics – subjects that had been the university's forte since the time of Sir Isaac Newton. Rose, however, had much more on his mind than his chosen subjects. Enrolled in St Catharine's College, for the first time in his life he encountered a group of young people who were not only fiercely intelligent, but also emotionally and ideologically committed to political change. With the Great Depression wreaking havoc on the global economy, and with Hitler and Mussolini already in control in Germany and Italy, Rose's Cambridge cohort set its gaze beyond the ivy-clad halls of learning. This was 'Red Cambridge'.

The atmosphere of the times was well captured by Kenneth Sinclair-Loutit, a Trinity College student and, by chance, a friend of spy-to-be Kim Philby: 'University undergraduates, themselves then mostly the children of prosperous families, were starting to have their consciences troubled by the plight of Hunger-Marchers and of those who, by the Means Test, were forced to sell their possessions before they could obtain the meagre dole payments.' For so many students of this generation, Cambridge brought with it a political awakening, and Sinclair-Loutit was dragged from the 'cosy shelter' of his Cornish life.[1] The charismatic young poet and communist John Cornford, born in the same year as Rose, was one of the poster boys of this student generation. He cut a handsome figure around Cambridge, though dressed in ragged trousers to emphasise his solidarity with the workers.[2] Soon he would sacrifice his life in the great symbolic battle of the times, the Spanish Civil War, killed on his twenty-first birthday.

Much of this was alien to Fred Rose. Suburban London was exposed to the troubles of those times much more than provincial Cambridge, but Rose was far from politicised when he entered university. Like many undergraduates, he was instinctively but apathetically conservative in his outlook. He had been exposed only to his parents' unswervingly Tory views, which accorded with their middle-class aspirations. Frances Rose harboured ambitions that her son would one day gain life membership of the Conservative Party. Little did she know how things had changed around the quadrangles of Cambridge. For what Eric Hobsbawm labelled 'the reddest and most radical generation in the history of the university', not only did conservatism fail to address the pressing issues of the day, but democracy as these young women and men knew it was not up to the challenge.[3]

Rose's conservative inclinations were not the only impediment to him finding favour with Cambridge's political avant-garde. His efforts to assimilate confronted a seemingly intractable problem. His south London accent made him stand out as a 'scholarship boy' in an enclave of wealth and privilege. He had always been the darling of the theatrical women in his mother's London circle, but the bright, politically astute young women at Cambridge were altogether different.

One of the most radical was Margot Heinemann. The daughter of a German Jewish banker who supported the Labour Party, she had won a scholarship to Newnham College, where she became intensely interested in left-wing politics. In 1935 she fell in love with Cornford after they met within the ranks of the Communist Party of Great Britain, the CPGB.[4] At first Heinemann almost disdained speaking to Fred Rose when he expressed his homespun conservative views, but in 1934 she encouraged him to visit the unemployed miners in the Rhondda Valley with members of the Cambridge University Labour Club.[5] He took away lasting memories of 'haggard unemployed miners and their wives and the miserable diet on which they lived'.[6]

Later that year Rose experienced an unemployed men's camp at Consett in County Durham, the heart of the coal-mining district, an important centre for the iron and steel industry, and, like the Rhondda Valley, devastated by the Great Depression. Many of these men later joined the

Hunger Marches to London. Rose was struck by the palpable 'class barrier' between the unemployed men and the Cambridge students responsible for running the camp. These were students from wealthy families who arrived at Consett in their own expensive cars. By his admission Rose was still 'a political babe in the wood', yet subconsciously an irreversible questioning of his values had been set in motion.[7]

While the Cambridge years led Rose to reflect on the values he had absorbed unquestioningly in his youth, he was not moved to join any party, though he mixed with a number of Cambridge communists apart from Heinemann and Cornford. One was the dashing Ceylonese student Pieter Keuneman, who later married activist Hedi Stadlen.[8] A figure of some social prominence in his college, Pembroke, and beyond, Keuneman served stints as president of the Cambridge Union and editor of the magazine *Granta*. At that time he was one of the university's WOGS – 'Western Orientalised Gentlemen' – though Rose came to wonder whether 'gentleman' quite fitted Keuneman, already a searing critic of the British Raj. Then there was Oskar Spate, the distinguished geographer who flirted with communism during his time at Cambridge, and with whom Rose shared a geography tutor.[9]

Rose's college, St Catharine's, was well into its fifth century, yet it was one of the humbler Cambridge colleges. With its open courtyard it was a distinctive landmark in central Cambridge, not far from King's. Rose found the freedom of living away from home and the students' casual meetings and luncheons in each other's rooms exhilarating. They would often stroll into town for coffee between lectures or take in a foreign film. He took up smoking and developed a taste for cigars, considered to be *de rigueur* for, as he put it ironically, 'those who aspired to be heroes'.[10]

The stumbling blocks of his accent and politics were soon overcome. Sport, he found, was a great entrée into Cambridge's social life. He occasionally missed lectures and practicum classes to play rugby, which he did with great enthusiasm. Tall and thin by build, he was ill-suited to his place in the second row, yet he played at every opportunity, on occasions even breaking into the college's First XV.

His diffidence with women, too, evaporated. Keen to meet female students, Rose invited Elisabeth Powys Fowler to dances at Cambridge hotels. He showed a particular interest in the daughter of a Church of England parish priest, offering to attend a service with her in the college chapel. She coldly refused, with the assurance that she had no interest in religion, thenceforth their contact dwindled to coffee between lectures and browsing in bookshops. He had arrived at Cambridge as an eighteen-year-old virgin, and sex was a subject never mentioned at home. His father's puritanical attitude once brought a discussion between his mother and aunt on the plays of Oscar Wilde to an abrupt halt when he entered the room. At Cambridge, attitudes to sex were decidedly liberal; even homosexuality was not concealed.

Amid the plethora of social distractions, Rose attended a few lectures in physics and chemistry, but was more assiduous in attending lectures in a discipline in which he acquired a new interest – geology. From 1935 one of the lecturers was Fritz Loewe, a German internationally renowned for his participation in 1929 in an expedition to the Greenland ice cap. He had returned with some acclaim, his toes lost to frostbite. Nazi Germany had no place for Jewish heroes, so an offer to teach at Cambridge probably saved Loewe's life. Two years later he would be in Melbourne, where he would find Fred Rose among his students, and where Vice-Chancellor Raymond Priestley praised 'his really fine attitude to a world which has deprived him of all his toes, of his livelihood, and of his country'.[11]

The Christmas recess in 1934 saw Rose return to the bosom of the family, as always, deeply ambivalent. His relationship with his father remained one of 'armed neutrality'. Despite his mother's concern, for it was mid-winter, to escape the oppressive domestic atmosphere on Boxing Day, Rose set out to hike back to Cambridge, ten days before the start of term.[12]

To fill in time, he first struck out in a north-westerly direction, taking in the bucolic scenery. Then he turned eastward toward Cambridge, following a route that required stopping at two hostels a couple of days apart. At each of them extraordinary, even life-changing, events occurred. At Hemel Hempstead he encountered the sexual advances of the young housekeeper when her husband left for work. Rose was unmoved as she ran her fingers through his hair, his hiking schedule foremost on his mind. When she briefly left the room he made an abrupt departure, but during the next two days on the road he pondered over his reaction to the housekeeper and its significance for what he called 'the more general question of his relationship to women'.[13]

The next stop at Saffron Walden provided a more auspicious encounter. Saffron Walden was a market town with longstanding Quaker connections.[14] At Illawarra, a youth hostel run by a couple of Quaker women, Rose was immediately attracted to the quiet German *au pair* Edith Linde. Her dignified demeanour and unadorned beauty, accentuated by simply styled hair drawn back from her face into a neat bun on the nape of her neck, gave an impression of order and composure that impressed the young undergraduate. He was elated that evening to find Edith at the table shared by his elderly hostesses. He effortlessly charmed the two older ladies, though Edith later confessed she had found his conversation boring. Nonetheless, for the first time Fred Rose had fallen in love, and despite Edith's initial coolness he was determined to see her again.[15]

It took a mere three hours to hike to Saffron Walden from Cambridge. Rose made fortnightly visits to pursue his courtship under the 'eagle eyes' of the two elderly chaperones at the hostel. His persistence succeeded, and though there was no intimacy between them, Edith was prepared at least to see him, and they spent many hours talking. Rose was able to discuss openly with a woman of his age political issues and world affairs about which, it soon became clear, she was extremely well informed and held firm views. In matters of sexual politics, too, there was a good deal upon which they agreed. Rose had adopted enlightened views concerning equality of the sexes and the role of women in society. He had seen women in his own family pursue economic independence and their own social interests and saw no reason why women should be discriminated against in either academia or the domestic sphere.

Edith had strong views on issues of race. Though not Jewish herself, she frequently articulated her loathing of anti-Semitism and reported her experience of it in Germany. She also made it clear that she considered it a menace in Britain, too, and on one occasion travelled into London, with Rose, to register her disapproval of a march staged by Oswald Mosley's Blackshirts. Together they witnessed the clash between the fascists and their opponents. For him it was 'a complete eye-opener' and 'the beginning of a change in my political orientation'.[16] His awareness of his father's anti-Semitism served only to confirm his newly won insights.

In fact, Edith was in England for political reasons. Her progressively inclined lawyer father Richard Linde was deeply concerned about the course Adolf Hitler was steering in the 'New' Germany. Linde had sent Edith to the progressive Luisen-Mädchenschule in central Berlin, where she counted many Jews among her fellow students and the Quaker Elisabeth Abegg among the teachers. After school her intention was to study science at university, but her strict refusal to join a Nazi youth group scotched that plan.[17] With her prospects of receiving further education in Germany curtailed, Edith was sent to England to prepare for study there. Her father had tapped into his wide-ranging British and Quaker connections to get Edith the *au pair* job in Saffron Walden, and with it the chance to become fluent in English and prepare to study physics at a British university. She and her anglophile father were politically of one, fervently anti-fascist mind.

In time Fred and Edith became lovers, but when she moved to the outer London suburb of Kingston, he could see her only if he made an expensive journey to the capital by train. Worse was to follow. In 1935 Hitler decreed that all foreign currency earned outside Germany must be brought back to Germany. A year later, Edith Linde returned home to Berlin.

Edith's German world was not a complete mystery to Rose. In 1934 he and his friend at St Catharine's, 'Tommy Tucker' (Theodore Lake), had embarked on a six-week cycling adventure across Europe that had taken them deep into Hitler's Reich. He was in the Rhineland on the 'Night of the Long Knives', and in a small town he witnessed the euphoria of the crowds as the Hitler Youth leader Baldur von Schirach was driven through the streets in an open vehicle, his hand raised in a Nazi salute. Rose was still a political naïf with a decidedly phlegmatic English temperament, but he was taken aback at this flagrant display of Teutonic bad taste.[18]

In the following year Rose and Tommy Tucker craved a new continental adventure, hoping to impress their fellow students and Rose's new love. Edith had told Rose about the dire situation for Jews in Nazi Germany and had given him names of some of her friends as well as her father's address in Berlin. Moreover, word had passed around Cambridge about a student organisation set up to assist Jews in smuggling money or valuables out of Germany. One of the locations where this activity was occurring, it seems, was Mainz, not far from the border with France, and it was here that the heroism of the two young adventurers was tested.

The prelude to that test occurred when they stopped for coffee in the Metz railway station, Union Jacks fluttering from their handlebars. Jean, a Frenchman, engaged them in English conversation and enlightened them about the Germans' maltreatment of Jews. He then made them an offer of monetary assistance that, he claimed, would benefit not only them but German Jews as well. Should they accept a simple mission, they would be able to finance a few more days of holiday in Germany with clear consciences.

The German government allowed the purchase of 'Tourist Marks' outside Germany aiming to promote tourism in Germany, but also boosting reserves of foreign currency to support the German rearmament program. The plan put to Rose and Tommy was to buy German tourist cheques in Metz, cross the border and cash the cheques at a bank in Germany, and then hand the cash to Jean, who would provide the lads with a daily allowance and keep the rest. This, according to Jean, would be used to assist German Jews to escape the country.[19]

The system seemed to be working until the third day. As the young Englishmen left a bank in Mainz with their cash, they were confronted by a German official in civilian clothes who detained them for questioning and conveyed them to the local prison. Following fifteen days of detention and a fine of 800 marks, paid reluctantly by George Rose, the young 'heroes' were released. They had daringly filched proof of their adventure – a monogrammed prison towel and Nazi prison garb – and returned home proud of their bold efforts to assist the Jewish cause. In Rose's considered judgment, formed many years later, the spell in a Mainz gaol was a watershed in his political development.[20]

In May of that year Rose sat for his natural science Tripos part one, with examinations in physics, chemistry and geology. Disappointed at achieving the Upper Second and not the First Class Honours he felt were his due, and daunted by the prospect of more rote learning in geology, Rose considered studying anthropology for his final year.[21] He would have to study hard to cover the two-year syllabus in one year for the final examinations in May 1936, but it was a challenge he accepted.

The almost legendary Alfred Cort Haddon had inspired him. Initially a biologist, A.C. Haddon had turned to anthropology and made an international reputation for himself, above all on the basis of his prominent role in the Cambridge Anthropological Expedition to the Torres Strait in 1898–99. By the time Rose came to know him in Cambridge, Haddon was an octogenarian, retired a full decade. Nonetheless, he remained a significant and influential public intellectual, as Rose discovered when Haddon spoke on his latest book *We Europeans*.[22] Co-authored with Julian Huxley and A.M. Saunders, the book was in Rose's judgment a 'damning scientific and political criticism of Nazi anti-Semitism . . . [and a critique of] the racism implicit in the United States of America's immigration laws'. It confirmed much that Rose had witnessed and that Edith Linde had reported about the plight of Jews in Germany. Rose was bold enough to ask Haddon what German intellectuals should do to combat anti-Semitism and racism, to which Haddon replied darkly, 'I fear they'll do nothing.'[23]

Haddon's influence on Rose was profound, although Haddon had no teaching role. Rose studied anthropology under J.H. Hutton, a former civil servant and ethnographer in India, and T.C. Hodson, who was attached to St Catharine's, where he had rooms for tutoring. The task these men were assigned was identical with that given to academic anthropologists at that time throughout the British Empire, including Australia, namely to train a generation of colonial public servants.[24] As a scholarly discipline at Cambridge, despite all the efforts and achievements of Haddon, anthropology was at best marginal, at worst a 'disaster'.[25]

Cambridge's deficiencies were especially glaring in regard to Australia. Rose received a general grounding in physical anthropology, archaeology and prehistory, material culture and selected geographical areas. But as preparation for a specialised interest in Australian anthropology Cambridge offered next to nothing – there were no lectures on Australia, or even Oceania.[26] Rose's fascination was not triggered by his Cambridge teachers but by the enigmatic Polish anthropologist Bronisław Malinowski, who was included on the Cambridge reading list but not the syllabus.

Malinowski's institutional base was the London School of Economics. His groundbreaking classic *Argonauts of the Western Pacific* created a paradigm shift in British anthropology.[27] Rose read *Argonauts* with fascination and immediately became, as he later put it, an 'uncritical adherent' of Malinowski's approach.[28] Malinowski's book was about the Trobriand people who lived on a small chain of islands north-east of New Guinea, not about Australia.[29] As Rose contemplated how he might make his own mark in anthropology, he struck upon a strategy whereby he could combine Malinowski's new fieldwork methodology with a journey to distant Australia, where, as he learned from Haddon, there was still much work to be done 'before it was too late'. As Rose put it with characteristic self-belief, 'If Haddon was right in what he had told me, I could do the same [as Malinowski] for some groups of the Australian Aborigines'.[30]

Rose's new-found passion for anthropology buoyed him through preparations for the archaeological and anthropological Tripos in May 1936. This time he was 'well satisfied' with his results, having gained Second Class Honours in the First Division. Hodson was sufficiently impressed to suggest he might read for a doctor's degree. Rose knew that under Hodson's supervision he would inevitably have to specialise in India, a prospect that held no attraction for him.[31] His sights were firmly set on Australia.

Rose had imbibed the atmosphere of 'Red Cambridge'; he had been touched by exposure to the human damage wrought by the Depression, and had been alerted to the dangers of fascism and the inequities of the British class system. Politically, like so many of his generation, his thinking had drifted to the left, but at this time it does not seem to have gelled into anything more tangible than a vague sympathy with the millions whose lives were ravaged by the failings of capitalism or the evils of fascism.

The seductive powers of hindsight might prompt speculation as to whether at Cambridge Fred Rose joined the ranks of those whose loathing of fascism led them to engage in espionage for the Soviet Union.[32] Yet there is nothing that connects Rose directly with the 'Cambridge Four' – Kim Philby, Guy Burgess, Donald Maclean and Anthony Blunt – even though all were students at Cambridge in the 1930s.[33] When he left Cambridge in 1936, Fred Rose was certainly not the innocent who had enrolled three years earlier, but there is no evidence that he was a spy. At least not yet.

3. Australia: First Contact

After graduating from Cambridge in the middle of 1936, Rose worked as an analytical chemist in the Telegraph Construction Company in Greenwich to scrape together enough money for a one-way fare to Australia. His dream was to make a name for himself as an anthropologist, but beyond that the details were few and the need for resourcefulness correspondingly large. By Christmas, with help from his mother's savings, he had the £37 required for a passage on the SS *Rotorua,* departing London on 7 January 1937.

Before he left, he and Edith had arranged via airmail to spend a secret New Year's Eve together in Brussels. But when the *Rotorua* steamed out of the London docks at midnight in drizzling rain, the only person who came to bid Rose farewell was his sister's friend Rosa Davis. With Fred still not on speaking terms with his father after his hair-raising escapade in Mainz, the family had been told to stay at home.[1] The crossing of the equator, marked in the usual way by partying on deck and a severe case of sunburn, also ended a phase in Frederick Rose's life. He would never again call England home.

After a two-week stopover in New Zealand, Rose disembarked from the *Wonganella* on an overcast Sydney day in April 1937. His only possessions were a suitcase and a second-hand trunk from a pawnshop in Brixton Hill. Its original initials had been erased and replaced with 'F.G.G.R.'. His mother had supervised the packing and included a three-piece double-breasted suit, a dinner jacket and evening dress suits with corresponding waistcoats, dress shirts and ties, all of which were untouched two decades later. The few books Rose brought to Australia were a curious collection for a budding anthropologist: a three volume edition of Tolstoy's *War and Peace, The Week-End Book* and the complete *Poems of Today,* a gift from Rosa

Davis for his 21st birthday that he retained throughout his 'lifetime of peregrinations'.[2] He had been warned that Australians were quite 'uncouth and uncultured and only interested in material items', suspicions that appeared to be confirmed by the dockers working on Sydney's wharves. An exceptionally tough-looking group, their broad Australian accents rendered them almost incomprehensible.[3]

These first impressions of Australia were strengthened on arrival at his hotel in Kings Cross. The Great Depression had visibly demoralised the city, bringing record unemployment and bouts of civil unrest. Troubled times found expression in the politics of the day, too. On one end of the spectrum there was a Communist Party of Australia, the CPA, founded in the aftermath of the Great War. On the other an ultra right-wing movement called the New Guard flourished. It was said to have over 50,000 members within Sydney alone. Like Oswald Mosley's Blackshirts in London, the organisation's activities rapidly descended into street violence and thuggery.

During the depressed 1930s Sydney's Domain had rapidly become a shantytown for the unemployed, and as described by Simon Bracegirdle – a contemporary observer and later friend of Fred Rose's – it also became the Sunday equivalent of Speakers' Corner in London's Hyde Park. Political subjects ranged from the Single Tax League to Karl Marx, 'while in the nearby rooms of the Friends of the Soviet Union, Professor Frank Cotton gave lectures on his visits to the Soviet Union'. For the unemployed, 'dole tickets could be exchanged for a two course meal for five pence at the Bridge Café' or a more 'up-market three course meal at the nearby Brigade café'.[4] Bracegirdle describes a bohemian Kings Cross, where 'knockabout' identities Peter Finch and Chips Rafferty entertained the locals. Finch, who had married a ballerina from a visiting Russian ballet company, gave 'a moving recital of Engels' speech at Marx's funeral to a large Communist Party gathering'.[5]

For several weeks Rose stayed in Surry Hills with two elderly White Russian women who had fled to Australia in the wake of the Bolshevik Revolution. Although they were probably politically right wing, according to Rose they were 'prepared to collaborate' and were avid readers of 'progressive journals' and possibly subversive material from the Australia–Soviet Friendship Society and the Communist Party Bookshop.[6] Rose was not averse to acquainting himself with 'progressive' developments in the Soviet Union, and he too became a keen reader.[7] However his immediate concerns were more mundane – he was running out of money. He found work as a physicist in the Amalgamated Wireless Australasia factory, then left to work as a chemist in Fitwell Products, a smaller factory closer to his new lodgings, a rented room in Railway Terrace, Lewisham.[8]

Rose lost no time in paying a visit to Adolphus Peter (A.P.) Elkin, Professor of Anthropology at the University of Sydney. At that time, and for many years to come, Elkin was the doyen and puppetmaster of Australian anthropology. If Rose were to have a future in the discipline in Australia, he would need Elkin's support.

Although Elkin was among the first of the professional anthropologists in Australia, he stood in a tradition that reached back to the previous century, when anthropology was commonly the domain of enthusiastic amateurs. One of them was the senior Victorian public servant Alfred William Howitt, who had corresponded with Lewis Henry Morgan, father of American anthropology.[9] Together with Lorimer Fison, a missionary anthropologist in Fiji, Howitt in 1880 had written the book *Kamilaroi and Kurnai*, which became something of a nineteenth-century classic.[10] The University of Melbourne's Foundation Professor of Biology, a brilliant young Oxford graduate named Baldwin Spencer, similarly had achieved international fame through his collaboration with the Irish postmaster Francis James Gillen in the study of *Native Tribes of Central Australia* (1899), *The Northern Tribes of Central Australia* (1904) and *The Native Tribes of the Northern Territory* (1914).[11] Research conducted among the Aranda and Loritja people of Central Australia by the German missionary pastor Carl Strehlow had led to the publication of seven important and influential volumes.[12]

By Rose's time the discipline rested on firmer institutional foundations; a new generation of anthropologists was shaping attitudes and applying different approaches to fieldwork. Whereas the study of totemism inspired by James Frazer[13] had been the main preoccupation of Spencer and Gillen, a British fieldworker named Alfred Reginald Brown (later Radcliffe-Brown) arrived in Western Australia in 1911 trained in a 'scientific' approach developed by his mentor W.H.R. Rivers. This was the 'genealogical method', with which Brown mapped the kinship connections of the Aborigines imprisoned on Bernier Island and then across the country, leading to the publication in 1930 of *The Social Organization of the Australian Tribes*.[14] Considered a triumph of 'scientific' inquiry at the time, while acknowledging the central place of kinship in Aboriginal society, Radcliffe-Brown failed to connect this to the cruelty of the isolation that his Aboriginal informants suffered from being imprisoned on Bernier Island and the growing practice of removing 'half-caste' children from their parents.[15] Nonetheless, when anthropology established its foothold in the academy in Australia – the first department was established in Sydney in 1925 – it was Radcliffe-Brown who became the foundation Professor of Anthropology in Sydney.

He did not last long there, abandoning Sydney for Chicago in 1931.[16] But before departing, Radcliffe-Brown gave the career of his successor Elkin a crucial boost by helping him secure Rockefeller Foundation funding to undertake fieldwork in the Kimberley in Western Australia. Elkin became lecturer-in-charge of the department and, soon, professor; he also took over from Radcliffe-Brown the editorship of Australia's flagship anthropology journal *Oceania* and chaired the Australian National Research Council's anthropological committee.[17]

Elkin ruled his domain with a firm hand. An Anglican minister by background, he was an unlikely incumbent, given that the primary rationale for establishing the discipline had been to train officers for service in Australia's own recently acquired colonial empire. New Guinea, not Australia, was to be the primary focus of academic endeavours. As for methodology, the study of kinship was the central pillar of the discipline; indeed, it became 'what logic is to philosophy or the nude is to art'.[18] Australian and British social anthropologists of the day were preoccupied with it, and Fred Rose was no exception.

The initial signals in Sydney augured well for Rose, who later recalled Elkin suggesting that 'he would probably be able to get some kind of a job in the university'.[19] As a first test of observing kinship practices in the field, Elkin suggested Rose visit the Aboriginal settlement reserve at La Perouse on Botany Bay. The trouble was that at this time there were few Aborigines living in Sydney, and fewer living in circumstances even vaguely resembling traditional communities. Rose found those he encountered around Botany Bay a 'very depressed group', far from what he envisaged for his studies. If he were to observe Aborigines still living in 'pristine' situations, then this would need to be done far from Sydney, and, as he believed, sooner rather than later.[20]

The communities best suited to Rose's purposes were in the tropical north. He needed to be able to travel there and remain for a sustained period. The plan he devised was to become a meteorologist, and to have himself posted to a location in the far north, where the expansion of the aviation industry would give him every chance of employment. If successful, he would be able to live in the immediate vicinity of indigenous communities and receive a regular income to support whatever fieldwork he could manage during his leisure.

He headed south to Melbourne for training. In 1921, a small research section had been created in the Australian Meteorological Service. In the early 1930s it was located at the Central Office of the Bureau of Meteorology in Melbourne, under the charge of Henry Barkley.[21] Rose stayed with his mother's cousin Beattie Eaton and her husband Charlie, a pilot in the First World War and now a squadron leader living at Point Cook between Melbourne and Geelong.[22]

In Melbourne Rose became friends with Richard Cohen, a fellow student on the meteorological course. During the breaks in their studies, the friends would take their rucksacks and go hiking in the forest areas near Melbourne.[23] Many decades later Cohen wrote an obituary for his youthful companion Fred Rose, recalling him as 'tall, gangly, erudite and thoughtful, typical of what I imagined to be the product of the old universities of Britain. He was a gentle person with a delicate sense of humour'.[24] Another student,

John Lillywhite, recalled that Rose was 'terribly terribly British', and that he was 'more interested in anthropology than in meteorology and was using this training course as an excuse to get to the Northern Territory'.[25] On both counts he was right.

Coincidentally, the chief lecturer of the new course in meteorology was Fritz Loewe, the German Jewish Arctic explorer who had found refuge from Hitler in Cambridge, and had arrived in Australia just weeks before Rose.[26] In Melbourne he was distinguished by his poor English, a limp – the consequence of his Greenland heroics – and, according to Rose, 'a certain aura'.[27] Beyond their Cambridge connections Rose had a practical reason to establish contact with Loewe. He was contemplating inviting Edith Linde to follow him to Melbourne, where, he imagined, she could finally engage in university study. Loewe, fully attuned to the needs of those wishing to leave the Third Reich behind, kindly offered his assistance.[28]

Even before he finished his training, Rose knew he would be sent to the Northern Territory. His destination would be Groote Eylandt, the most remote location on offer, welcome news for the budding anthropologist. However, he would need to get some experience in Darwin before setting up a weather station on Groote. In preparation for the move north he tapped the available resources of the University of Melbourne's library, devouring the relevant books and journal articles on anthropology.

He also solicited advice from those who were the experts in the field, one of whom was the polymath anatomist Frederic Wood Jones. Wood Jones's sweeping interests extended to Australian Aborigines, and when Rose met him, he was working on the collections of his University of Melbourne colleague Donald Thomson. Happily for Rose, before long Thomson also turned up in Melbourne, fresh from a lengthy 'pacification' expedition in northern Australia. Like Rose, Thomson's scholarly pursuits had turned from the natural sciences to anthropology; he had taken a diploma in the discipline at the University of Sydney under Radcliffe-Brown. After the publication of sensational reports of multiple murders in the Northern Territory in the early 1930s, he travelled to eastern Arnhem Land as a representative of the Commonwealth government, charged with investigating the background to the violence and calming the volatile situation. He had gone a long way toward earning the trust and respect of indigenous people there, but also the skepticism of many Europeans, including Elkin.[29]

Thomson was able to give Rose the most current advice available on Australia's far north. The indigenous population of Darwin, he explained, was now 'completely de-tribalised'; Rose should therefore concentrate on working amongst the Aborigines along the railway line south from Darwin to Birdum, where he would get valuable experience.[30] It was wise counsel, followed in due course by Rose.

Rose's formal appointment to the Meteorological Branch as a Meteorologist Assistant Grade One came in September 1937.[31] His passage to Darwin was via Sydney, where he cooled his heels for three weeks waiting for SS *Merkur* to set sail. A short stop in Brisbane allowed him to catch up with his uncle Harry – his mother's brother – and Harry's wife Hilde. His abiding memory of Townsville was eating his first mango, while Thursday Island brought the first exposure to a polyglot community in Australia, a brief foretaste of Darwin.[32]

On the other side of the world travel preparations were also underway. With encouragement from Fred, and with the promise of support from Fritz Loewe, Edith Linde and her father were preparing for her to leave Germany and gain the university education she had long anticipated. Richard Linde would pay for her voyage to Melbourne, where she would arrive in April 1938. Rose undertook to divert a good part of his salary to provide her with a stipend so that she might live comfortably and devote herself to her studies. In time he would arrange for her to visit him.[33]

4. Darwin

Rose's first impressions of Darwin, recorded in the early hours of a December day, confirmed his expectations of the tropics. As SS *Merkur* pulled into the harbour to disgorge its human cargo, Rose lay naked under a sheet, an electric fan cooling the beads of sweat as they formed on his brow. Stirred to wakefulness by the prospect of encountering the colonial outpost in which he had invested so much hope, he made his way to the deck. There he was greeted by the scent of frangipani and the outline of palms, filling with colour as the sun climbed languidly over the horizon.[1]

Daylight delivered clearer views. Rose made out a line of low red cliffs with a road running along their base, bordered by an undergrowth of tall, rank grass. Atop the cliffs was a row of white bungalows, exemplars of Darwin's distinctive architecture, perched on stilts and boasting large shutters. Their inhabitants were the representatives of the white bureaucratic caste. To the right their neighbours, denizens of a row of corrugated-iron cottages, were of more modest status. This, Rose came to learn, was Cavenagh Street, Darwin's Chinatown. As that first day wore on, the temperature rose, and clouds of insects emerged from the stinking mud to feast on his bare skin. Darwin, as he later put it, 'was rapidly losing its romance'.[2]

Bureaucrats in Canberra in the 1930s harboured grand visions of a Darwin that would provide an enticing gateway to Australia for the growing number of travellers arriving by plane. Under Commonwealth rule since 1911, as under South Australian rule in the decades before then, bold designs for the 'Territory' were customarily revised to more moderate goals before being quietly abandoned altogether. Inevitably, it seemed, harsh logistical and climatic realities rendered Darwin the colonial visionary's nightmare, a place of, in Fred Rose's words, 'sin, sorrow, sore-eyes, sand

and syphilis'.[3] On the other hand, those who accepted the town for what it was – a hot, rough, melting point, open as much to tropical Asia as to the continent sprawling southwards – experienced an allure they could not shake. They were the ones who stayed.

In 1937 there were just 2000 or so souls who, by choice or obligation, resided in Darwin. It soon became clear to Rose how distinct the strata in this tiny society were and how rigidly its hierarchy was enforced. At the very peak were the Administrator and his wife, their residence an expansive white building overlooking the harbour. Immediately below them were the pearlers, whose long-established social eminence derived from 'old' money. Then, in Rose's view, came the families propelled upward by an industry that still had a future, the cattle industry. The dwellings of the Vesteys and the Bovrils in Darwin were the visible signs of British meat monopolies based on the ownership or lease of land on a scale that defied the imagination.[4]

Then came the public servants like Rose himself, playing a variety of roles on what was typically a three-year tour of duty. Salary levels varied, with medical officers better paid than bureaucrats, clerks or, for that matter, budding meteorologists. Nonetheless, they all stood above the class of small business-people and men of the cloth.[5]

At the bottom of the white social pyramid was the working class, who even before Rose's time had garnered a reputation for militancy. During the Depression, Darwin became known in some quarters as 'Little Moscow'.[6] Among the radical elements of Darwin's proletariat were waterside workers from a multitude of ethnic backgrounds – Italian, Greek, Spanish, Chinese, Malay and Aboriginal–Asian – and they were a potent political force. At that time some eighty of them were members of the waterside section of the North Australian Workers Union (NAWU), which by 1940 was under communist control.[7] Next to these blue-collar workers with jobs were the ranks of the unemployed, many of them camped on Mineral Beach and living in humpies.[8] Some – known in the vernacular as 'combos' – had established relationships with indigenous women and had thereby cemented their position at the margins of European society.[9]

Social stratification was nothing new to an Englishman like Rose, but Darwin offered the less familiar dimension of colour. Below the whites were the Japanese and Chinese. The former had been brought to the Northern Territory as indentured pearlers serving the burgeoning labour demands of European master pearlers. The Chinese were farmers and shopkeepers and in their politics, as Rose noted, 'Kuomintang to a man'.[10]

Then came the 'half-castes', in almost all cases people of mixed indigenous and European descent, but with other variations as well. The white authorities viewed them differently from the 'full bloods'; theoreticians of race even applied scientific-sounding names to denote various gradations – 'quatroon', 'octoroon', and so on. In the vernacular they were simply 'half-castes' or 'half-bloods'. Victims of the overweening arrogance and condescension of the Europeans, they were placed in the missions, settlements or homes of Europeans, to be taught the ways of the white world in the expectation that, over generations, the 'black' would be 'bred out'. In Darwin many of them inhabited the dilapidated corrugated-iron huts of the Kahlin Compound just south of Myilly Point, where white administrators hoped to keep an eye on them.

Standing on the second-to-bottom rung of the social ladder were, in Fred Rose's view at least, the so-called Koepangers, people from the island of Timor, where Koepang was the major port. Like other Asians working in the pearl-shell industry, they were in Australia because that industry had been specifically exempted from the *Immigration Restriction Act*.[11]

At the bottom of the ladder were the Aborigines. The traditional people of the area where Darwin was established were the Larrakia. Although Aborigines were a large portion of Darwin's population, very few identified as Larrakia. The reason, as Rose learned, was not that they had been massacred or poisoned, but rather that a more subtle process of extermination was under way: 'From their paramours the women contracted venereal disease or leprosy, passed it on to their own menfolk, and the circle was complete.'[12] As a cruelly ironic reminder of the fate of the now absent locals, the white bureaucracy had bestowed the name Larrakia Point on the area inhabited by its better paid members.[13]

In those days Darwin's airport was in the suburb of Parap, about four kilometres from the Administrator's residence and the harbour. Rose was delivered from the wharf to the Parap Hotel, adjacent to the airport, by Inspector of Aerodromes Jim McCormack.[14] From the hotel it was a short walk to the airport administration building, where Rose was to perform his daily duties. The Parap housed at any time some fifteen to twenty other guests in its sleeping quarters, arranged in pairs with a common dressing room. Divided into three main parts, the pub seemed to represent a microcosm of Darwin society:

> *The toilets for the drinkers at the public bar and the shacks used by the Aboriginal servants were the out-buildings. The Aborigines had no toilets, they used the bush. The second part, on the ground floor, consisted of the kitchen, dining-room and the public bar, while the third, supported on ten-foot steel girders, was the sleeping quarters, toilets and bathrooms of the permanent guests. The second and third parts were adjacent so that the sleeping quarters of the permanent guests provided an excellent shelter from sun and rain for the 'regular' drinkers.*[15]

Rose shared his dressing room with a journalist named Philip Winter, the Darwin correspondent for the Sydney *Daily Telegraph*.[16] In time it became apparent to Rose that Winter was afflicted with tropical neurasthenia – in the language of the locals, he had gone 'troppo'.[17] Winter had been asked by Xavier Herbert to check the proofs of *Capricornia*, his rambling epic novel set in northern Australia. Winter's fragile health meant he was barely up to the job, so he passed the weighty manuscript on to Rose. Having spent just over a year in Australia, Rose was still homesick and still thinking and acting 'as a somewhat precious young Englishman'. Reading Herbert's work confirmed his preconceptions of Australians, namely that they were 'an uneducated and uncultured conglomerate of people'. In time Rose would come to consider *Capricornia* a masterpiece, but for now it was just 'uncouth'.[18]

Curiously there is no indication that Rose and Herbert ever met, though Rose might have found much to admire about Herbert. In the first half of

1936 Herbert was trying to wean himself from his literary ambitions by serving a stint as relieving superintendent in the Kahlin Compound.[19] He garnered something of a reputation as a champion of indigenous rights, which would have endeared him to Rose, as would Herbert's membership of the North Australia Workers' Union.[20]

Rose's work at Parap was intended to provide him with supervised training in advance of his transfer to Groote Eylandt. Anthropology had to play second fiddle, and Rose also had to be wary that his extra-curricular activities did not expose him to the suspicion that he was motivated by sexual desire. To forestall any such accusations – at least that was his explanation – he resolved to establish a relationship with a white woman. In a town where just one in four residents was white, this was a challenge. Rose met it with the complicity of a married woman some years his senior. Perhaps in his homesickness she reminded him of his redoubtable mother and aunts. An energetic hotel manager and keen golfer, her marital status appears to have offered no moral or practical obstacle; her husband was, as she confided to Rose, 'sexually incompetent' but 'very jealous', and judging by his florid complexion addicted to the bottle. Rose avoided the wrath of the cuckolded drunk, which was just as well, because in a sober state he was known to be a dab hand with a rifle.[21] In time Rose hoped to be reunited with his German fiancée Edith Linde, but this was a card he played close to his chest.

As an 'upper-grade' member of the white establishment, Rose was expected, so he was informed, to don a white poplin suit, which should be changed daily.[22] In steamy Darwin this requirement had more to do with sartorial symbolism than good sense. Within two days of his arrival in the township Rose dutifully reported to Darwin's number one tailor, Fang Chong Loong, in Cavenagh Street. There he made the acquaintance of Grandfather Fang, who sported a straggly beard and loose flowing robes and munched on sunflower seeds. Fang, who might have been among the original coolies brought to build the Darwin to Pine Creek railway in the 1870s, spoke only Cantonese. It was his Adelaide-educated, immaculately attired grandson who served the customers. Rose rejected the approved options of white or khaki – the latter because it reminded him of military discipline – and plumped instead for an unobtrusive grey. He soon came to rue his mistake, his grey suit appearing to explain his exclusion from all social occasions. Even the customary invitation to one of the select gatherings hosted at the Residency did not come his way.

Rose's efforts at anthropological fieldwork in and around Darwin were earnest but doomed from the outset. He shared the common view of the day that to make an original contribution to anthropological knowledge in Australia he needed to do his fieldwork in the far north. The professional consensus was that the Aborigines of the south-east were 'not authentic'; they were viewed 'as people who did not live as Aborigines, as people who had lost their "Aboriginal" culture and had only a fragmented memory of their (past) culture'.[23] The trouble was that in Darwin the 'authenticity' Rose sought was a chimera, as Donald Thomson had cautioned in Melbourne. Rose would need to put Darwin far behind him.[24]

Thomson's counsel was not easily followed. On his first trip south along the rail line the train got only as far as Pine Creek, where damage caused by heavy rains prevented progress. The unperturbed crew and passengers promptly disembarked and staged an impromptu 'gin party'. A day later, its supplies of alcohol depleted, the train returned to Darwin.[25] A second effort some time later got Rose as far as Birdum, but then he had to return to Darwin, and his meteorological duties, almost immediately.

These early forays into fieldwork, as Rose recognised later, were amateurish and ill conceived. His contacts with Aboriginal people bore little scientific fruit, though they were important in other ways. If he had come to Australia armed with the rudiments of a political philosophy marked by sympathy with the marginalised and oppressed, that philosophy broadened to embrace a compassion for those subjected not just to social but to racial persecution.

His evolving views accorded well with those of the Queensland-born bushman Bill Harney, whose company Rose sought. Harney was a well-known figure in Darwin, but Rose had a very particular reason to visit him – Harney knew Groote Eylandt just about as well as any white man.

Rose found in him a man of little formal education yet great erudition, capable of quoting not only chunks of Shakespeare and Milton but also Greek and Latin classics. Asked how he knew them, Harney replied pithily, 'I read 'em.'[26] After serving on the Western Front in the Great War, Harney had worked at various jobs and developed a politics that earned him the moniker 'Bill the Red'.[27]

Of greater interest to Rose were the years when Harney had trepanged on Groote Eylandt. It was there he had met his wife, a 'half-caste' woman named Linda Beattie, taken from her mother on the mainland by missionaries in their civilising zeal and placed in the mission at Emerald River.[28] The first time Harney saw her 'she was in a four-span dragging cypress pine out of the scrub to the Mission sawmill'.[29] The mission itself was 'like a fortress surrounded by barbed wire'.[30] After their marriage the Harneys had moved to Darwin, but both Linda and their daughter died of tuberculosis.[31] As Rose planned his Groote Eylandt fieldwork, the advice Harney gave him was invaluable.[32]

Not everyone in Darwin took to Fred Rose. His boss at the meteorological office, George Mackey, found little to recommend in his new charge. He later recalled having to 'endure' Rose for about six months. One event stuck particularly firmly in Mackey's craw. Early one morning Mackey was hauled from his sleep because Rose had not presented for his duties at the airport. Brimming with resentment, Mackey hurried to carry out the required balloon observation. Eventually Rose arrived, 'clumping down the road in heavy boots unlaced, and only partly dressed about half an hour after he should have been on duty'.[33] At the heart of the resentment, in all likelihood, was not simply the neglect of duty but rather a pattern of behaviour that men of Mackey's ilk found troubling, namely Rose's 'fraternizing with the natives, to the extent of visiting them in their bush camps'.[34] As far as Mackey was concerned, Rose's 'going native' was no more than an affectation, laid on with a trowel.

George Mackey was not the first person to take an instinctive dislike to Fred Rose, and he would not be the last. Rose, it seems, was a man who unwittingly invited quick and decisive judgment. Many found him congenial, welcoming and warm; they were neither intimidated by the Cambridge erudition nor threatened by his vaulting ambitions. Others, like Mackey, suspected that more complex forces were at play, and that Rose's affability was a screen deployed to conceal darker motives. On this occasion, whatever the source of his enmity, Mackey was in no position to stand in Rose's way. His job done, Mackey could heave a sigh of relief as his charge boarded a flight from Parap and disappeared below the eastern horizon.

5. Groote Eylandt

Shaped like a postage stamp frayed around its edges, Groote Eylandt is in the western reaches of the Gulf of Carpentaria, some 50 kilometres from the Australian mainland's Arnhem coast. Its archaic Dutch name gestures to its size; at about 60 kilometres from top to bottom, and a little less from side to side, it is indeed a 'large island', the largest in the Gulf. Groote was writ large, too, in the life of Fred Rose. His career as an anthropologist was linked inextricably with it; from the first to the very last, his thinking was informed in some way by the experience and knowledge he gained on Groote Eylandt.

The Dutch first visited Groote in 1623, when the vessel *Arnhem* sailed through the gulf. The name was bestowed later, when Abel Tasman in 1644 explored the Carpentaria coast and the islands sprinkled off it. Distrustful of the early Dutch charts, the British sent Matthew Flinders to perform a detailed hydrographic survey of the region during his circumnavigation of the continent. He sailed around Groote Eylandt in January 1803, on multiple occasions dropping anchor off its shores, but neither Flinders nor his crew set foot on the island. Flinders did, however, see enough to surmise that Groote and neighbouring islands might for some time have been receiving 'Asiatic visitors'.[1] These were the Macassans, so called because they operated mainly from the port of Makassar in Sulawesi – formerly Celebes.[2] For an unknown time the Macassans had been visiting these waters to dive for trepang (also known as sea cucumber). They would cure it in camps they established on the mainland and various islands, including Groote, and return year after year. Their product prepared, they would depart in their fleets of fully laden *prau* for Timor, where they would sell it to Chinese merchants, convinced of its aphrodisiac qualities.

The merchants in turn would make handsome profits selling the delicacy to their countrymen. Trepanging was, in effect, Australia's first export industry.[3]

Though their presence was temporary, the Macassans' impact on Groote Eylandt and elsewhere was permanent. They taught the people of Groote, the Anindilyakwa, to make dugout canoes, and they brought to the island iron, glass, cloth, pipes and tobacco.[4] Their legacy is visible in the very countenance of some of the Anindilyakwa, in their language, their art, and in the tamarind trees growing to this day along the island's shores. But by the early twentieth century Macassans were no longer welcome in Australian waters, at least not as far as the white Australian authorities were concerned. From 1907 Macassan trepanging formally ceased, largely to clear the seas for the commercial activities of the new European masters, eager to exploit the natural bounty of the Gulf's waters, above all trepang and pearl shell.[5] The Japanese, too, became aware of the riches that might be extracted from those waters. As Europeans and Japanese vied for the upper hand, the Groote Eylandters and their neighbours across the straits at places like Bickerton Island and Caledon Bay could wax nostalgic about what by now seemed the gentler days of the Macassans, who returned home at the end of each trepanging season. By the time the European presence was well established and irreversible, to the Anindilyakwa the Macassan period seemed a golden age.[6]

The missionaries followed in the wake of the explorers and commercial interests, arriving on Groote relatively late. In 1920 the island was gazetted as a Native Reserve.[7] Within a year the Church Missionary Society (CMS), affiliated with the Church of England, established a mission at Jadigba on Emerald River near the south-western coast. For a time the Emerald River Mission had few consequences for the Anindilyakwa people, since the Anglicans saw their primary, God-given role as 'saving' 'half-caste' children, who were separated from their families and brought to the island. In the 1930s, however, the missionaries began to impose their endeavours on the locals, hoping for multiple conversions among the island's population of some 300.[8]

To anthropologists, Groote Eylandt promised much, its very insularity its most attractive feature. The island seemed to offer the opportunity to study 'primitive' society untouched by the corrupting influence of the outside world. This was true to an extent – European contact might have stretched back centuries, but until the establishment of the mission it was minimal. What was less well appreciated was that the Anindilyakwa were not a fully self-contained community, not least through their prolonged exposure to and dealings with Macassans. Moreover, with the founding of the CMS Mission at Emerald River, the profound social and cultural changes began to accelerate.

In 1921 Norman Tindale of the South Australian Museum was the first of the anthropologists to reach Groote. He had sought and gained permission to become a member of the CMS and to contribute to the establishment of the Emerald River Mission; for him missionary and scientific work went hand-in-hand. Tindale's primary duty on Groote Eylandt was to gather specimens for his museum, which he did with great success. In the process it became apparent that Tindale possessed the knack of engaging with the locals and creating a willingness among them to impart the kind of knowledge that fed the appetite of the social anthropologists of the day – information about the organisation of kinship and totemic systems.[9] He had arrived armed with Baldwin Spencer's personal copy of *Notes and Queries in Anthropology*, and he sought to put it to use.[10]

Two prominent visitors arrived later in the decade, both of them guests at the Emerald River Mission. One was the multi-talented South Australian explorer and adventurer Hubert Wilkins; the other was a special commissioner by the name of J.W. Bleakley, sent to the region by the Commonwealth government. Both wrote favourably of their missionary hosts, yet both expressed reservations about the policy of separating 'half-caste' children from their parents, which at that time was still the mission's *raison d'être*.[11] Donald Thomson came in March 1935 after the killing of five Japanese trepangers and three Europeans around Caledon Bay and Woodah Island; Thomson was to play the role of Commonwealth-appointed peace broker.[12] After his two tours of East Arnhem Land Thomson returned south, voicing his firm view that non-indigenous people should be excluded from Arnhem Land.[13] It was quietly ignored.

Indeed, on Groote Eylandt the process of change was about to gather pace. One of its prime agents was an Englishman, Fred Gray. Born in England in 1899, Gray had migrated to Australia in 1924. For a number of years through the second half of that decade he worked as a pearler in Broome, but by the following decade he was making his living as a trepanger around the islands and coastline of East Arnhem Land.[14] As his trepanging operations had been based at Caledon Bay, Gray was well acquainted with the brutal events that had brought Donald Thomson to Arnhem Land.[15]

As Thomson's pleas fell on deaf ears, Gray continued to trepang in the waters around Groote, sometimes setting up base on the island. Though devoid of proselytising zeal, he met on occasion with the missionaries at Emerald River, indeed he was their guest every Christmas from 1935 to 1938. They seem to have held him in high esteem, high enough to invite him to join them as a missionary, an offer he declined politely.[16]

By the last of those Christmas gatherings on Groote Eylandt great changes were in the air – quite literally. Qantas Empire Airways was on the point of constructing a flying-boat base at Port Langdon on the north-eastern side of the island. When built it would present exactly the kind of interference in the lives of the Anindilyakwa that Thomson feared. As Gray was about to depart for Caledon Bay, missionary Philip Taylor asked him if he would soon return to Groote Eylandt to 'look after the natives of the Island near the new flying boat base on behalf of the Mission'. His brief would be to ensure 'that there was no undue contact made between the natives and the whites who would be coming to the flying boat base'.[17]

Gray accepted the offer, and from Emerald River in the south-west made the long trek to Port Langdon on the north-east coast. He was accompanied by three Yolngu men from the mainland at Caledon Bay and a Yolngu woman. Together they herded forty goats across the island, an impost that stretched the journey to four days.[18] On arrival the party set up camp among the tamarinds planted in the distant past by Macassans.

From this site the shores of Port Langdon swept east and then north.

Reaching out into the port was an isthmus that tapered to a spit, curling southward in the shape of a seagull's beak. It was on that spit that the flying-boat base was to be built. The curve of the land enclosed a stretch of water that had at one point had the regal name Princess Elizabeth Bay bestowed upon it. When it was recognised that no regal assent had been issued, and indeed that such nomenclature might not have befitted the modest lagoon, it was quickly renamed Little Lagoon in honour of the hydrographer who had keenly recommended it.[19] From the proposed site of the base a long walk following the gentle curve of the lagoon led to its southern shore and to the site chosen by Fred Gray. In honour of its Macassan past, it was given the name Umbakumba, meaning 'little waves'.[20]

Soon after Gray's party arrived with its herd of goats, Gray's ketch the *Outuli* appeared, having taken the sea route from Emerald River, crewed by indigenous men. With the ketch came the crucial supplies that, along with the goats, enabled Gray to establish a self-supporting settlement, complete with fruit and vegetable gardens. The people who stayed with him would be allocated their own land on which, so Gray's dream went, they would be able not only to feed themselves but sell excess food to the nearby flying-boat base. Before the construction teams arrived to begin work on the base, Gray gathered local people around his 'settlement' – so called to distinguish it from Church-run missions – removing them from the stretch of land where the base would soon be built on the sandy soil.[21]

At first the Commonwealth accepted Gray's presence at Umbakumba, but over time concerns arose. There was a greater level of contact between base personnel and the locals than envisaged, since not only did Gray oversee the involvement of indigenous workers in building the base, but his settlement eventually provided vegetables, milk and poultry to the base mess.[22] Gray's role had become one of regulating contact rather than preventing it. The Chief Protector of Aborigines in the Northern Territory, Dr Cecil Cook, whose brief was evident in his very title, raised the alarm among the bureaucrats in Canberra. He was anxious to shield the locals from the construction of the base, lest it 'should later prove to have been the first step in their utter demoralization'.[23]

In reality Fred Gray was not the source of the problem, just a symptom of it; the base would inevitably accelerate and intensify a process already in motion. Long-range flying boats departing the UK would hop their way eastward across the northern hemisphere then into the southern. After reaching the Australian continent at Darwin their limited range demanded a refueling stop further east, before continuing the journey to Townsville. From there the coastal route would deliver them eventually to Sydney's Rose Bay.[24]

Air and sea surveys had suggested Groote as the best refueling site and pinpointed the lagoon sheltered within Port Langdon as ideal. An area of 2800 hectares was excised from the Groote Eylandt portion of the Arnhem Land Aboriginal Reserve, and the Shell Company – which had the contract to provide refueling services – was granted a 21-year lease. The area included a significant part of the surface of the lagoon on which the flying boats would alight.[25] The base proper was to be built on the sand spit, covering an area about five kilometres long and a kilometre wide.[26] The land was formally handed over to the control of the Department of Civil Aviation, which took on the task of building the base, while the project of installing a fuelling depot was entrusted to Shell.[27]

On 13 March 1938 a vessel ferrying Shell's men, supplies and material reached Port Langdon.[28] In early May the construction crew for the base proper arrived, contracted by the Department of the Interior's Works and Services Branch. They set to work with aplomb, building a short jetty into Port Langdon in readiness for the arrival of further supply vessels. Their supervisor, Mr Swingle, drove his underlings to a punctual conclusion of their tasks.[29]

Then came a complement of men from the Department of Defence's Civil Aviation Board. The key person was the base's control officer, under whom served a wireless operator, a wireless engineer, a coxswain, a boat-hand, a base engineer and a cook, all of them braced for a stint of tropical service. They were quite a different group from the construction workers, and tensions between the two groups would soon flare.[30]

When the initial construction work was completed, the missionary

Philip Taylor from Emerald River suggested it was time for Fred Gray, his job done, to pack his things and return to Caledon Bay. Gray would have none of it. The government, at first, also supported Taylor's view that Gray's work was over; and Cecil Cook applied pressure from Darwin. The decisive intervention appears to have come from Minister of the Interior Senator Hattil (Harry) Foll, who visited the base. With the backing of the Civil Aviation control officer, Gray was able to persuade Foll that if Umbakumba were abandoned, Aborigines would be all over the base. Foll directed that Gray be permitted to remain on the area of land he wanted. Taylor was displeased but could not trump a ministerial intervention. His relations with Fred Gray became strained, but at Umbakumba Gray did not want for friends. Forfeiting his salary, he set about establishing a community that with modest means would meet the needs of those who chose to gather there, as well over a hundred Aborigines from the western side of the island did.

By the middle of 1938 the base, its buildings not yet complete, was sufficiently ready to receive its first flying visitors. On 5 July the Qantas Empire Airways flying boat the *Cooee* splashed gently into the waters of Little Lagoon, on its way from Sydney to Singapore. Just hours later, the base received its second visitor, *Challenger*, approaching from Darwin and carrying passengers on the inaugural flight from London to Sydney. Three figures who had boarded in Darwin emerged from the aircraft to terminate their travels on Groote. One was the tall, thin figure of Cecil Cook.[31] One-eyed in at very least the literal sense, the Chief Protector of Aborigines was eager to learn whether the base was keeping the promise of separating its personnel from the island's Aborigines. Then there was Fred Gray, who had been to Darwin on business. Lastly there was the base's new meteorologist – twenty-three-year-old Fred Rose.[32]

6. Island Days

That flight from Darwin to Groote Eylandt signalled the beginning of two important friendships for Fred Rose – one with Fred Gray, and the other with Groote Eylandt and its people. As he emerged from the plane, Rose had the appearance of an emissary of empire: 'With my rifle over my shoulder, case in either hand and my poplin suit, shoes and socks as a bundle under my arm, I struggled to the shore.'[1]

His parents approved of their son's front-line involvement in a grand imperial enterprise. He sent them a newspaper article announcing his transfer, prompting his mother to send him some 'new white shirts in time to be of service'.[2] Even his father abandoned his customary aloofness to express paternal approval, writing, 'Dear Fred, Your letter to hand as usual with the cutting from the newspaper. We thought it a really good photograph of you as does everybody else who has seen it . . . No doubt you are busy at G.E. and the letters you send are very interesting as are also the snaps.'[3]

The formal plan was for Rose to assume control of the meteorological office crucial to the functioning of the new air base. But Rose's plans were more ambitious and devoted primarily to activities outside his official duties. It was on Groote Eylandt that he hoped to fulfill the task he had set himself on leaving Cambridge, to achieve a triumph of Malinowskian fieldwork in a region where white civilisation had not yet made its mark.[4]

Rose kept a diary during that seven-month tour of duty on Groote Eylandt. His intention ultimately was to write a book based on his experiences, and decades later he would make several fruitless efforts to hawk to publishers a typewritten manuscript bearing the titles 'Carpentaria Ripples' and 'Ripples in the Gulf'. In the end he resigned himself to depositing copies, along with his diary and a collection of letters, in the State Library of New South Wales and the National Library of Australia in Canberra.

The other Fred, Fred Gray, figures prominently among the *dramatis personae* of Rose's 'Ripples'. When Rose first saw him on the flight from Darwin, he assumed that Gray was a missionary: 'Dressed in immaculate white he seemed out of place going to Groote Eylandt. Of ruddy complexion, with kindly eyes set in a long, slightly ascetic face, with a firm but generous mouth, I imagined him more at home as a youngish clergyman in a country vicarage in England than here, although his gnarled hands, with gaunt fingers betokened long exposure to the tropical sun.'[5] Gray was no missionary, at least not in any religious sense, but his knowledge of the region and his commitment to the wellbeing of those who lived there soon earned Fred Rose's greatest respect.

What impressed Rose most was the easy manner of Gray's interactions with the locals. It was quite different from what Rose had witnessed in Darwin, 'where they were bullied, and what a word would not make them do, a hob-nailed boot probably would'.[6] Gray's philosophy was refreshingly enlightened: 'They have to be treated as strictly logical beings. They argue from different premises to ours but their argument is just as logical.' Moreover, as Gray counselled Rose, 'The first thing to remember is never to give the aboriginal something for nothing. The fault that most white people have when they first come into contact with aboriginals is that they are too fond of giving presents to get on good terms. This does not engender respect, rather does it do the opposite. And then when the presents stop, the natives resent it.'[7]

Gray had embarked on an experiment whose results were not yet known. He was attempting to change the economic foundations of the lives of those who gathered at Umbakumba. The plan was that they would receive plots of land to cultivate, and goats and fowls to raise. In time each would become, to use Rose's terminology, a 'sedentary agriculturalist', with full rights to sell surplus produce or exchange it for other goods. If the plan worked, then not only the economic structures but the ways of thinking of the Anindilyakwa would be transformed. And if this occurred in Umbakumba, then according to Gray's ambitious reasoning, the principle of indigenous economic progress could extend throughout the region.[8]

Gray's approach contrasted strikingly with that of the missionaries, who every now and again would make the trek across the island from Emerald River to visit Umbakumba and, as Rose observed on one occasion, conduct services:

> *I was never more strongly impressed with the stupidity of trying to 'make' the aboriginals Christian. They sang the hymns well. They knew them by rote and it may be sacrilegious to say so, but it reminded me of a community sing-song or a concert hall turn. But the Christian ethics and dogma which Taylor retailed, the aboriginal could not understand either because the language in which it was spoken was not intelligible to all, or because it would pass clean over his head.[9]*

Rose's own excursions from his digs at the base to Umbakumba on the other side of the lagoon were either by a five-kilometre paddle in a dugout canoe or a walk of twice that length following the shore. In time the two Freds came to an arrangement whereby Rose would walk to the end of the sand-spit and flash a light in the direction of Umbakumba, and Gray would respond by sending a launch to pick him up.[10] These expeditions by Rose provoked the ire of the base's works supervisor, Swingle, who threatened to deprive Rose of his tent accommodation and the food served in the communal mess. For a time, until 'the old bastard' Swingle and his men packed up and left, Rose kept his distance from Umbakumba.[11]

That presented him with a quandary. Edith Linde had arrived in Australia. She was now installed in lodgings in Carlton and writing him plaintive letters. She was relieved to be away from Germany at a time when the regime was steadily tightening the screws on people like the Lindes. A letter from her father, she told Rose, 'made me realize again how glad I can be to be in Australia. The GESTAPO had been informed that I have gone to Australia and now my father has been asked: Why did I stay in England for two years and why have I gone to Australia? It is too ridiculous'. She had reached Australia safely, but she felt lovesick and lonesome, conscious that a continent separated her from her 'dear Freddie'. Perhaps it was her father's Quaker contacts who triggered an invitation to Edith to attend a social evening held by the Society of Friends,[12] yet her loneliness remained unalleviated. In one letter to Fred her despair was almost palpable: 'I find it the hardest I have ever undertaken, trying to study in a foreign language which requires a lot of concentration and ability, which I am little able to concentrate. I am too much a hopeless dreamer. Nothing seems to matter to me except you, and yet I cannot see you.'[13]

Plans for Edith to visit Rose were soon advanced. Fred Gray had voiced no objection to accommodating Edith at Umbakumba, so in July Rose wrote to Cecil Cook requesting a permit for her to stay there for up to a month.[14] Cook did not reject the request outright, but in his reply he pointed to the uncertainty surrounding Fred Gray's tenure at Umbakumba. If Gray were asked to leave the island very soon, Rose's plan would come to nothing.[15] For Rose this was a reason to postpone the visit, and on the very day he received Cook's letter he wrote to Edith to explain the dilemma. His revised suggestion was to wait until the work on the base had finished and the workmen from the Department of Interior had left, probably in November. By then Fred Gray's tenure would be more certain.[16] Then another option presented itself – missionary Philip Taylor's sister Elizabeth had told him that visitors were always welcome at the Emerald River Mission. Rose decided to make a renewed application, this time with the insertion of a clause that rendered the tenuousness of Fred Gray's position at Umbakumba irrelevant – 'NOT DEPENDENT GRAY IF NECESSARY STAY WITH MISSIONARIES'.[17] A permit for Edith was issued on 4 August.[18]

Strictly speaking, the permit was for a stay at the mission, but Rose considered that there could surely be no objection to Edith staying with Fred Gray at Umbakumba until the mission lugger arrived to take her to Emerald River. Rose was eager that no one at the base should know of Edith's visit, indeed that she should spend no time there. But by the time she finally arrived on 17 August, rumours were rife, and one colleague on the base confided to Rose that a 'little lass' with a 'sickly smile' had arrived on the plane from Townsville and been taken to Umbakumba. 'She seems to have as much sex-appeal as a crayfish', he offered. 'If she used some paint and powder, she would be quite attractive.'[19]

Swingle was as insistent as ever that Rose, like his workmen, should be confined to the base. Rose was equally determined that the 'whim of a small-minded cantankerous old man' would impede neither love nor fieldwork. Ignoring all advice to the contrary, Rose made his way across the lagoon to visit Edith at Umbakumba as soon as he had completed his meteorological duties. The first meeting was especially memorable: 'Edith came down to meet me as I came ashore. No! My God she had not changed ... her eyes were as fresh as that last time I had seen her, New Year's Day, twenty months ago in Brussels.'[20]

For a short time fortune favoured the young lovers. The lugger would not be able to sail from Emerald River to pick Edith up, so she would have to spend her vacation entirely at Fred Gray's settlement. After a brief flurry of rumour and innuendo, 'like a hen roost with a lot of old fowls clucking away', the workers at the base mercifully seemed to forget that a woman had been escorted from a westbound Catalina.[21] As for Rose's sorties across the lagoon, they were surely in the interest of his anthropological fieldwork. But Swingle stuck his nose into Rose's business once more, and reissued his ultimatum emphatically. From that point Fred and Edith's trysts would need to be staged under the cover of darkness. An arrangement was reached with Gray; he would deliver Edith to the end of the spit at 8 pm every evening – and into the waiting arms of Fred.[22] The location was no *locus amoenus*, but the couple made do:

> ... *there was no moon, although we had the stars. We had no palm trees waving gently in the tropical breeze; we had only saltbush, an odd stunted ti-tree and mangroves. It was dead calm and the faint clammy stench of the mangroves pervaded everything, even the sand on which we were lying. A few days previously a crocodile had been seen at the end of the spit where we were now and it was only a week ago, that Gray had shot one in the passage into the lagoon, between the spit and his place.*[23]

More conventionally the question of marriage was raised, as it had been tentatively in England, where Edith's skepticism first emerged. In her modern view a woman virtually became a slave upon marriage; she was obliged to accede even to unreasonable wishes. If she chose to remain unmarried, her freedom was limited only by her own choices; she saw no reason to forbid sexual relations between a man and woman if they were not married. On Groote Eylandt Edith's thinking had not fundamentally changed. Her plan was to continue the relationship as it was at least until she gained her degree. Rose's views, by contrast, were shaped by the politics of the day. If war broke out, he told Edith, then as a German citizen she would be regarded as an enemy alien. Were they to marry, however, she would automatically become a British subject and not face the bleak prospect of internment.[24]

On 26 August Edith boarded the eastbound flight from Little Lagoon. Fred was not present to bid her farewell. 'Indifference', he feared, 'might be too difficult for me to affect'.[25] As for Edith, she had much to contemplate on the long return flight to Melbourne. She had her own reasons to resist marriage, but the louder the dogs of war growled over the coming weeks and months, the more she was inclined to abandon her reticence.

When Swingle and the remnants of his construction team finally left the base in November, Rose abandoned any obligation to remain there. He stepped up his fieldwork, recording kinship terminology and making notes furiously. In this he continued to have the unstinting support of Fred Gray, who had well-established connections with the local people drifting in growing numbers to Umbakumba. Rose's other pillar of support was the indigenous man Kulpejer (or Kulpaja) Bara, who had crewed with Gray and was a member of the party that had herded goats to Umbakumba. He was an invaluable interpreter for Rose, for whom languages had always been an Achilles heel, and for complexity the language of the Anindilyakwa turned Latin into a stroll in the park.[26]

By pre-European standards the island's population of 300 created a relatively high density, sustained with a year-round sea-hunting economy. Rose was under no illusion that this society would remain forever shielded from the outside world. To the trained anthropologist the signs of Macassan contact were evident enough, both in the islanders' physical appearance and the iron cold-hammered into their spear points.[27]

Yet the pace and profundity of the Macassan influence were nothing compared with the changes heralded by increasing contact with Europeans. The best-intentioned efforts of protectors of Aborigines and others to separate the indigenous people from the Europeans were doomed to fail, both around the flying-boat base and elsewhere. With the mission in the west and Fred Gray's settlement in the east, the lives of the Anindilyakwa were already becoming more sedentary. Polygyny, practically the norm on the island, was condemned and forbidden by the missionaries at Emerald River, who refused men baptism until 'all the wives other than the first were put away'.[28] Fred Gray, too, moved to stamp out the practice. Rose had hoped to engage in 'salvage anthropology', recording a 'pristine' indigenous society before it disappeared entirely, but by 1938 he was already too late.

Time was not on his side. At the end of the year the wet season set in; the combination of rain and oppressive heat produced among the Europeans a tropical torpor. Merely to carry out his formal tasks at the base became a trial for Rose; to pursue his passion in his spare time was too much. After Christmas Rose could not even muster the energy to keep a daily diary. Decades later he wrote: 'Those last few weeks on Groote Eylandt, when I, streaming perspiration, had sat at a mess table regularly each evening for an hour or two, had assumed the proportions of a nightmare.'[29]

If the recollections of Fred's Darwin nemesis George Mackey are correct, it was proposed that Rose would return from Groote Eylandt for another tour of duty in Darwin. But Mackey would not have him back. Rose was not to be lost to the northern tropics entirely, however. Further to the west a position as meteorological officer was available in Broome, and Rose took it.

7. Broome

Before Rose could take up his new post in Broome, there was personal business to attend to – marriage. By this time both he and Edith had adopted a pragmatic attitude. War appeared ever more likely, and with it the prospect that as a single woman of German citizenship Edith would be treated as an 'enemy alien'. Upon marriage to Fred she would automatically become a British subject, and the prospect of internment would recede.[1] They decided that Edith should cross the Nullarbor by train from Melbourne, while Fred would fly from Groote to Darwin and from there travel down the west coast. Their nuptials would be celebrated in Perth, *terra incognita* for them both.

The fly in the ointment proved to be Fred, who missed his flight in Darwin and scrambled to make new arrangements. In desperation he sent a telegram to Kalgoorlie, hoping it would reach Edith when she changed trains. Unbeknown to Rose, it did not. He took the next available flight to Alice Springs, only to become stranded there for three days because of heavy rain. The irony of a meteorologist being stranded by an unexpected 'wet' in one of the driest regions of the world cannot have escaped him. After a day's further delay in Adelaide, Rose finally headed west, just as Edith was beginning to fear that her fiancé had lost his nerve. Her sinking hopes were revived when she noticed the name 'Rose' on a passenger list for a flight originating, curiously, in Adelaide. The couple met at Perth aerodrome for the first time since their Groote Eylandt encounters the previous August.[2]

The wedding was a modest affair. Fortunately a clerk at the Registry Office found space in the schedule for a civil ceremony the day after Rose's arrival. The ceremony went ahead on 3 March with the participation of a willing passer-by who acted as witness – the couple otherwise did not know a soul to call upon. When the officiating clerk asked the groom to place a ring on his bride's finger, Rose to his embarrassment did not have one. Edith chimed in with, 'I do not require a ring to show that I am married'.[3] From its very beginning it was to be an unconventional marriage. A day or two later Rose headed for Broome, while Edith returned to Melbourne and her studies.

On arrival in Broome on 8 March Rose was, by his own admission, still a 'brash young English university graduate', although homesick no more.[4] He had now experienced fifteen months in the tropics, sufficient time to steel him for a quick acclimatisation to Broome's weather and to the social realities of a multi-ethnic imperial outpost with its hard edges still intact.

At this time the European population of Broome was outnumbered by its Japanese residents, whose presence was vital to the pearling industry. As divers and lugger crew the Japanese had brought skills and experience on which the Europeans came to depend.[5] While the international climate was bringing strains to that relationship, overall Broome was proving a successful enterprise in multiculturalism. As elsewhere in Australia at the time, the indigenous population around Broome had fewer grounds for optimism. A royal commission conducted by Perth magistrate H.D. Mosley had concluded: 'There is little, I think of importance, which should be done to better the condition of the Kimberley natives [...] the huts in which they live, made of bush material – bags, and sometimes flattened petrol tins – are suitable to their needs. Anything more elaborate would not be appreciated by them.' Mosley's dire predictions about the future of the 'half-castes' were even more chilling: 'At the present rate of increase the time is not far distant when they, or a great majority of them, will become a positive menace to the community; the men useless and vicious, the women a tribe of harlots.'[6]

Rose took a room in the Continental Hotel. After war was declared in September, Edith joined him from Melbourne, and they moved into a small, two-roomed shack opposite the hotel. Some months later they shifted to a larger house only slightly further away. Although a vicious war of sorts was now being fought on the other side of the world, in Broome Edith suffered no discrimination at all. Indeed, her presence provided a bonus for Rose. No longer could he be accused of carrying out his anthropological investigations as a pretext for gaining access to Aboriginal women.[7] Nonetheless, it was resolved that Edith could hardly sit out the entire war before resuming her studies. In late March or early April of 1940 she left Broome, not to return to Melbourne but to study at the University of Sydney tropical medicine and linguistics, topics that would complement Rose's anthropological interests.[8]

As in Darwin, the public service in Broome formed a distinctive caste. The main difference was that in Broome there were two sets of civil servants, Commonwealth and state. Another social distinction concerned indigenous labour. State civil servants could call on Aboriginal prisoners, chained together around the neck, to work in their gardens. Under the supervision of a white, carbine-wielding gaoler, they would be marched out each morning to perform their duties. It was the first time Rose had witnessed humans chained together, and he felt it plumbed the very depths of humiliation.[9]

And as in Darwin there was both a colour bar and a Chinatown, but the church had a stronger presence. In Broome there was a Catholic bishop who was German, as were the priests and brothers. Some 100 kilometres north of Broome at Beagle Bay was a Catholic mission, imposing its beneficence on the Nyul Nyul people of the area. The first missionaries had arrived in the Kimberley in 1884, but it was a group of French Trappist monks who undertook the first proselytising efforts in the reserve at Beagle Bay. When their support was withdrawn, the German Pallotine priests and brothers took over at the turn of the new century. In 1935 a major cyclone flattened the mission, but a worse disaster, not of natural causes, was to follow. When war broke out in 1939, several of the German priests and brothers were interned, first in Broome, then in Melbourne.[10]

In Broome Rose formed a close relationship with a Nyul Nyul man, perhaps in his sixties, who went by the name of Casimir. Separated from his people at about the age of five, he had been taken to Melbourne, arriving there on the same day Ned Kelly was delivered to the gaol. When Rose met him in Broome, Casimir was not working, and Rose needed a cleaner to work in the house-cum-office being built for the meteorologist. As the building was being completed, Casimir went home to Beagle Bay for a break, but was soon back in Broome doing menial work at the Continental Hotel. When Rose asked him why he had returned so soon, Casimir replied that the police had fetched him for Mrs Locke, the owner of the hotel. This created something of a quandary for Rose, who had understood that Casimir was to work for him. Casimir indicated that he still wanted to work for Rose, but that Mrs Locke had 'got' him. Rose pointed out to him that the law had recently changed, and it was now possible for Aborigines to quit their employment without fear of being returned to their employers by the police. He pressed Casimir to give the hotel a week's notice. A short time later Casimir turned up at Rose's new house with a small bundle of possessions.[11] Rose paid him ten shillings a week, double the statutory wage for an Aborigine at that time. Casimir was not only of benefit in cleaning the house and the meteorological office, but as a fully initiated Nyul Nyul man he was an extremely valuable source of ethnographic knowledge.[12] If Rose was finally to make an impact as an anthropologist, he needed people like Casimir in Broome, just as much as he had needed Kulpejer on Groote.

Rose was not alone in sympathising with the likes of Casimir. The newly arrived doctor Alec Jolly was determined to break Broome's colour bar. Jolly had arrived in Broome with some pedigree as a radical. During his student days in Melbourne he had been active in the campaign for Egon Erwin Kisch, the radical Czech–German journalist whom the Lyons government had sought to prevent landing on Australian soil in 1934. Famously the efforts of Attorney-General Robert Menzies had failed. According to Fred Rose it was Alec Jolly who handed Kisch a note advising him to jump from the ship as it pulled away from the wharf in Melbourne.[13] In Broome the young doctor's sympathy for the underdog manifested in his hospital surgery hours. In contravention of the tradition of separate times for whites and others, Jolly insisted on the same opening times for all.[14] For Fred Rose that was enough to detect in Jolly a kindred spirit.

In the end Jolly proved much more than that. Of all the men and women whom Rose encountered in his years in the Australian tropics, it was Jolly who had the greatest impact. Born in Norwich in 1910, Jolly graduated with the degree of MBBS from the University of Melbourne in December 1935, taking Honours in medicine, surgery, bacteriology, physiology and pathology. For the next couple of months he worked in the midwifery ward at Bendigo Base Hospital, before commencing in February 1937 a year-long stint as resident medical officer, then registrar, at the Alfred Hospital in Prahran. After that he held a series of locums, followed by a return to the Alfred and an appointment to the position of assistant pathologist. Asked to provide references for their junior colleague, none of the doctors at the Alfred could find an unkind word to say about him.[15]

In April 1940 Jolly had applied for the position of medical officer in Broome offered by the Western Australian Public Health Department. With enthusiastic testimonials provided by a number of doctors, he was a strong candidate, and by early June he had the job. It would see him offering his services as far away as the Beagle Bay mission.[16]

Jolly's competence as a doctor was a matter of interest to the Roses, because by now Edith was pregnant. If there had been no decent medical service in Broome, Edith might have chosen to remain in Sydney for the birth. As both she and Fred were assured of their friend's skill, it was decided that Edith should return to Broome in time to give birth there. Moreover, the prospect of spending time with Alec Jolly, his wife Babs and their young daughter must have been of some comfort.

On 17 January 1941 the Roses became a family of three. Kim was named for his place of birth, the Kimberley. Rose had become a father at the age of 25, Edith, just five months older, had already turned 26. There were great celebrations through the night at their house, as half the town turned up with copious quantities of alcohol. From the hospital just down the road, an exhausted Edith was not as impressed with the nocturnal revelry, which kept her awake until dawn.[17]

At their very first meeting Rose had piqued Jolly's interest with his discussion of his anthropological pursuits. The widely read Jolly was by no means ignorant of the discipline and enquired whether Rose was familiar with Lewis H. Morgan's book *Ancient Society*.[18] Rose did know of Morgan and was vaguely aware that he had written a work of some significance in the previous century, a sweeping history of the evolutionary stages of human society, but that was the extent of Rose's knowledge at that time.[19] Unperturbed, Jolly took the discussion a step further. Had Rose read Friedrich Engels' book *The Origin of the Family, Private Property and the State*? Rose admitted that he had not heard of Engels, let alone read any of his works. Jolly explained that before his death in 1883 Karl Marx had read and made notes on Morgan's *Ancient Society*. These notes were subsequently taken over by Engels and used as a basis for his book, which, published in 1884, was to become the seminal work for any anthropologist of Marxist persuasion.[20] In it, Engels not only reviewed the course of history in a manner deeply indebted to Morgan, but he also looked to the future, beyond the age of capitalism in which he and Morgan lived.[21] Though Jolly was no anthropologist, he knew his Marx and Engels, and he could hold forth with the competence of an impassioned polymath on any number of topics, including the history – and future – of humankind.

Thus began a partnership that brought together curiously complementary skills and capacities. Rose had a formal training in anthropology from Cambridge and an understanding of fieldwork gleaned from such luminaries as Haddon, Malinowski, Radcliffe-Brown and Elkin. Jolly for his part had no such training, but he had read Morgan and Engels and, as Rose noted, 'had mastered and moreover clearly remembered their basic content'.[22] And although they stood in different intellectual traditions, they had both come to anthropology via backgrounds in the natural sciences. Moreover, their scientific conception of the discipline was matched with a deep compassion for the people they hoped to understand better.

Rose and Jolly were well suited on a practical level too. Through his medical work Jolly had access to a wide range of potential subjects; at the Aboriginal Hospital he treated patients who came from as far afield as Wyndham or the region along the track to Port Hedland and who might, with gentle persuasion, agree to be interviewed.[23]

Bringing their scientific training to bear, the task Rose and Jolly set themselves was to test a theory, one which had its origins in Morgan but had largely been embraced by Engels. The idea was that over the course of evolution humans had learned to avoid incest. It was not a conscious avoidance, but rather it came about in a 'groping, spontaneous' way, as if humans instinctively understood that inbreeding inhibited human progress.[24] When Rose and Jolly consulted Radcliffe-Brown's study of Australian kinship systems in the journal *Oceania*, they noted that some of these systems were identified as matrilineal, others as patrilineal.[25] The latter were considered surprising, because Morgan and Engels had assumed that the emergence of patrilineal systems would not have occurred until a later stage in human social development – that is to say, on the threshold of class society, and with the 'defeat' of the female sex. So why was it then, Rose and Jolly asked, that in apparently primitive communities like those in Australia, patrilineage had, in some instances at least, already established itself?[26]

In search of answers they collected their own kinship data, consulted with experts in the field, and produced a manuscript with their findings. Its title indicated the bold purpose of fitting the Australian story into a much larger one: 'The Place of the Australian Aborigines in the Evolution of Society'. The line they wished to take was anticipated unambiguously in the subtitle: 'A vindication of Lewis Morgan'.[27] The challenge was to find a journal that would publish it. A date stamp on a copy of that original manuscript suggests that it was completed in December 1940, but it would be some time before a journal was found.[28] Eventually, and through the good services of Rose's mother in England, the article appeared in 1943 in the Cambridge journal *Annals of Eugenics*.[29]

Apart from the title of the journal that published this first major scientific work, there was much about the article that, with the passage of time, would make the more mature Rose blush. Nonetheless, it is a good indicator of where his anthropological thinking stood at the time, and it was a far cry from the establishment position. Rose and Jolly took the view that societies all over the world passed through particular stages of development from primitive to higher forms. Any society at any time was in a state of social evolution, some more highly evolved than others. Where American Indians as described by Morgan had reached a relatively advanced stage of development, the Australian Aborigines as observed by Rose and Jolly and by the likes of Elkin and Radcliffe-Brown were at an earlier stage.[30] In grappling with the evidence of the existence of a variety of stages of social evolution, Rose and Jolly looked to the role of taboos. At the beginning of history, they contended, humans were promiscuous, but over time ever more sophisticated taboos proscribed particular relationships and promoted liaisons with people of alternative 'lineage'. In Australia, they claimed, the advance of history meant that there were no longer any examples of 'one-lineage' societies, that is, societies in which all members traced their origins to a common ancestor. Such societies were common in antiquity and might still exist on isolated islands but were no longer to be found in Australia. They argued that in Australia there were a number of variations of more advanced societies, with more developed taboos forbidding incestuous relations and thereby producing 'good effects', ranging from two-lineage societies up to four-, six- and eight-lineage.[31] All these societies needed to develop new relationship terms, which would in effect codify what was permissible and what was not. 'The evolution of the social structure of a primitive society', they concluded, 'is such as to make the marriage of close relations progressively more difficult'.[32]

Despite its scientific tone, the essay carried a political sting in its tail, as the authors offered gratuitous policy advice with some echoes of Donald Thomson:

As far as the Australian aboriginal is concerned a policy of complete autonomy under guidance is recommended, with contact between white and black men strictly forbidden. The guidance should be given by anthropologists and not by such people as untrained missionaries or policemen, whose objects are almost invariably diametrically opposed to the well-being of the aboriginal: the one attempting to graft a worthless form of Christianity on to the shattered beliefs of the aboriginal, the other to enforce the white man's law.[33]

The collaborative fieldwork in Broome led to one other published article, an investigation of the mother-in-law taboo among Australian Aborigines.[34] At first glance, Jolly and Rose contended, there seemed no impediment to relations between son-in-law and mother-in-law; such sexual relations did not appear to be 'physiologically incestuous'. It was a taboo that had 'defied explanation in terms of incest avoidance'.[35] Why then, they asked, had such a taboo arisen? The answer they provided was that in the context of 'gerontocratic polgyny' as it existed in Australia, there could be a biological impediment after all. An older man might take as one of his wives a young woman whose mother might be of a similar age to himself, or even younger. It was possible that a man might thus become the biological father of his own wife. In Rose and Jolly's words, intercourse between mother-in-law and son-in-law, 'gives rise to conditions suitable for the worst of incest, i.e. that between parent and child'.[36] This would undoubtedly have harmful biological consequences, and that, they reasoned, was why the taboo had come about.

It was quite a feather in Rose's cap that this co-authored article appeared in the prestigious journal *Man*. Yet it was in the realm of politics that his intellectual proximity to Jolly was most evident, as their reactions to a trial staged in Broome revealed. A missionary in Kunmunya had condoned a marriage that breached tribal law. Two murders ensued; the perpetrators were arrested, tried, and sentenced to lengthy jail terms. Jolly dispatched a letter of protest to the Commissioner of Native Affairs in Perth, placing the blame for the murders squarely on the shoulders of the mission.[37] Rose vented his anger in a letter to the *West Australian*. He targeted first the court for ignoring tribal law, and what was plainly a case of 'a tribal murder'. Like Jolly, he reserved his most cutting vitriol for the missionaries. His final paragraph presented a stark choice,

The missions are thus doing the greatest damage both physically and morally to the aboriginal by sanctioning such marriages. If we wish to exterminate the original inhabitants of this continent we are setting about it in the right way. If we do not wish to do this, the remedy is

plain – force the missions to obey the marriage laws of the aborigines or abolish the missions. These are the only two alternatives if scientific reasoning is to take the place of blind prejudice.[38]

With that Rose had crossed a Rubicon of sorts. Sympathising with the underdog was not new to him, but going public with his views was. Thanks above all to Alec Jolly, he had been radicalised, and he knew the colour of his views.

8. Groote Revisited

By May of 1941 Rose had accumulated enough leave to absent himself from his meteorological duties in Broome for four-and-a-half months, time he was determined to devote to anthropology. He had managed to do valuable work through his collaboration with Jolly, but earlier stints in Darwin and on Groote Eylandt had produced paltry results. The plotted return to Groote would be different.

What did it mean to be an anthropologist in Australia at that time? What kind of knowledge did anthropologists imagine they were gleaning from spending months living among indigenous people, in Australia or other parts of the world? By his background and training, Rose stood in a tradition of social anthropology that purported to offer an understanding of the societies over which Britannia ruled. Indeed, nearly all the influential fieldwork of British social anthropologists was carried out in some part of Britain's empire, and nearly all was a contribution to the maintenance of indirect rule.[1]

At the heart of the discipline as it evolved in the nineteenth century was the study of kinship systems. To outsiders, as A.P. Elkin's biographer Tigger Wise puts it, kinship was 'one of the drearier and most puzzling branches of anthropology, an apparently useless mumbo jumbo full of cross-cousins, MMBDDs (mother's mother's brother's daughter's daughter), cognatic descent, Aranda-type systems and mother-in-law avoidance'.[2] But to insiders, like Fred Rose, kinship was at the very core of their discipline; most of their research was devoted to it. The argument, implicitly at least, was that to understand kinship bonds was to hold the key that would open the door to an understanding of any society. They were 'the pivot around which daily life revolves in many societies – providing security, governing

60

interactions, exacting loyalty, demanding obligations. If you can just get a grip of the kinship rules, the aficionados believe, you should be able to get straight to the roots of that culture's social organization'.[3]

The intellectual father of kinship studies was W.H.R. (William Halse Rivers) Rivers, a Cambridge doctor, academic, psychologist, anthropologist and member of the first Cambridge expedition to the Torres Strait in 1898. His abiding intellectual ambition, consistent with the spirit of the Victorian era, was to create a unified 'science' of anthropology. And for Rivers, marriage and kinship were simply 'bodies of dry fact' that could be singled out from other 'low forms of culture' and studied in 'relative isolation'.[4] He held the dogmatic belief that marriage rules were the key to understanding any system of classificatory kinship, for it was through marriage that 'every individual born into a society [was] assigned a definite place in that society'.[5] Typically for him, as for nineteenth-century students of various forms of Aboriginal kinship, the task 'was not just to classify [kinship systems] but to fit these types into a *succession*: to transform taxonomy into a sequential typology [...] each type must represent a stage in an evolutionary progression'.[6] Following James Frazer, Baldwin Spencer, like many others, characterised this progression as a journey from magical practices to religious beliefs and eventually to scientific truth.[7]

The method Rivers devised for mapping the kinship and the marriage laws of 'native' societies was explained in his 1900 publication 'A Genealogical Method of Collecting Social and Vital Statistics', better known by the shorthand label 'Genealogical Method'.[8] Haddon had written to Spencer enthusiastically endorsing 'its great value and objectivity', though even Rivers himself had begun to express some doubts 'as to whether the method was applicable to extended societies, as to tiny island communities'.[9]

Such relationship and marriage 'mapping' initially seemed orthodox enough to Fred Rose, but perhaps it also bore the imprint of its own genealogy. Rivers was the son of Anglican clergyman Henry Rivers. The young William had plenty of time during the tedium of regular Anglican church services to contemplate the pages of *The Book Of Common Prayer of the Church of England*, where on the last page (before the 'Hymns Ancient and Modern'), was 'A Table of Kindred and Affinity, wherein whosoever are related are forbidden in scripture and our laws to marry together'. The table clearly set out thirty categories of kin (for both men and women) who were forbidden 'in scripture and our laws' as marriage partners.[10]

Rivers' impact on the discipline of anthropology reached its apogee around the turn of the century and was maintained well into Rose's time. His method was succinctly and usefully outlined in the fifth edition of *Notes and Queries on Anthropology* (1929), which Rose used as his fieldwork manual.[11] The 'Genealogical Method' confidently asserted that 'nothing gives more insight into the intimate nature of social organization than the mode of naming relatives'.[12] The manual advised the collection of extensive pedigrees using just five terms of relationship – father, mother, child, husband and wife – while cautioning against using terms such as brother, sister, cousin, uncle or aunt.[13]

The schematic kinship groupings, or relationship systems, which emerged through this method of recording brought 'savage' societies into the ordered field of vision of modern Western science.[14] The simple genealogies and kinship diagrams were visual, abstract expressions of the principles of social organisation.[15] Moreover, given the urgency of investigating 'vanishing peoples', such diagrams seemed to offer anthropologists an efficient 'short-cut route' into the workings of the societies they believed were hurtling toward extinction.[16] The kinship diagram was soon established as 'a central motif in modern anthropological analysis', providing an air of scientific integrity to the nascent discipline and its practitioners. [17]

In Australia Rose continued to read the latest work in the field of British social anthropology. The assumption that to 'do anthropology' in Australia meant studying kinship with the aid of the methodology established by Rivers remained fundamentally unchallenged. On Groote Eylandt, Rose would attempt to apply the 'Genealogical Method', but in a distinctive way, tailored to the conditions in which he worked. After four years in the Australian tropics he approached his task with enthusiasm and determination.

Though barely two years had elapsed since his first stint on Groote, much had changed. At the base there was no one he knew from his earlier sojourn. To counter the impact of isolation, a policy of rotation after just one year had been introduced. Across Little Lagoon at Umbakumba it was a different story. Fred Gray was still a presence, his settlement flourishing. More ground was now under cultivation, the range of crops had extended to cassava and sweet potatoes, supplemented by poultry, cows and goats. Happily for Rose the general social conditions under which the people lived had hardly changed.[18] The one exception concerned the women, who had lived in seclusion when he was there in 1938–39 and were very rarely seen. By 1941 they were more visible, and no longer wearing bark coverings but donning hessian flour bags, dresses imported by Fred Gray, or even cast-off men's singlets or shirts. The sense of shame that might have forbidden them from exposing their breasts and pudenda had not yet established itself.[19] Rose could not predict the rapidity with which transformations would occur in the coming years, but in 1941, it seemed to him, the people 'were changing their way of life at their own pace'.[20]

The wider political context of Rose's second visit to Groote was quite different from the first. With some prodding from Elkin in Sydney, Minister for the Interior John ('Black Jack') McEwen undertook a tour of the north in 1938 and on his return to Canberra started implementing a new strategy. Its keystone was that the areas of Health and Aboriginal Affairs, which during Cook's tenure had sat under the one umbrella, would be separated. The Chief Protector of Aborigines, hitherto the medical doctor Cecil Cook, would be replaced by a Director of Native Affairs, while responsibility for health would be shifted to a Chief Medical Officer. Cook's job was effectively split in two. Asked which area he wished to lead, he is alleged to have huffed, 'Both or neither.'[21] Neither it was. Slighted after many years of dedicated, energetic and well-intentioned service, Cook chose to leave the Territory altogether and take up a medical post in Sydney.[22]

McEwen was accompanied on the tour by Ernest William Pearson Chinnery, who studied anthropology under Haddon at Cambridge and had seen many years colonial service in New Guinea.[23] Before the year was out, Chinnery was appointed Director of Native Affairs in the Northern Territory and Commonwealth Adviser on Native Matters. The appointment was later described as 'a consequence of a Country Party minister and a university professor's machinations'.[24] By April 1939 Chinnery was setting up his office in Darwin.[25]

Chinnery adopted a new approach to Aboriginal affairs, backed staunchly by Secretary of the Department of Interior Joseph Carrodus, a New Guinea veteran and former acting administrator of the Northern Territory.[26] Like the appointment, the new approach betrayed the influence of Elkin, envisaging as it did a process of indigenous adaptation to European ways. Eventually Elkin would champion the term 'assimilation', but a proto-version of it was already in operation from the eve of war. Aborigines were to be given useful occupations; rewards would be dangled before them where signs of successful adaptation emerged. There was a role for missions as partners in this process; Donald Thomson's separatism was rejected. The voices of those who thought it might be time to hand control of Aboriginal affairs to the Aborigines themselves, were effectively drowned out.[27]

Fred Rose now needed to turn to Chinnery for assistance in planning his visit to the Aboriginal reserve on Groote Eylandt in 1941. Chinnery, it seems, had misgivings. They related to Rose's lack of formal affiliation with a university or similar scientific body. Rose was a meteorologist hoping to do fieldwork on his own initiative while on leave from his job. It was Elkin who set Chinnery's mind at rest, vouching for Rose's credentials and in effect affording Rose the patronage of Sydney University's Department of Anthropology.[28] At this time Elkin's influence in matters anthropological had reached an apogee, stretching far beyond the hallowed halls of academe to Canberra, Darwin, and even Umbakumba.

Two main theoretical problems had exercised Rose's mind since he was last on Groote. One of them concerned the distinction between pater – that is, the man who played the role of father in a social sense – and genitor, that is, the biological father. He had hoped to address this issue by having Edith trained in in blood-grouping techniques at the University of Sydney. Theoretically a simple blood test should be able to reveal in which cases pater and genitor were identical.[29] The question remained unanswered. On Groote Edith was too busy looking after baby Kim, and the work was not carried out as had been planned. Later Rose lost interest in the question, for he came to realise that, as far as the Aborigines were concerned, 'under traditional conditions the question of whether pater and genitor was one and the same was quite irrelevant for them'.[30]

The second question was how best to record and understand the social organisation of the people on Groote Eylandt. Conventional though this line of enquiry may have seemed, his experiences with Alec Jolly in and around Broome had produced quandaries. In Broome, Rose had essentially applied Rivers' 'genealogical method', using pidgin English to ask his questions. In doing so he was following in the footsteps not only of Rivers but also of Elkin and Radcliffe-Brown, both of whom had worked in the Kimberley. Rose and Jolly found there were significant numbers of exceptions and variations to the ideal types of social organisation as previously posited by Elkin and Radcliffe-Brown. At the time Rose believed that these anomalies did not invalidate his general findings, but they triggered doubts about the validity of the method employed.[31] How 'real', he began to wonder, were particular 'ideal' types of social organisation to which Aboriginal societies conformed?

When he arrived back on Groote, Rose resolved to try a different approach, the central component of which was photography. By itself that was hardly revolutionary, especially as Rose would have been familiar with Haddon's extensive use of photography in 1898.[32] Rose's intentions, however, were different from Haddon's. His aim was not to record a 'dying race' but to determine kinship classifications with a higher degree of accuracy. As he put it: 'Some other method had to be found which would easily and efficiently identify one aborigine from another. This was clearly photography. A photograph taken with reasonable care even by a tyro will identify a person with a high degree of reliability and an aborigine can identify one of his relatives by a photograph with as much certainty as a white man can.'[33]

On Groote Eylandt Rose photographed as many of the islanders as he could and asked *them* to identify each other in their own way, rather than pose the standard Eurocentric kinship questions. After all, what did the terms 'mother', 'father', and so on mean to *them*? This method had the obvious advantage of de-centering 'ego' in the tradition of a Western-style family tree and placing the emphasis on an *Aboriginal* classification of kin. It was 'a method of showing *how people use kinship terms towards each other*, NOT the tracing of descent through generations'.[34]

Rose did most of this work from his base at Fred Gray's settlement at Umbakumba. Ideally he would have been able to do all his fieldwork as a 'verandah anthropologist'. That is, he would remain in the settlement, and the people would come to him. Indeed, if he had wanted to interview only males, such an approach might have sufficed. But as his study was to include women, who were still reluctant to emerge from the bush, he eventually had to leave the settlement. In June, photographic equipment in tow, and with the aid of Kulpejer, he set off on his travels, which took him as far as the mission station at Emerald River on the other side of the island.[35]

To complement the use of the camera, Rose designed a single-page table for every subject in the study, showing how each was related to the others photographed.[36] Using the photographs, the 'English Name', 'Native Name', 'Sex', 'Spouse', 'Age', 'Moiety', 'Locality', 'Totems', 'Father' and 'Mother' could be more accurately ascertained and added to the table, which with its collected data assumed the form of a kind of matrix, a head-and-shoulder portrait attached in the corner.[37] Instead of relying on pidgin English, Rose solicited his data as a short series of questions in the local language. A short history of the individual was added to the tabular data under 'Notes', and data on cicatrices and circumcision were included on the bottom left-hand side of the table.[38] For females a different approach was necessary. To overcome shyness, their husbands helped them identify the photographs. When a man had several wives, they would be arranged in a semi-circle around the husband; he would describe who the subject was, and each of the wives in turn would give their relationship to the various people in the photos.[39]

Of the estimated 325 people on the island at that time, 219 were photographed,[40] and approximately 25,000 identifications were made.[41]

Apart from anything else, it was a significant and impressive logistical achievement. The mass of data would present Rose with the possibility, when all the interview and collection work was done, of forming an objective picture of the overall kinship organisation on Groote Eylandt. Were it to indicate the kinds of anomalies that the much more limited work performed in the Kimberley had suggested, then this data set held out the hope of explaining them more adequately.[42] That, at least, was the theory.

The analysis, however, would have to wait. His leave completed, Rose headed back to Broome and to his other life as a full-time civil servant. It would take much longer than he could possibly have anticipated to draw conclusions and disseminate them. A first attempt was made in 1944, when Rose wrote to then Minister for the Interior J.S. Collings, inquiring whether the Commonwealth might consider publishing his outcomes. He told the minister that he had worked them into a paper some 400 pages in length, accompanied by a similar number of photographs.[43]

Rose was knocked back. The minister had turned to Elkin and Chinnery for advice. By this time Elkin was familiar with the findings Rose and Jolly had published on the basis of their fieldwork in the Kimberley; perhaps it coloured his assessment of Rose's Groote Eylandt work. In his report for the minister, Elkin decried the 'very poor quality' of Rose's previous published papers and moreover maintained that Rose did not understand indigenous kinship systems. He advised firmly against publication, on the basis it might attract the scorn of genuine specialists in the field. His reservations were shared by Chinnery.[44] As a sop Elkin hinted that he might publish the photographs and the statistical data in *Oceania* if Rose revised his interpretation. Rose was not about to kowtow to Elkin, and Elkin was a similarly immovable force. Publication would have to wait.[45]

A strange thing had happened to Rose during his fieldwork in June, an event that signalled that Groote Eylandt was becoming increasingly connected to the rest of the world. As Rose approached the mission at Emerald River, a white woman from the mission approached him, seemingly to greet him, an unexpected white visitor. But she had different intentions, uttering the words 'Hitler's finished', with what Rose described as 'malicious satisfaction'.[46] She went on to explain that Hitler had just invaded the Soviet Union. It was rare for Rose to concur with a missionary, but in the hope expressed they were of one mind.

Operation Barbarossa changed world politics overnight, yet it had no immediate impact on Rose. He carried on with his fieldwork until his leave ended in September. In the longer term, though, he and his family would not remain immune from the drama being played out on the other side of the world.

9. The War of the Roses

As the Wehrmacht rolled eastward and the future of the Soviet Union hung by a thread, Stalin had no choice but to throw in his lot with Britain. His pact with Hitler lay in tatters. Pushing all his reservations aside, Churchill accepted the logic of the looming catastrophe and welcomed his new ally, fervently hoping that Stalin might conjure some kind of military miracle to save not just his own skin, but all of Europe.

Attitudes to communism changed, as Stalin, hitherto the ruthless despot, was reinvented as an avuncular figure invested with the task of rescuing the globe from barbarism. Communism and communists were no longer to be feared and despised but were welcomed warmly into the antifascist fold. In the previous year, just a couple of weeks after Dunkirk, the Menzies government had declared the Communist Party of Australia illegal, but now a spirit of cooperation prevailed. In Western Australia the acclaimed novelist and ardent communist Katharine Susannah Prichard threw herself into organising events that would capture the new spirit. An Australia–Russia Goodwill Congress, of a kind replicated throughout the country, was staged in Perth on 28 March 1942. As Prichard soon reported to one of her Moscow correspondents, *International Literature* editor Timofei Rokotov, the event was a great success in expressing the newfound antifascist ecumenism. The venue was festooned with a banner declaring, 'For Life and Liberty – Death to Fascism'. Alongside it were the flags of the Allied nations and a series of enlarged portraits of Roosevelt, Churchill, Stalin and Curtin, Prime Minister since October 1941. Prichard took her place alongside the recently retired Professor Walter Murdoch and the Reverend Canon John Bell in addressing the gathering.[1]

When the global conflict stretched to the Far East, Broome was no longer a backwater but a site of contestation. After Pearl Harbor, Broome's residents followed the progress of the Japanese juggernaut by tuning into radio broadcasts from the UK and from a Bandung radio station still in Dutch hands. The news was alarming. Before long the Dutch air force was evacuating refugees from Java to Australia, Broome their first port of call. At times the Roses had half a dozen such refugees camped on their front verandah.[2] As the threat to Broome itself grew more acute, Edith and Kim were among the women and children evacuated south to Fremantle by ship. It was an anxious voyage for Edith, as the vessel hugged the shore for fear of enemy submarines. In those waters just weeks earlier HMAS *Sydney* had been sunk by the German auxiliary cruiser *Kormoran*, so Edith hastily prepared a makeshift harness to swim ashore with Kim on her back in the event of an attack.[3]

Then Japanese forces struck the Australian mainland. A first raid was staged on Darwin on 19 February 1942, causing widespread loss of life and material damage. Broome braced itself for an attack. In the month of the Darwin raid American forces arrived to bolster defences on the Kimberley coast. Dutch military personnel also arrived from the Dutch East Indies as they fell under Japanese control. Already a multicultural settlement where Japanese outnumbered Europeans, Broome took on the character of a melting pot to which an uncomfortable amount of heat was being applied.

On the morning of 3 March 1942, Japanese aircraft based in Timor appeared over the horizon, their main targets aircraft and boats. Undeterred by the six rifles of the puny Broome Voluntary Defence Corps, the aircraft stayed about an hour wreaking havoc until their dwindling fuel supplies forced a departure.[4]

Rose not only witnessed the Zeros as they swooped over the town, he had a grandstand view. They disturbed him as he was taking a late breakfast at the meteorological office, perilously located between the harbour and the aerodrome. When it seemed too hazardous, he and the meteorological observer George Sneed ducked down into their air raid shelter until the danger had passed. Rose did not join the convoy heading south after that first raid, electing to stay in the largely deserted town, with every expectation that the attack would be followed by an invasion. Unusually for the indigenous population, most of whom went bush, Casimir remained with Rose and Sneed, assuring them that if there were an invasion, he would guide the two of them into the bush and look after them.[5] With the rest of the hardy souls who remained, they gathered together what weapons and ammunition they could find, converting the meteorological office into an arsenal.

Rose departed Broome in April, armed with two revolvers and 20 or 30 rounds of ammunition. He was following instructions, since a RAAF meteorologist would take over the office. Rose's brief was to make his way to Perth by any means available, but to destroy the code books, used to encode messages sent by radio to aircraft, before he left. These were kept in a tin box, safe from the ravages of termites. And it was precisely because the box was impenetrable that Rose stored in it about half a dozen notebooks with ethnographic data from his Groote Eylandt fieldwork – though thankfully not the kinship data, too large for the box. When Sneed followed Rose's instruction and burned the code books, he consigned the precious notebooks to the flames as well. It was, Rose ruefully observed, a 'minor tragedy'.[6]

The journey south proved as hazardous as the Japanese raid. Rose had ignored meteorological data suggesting a cyclone – unlikely at that time of year – was approaching the coast. As Rose and his travelling companions approached the De Grey River in the Pilbara, the wind picked up, and it began to pour. They were told they would need to travel eighty kilometres upstream to cross the river, which for the best part of the year consisted of little more than a string of waterholes. Now, however, it was clear that the heavy rain would cause a flood, and it would be a race to reach their destination – a sheep station on the southern side of the river – before a wall of water trapped them. By the time they reached the crossing point there was a howling hurricane. The river flats were already too wet to support the truck, so it was abandoned on high ground, while the passengers made their way to the assumed site of the homestead on the river flats. As Rose told the story years later, they had a narrow escape. Three Aborigines with half a dozen horses emerged out of the torrential rain to guide them to the homestead and safety.[7]

In Perth, Rose rejoined Edith and Kim and recommenced his meteorological work. Edith had rented a house in Maylands, not far from the civilian aerodrome. But then, unsurprisingly, Rose was given work with a military dimension. At that time US Navy Catalina aircraft were making reconnaissance flights over the Indian Ocean, for which he made meteorological forecasts. To do so he was attached to the weather bureau in Perth, where he joined a group of civilians and RAAF personnel. For convenience the Rose family moved into a house in Dalkeith, just downriver from the city centre.[8]

For a while Rose contemplated making a more direct military contribution. At the outbreak of war it had been suggested he might join the RAAF, which needed trained meteorologists. He was not averse to the idea, but enlistment would need to take place in distant Melbourne, so at that point the idea came to nothing. When Japan entered the war, it was revived, because the RAAF would need to expand its operational capacity in northern Australia, whose weather patterns Rose knew so well. There were numerous precedents of weather officers trained by Fritz Loewe transferring to the RAAF at the rank of flight lieutenant. Despite his considerable tropical service, Rose was told he would be assigned the humbler rank of flying officer. Without the offer of rank equivalent to those with similar experience, Rose refused and retained his civilian status. At another point he did, however, contemplate joining the military unit headed by the anthropologist Donald Thomson, which included W.E.H. (Bill) Stanner as well as a number of Aborigines, charged with acting as coast watchers to intervene in the case of a Japanese landing in the Northern Territory. Indeed, Rose claims that he made application to this unit, 'as with my experience of the Aborigines it seemed something I could usefully do. However, the Australian military bureaucracy insisted that I remain a meteorologist and I was so-called "man-powered" as a civilian meteorologist'.[9]

In Perth he met up again with Alec Jolly, whose presence there was a matter of some controversy. Jolly was among those who had beaten a retreat from Broome after the Japanese attack. Some thought that as Broome's medical officer and acting resident magistrate he had duties to perform in the wake of the raid and should have stayed. They insisted he return. Jolly found an unlikely ally in Lieutenant Colonel Richard Legge, who commanded the American forces in Broome at the time. Legge, who took the decision to evacuate the Americans, testified that Jolly was among the last to leave the town, that he had stayed on sufficiently long to treat the injured, and that among the mere twenty or so who chose not to leave there was an RAAF doctor. It was by no means a case of desertion of duty, Legge insisted, because nothing was to be gained by Jolly remaining.[10]

Jolly was not going to let accusations of cowardice or treachery go unchallenged and put pen to paper to defend his actions. Some of the townspeople, he noted in his letter of 27 March to the Minister of Civil Defence, had taken the attitude 'if the Japs come the best thing we can do is to do business with them'. The male population – Americans and Dutch included – spent most of the time in a state of intoxication, and Jolly became involved in the shutting of the hotels by arrangement with the publicans. At that point he reviewed his own circumstances: 'I saw no reason why my wife and children should be left beggars because of a lot of semi-intoxicated pearlers who did nothing for themselves but talk about defending Broome to the very last and drawing maps on bar counters with fingers dipped in beer.' On the day of the raid Jolly had tended to the wounded at the jetty, then made his way to the hospital to help with dressings and evacuations. But with Legge's firm encouragement he left Broome at midnight of 4 March, having 'no intention of sitting in the bush drinking beer and whisky waiting for the invaders to turn up'.[11]

Jolly was no coward. After heading south, he left the public service and worked at a medical practice at Midland Junction, just east of Perth, before choosing to serve in his adopted country's armed forces. His record shows that he enlisted in the Royal Australian Medical Corps in October 1944. By the end of the year he was sent on overseas service on the island of Morotai and then in Borneo, attached to an Australian camp hospital.[12]

Before that he spent time with Fred Rose in Perth. There was no chance of anthropological collaboration, yet there was much to discuss. One topic was membership of the Communist Party. It was a delicate topic, because the Curtin government preserved Menzies' ban on the CPA until December 1942. To join before then could have devastating consequences, especially for a public servant like Rose. Nonetheless, the politics of the day now seemed refreshingly simple: 'Nazi Germany was my *bête noire*, followed by the two other axis partners, Italy and Japan.' And for Rose 'it was the Red Army and the Soviet people that had shown at the gates of Moscow and Leningrad and were still showing at quite unpronounceable places that the Nazi Wehrmacht could be held. Naïve perhaps, but this was for me conclusive evidence of the moral and social superiority of the Soviet system led by the communist party and I wanted to join the Australian Communist Party to learn more about it'.[13]

From that point until the end of his life, Rose would remain a member of a communist party. The timing of that initial commitment had much to do with the geopolitics of the day, but it had also been a long time in the making. Exposure to the misery of Britain's Depression-struck unemployed, 'Red Cambridge', incarceration in a Nazi jail, and the firsthand experience of the wretchedness and exploitation of indigenous Australians had pushed him in that direction. A string of mentors, witting and unwitting, had done their bit as well: Margot Heinemann, Edith Linde, Bill Harney, Alec Jolly. Marxism met a pressing intellectual need; it gave the young scientist what appeared a comprehensive and internally consistent framework to help him understand not only his chosen discipline but the entire world. Emotionally, too, communism had much to offer. The Party became Rose's bedrock; he would build his world on it.

There was no hint of opportunism in his decision to join; he was and remained a member out of deep conviction. Neither was his decision to join an act of spontaneity sparked by an apprehension of crisis. He was no callow revolutionary, swayed by the slogans of the day. On the contrary, at twenty-seven he was a mature adult, had seen much of the world, and had been aware of the possibility of becoming a communist for some time.

A family portrait of the Rose family. Standing are Fred's father George, his older sister Dora, and Fred himself, dressed in a sailor's suit. Seated are Fred's mother Frances and, on her knee, Donald. Donald was to die in 1933 at the age of 13. (Rose family collection)

Rose's rugby team at Whitgift Middle School. Rose is in the back row, third from the right. (Rose family collection)

Rose at about the time he commenced his studies at St Catharine's College Cambridge. (Rose family collection)

Edith Linde and her sister Ruth at the Linde home at Hohen Neuendorf just north of Berlin in the late 1920s. The villa behind them became the hiding place for Jews, forced labourers and POWs on the run from the Nazi regime. Eventually the two sisters would live on opposite sides of the Berlin Wall. (Rose family collection)

Courting. Fred Rose and Edith photographed by each other on a day out together. (Rose family collection)

Flying-boat base at Port Langdon on Groote Eylandt. Constructing the jetty into Little Lagoon, August 1938. (Rose family collection)

Shell Company employee Henry with
a stingray shot from the jetty at the
flying-boat base, September 1938.
(SLNSW Frederick Rose papers, Box 3)

The CMS missionary Philip Taylor and his sister
Elizabeth visit Fred Gray at the latter's still unroofed
house at Umbakumba, July 1938.
(Rose family collection)

Fred Rose with fly net on ridge of sandhills to the north-east of the flying base and
boundary of the Aboriginal reserve on Groote Eylandt, 1938. (Rose family collection)

Aborigines on board
Fred Gray's schooner
Outuli, Groote Eylandt,
1938.
(SLNSW, Frederick
Rose papers, Box 3)

Christmas Day 1938.
Fred Gray, dressed
characteristically
in white, with
unidentified
Aborigines and
the Shell Company
employees Hughie
Polden, Percy Stamp
and Doug O'Reilly
at Umbakumba.
(SLNSW, Frederick
Rose papers, Box 3)

Rose's fiancée
Edith Linde with
Fred Gray's bitch
Bunty in front of
Gray's house on
Groote Eylandt,
August 1938.
(Rose family
collection)

Broome 1941. Fred Rose on the left with son Kim. Next to them is Alec Jolly with his daughter on his shoulders. (Rose family collection)

Rose and Groote Eylandters Nertichunga, Machana and Nabia, Groote Eylandt, 1941. (SLNSW, Frederick Rose papers, Box 5)

Edith Rose in front of Fred Gray's house at Umbakumba, May 1941. (Rose family collection)

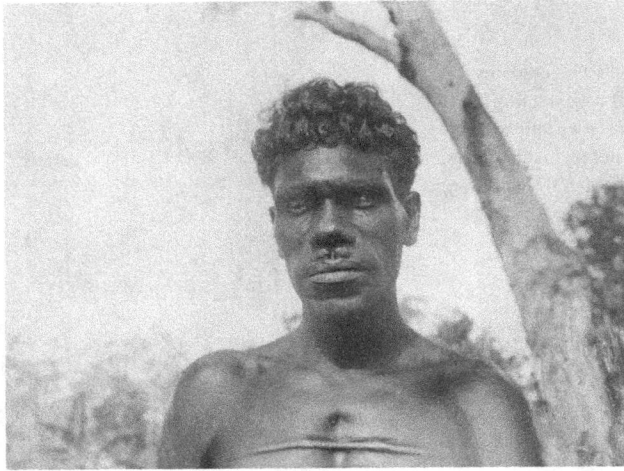

Kulpejer (or Kulpaja) Bara. Kulpejer had crewed with Fred Gray; he helped Rose and later Peter Worsley perform their anthropological fieldwork on Groote Eylandt. The method adopted by Rose was to take photographs of as many people as he could, with the result that Kulpejer himself became an object of study. (SLNSW, Frederick Rose papers, Box 5)

Richard Linde. Because of his Anglophilia Edith's father later came to be addressed by his grandchildren as 'Sir Richard'. An uncompromising anti-fascist, Linde hid refugees in his home in Hohen Neuendorf outside Berlin and welcomed the arrival of the Red Army in 1945. (Rose family collection)

Rose the dedicated public servant strides to work, 26 November 1946. (Rose family collection)

Stranded without radio contact at Umbakumba during a period of torrential rain at the very beginning of the Mountford Expedition, Rose is among a small group who make their way by foot across the island to Angurugu to use the mission station's radio. Pictured are Quart-pot, Rose, Bukanda and Kulpejer. (Rose family collection)

Walter Seddon Clayton, the elusive communist spymaster, was a visitor to the Rose house in Froggatt Street Canberra. (National Archives of Australia A6119 941)

Charles Chambers Fowell Spry. In 1950 Spry was appointed Director-General of the Australian Security Intelligence Organisation (ASIO), founded by the Chifley government the previous year. Spry's prime goal was to crack 'The Case', that is, the network of communists and sympathisers who were passing intelligence to the Soviets. (National Archives of Australia A9626 8)

Gathered on the stoop of the Rose house at 25 Froggatt Street in December 1951 are Edith, Kim, Ruth and Sonja Rose along with their visitor Bill Harney, an almost legendary outback figure, who advised Fred Rose on undertaking anthropological fieldwork in the Northern Territory. (Rose family collection)

Peter Worsley came to Australia in the expectation of going on to New Guinea to undertake fieldwork, but a government ban foiled that plan. With the help of Fred Rose and Fred Gray he was able to work on Groote Eylandt, which became the subject of his doctoral dissertation. Worsley went on to become Professor of Sociology at the University of Manchester, from where he remained in touch with Rose. (Julia Worsley)

Circular Quay, Sydney, June 1953. Edith, Sonja and Ruth look anxiously toward Fred and Kim, who remain behind. Between their departure and the family's reunion lie more than three years and countless vicissitudes on both sides of the globe. (Rose family collection)

His decision was not taken lightly, rather it was the result of the careful reasoning of a sharp intellect, mixed with an instinctive compassion for the underdog. He was totally convinced that it was the right course to follow, and over the remaining decades of his life he would never be persuaded otherwise.

Rose was not alone in his attraction to communism's dubious charms. After Barbarossa, membership of the CPA – renamed for a time the Australian Communist Party (ACP)[14] to foreground its patriotic credentials – spiked. Such was the level of public support that it operated relatively openly in defiance of its proscription.[15] And when the ban on the CPA was finally overturned near the end of 1942, thousands more abandoned their misgivings and took out membership.

Rose noted that at first he and Jolly were treated with some suspicion when they arrived at Party gatherings, presumably mistaken for plain-clothes policemen. They would have looked the part. Rose was close to six feet tall, strong and fit, while the older and stockier Jolly still looked every bit the pugilist he had been in his youth. In time they were able to convince the WA branch of the CPA of their bona fides. Rose joined, while Jolly, whose earlier membership in Victoria had lapsed, rejoined. Rose's sponsor was Katharine Susannah Prichard, a founding member of the CPA in 1920, a staunch advocate of Aboriginal rights, and, in time, not just a 'comrade' but a close friend and patient of Alec Jolly at Midland Junction.[16]

Living as he did in Dalkeith, Rose joined the branch in nearby Nedlands, many of whose members were associated with the University of Western Australia. In that regard the branch reflected the changing demographic of the CPA during its growth phase. What had formerly been a party of largely blue-collar workers and the unemployed was attracting ever increasing numbers of 'intellectuals' and white-collar workers. One of the leading figures in Nedlands, according to Rose, was the physicist Sid Williams. Kim Beazley attended a number of meetings. When Rose noted to fellow members that Beazley had stopped attending, he was told in hushed tones 'the party wanted him to join the Labor Party, presumably to red-ant it'.[17]

The CPA activities Rose pursued most avidly related to the plight of

Aborigines. He gave a couple of talks addressing that topic on what he described as 'a regular progressive program on one of Perth's radio stations', facilitated by Bill Beeby and financed by the 'Anti-Fascist League', in all likelihood one of the CPA's fronts.[18] Through the Party, Rose became acquainted with Don McLeod, an activist who became a leader of the Aboriginal station workers' strike on Pilbara sheep properties in 1946. When Rose met him he had been attempting to acquire a property in his own name for Aborigines to run, but the Western Australian government had stymied him, and he had turned to the CPA for support.[19]

The Party soon picked up on Rose's expertise. Prichard suggested he write a pamphlet on the Aboriginal question. To that time the CPA had hardly distinguished itself in promoting the Aboriginal cause, but just prior to the war Tom Wright, secretary of the Sheet Metal Workers' Union and a former CPA general secretary, had written a pamphlet, *A New Deal for the Aborigines*, with a foreword by Prichard.[20] One of his sources was the anthropologist Olive Pink, who with the support of A.P. Elkin and the Australian National Research Council had undertaken research in Central Australia in the mid-1930s.[21] After a falling out with Elkin she received support from Quakers and from Wright's union.[22] Wright had also drawn heavily on the work of Donald Thomson in Melbourne – who was certainly no communist.[23] Following Thomson, Wright had argued for the complete segregation of Aborigines and the preservation of their traditional ways of life. And in line with the widespread assumptions of the day, for him that meant distinguishing between 'full-blood' and 'half-caste' Aborigines and treating them differently.

Prichard might have hoped that Rose could provide the Party with a distinctively communist perspective on the issue. Yet with Wright's views already in print, Rose could not disregard the thinking of the tacitly acknowledged 'expert' in the area. When Rose's views were delivered to Wright, the latter wrote a 'devastating criticism', which very nearly persuaded Rose to quit the CPA. Wright's comments to Rose's mind were 'quite unqualified and in several respects rather stupid'. Nonetheless, he chose to swallow his pride and observe Party discipline.[24]

While Rose affirmed his loyalty, it was decided that Edith as a previous German national would be better served avoiding membership until the Party became legal. When that occurred, both she and Fred threw themselves with the enthusiasm of novices into Party work, 'selling the party press and publicity material and chalking and painting up slogans in the neighbourhood'.[25]

There were limits to the time Edith could make available for such work. On 20 April 1943 she gave birth to a daughter, Sonja; Kim was just over two years of age.[26] Moreover, at the height of the war, and with bombing raids on German cities becoming ever more frequent, many of her thoughts must have been with her family on the other side of the world.

It was not just bombs that threatened her father's wellbeing. Richard Linde, born in Hannover in 1880, had climbed from the humble rank of metalworker to become a patent attorney of international repute. Politically, however, his views remained firmly anchored on the left of German politics, albeit on the social democratic rather than the communist left. Having lived in England for some years, he personified the kind of cosmopolitanism his political enemies despised. As an active freemason, too, he could expect no sympathy from Nazis.[27] As Hitler turned ever more ruthlessly on his enemies at home, Richard Linde and his ilk had much to fear, especially when Linde took the immensely courageous decision to throw in his lot with the resistance. He attached himself to a group built around Ernst Strassmann and Hans Robinsohn, whose opposition to Nazism derived from Quaker principles of the renunciation of violence and love for one's fellow human beings. In the Linde family villa at Hohen Neuendorf just outside Berlin, anti-Nazi political meetings were held and English radio broadcasts monitored intently. The latter revealed the extent of the crimes committed by German forces in the East, strengthening the group's resolve to save as many of the persecuted as they could. In time the Linde home became a refuge for a number of Jews, escaped slave labourers and prisoners of war. Overall the network to which Linde belonged protected some eighty people, finding them food, shelter and clothing and furnishing them with false papers. In the end it was only with much good fortune that Linde escaped arrest and the even more drastic consequences that would have ensued.[28]

For a time Edith faced her anxieties without Fred, who in June 1943 was transferred to Melbourne to take up a position as climatologist at the Central Weather Bureau in Carlton. He rented a room in Drummond Street, just a couple of doors from his place of work, while Edith and the children waited several months to get berths on a train across the Nullarbor. In November Fred and Edith reunited and began to refocus their energies in the service of the Party. Fred was soon elected chairman of the Carlton branch, and then of the entire Carlton zone.[29] It was a role that brought him into contact with members of the Melbourne University branch, both students and academics.

After the hellishly hot summer of early 1944 the Roses abandoned the cramped quarters of Drummond Street for half a furnished but crumbling house in Bay View Terrace in South Kensington. The location was less than ideal, since in certain winds the stench of the nearby Footscray slaughter-yards and boiling-down factory overwhelmed the house and its occupants. Noise, too, was a constant irritant. Two fibro sheets separated the Roses' abode from their neighbours the Gardiners, who also had two children.[30] With the move to Bay View Terrace came the transfer for both Fred and Edith to the South Kensington branch of the Party, and with it contact with the Free German Movement, the *Freie Deutsche Bewegung*. This group of German refugees hoped that even in the Antipodes they might make a contribution to liberating their homeland. Among them was Heinrich Eggebrecht, a Berlin baker who had come to Australia on the notorious *Dunera* and been interned as an 'enemy alien'.[31] Another was Klaus Wilszynski, the son of a Jewish dentist from Berlin and destined to become a senior journalist with the East German *Berliner Zeitung*.[32] Then there was Walter Kaufmann, also from Berlin, whose Jewish adoptive parents were murdered in Auschwitz. The 'baby' of the Germans on board the *Dunera*, Kaufmann, like Eggebrecht and Wilszynski, would return to Germany after the war, accompanied by his Tasmanian-born wife Barbara, and renew his acquaintance with the Roses there.[33]

There were artists, too, in the circle of friends the Roses established in the small South Kensington branch, among them Vic and Ailsa O'Connor. Vic was part of a 'Realist Group', which included Yosl Bergner and Noel Counihan, both communists. The Viennese-born Bergner, who had joined the Richmond branch of the CPA,[34] was building a reputation as an artist with a talent for depicting the misfortunes of working-class Australians. Counihan had joined the CPA as early as 1933 after serving his time in the Young Communist League. He worked as a cartoonist for several newspapers until Bergner persuaded him to paint, which he did in the social realist style of the day.[35]

Membership of the South Kensington branch also brought Rose into contact with Ted Hill, who for a time had responsibility for that branch and sometimes attended its meetings. As a member of the Victorian state committee of the CPA, Hill would have been the most senior communist known to Rose. A lawyer by profession, his occasional attendance at branch meetings would make for a lively gathering. Hill was inclined, as Rose noted, 'to rub people up the wrong way'.[36]

Whether judged by the breadth of its activities or simply by the numbers and diverse demographics of its members, the Second World War marked the halcyon days of the CPA. By the end of 1944 a peak membership of 23,000 was reached, and the communist Fred Paterson had been elected to the Queensland parliament.[37] The prewar distrust of communism largely evaporated, as Australians evinced huge goodwill toward the Soviet Union as it battled for its very survival, turned the fortunes of the war in Europe, and then eventually turned Berlin into the grave of fascism.

With the war at an end, neither the goodwill toward the CPA nor its healthy membership numbers would last. In time the apparatchiks – Ted Hill and his kind – would strengthen their grip on the Party in Australia, just as Moscow would demand unquestioning obedience from communist parties throughout the world. Many of the 'bourgeois intellectuals' abandoned the Party when administered their first dose of postwar discipline, and the CPA entered a period of inexorable decline.[38]

In the eyes of Ted Hill and others, Fred Rose with his middle-class roots,

Cambridge education and public service job, was a 'bourgeois intellectual'. Yet he was not one who would abandon the Party when its fortunes turned after the war, or at any time thereafter. In the case of Rose, the intriguing question is not so much why he joined the Party in the first place, but rather why he stuck with it, while so many others found so many reasons to consign their Party badge to the rubbish bin. The difference was that Fred Rose was a communist by unstinting conviction. Even when he disagreed with the Party line – as he did in the Tom Wright affair – he took the view that the greater good would be served through obedience and unwavering commitment.

Alec Jolly was made of similar stuff. Even as his medical practice thrived, Jolly maintained his devotion to the Party well after the war was won. In her memoirs Dorothy Hewett recalls Jolly as the only communist member of the Midland Council.[39] He continued his friendship with Katharine Susannah Prichard, remaining her personal physician to the final days of her life. 'Each day', Prichard's son Ric Throssell later wrote, 'when Dr Alec Jolly called to see Katharine on his way to the surgery in Midland Junction, she had a cup of tea ready for him'. As Jolly held forth on all manner of topics, the ageing Prichard would curl up in her chair, 'trying to look as if she could grasp the dimensions of time in space, theories of inherited immunity or the origins of consanguinity taboos'.[40] Jolly was present as Prichard drew her last breath. Summoned from his work in Canberra in 1969, Throssell arrived at his mother's home, Greenmount, to hear Alec Jolly 'crying out in his own grief: "God, who am I going to talk to now?"'[41]

10. Postwar

During the war Rose had been 'manpowered'; he had little choice but to remain in his assigned position as climatologist at Melbourne's Central Weather Bureau. With victory in the Pacific Rose was free to explore new career options, whether in the public service or outside it.

In desiring change he imbibed the spirit of the times. The end of war brought new possibilities for those who had survived and for Australia as a whole. War had cut some of the apron strings that tied Australia to Britain. In some quarters, at least, the realisation set in that Australia's future lay not only in the new bond formed with the United States, but also in asserting a presence in its region. The conflict had set this process in motion; Australia had focussed its energies on the Japanese threat from the north, and, in doing so, had taken giant steps in developing its own northern regions. The most far-sighted of Australia's planners knew it would be disastrous to retreat from those advances.

Rose naturally discussed his future with the Party. He conveyed to his comrades the notion that he might commence a career as an academic anthropologist, but also his skepticism as to its feasibility. Elkin's position as doyen of Australian anthropology was not yet seriously under threat in 1945; he continued to rule his department in Sydney with a 'cold megalomania'.[1] As he had already passed damning judgment on Rose's work, there was no hope of him lending support to any application Rose might make for an academic post. Rose nonetheless threw his hat into the ring, applying for a research fellowship at the Australian National University (ANU), only to be knocked back, he surmised, on 'ideological grounds'.[2] In 1946 he lodged a hopeful application for a chair of geography and anthropology at the University of Wales Aberystwyth. Elkin's grasp did not extend that far, but in this instance, too, Rose was unsuccessful.[3]

Destined to remain for now in the public service, but keen for a change of direction, one possibility was to move to a position in the administration of the Northern Territory. That would have been a simple option because it did not entail moving from the Department for the Interior. The other was a move sideways into another department, where he might apply his knowledge of indigenous Australia. As it happened, the position of Senior Research Officer in the Regional Planning Division of the Department of Post-War Reconstruction was gazetted. Rose applied and was successful.[4]

The Department of Post-War Reconstruction had been established on 22 December 1942. Early the following year a director-general had been appointed; core staff were transferred from the Reconstruction Division of the Department of Labour and National Service. The government gave it the ambitious brief to prepare the transition from a wartime to a peacetime economy through the provision of planning and coordination services. In practice this would mean collaborating with other Commonwealth departments as well as state governments and other authorities. An inspired choice was made for the position of secretary in the new department – the mercurial economist Herbert Cole (Nugget) Coombs.[5]

Coombs and his department would prove an ideal fit for Rose's abilities. Under Coombs's guidance the department would not lose sight of the importance of developing northern Australia, both through promoting the Commonwealth's Northern Territory and through working together with Queensland and Coombs's home state of Western Australia. Moreover, as would become increasingly apparent later in his career, Coombs was deeply interested in indigenous Australians and how they might be integrated into the modern Australia he envisioned. As for Rose, there would have been few public servants with a better knowledge of northern Australia than he, and his abiding interest in anthropology could be regarded as an asset rather than a liability.

If there was one disadvantage in this new post, it was that it required a move to Canberra. Since the births of Kim and Sonja in Western Australia, another daughter, Ruth, was added to the brood in January 1946. Rose had to leave behind his wife and three children to join the influx of public servants into the hostels of Canberra. For a time he occupied a room in the Acton Hotel, while he awaited more adequate accommodation for the family. Not until near the end of 1947 could he rent a house, a red brick bungalow at 25 Froggatt Street in Turner, bordering the dairy pastures that Canberra was engulfing. Its previous occupant, the diplomat Arthur Malcolm Morris, had departed to take up an overseas posting.[6]

Rose was placed on the North Australian Development Committee (NADC), where he worked under its executive officer Grenfell Ruddock. Rose was particularly interested in what the NADC might do for the advancement of Aborigines in northern Australia. In this area, as in others, there was continual pressure from the states to free up Commonwealth funding, purportedly in the interests of Aboriginal advancement. Rose struggled to find much sincerity in the states' actions, indeed it appeared to him that the state representatives were 'chauvinistic and discriminating' in their attitudes. Coombs, by contrast, took a more sanguine view, in fact he was 'the only one who took a positive attitude towards them [that is, Aborigines] as human beings'.[7]

The NADC also dealt with issues ranging from the agricultural, pastoral and mining industries, to transport and infrastructure, fishing, health, housing, education and immigration. For Rose there was much liaison work to be done, indeed liaising was at the very core of his working life. He became very well connected in and outside the public service, in Canberra and in other parts of the country. He knew and was known by people in high places. Authorship of policy, too, was part of his brief. He prepared reports for the Prime Minister and the relevant state premiers; he even drafted letters for the Prime Minister's signature expressing Commonwealth views on the committee's recommendations.[8]

In the performance of all of these tasks, there appears no suggestion in the public record that Rose was anything other than a competent and diligent public servant. A large part of his very considerable intellect was devoted to the conscientious performance of his duties. Yet it was also a feature of Rose's personality that he could compartmentalise his various spheres of thought and action. These compartments were quite watertight;

the contents of one need have no impact on goings-on in another. So it was, for example, that the diligent public servant could also be the engaged anthropologist, even if the work of the latter had to be confined to his hours after work or during holidays. Similarly, the diligent bureaucrat Fred Rose, who by day carried out his obligations in the service of a modern capitalist state, by night and in his free time devoted his energies to planning the overthrow of that very state. Rose might have left the South Kensington Branch of the CPA behind, but white-collar Canberra, too, had its communists, and Rose was one of them.

The transfer of his CPA membership to Canberra was a mere formality. And while sleepy Canberra was hardly a hotbed of political radicalism, for Rose it was within striking distance of Sydney. Occasionally he would travel to CPA headquarters in Sydney's George Street to meet with members of the central committee and discuss the pressing issues of the day with them.[9]

There were matters of some gravity to tackle, as the Party struggled to adapt to the postwar order. The CPA's 14th congress was staged in August 1945, just as the war in the Pacific was hastening to an end with the horrific bombings of Hiroshima and Nagasaki. Its resolutions oozed with pride in victory and confidence in the future. Fascism was vanquished, new 'people's democracies' were being established, the labour movement was stronger and more united than ever before. In Australia the Communist Party had supported all the Labor government's necessary war measures; 4000 Party members had fought in the armed forces, and many had lost their lives.[10] But with peace secured, the task now was to guard against the re-emergence of the forces of reaction, both in Australia and beyond. It was stirring rhetoric, though strangely quiet on the question of what the new order might offer Australia's indigenous people.

Behind the scenes matters were different, and in some CPA quarters at least there was a recognition that the Party had to engage with Aboriginal issues to a much greater extent than before the war. To do so would require placing the Party's thinking in this area on a firm scientific foundation, and it was acknowledged that Rose possessed precisely the knowledge that could be helpful. One security report from the time has it that Rose was the

CPA's 'official anthropologist'.[11] He was encouraged to express his views, and did so in the pages of the Party's theoretical organ, *The Communist Review*, concealing his identify as a public servant by publishing under Alec Jolly's name. Moreover it was suggested that the Party needed a coherent and updated articulation of its position on Aboriginal issues, supplanting Tom Wright's prewar tract *A New Deal for the Aborigines*. And who was better qualified to deliver an informed diagnosis of current ills and an ideologically grounded program to address them than Fred Rose?

Rose took up the challenge, aware that it would be no easy task. The truth was that in the world of anthropology ideas were in a state of flux, if not upheaval. In Europe the Holocaust had demanded a fundamental questioning of the 'science' of race that had informed so much anthropological thinking through the first half of the century. Rose's fieldwork in Australia had led him to doubt some of the basic tenets of British social anthropology. The influence of Alec Jolly had steered him toward the works of Morgan and Engels, yet his views were not yet fully mature. To meet the CPA's request would require him not only to meet the Party's needs but to clarify his own views.

When he had completed his task, Rose concealed his identity by adopting the *nom de plume* 'Jagara', the name of an Aboriginal group originally from the Brisbane area.[12] Over its sixty-four pages, Jagara's *Frederick Engels, Lewis Morgan and the Australian Aborigine* demonstrated that Aboriginal society on Groote Eylandt was not dying out in a Darwinian contest with a superior white race of British colonists. Rather, the Aborigines, who had applied intelligent insights to reproduction, had ensured their survival by making the 'right' marriage choices, which meant avoiding incest through the practice of exogamous marriage.

Any reader possessing a close familiarity with recent developments in Australian anthropology could not have mistaken the voices of Fred Rose and Alec Jolly in Jagara. The homage to Morgan and Engels, the Australian examples provided, and the distinctive approach to kinship studies were faithful echoes of the works Rose and Jolly had published under both their names in *Annals of Eugenics* and under Jolly's name alone in *The Communist*

Review. By 1946, however, Rose was adding a sharper political thrust to the expression of his ideas. He urged his readers not only to return to the study of the classic works of Morgan and Engels but also to promote 'the tasks of the Australian Labour Movement in relation to the problem of the Aborigines'.[13] The pamphlet was written for the labour movement and for Aborigines, but also expressly against the 'reactionaries'. Those reactionaries, Jagara proclaimed in unison with Engels, would have to give way in the end to Morgan's evolutionary theories.[14]

After that combative polemical flourish Jagara concluded on a curiously diffident note: 'It is recognized that owing to restricted or incorrect data some of Morgan's and consequently some of Engels' conclusions on primitive society need to be revised.' It seemed a misplaced concession of doubt in an otherwise brashly assertive tract, yet it pointed to a genuine uncertainty that would not go away. Far from being a minor irritant in Rose's project of developing a Marxist theory of anthropology for his own times, the issue of the reliability of Morgan and Engels was soon to turn into a major stumbling block.

What Rose could not know at the time was that in the Soviet Union anthropological thinking had taken a different turn under the direction of Josef Stalin. Even as Soviet forces were locked in desperate battle against German invaders, Stalin exercised a powerful influence over the sciences in the Soviet Union, and anthropology was no exception. In the biological sciences, the infamous Professor Trofim Lysenko, who held sway in Stalin's scientific court during the late 1930s and 1940s, had convinced Stalin that 'eugenics, genetics and fascism were all cut from the same cloth'.[15] As a result, Stalin re-emphasised his conviction that 'Marxism [was] not a biological science but a *sociological* science'.[16] As Fred Rose later came to realise,[17] Stalin was almost certainly swayed also by the German anthropologist Heinrich Eildermann, who in his 1921 seminal work *Urkommunismus und Urreligion* (Ancient Communism and Ancient Religion) had had the temerity to claim that in one fundamental point Engels was wrong.[18] Eildermann's work was translated into Russian in 1923, though it was a couple of decades before Stalin – or at least those entrusted with adducing the evidence to prove Stalin's infallibilty – conveniently rediscovered the German's bold thesis.

Where Engels went wrong, according to Eildermann and Stalin, was in staking a claim for the role of biology, of human reproduction, in shaping the course of human history. Engels in his foreword to *The Origin of the Family* had contended that social structure was determined *not only* by the conditions of production of material goods, *but also* by the conditions of production of humans themselves. His precise words were: 'According to the materialist conception, the determining factor in history is, in the final instance, the production and reproduction of human life.'[19] Stalin disagreed. In his view a materialist interpretation of history was *all* about the mode of production and had *nothing* to do with biology or reproduction. Engels had failed to acknowledge that the mode of production *alone*, that is, the *economic* base of any society, determined that society's nature and its development. In other words, Engels had lapsed into 'biological determinism', seeing the form of the family as itself the product of a particular set of material circumstances, and mistakenly concluding that the form of the family helped shape social development.[20] This was in Stalin's view a philosophical dualism, which stood in contradiction to the 'monistic view of history which Marx and Engels [had previously] worked out'.[21]

Stalin's critique of Engels had first surfaced in 1943 in the Soviet theoretical journal *Pod Znamenem Marxizma* (Under the Banner of Marxism).[22] Knowledge of the so-called 'Stalin Criticism' first reached Australia in an English translation in the December 1944/January 1945 issue of *The Communist Review*.[23] At first Rose had laconically dismissed the controversy as mere 'hairsplitting' over Engels' foreword and no reason to throw out the proverbial baby with the bathwater. The diffident conclusion to his Jagara pamphlet was a concession that perhaps Engels was not absolutely right on every point, but that was as far as it went. Others, though, took the so-called 'Stalin Criticism' more seriously, and Rose found himself 'in a minority amongst Australian Marxists'. Pedantic though it must have seemed to many, the controversy refused to die away.[24]

Not until the middle of the 1950s did Rose fully absorb the impact of the 'Stalin Criticism', and in such a way as finally to proclaim Engels' – and therewith his own – error of 'dualism', that is, of placing an inappropriate emphasis on biological factors in understanding changes in human society. After some ten years of debate he conceded that Stalin was absolutely right and that he and Engels were guilty of using 'an evolutionary and not a dialectical-historical method'.[25] In May 1955 Rose eventually submitted to the CPA's secretariat in Sydney a thirty-three-page report which concluded: 'Engels was incorrect on the point at issue and in philosophical terms had made an error of "dualism".'[26] It was a formal recantation, a confession of '16 yrs of idealism', in order 'to demonstrate the weaknesses which I personally have shown both theoretically and in other directions'.[27]

The ultimate result of the 'Stalin Criticism' was that, as he put it less formally, he 'was left like a shag on a rock without a feather to fly with'.[28] Nonetheless, from that point in his intellectual development he would never again fundamentally shift his thinking. In his anthropological work Fred Rose manifested the conviction, the zeal and even the arrogance of the convert. From that time forth until his dying day, in his anthropology as in his politics, Rose remained an implacable advocate of an orthodox Marxism that brooked no alternative.

11. Monty

Rose's working life after the war bore little resemblance to what he had envisioned for himself a decade earlier. His routine was that of the Canberra public servant, setting off to work each day from quintessentially suburban Turner. Having dedicated some eight hours of his intellectual labours to the task of ensuring the smooth running of the country, he headed home to his wife and three children in their cosy Froggatt Street bungalow. But Rose was itching to get back to fieldwork and to Groote Eylandt. Finally, when in 1948 an opportunity presented itself for him to cast off his public servant's white collar and tie, to don the pith helmet of the anthropologist and head back to the tropics, he jumped at it.

The man who made it possible was Charles Pearcy Mountford – 'Monty' – a former tram driver turned anthropologist. The idea for an expedition to northern Australia had arisen in 1945, when Mountford conducted a lecture tour of the United States organised by his then employer, the Commonwealth Department of Information. His tour included a photographic presentation to the National Geographic Society at Constitution Hall in Washington, where an audience of over 4000 greeted his lecture with enthusiasm beyond his wildest dreams.[1]

It was in large part American money that converted the idea into reality just three years later. The Smithsonian Institution contributed a very significant sum, as did the National Geographical Society.[2] In Australia, even in the austere postwar environment, there was firm support for the expedition. Lessons had been learned from the war. If future threats of invasion were to be thwarted, according to the contemporary postwar strategic orthodoxy, the north had to be developed.[3] Moreover, the Labor government saw great public relations potential in a showcase of

US–Australian collaboration, and with it a timely distraction from the waning popularity of Ben Chifley's socialism.[4] This was especially true in the case of Minister for Immigration Arthur Calwell, who spruiked the forthcoming expedition with a passion. A number of ministries pitched in to aid with logistics, and it was at the Commonwealth government's expense that three scientists from the Australian Institute of Anatomy were included in the expedition.[5] Both the Australian Museum in Sydney and the Institute of Anatomy in Canberra lent generous support.[6] Whether American or Australian, all expedition members were treated like VIPs and given official receptions in various parts of the country.[7]

Mountford, his salary and expenses paid by the Commonwealth, was appointed leader. In the opinion of his detractors, Mountford had shortcomings as an anthropologist, having left school at just eleven and entered the discipline through one of its many back doors. Working as a mechanic for the Darwin Post Office, he had made occasional visits to the Kahlin Compound. Back in Adelaide he pursued his interest more formally through collaboration with Norman Tindale, who had a professional base in both the South Australian Museum and the University of Adelaide.[8] In time the amateur Mountford established a record of research that outshone many of his professional colleagues.[9]

No one's feathers were more ruffled by the decision to bestow the leadership on Mountford than those of A.P. Elkin. Still holding the chair of anthropology in Sydney, and still expecting to pull the discipline's strings throughout Australia, it was Elkin who had apparently vetoed Mountford's 1940 application for a Carnegie Fellowship to study Aboriginal art in the Western Desert.[10] Elkin construed Mountford's 1948 appointment as an attempt to undermine his authority; he responded by dispatching his loyal protégés Ronald and Catherine Berndt on a research mission to Yirkalla, arranging salaries and expenses for them as well as the cooperation of mission bodies and personnel. It was an ultimately futile attempt to thwart Mountford.[11]

Of course, anyone who got on Elkin's wrong side was likely to find favour with Fred Rose, and perhaps Mountford knew, or intuited, Elkin's attitude to

Rose. As early as 1945, having got wind that a major expedition was in the offing, Rose had broached with Mountford the prospect of involvement.[12] In Rose's recollection, he and Mountford discussed 'the problems of scientific personnel' in Canberra and Adelaide.[13] One of the suggestions Rose made would have helped in small measure to address the gender imbalance among the scientists. He recommended that the anthropologist Pamela Beasley be included. He would have known that Beasley was the sister-in-law of John Wear Burton, Secretary of the Department of External Affairs. Almost certainly, though, he did not reveal that she and her husband were members of the CPA.[14] In any case, Rose's idea in this instance came to nothing.

In other regards Rose's influence in the planning of the expedition is apparent. The first leg of the anticipated seven-month expedition was to be devoted to Groote Eylandt, and few European Australians knew the island as well as Rose. It was resolved that the expedition's first base for a full three months would be at Umbakumba; its first host would be Rose's old mate Fred Gray. This offered the prospect that Gray's pearl lugger *Wanderer* would transport the scientists to different locations along the Arnhem Land coast and to the other base camps at Yirrkala and Oenpelli (today more commonly Gunbalanya).[15]

This was not to be a purely anthropological expedition, even if anthropology was Mountford's passion. The seventeen members were drawn from various stakeholder institutions, representing a diverse range of disciplines. The deputy leader, Frank M. Setzler from the Smithsonian Institution, for example, took on the role of archaeologist, in which capacity he managed to pilfer a large collection of human bones from mortuary caves and other burial sites. Apart from Mountford himself, an honorary assistant in ethnology at the South Australian Museum, anthropology was covered by Fred McCarthy from the Department of Anthropology at the Australian Museum.[16]

Seven years had passed since Rose had been on Groote Eylandt, and much had changed. The greatest impact of the war had occurred after his departure. Northern Australia was a battle zone, and Groote Eylandt was part of it. The flying-boat base was handed over to the RAAF; its prime functions were military. Aborigines were accorded a role in defending the country; in the Gulf of Carpentaria they could draw on a long tradition of viewing the Japanese as outsiders to be repelled. As for their relations with Europeans, instead of distancing themselves from the air base, Gray's settlement and the mission had become integrated into the social structures mandated by the defence effort. The men were employed and fed primarily by the RAAF and the Main Roads Commission. In their military functions they worked in much the same way as white people. They learned, as Rose observed, 'that white men were not just policemen or missionaries but also human beings who laboured like themselves'.[17]

The transformation of the island's traditional social and economic structures was profound and irreversible. Before the war the centre of the islanders' life had been the bush or the seashore; now it was in camps supervised by whites in military uniforms. Under bush conditions polygyny made sense, but now it disappeared entirely. Initiation had been necessary to teach the young men the tribal code of ethics and the skills and lore of the bush required by a hunter. When food came from a tin or a flour bag, bush skills were less useful; initiation, too, had changed, although it was still practised.[18] Rose had witnessed the early stages of these changes back in 1941. By the time he returned in 1948, it was evident that the traditional lifestyle was disappearing.[19]

Another change he observed was the hardening of the division in the island's population between west and east. On the western side of the island the mission had been moved in 1943 from Emerald River a short distance north to Angurugu.[20] Dormitory life became the norm for the older children there, while schooling was made general for the mission children in 1944. On the eastern side of the island, similar trends were observable at Fred Gray's Umbakumba settlement, where some of the children were moved into dormitories. No qualified teacher was available, at least not until Gray married one. In desperation perhaps more than in love, he had sent a telegram proposing marriage to Marjorie Gray, an old friend in England. Fortunately she accepted, and when they married in Melbourne in 1946,

Fred Rose was best man. By the time the Mountford Expedition arrived at Umbakumba, she was deeply involved in pastoral and educational duties. In effect the population of the island was separating into two distinct but arbitrarily formed groups. One, consisting in part also of Bickerton Islanders and mainlanders, was centred on the CMS mission at Angurugu, where the efforts to spread the word of God continued unabated. The other gathered around Umbakumba, where Fred Gray's secular – but still fundamentally European – worldview prevailed.[21]

The military presence disappeared almost overnight in 1945. First the personnel departed, and elements of infrastructure followed. Most crucially, technical advances in aviation accelerated by the war meant that the air base on Groote Eylandt became redundant, even for civilian aviation use. The flying boat's days were as good as over, as land-based aircraft with vastly superior ranges replaced it. Planes from Britain now landed in Darwin and then flew directly to Sydney. What equipment could be salvaged from the Groote Eylandt base was packed up and sent south; anything useful that remained might find its way across the lagoon to Umbakumba. The rest was abandoned to the ravages of tropical nature and, with that, rapid decline into a state of ruin.

The conundrum facing Fred Gray and Umbakumba was that his settlement's *raison d'être* disappeared with the base. In principle Umbakumba's function had been to ensure a separation of the indigenous population from the interlopers; in reality under Fred Gray's guidance it had developed a symbiotic relationship by supplying the base with goods in exchange for money used to improve its amenities. Without the base, it was difficult to envisage a future.

It was at this point in Umbakumba's history that the Mountford expedition arrived on the island. Fred Rose was among the first to arrive by seaplane at Little Lagoon, re-enacting a flight he had first taken more than a decade earlier. Fred Gray was there to greet the party warmly. The base, Rose immediately noticed, was deserted, and the jetty warped – decay was already setting in. Among the people, too, the signs of change were immediately obvious: 'All the Aboriginal women and even the little girls were wearing dresses. The men were wearing khaki shorts – in a few cases, shirts as well. The seclusion of the women was a thing of the past and they moved without embarrassment among the men.'[22]

Soon the first disruptions to the expedition's carefully laid plans began to unfold. No one could have anticipated the wildness of the approaching weather. More troubling though was Fred Gray's news that the vessel dispatched from Darwin with expedition equipment and supplies had not arrived. Then it was discovered that neither Mountford's nor Gray's radio transmitter functioned. The expedition was cut off from the outside world, and food supplies were fast diminishing. After ten days the situation was critical. Communication with Darwin was paramount, but faced with torrential rain and the stark reality that the nearest transmitter was more than fifty kilometres away at Angurugu, the only option was for some expedition members to walk there.

Fred Gray offered to take a small party as far as Thompson's Bay on his old barge, left behind when Shell abandoned Groote Eylandt. Undeterred by a strong northerly and driving rain, Rose, Mountford, the patrol officer Gordon Sweeney and four Aboriginal guides set off with a small ration of food, ground sheets as rain capes and cheap straw hats as head covers. Just 150 metres out to sea, disaster struck. In howling winds and a heavy swell, the barge lost power. As the motor spluttered and chugged, Gray shouted above the noise of the howling wind for Rose to take the wheel, while he attempted to coax the engine to full power. Tied together only by 'bits of wire string and old rag', had it died, the barge and its passengers would have been dashed onto rocks in minutes. 'We can't make it,' Gray called out as he swung the barge around and headed back to the lagoon. As they heaved to off Umbakumba beach, Rose was violently ill, perhaps as much from anxiety as seasickness.[23]

With only a mug of tea under their belts, the party commenced a cross-island trudge through tropical rain to Angurugu. They followed the old Army track, but the Army had been gone for two years, and parts of the track had become a raging torrent. Three or four swollen creeks were successfully negotiated, Rose stripped down to just boots and hat, entrusting his rucksack with camera to his more sure-footed Aboriginal companions. Then a more daunting torrent presented itself – by Rose's estimate some 400 yards wide.[24] All that remained to guide them across were the two surviving tree trunks of what had once been a bridge. The sight of Rose trying to cross the swollen creek straddling these logs, stark naked except for his old straw hat, was a cause of much hilarity among the guides who, while clutching rain capes under their arms and rucksacks on their heads, crossed the creek with nimble ease.[25]

The mood altered abruptly when it was Mountford's turn to cross. He fell and was swept rapidly downstream. One of the guides jumped into the swollen creek to rescue him. A sodden Mountford and his rescuer were later found clinging to the branches of a tree, hundreds of metres away. As darkness fell, the party became entirely dependent on the skill of the Aborigines to lead them on the last stage of the journey and across one last watercourse, the Angurugu River. The guides negotiated it with the aid of a rope stretched from bank to bank; Mountford, Rose and the others chose to wait until daybreak before crossing for a hearty breakfast at the mission.[26]

Frustratingly, poor reception meant that another thirty-six hours would pass before radio contact could be made with Darwin. To everyone's relief, it was eventually established that the landing craft, the fittingly named *Phoenix*, had miraculously reappeared at last, and the expedition members aboard were reported well. It had gone ashore on one of the many islands off Arnhem Land. Some suggested that the owner captain and his crew had celebrated his birthday too enthusiastically and lost their way. Happily, the supplies and equipment were intact, and in the meantime a shuttle service of RAAF Catalina flying boats was organised to relieve those waiting at Umbakumba.

The unscheduled visit to Angurugu brought Rose a quite unexpected discovery before his long walk back across the island. On the evening of the first day at the mission the Aborigines performed a traditional ceremony for a dead baby. What surprised Rose was the location, right in front of the mission house, and the missionary's tolerance of the event. The next day Rose was again at the Aborigines' camp to learn more about the maintenance of traditional culture in the very shadow of the mission. Three older men, Banjo, Kaleeowa and Baranboo, indicated they wanted to show him a ritual site, but he first had to promise not to pass the information on to the missionary. With two younger men they set out west along the Angurugu River until, after a couple of kilometres, they came across a circular clearing with three brush huts. The missionary knew nothing of this in 1948, but Norman Tindale had known of it as a result of his fieldwork in 1921. According to Tindale, under each hut were buried painted wooden slabs; they were used in totemic rituals to conjure the multiplication of certain natural species.[27] Rose knew of Tindale's findings but had not seen such a site himself, so now he was keen to establish whether these huts in the clearing contained such slabs. Without needing to ask, one of his guides dug up three of them, all bearing traces of ochre and pipe clay designs. Altogether nine were unearthed, some badly eaten by termites.[28]

The slabs, Rose knew, were associated with rituals of a kind which neither he nor Tindale, nor indeed any European, had ever witnessed. He asked Banjo and Kaleeowa, the heads of the two patrilineal moieties on the island, if the rituals might be performed so as to be recorded by the expedition. Their answer was that a performance was indeed possible, but not close to the mission. It was decided that it would occur at Umbakumba when the food supplies arrived. In the meantime Banjo, Kaleeowa and Baranboo would walk with Rose to Umbakumba to make preparations and select a site. Rose was amazed that despite the obvious changes that had taken place on the island, and despite the presence of missionaries for over a quarter of a century, such manifestations of traditional culture still existed. Alas, Rose had to return to Darwin before the performance took place.[29]

By the time Mountford's party finished its business on Groote, Rose was back at his desk in Canberra. From afar he would have traced the expedition's progress over the months that followed. Delighted though he must have been to participate for at least a time, his efforts brought him little recognition. His personal and professional reputation in Australia would be impugned by the time the multi-volume official expedition account was published, his name almost completely absent from its pages.[30]

In his introduction Mountford reports the early challenges confronted on Groote Eylandt, referring to Rose simply as 'a visitor'.[31] Rose had another reason to be disappointed. He had hoped to persuade either Mountford or Fred McCarthy to help him publish the findings of his own Groote Eylandt research. Before he returned to Canberra, he left a copy of the final manuscript of his study for the expedition's use.[32] That was as far as it went. As a very minor sop, copies were lodged with the South Australian Museum as well as in the Smithsonian Institute in the USA, but Rose must have despaired that the painstaking research he had carried out in 1941 would never achieve its due recognition.[33]

12. A Nest of Traitors

As Mountford and his team checked off the final stages of their Arnhem Land itinerary, tectonic political shifts were taking place in the wider world. With each passing month it became more apparent that global politics had fractured into two irreconcilable blocs. For a time there had been signs that the alliance formed to defeat fascism was crumbling. Those who still believed that the spirit of cooperation forged in the crucible of war might form the foundation of an enduring peaceful world order watched the mounting signs of tension with dismay. In 1948 a communist coup in Czechoslovakia showed that the Soviet Union was committed to exerting its will over a series of vassal states in eastern and central Europe. The Americans pushed through the introduction of a new currency in the Western zones of occupied Germany, provoking the Soviets into cutting off the land supply routes to the Western sectors of Berlin. For over a year western forces, including Australian pilots and aircraft, supplied West Berlin via an airlift unparalleled in history. With it the hope of creating a unified Germany disappeared. In May 1949 the Federal Republic of Germany was founded with its 'provisional' capital in Bonn; the Western-occupied sectors of Berlin were a distant island in a sea of communism. By October the Soviet zone of occupation in Germany, too, was promoted to the status of a nominally independent state, the German Democratic Republic. The Iron Curtain of which Churchill had warned in 1946 was now reality. It ran, as he had foreseen, from the Baltic to the Adriatic, and right through the middle of Berlin.

Just how Australia should adapt to the deterioration of relations with its former ally the Soviet Union was a matter of dispute. Under Labor's longstanding Minister for External Affairs Herbert 'Doc' Evatt, Australia vigorously advocated the construction of a world order based on the principle of collective security. Peace could be guaranteed only if widening divisions were healed and states worked together, not in competition. That meant acknowledging the emergence of the Soviet Union as a major player in world affairs and creating a commensurate place for it in the architecture of the postwar order; for Evatt, the centrepiece of that new order was the United Nations. He occupied the presidency of the UN's General Assembly from 1948 to 1949 and had helped draft the UN's Universal Declaration of Human Rights. Significant resources were committed from within his department in Canberra to make the UN the success that the League of Nations plainly had not been.

Australian conservatives saw the world and the prospects of peace differently. Alliance with the Soviet Union had been a marriage of convenience, the product of the existential threat posed by Hitler and the Axis. With the Axis defeated, the deep ideological differences between Western liberalism and Soviet communism would inevitably re-emerge. It was the obligation of the West not to bow to communism but to confront it and, eventually, defeat it. The best way to assure Australia's security was not through a misguided trust in the good intentions of the international family, but rather through strengthening the ties that had already served Australia well through good times and bad.

Foreign policy was one of the issues debated hotly during the election campaign of late 1949; it ended with the election as Prime Minister of Robert Gordon Menzies, now the leader of the Liberal Party, on 10 December. His Minister for External Affairs, Percy Spender, made it clear that a new era was dawning in the way Australia conducted its relations with the rest of the world. In an address to parliament in March 1950 he declared an end to Evatt's 'busy-bodying in other people's business' in the United Nations. Far from being able to meet Australia's security needs, the UN included among its representatives 'those who are working to disrupt the order we believe in'.[1]

The change of government had unsurprising personnel consequences, the most prominent of them concerning John Burton, whose term as

Secretary of the Department of External Affairs came to an end in June 1950. Burton, two weeks older than Fred Rose, had been appointed to that senior role in 1947 at the age of just thirty-two. The son of a Methodist minister, he had served as private secretary to Evatt before his spectacular elevation to a position from which, alongside Evatt, he shaped Australia's postwar foreign policy. With Menzies' triumph at the ballot box, Burton's days as a senior public servant were numbered; by the middle of the following year a successor was in place. After a time Burton took up farming on a property just outside Canberra, where he had many friends and acquaintances.[2] One of them was Fred Rose.

The change of government brought profound shifts in domestic policy too. The last months of Chifley's prime ministership had been plagued by industrial unrest, climaxing in a national strike by coalminers. The government responded by confiscating their union's assets, imprisoning its leader and raiding the offices of the CPA.[4] Labor, it appeared to many, had betrayed the working class, while Menzies' Liberals won the battle for the hearts and minds of middle Australia.

After the Mountford interlude Fred Rose returned to his public service position, performing his duties sufficiently conscientiously to earn promotion to the role of Executive Officer of the NADC. But Rose was restless, and he sensed that Nugget Coombs was losing interest in the work of the NADC and preparing to fry bigger fish.[5] He was right. By the end of 1948 Coombs had been appointed Governor of the Commonwealth Bank of Australia.[6] Rose, too, sought a new challenge.

One option lay in a move to the Department of External Territories. Formerly a branch of the Prime Minister's Department, External Territories was elevated to the status of a fully-fledged department, its main brief the administration of the territories of Nauru, New Guinea, Norfolk Island and Papua. After the war those overseas duties were preserved, while some intriguing additions were made, including control of the School of Civil Affairs, now rebadged as the Australian School of Public Administration.[7] One of the school's tasks was to teach courses in colonial administration.[8] That stuck in the craw of A.P. Elkin in Sydney, who thereby lost his monopoly in the training of budding anthropologists for overseas service.[9]

In October 1949 Rose was offered a job as Principal Research Officer in the Department of External Territories.[10] He could not have known when he applied how profoundly things would change after the election. Percy Spender was given the External Territories portfolio alongside the plum job of Minister for External Affairs. That meant that Rose's new department was closely linked with the bigger Department of External Affairs. The two departments shared the West Block, an administrative building just west of Parliament House, which meant that their officers had plentiful interaction.

Through all of this Rose remained a devoted member of the tiny Canberra branch of the CPA. In the time before Edith and the children had moved to Canberra from Melbourne, the CPA had been a kind of substitute family for him, as it was for many, and his commitment to this new 'family' remained undimmed. With wife and children now fully ensconced in Froggatt Street, his changed personal circumstances simply meant that his Party activities shifted increasingly to his own home.

There was nothing illegal about membership of the CPA, but the truth was that there were reasons why, by 1949, membership of the CPA attracted a level of attention unknown since Menzies banned it in 1940. Those reasons had much to do with the changing international climate, a climate that rendered communists like Fred Rose persons of great interest. More specifically, the attention directed toward him was intimately connected to new evidence that there was a network of spies operating in Canberra's public service, and that they were leaking intelligence to the Soviets.

The leaks had been going on for some time. The first Soviet diplomatic mission was established in Canberra in 1943. From that date Semyen Makarov, as resident head of Soviet espionage operations in Australia, was able to penetrate the Department of External Affairs, an important source for both British and Australian classified documents.[11] By November of 1947 the head of Britain's MI5 was informed that a decrypted Soviet telegram from about 1945 showed that a serious leak of British classified material had occurred, 'probably from the Australian Department of External Affairs'.[12]

Doubts about Canberra's capacity to keep secrets safe would soon have consequences for Australia's relations with its allies. After the war Australia became involved in the development of military technology, largely under British direction. Rocket technology was developed at a former munitions factory in Adelaide and a rocket range at Woomera, 500 kilometres north of the city. Australia would also provide test sites for British manufactured nuclear bombs on the Monte Bello Islands in Western Australia and Maralinga in South Australia.[13] The US, like Britain, was interested in what Australia could contribute to the development of its weapons program, but initial American enthusiasm had waned. In some US circles, most notably in the powerful Department of Defense, there was a deep suspicion that both Britain and Australia were security risks.[14] The Chifley government in particular was seen to be 'soft on communism' and therefore not to be trusted with sensitive material, which might be passed into grateful Soviet hands.[15]

This American uneasiness had become evident in London and Canberra by early 1948. The British requested that the Americans release to Australia all information relating to guided missiles, but the US Navy blocked the approval. In arguing that there was little need to share with Australia advanced research on guided missiles, the Navy voiced its distrust of the Chifley government. Australia, it claimed emphatically, was a *'poor risk'.*[16] The Navy was drawing on a CIA assessment made to President Truman in January 1948 that there were indications of 'a leak in high government circles in Australia, to Russia'.[17]

As the distrust of Australia impacted on American willingness to share intelligence with Britain, the British set about finding and plugging the putative Australian leak. In March 1948, during a visit to Australia, the Director-General of MI5, Sir Percy Sillitoe, accompanied by Roger Hollis of MI5's counter-intelligence section, advised Prime Minister Ben Chifley of a leak.[18] A confidential 1945 British paper on security in the western Mediterranean, several copies of which had been sent to the Department of Defence in Canberra, had been passed to Soviets, allegedly via an Australian source. Chifley undertook to prepare a report on the incident, but, when finally presented, it offered no clarification.[19] Next year Hollis was back again, this time accompanied by Robert Hemblys-Scales.[20] They presented further evidence of leaks, and insisted that the source was within the Department of External Affairs in Canberra.[21]

The solution, as the MI5 team impressed on its hosts, was for Australia to establish a single, powerful security authority with counter-intelligence capacities.[22] Chifley was loath to concede Australia's deficiencies, but something had to give, and it did. Following the British suggestion, and in the twilight of his prime ministership, Chifley resolved to introduce what was in effect an Australian version of MI5.[23] Its primary task would be to solve what became dubbed 'The Case', that is, the leakage of intelligence through Australian hands to the Soviets. With the aid of such a body, its proponents argued, 'The Case' would be finally solved, and Australia would be able to convince its British and American allies that it deserved their trust. The Australian Security Intelligence Organisaton (ASIO) came into existence on 16 March 1949.

ASIO was not created in a vacuum. Before the war the main security organisation in Australia was the Investigation Branch of the Attorney-General's Department. During the war it maintained its vigil, but it was aided in its tasks by the creation of a Security Service founded and operated by the Army, even if functionally it was under the control of the Attorney-General's Department. Without replacing the Investigation Branch, the Security Service took on a growing number of functions, keeping a close eye on those considered politically suspect and interning those it assessed as security threats.[24] Communists were among those watched especially keenly.

After the war a new body, the Commonwealth Investigation Service (CIS), was formed through the amalgamation of the Security Service and the older Investigation Branch.[25] For all the resources it inherited from its predecessors, the unambiguous advice from MI5 was that the CIS was not up to the task required in the politically charged climate of the Cold War. In the realm of counter-espionage especially, its successor ASIO would be beefed up with a capacity unimaginable in earlier times, and destined to expand as the years went by.[26]

ASIO was thus a creation of a Labor government; Menzies not only preserved it but expanded and intensified its activities. Colonel Charles Spry, a former Director of Military Intelligence (DMI), was appointed Director-General in July 1950.[27]

It is tempting to view Charles Spry as an inverted image of Fred Rose, viewed across a Cold War divide. The two men were of the same generation, Spry just five years older. Rose found a home in the disciplined environment of the CPA, Spry in the Army, going directly from Brisbane Grammar to the Royal Military College Duntroon. He was still in the Army when he took up his appointment as Director-General of ASIO. For a time in the 1930s he had served in the British Army in India, and there was much about the Brisbane-born Spry's persona that seemed quintessentially upper-class English. Perhaps it was the neat moustache or the similarly well clipped accent, or the visceral anti-communism he shared with Menzies. In any case, Spry committed the very considerable power he now possessed to the task of ridding Australia of the communist scourge. He performed his work with a passion that bordered on, and perhaps even tipped over into, paranoia.

The London-born Rose, in contrast, having lived in Australia for well over a decade, and having been identified at first as 'terribly English', by now seemed – and sounded – more Australian. If there was a certain inevitability in that process, he did nothing to resist it, even cultivated it. Temperamentally he was strongly attracted to the egalitarian ethos and democratic temper that prevailed, at least in the circles in which he mixed. For him the enemies were the reactionaries and conservatives like Spry, who fought to block the kind of progress Rose believed inexorable. In his sense of being locked in mortal combat with an implacable enemy, Rose, too, was inclined toward paranoia – and not without reason.

As his first priority Spry was determined to crack The Case, still unsolved. What the Australian authorities did not realise at first was that the British and Americans were already well on the way to doing so. During the war they had developed the capacity to decrypt and analyse Soviet cable traffic. Venona was the last and most enduring name given a top secret project initiated in 1943 under orders from the then American Chief of Military Intelligence, Carter W. Clarke; its purpose was the interception and decryption of Soviet cable traffic. It became 'the most closely guarded intelligence secret on both sides of the Atlantic'.[28] For at least three years even President Truman was not briefed on its existence.[29] Among Venona's precious spoils was traffic between the Soviet Legation (later Embassy) in Canberra from 'friends' in the Australian Department of External Affairs and Moscow.[30]

By 1947 American analysts had made sufficient headway in decryption to establish that there was significant Soviet espionage occurring in the US and Australia.[31] Combining American with British operations meant that by the first half of 1948 some of the Soviet intelligence traffic between Canberra and Moscow was being decrypted in near real time.[32]

What the Venona decrypts were suggesting to the elite group of counter-intelligence authorities who had access to them – including, from 1950, Charles Spry[33] – was the existence of an Australian leak in Canberra. The incomplete picture they revealed was that of a Soviet Embassy housing Soviet intelligence staff, including for a time Viktor Zaitsev, the first head of Soviet intelligence and putatively 'Stalin's top spymaster in the 40s'.[34] The Soviet agents had established links with a number of Australians, identified solely by a range of cryptonyms, and typically in public service positions with access to sensitive information.

Some of them were associated in one way or another with Doc Evatt, whether as officers in the Department of External Affairs in Canberra or as staff members in Evatt's Sydney office. The officers in External Affairs were Jim Hill (who bore the cryptonym 'Tourist'), Ric Throssell ('Ferro'), Dorothy Jordan ('Podruga') and Ian Milner ('Bur').[35]

The last was perhaps the most important of the 'nest of traitors'.[36] The New Zealand-born Milner was a man of great academic ability and erudition. As a student at Canterbury University College in Christchurch he had developed political views at odds with those of his conservatively inclined father, and there is no indication that his enthusiasm for the Soviet Union ebbed during his studies at Oxford.[37] After stints in the United

States and then back in New Zealand, Milner was lured to the University of Melbourne during the war by Macmahon Ball, who headed political science there.[38] One of his colleagues, and a friend for decades to come, was the dynamic young lecturer Charles Manning Clark.[39] Milner's career took a new turn when, at the suggestion of Paul Hasluck, he applied successfully for a position in Canberra in the Post-Hostilities Division of the Department of External Affairs.[40] He remained there until he took a position as a political affairs officer in the UN Security Council Secretariat in New York at the beginning of 1947.[41] Before then, as Venona revealed, he helped pass on a number of pieces of information to the Soviets in September 1945 and March 1946.[42] In July 1950 he abruptly departed to live and teach in Prague, where he remarried in 1958.[43]

Jim Hill (Tourist) had joined the CPA in 1937 or 1938.[44] During the war he served for a time in the Army, including a stint in the Northern Territory.[45] He had studied at the University of Melbourne, for a time under Ian Milner.[46] On the eve of victory in Europe he received word that an application he had lodged to become a research officer in the Post-Hostilities Planning Division of the Department of External Affairs had been successful. Burton, it seems, was keen to involve him in building close relations with the Soviet Union in the hope of overcoming the latter's suspicions of the West.[47] Hill was implicated in the passing on of British postwar planning documents in the period 1945–46.[48]

Ric Throssell, the son of Fred Rose's and Alec Jolly's friend Katharine Prichard, had seen active wartime service in New Guinea and then joined the Department of External Affairs; for a time he served in the Australian Legation in Moscow. In Canberra in the latter part of the war he worked with Hill in the United Nations section of the department.[49] At this time his mother was living mainly in Sydney. On occasion Throssell would visit and discuss his work and career prospects with her.[50] The Venona material suggested that Prichard (who carried the codename 'Academician') was passing on information given to her by her son.[51]

Dorothy Jordan was Ric Throssell's second wife; his first died tragically in Moscow. Jordan was a graduate of the University of Melbourne and a former member of the CPA branch there.[52] She held a position in Canberra in the office of the Minister for Post-War Reconstruction before transferring to External Affairs but had to leave the public service when she married Throssell. The Venona material on 'Podruga' is, as the historians of Venona suggest, 'sparse and unrevealing'.[53]

The two members of Evatt's staff in Sydney identified in the Venona decrypts were his private secretary Allan Dalziel ('Denis') and Frances Bernie ('Sestra').[54] The latter, a secretary, ultimately confessed to passing on a greater volume of material than her accusers had suspected.[55] She had been a CPA member in Sydney. After joining Evatt's staff as a typist in November 1944 she married the Viennese Jewish refugee, and communist, Max Gluck. From Evatt's office she, too, was passing on information to the Soviets.[56] As for Dalziel, a Christian Socialist known to have contact with Soviet diplomats, he has been assessed as 'the main person responsible for the leakage of the war cabinet and advisory war council documents'.[57]

In Canberra and Sydney there were numerous people, then, who had access to intelligence and who, Venona suggested, were prepared to share it with the Soviets. This still raised the question of how they might have passed it on. The Venona decrypts suggested an answer. The key intermediary, perhaps even the 'spymaster', was a man who went by the most unflattering of codenames – 'Klod'.

'Klod' – or 'Clode' or even 'Claude' – was Walter Seddon Clayton.[58] It was Clayton who organised 'virtually all Soviet espionage' in Australia.[59] He operated his spy ring by collecting information from his sources and passing it on to his Soviet contacts for forwarding via the Soviet Embassy in Canberra to Moscow. Clayton was a New Zealander by birth, but in 1930, at the age of twenty-four, had moved to Australia, where he joined the CPA and put at its disposal his considerable energies. When the Party became illegal in mid-1940 he went underground, and the security services lost track of him.[60]

With the onset of the Cold War, Clayton's devotion to the Party kept him busy. He put together a network of committed communists who were not on any Party lists, established a set of safe houses and dead-letter drops, and stored secretly the Party's printing press. By 1949 he had once more disappeared almost entirely from the public view.[61] All of this was preparation for the possibility that a new Menzies government, like the first one back in 1940, would declare the Party illegal. It was a well-founded fear. Yet the creation of a kind of parallel, underground Party was useful for another reason as well. As the Soviets cultivated an espionage network, hidden from the prying eyes of ASIO, Clayton's shadow Party would serve their needs as well.[62]

What did any of this have to do with Fred Rose? As the Cold War warmed up, and even before Menzies made his triumphal return to the prime ministership, membership of the CPA or association with known members invited a good deal of unwanted attention. The CIS kept tabs on Rose after his move to Canberra, and it made some interesting observations about his activity there. An informant brought to the attention of the CIS that in his capacity as member of the NADC Rose had attended meetings of the 'Rocket Bomb Committee'.[63] The CIS was not clear what this committee might have been but thought it likely to have been devoted to developments at Woomera and their likely impacts in central and northern Australia. In the same year, 1947, it was recorded that Rose addressed a meeting in Melbourne on the welfare of Aborigines in the vicinity of the Rocket Range, alleging 'that he was only interested in the political and not the scientific aspects of the project'.[64] In December of that year it was claimed that Rose had visited Western Australia and had been introduced as 'Scientific Adviser to the Communist Party'.[65]

There were other reasons, too, why Rose was a person of interest, and they had to do with the company he kept. With a population of just 20,000, Canberra was little more than a modestly proportioned country town, made for mixing.[66] The Rose household in Froggatt Street was among the most convivial places in town, drawing through its open doors a stream of public servants keen to establish some kind of social life away from their dreary hostels. Several of them were the sort of people who raised eyebrows in security circles.

Jim Hill was well known to Rose. It was not an entirely serendipitous acquaintance, as Jim Hill was the brother of the Victorian CPA heavyweight Ted Hill, whom Rose knew from his time in Melbourne. Hill had been living at 41 Froggatt Street Turner since 1946.[67] He was a close neighbour of the Roses.

Then there was Ric Throssell. He and Rose worked in the same building, the West Block, and one source has it that they would sometimes lunch together in the nearby gardens.[68] Throssell and Dorothy Jordan lived not far from the Roses, on Northbourne Avenue.[69]

And there was one more reason to take an interest in Fred Rose. Venona decrypts showed that one of the participants in the network of spies bore the codename 'Professor'. Who was Professor? Was it perhaps Fred Rose?

13. The Gathering Storm

The drama of Rose's life, seldom far from the surface, rapidly escalated as the twentieth century reached its halfway mark. On a personal level he received a surprising visit from his parents.[1] Fourteen years had passed, and his father had mellowed. His mother, still the capable, energetic person he remembered, must have been proud of her son's rapid promotion through the public service. The birth of a daughter, Nita, in October 1952 was an added delight, as was the experience of meeting charming new friends in Peter and Sheila Worsley. It would be a mistake though to assume that Rose's life was going to proceed toward a conventional happy ending, either personally or politically.

When Menzies commenced his second stint as Prime Minister, reasons of state bolstered his visceral anti-communism. The foundation of the People's Republic of China a few weeks earlier suggested that the Iron Curtain now stretched to Asia. In these troubling times, Menzies' devotion to the Anglo–American alliance was stridently unambiguous. He committed Australian forces to helping Britain defeat a communist insurgency in Malaya, and when war broke out on the Korean Peninsula, Australia sent in its troops.

As Menzies conjured an image of communism on the march across the globe, he also promoted a nightmare vision of democracy under siege at home. He enacted the Communist Party Dissolution Bill in the hope of removing the blight of communism from Australian politics forever. The Bill broadly defined as 'communist' not just CPA members but anyone who supported the principles of communism. Unionists, ALP members and peace activists ran the risk of being 'declared'.

Menzies' victory was short-lived. The Bill was challenged in the High Court by the CPA and by a number of trade unions, including the Waterside

Workers' Federation (the WWF) represented by Doc Evatt, who successfully argued the Bill was unconstitutional on the grounds that Australia was not at war.[2] Menzies persisted, turning to the instrument of a referendum to acquire the power he needed to destroy the CPA.

Had the referendum succeeded, the outcome for the CPA and its individual members would have been disastrous. All those declared to be communists would carry the burden of proof to establish that they were not. Public servants subjected to such a declaration would be dismissed from their jobs, while failure to cease activity in a banned organisation would be punishable by up to five years' imprisonment.[3] In bludgeoning communism into submission, Menzies allocated the function of blunt weapon to ASIO, whose role it would be to identify communists. It dutifully redoubled its efforts in keeping a close eye on existing suspects and searching out new ones.

The referendum was defeated by a narrow margin on 22 September 1951,[4] leading Menzies to weigh his options afresh. In doing so he sought counsel from the like-minded Charles Spry; together they resolved to continue the policy of ASIO's 'vetting' of members of the public service, establishing just who was a CPA member and who a sympathiser. The law did not allow the sacking of CPA members, but the determination that a public servant was a 'security risk' could, so it was hoped, lead to dismissal. Significant numbers were concerned, since by Spry's reckoning some 180 communists and sympathisers were employed in the Commonwealth public service.[5]

Even this more subtle approach of effecting dismissals through adverse security findings proved a bridge too far. In early 1953, Solicitor General Kenneth Bailey confirmed that the Public Service Board – the employer of Fred Rose and all Commonwealth public servants – 'had no legal right to refuse a job on security grounds to a qualified applicant'.[6] Rather than trying to change the law, Menzies simply continued ASIO's surreptitious vetting practice, with the widespread consequence that public servants who fell under suspicion might be transferred or at least have their duties changed so as to deprive them of access to sensitive material. The practice fell far short of Menzies' fantasies of 'emergency measures' including the internment of left-wing Australians.[7] Nonetheless, even in its diluted form, the collaboration of the conservative government and ASIO had a profound effect on the lives of many, not least the Roses.

The security agencies had known of Fred Rose long before ASIO was founded. What prompted their initial interest was Fred's relationship with Edith, a German, which gave rise to the suspicion that the couple might have been Nazi sympathisers. It would not be the last time that security speculation was ludicrously wide of the mark, but in this case the suspicion appeared to receive some credence from a bizarre observation. A Captain J.F. Bell of the Royal Australian Navy reported that he performed intelligence duties in the Northern Territory in the period 1941/42, and he came to know both Fred Gray and Fred Rose on Groote Eylandt. Fred Gray, in Bell's recollections, at one point produced underwear said to belong to Rose, with his name embroidered on it, together with a swastika.[8] If there was even a germ of truth to the story, it was perhaps an item purloined from a Mainz jail in 1935.

Though she had taken her husband's nationality on marrying Fred, Edith's German background attracted some attention during the war. While she spent some weeks studying tropical medicine in Sydney in 1940, she was asked to present herself to the Military Intelligence Section at Police Headquarters in Sydney. There were no grounds for concern, however, and the interviewing officer declared that she appeared 'harmless'.[9] Clearly Edith gave nothing away about Fred's politics either, because the most that could be said of him at that point was that he was 'obsessed with an idea – The Study of Anthropology'.[10]

After the war the CIS kept an eye on Rose, noting his activism in relation to the Rocket Range.[11] With the birth of ASIO and the struggle to solve 'The Case', Rose became the subject of much closer scrutiny. His multiple ASIO files give some insight into the lengths to which the service went. Some of the material in them was gathered by ASIO from its predecessors, but the bulk is from the ASIO era. Rose became the object of an observation regime that consumed substantial human and material resources. He was followed, his house was watched, his work diary (or 'date block') was checked, he was surreptitiously photographed, and his phone was tapped.

What ASIO lacked, however, was any evidence that Rose had direct contact with the Soviets, whether with Soviet Embassy staff in Canberra or, on his trips to Sydney, with the TASS press agent. The closest they came was to note that Edith Rose attended Russian classes in Canberra between 1948 and 1950. Fred, the report ingenuously conceded, 'attended on only four occasions, mainly to please his wife'.[12]

In 1951 Rose's job changed, but for reasons that had nothing to do with security. A departmental reorganisation brought about the formal demise of his Department of External Territories and, on 11 May 1951, the creation in its place of the Department of Territories. Much remained the same, including the continuation of Paul Hasluck as the responsible minister. The main difference lay in the extension of the department's administrative duties to the Northern Territory, duties transferred from the Department of the Interior.[13]

The restructuring brought with it a new definition of Rose's role. He was now 'Principal Research Officer, Research and Development Section, Department of Territories'. Under the direction of the Assistant Secretary (Research and Development) he was responsible for carrying out 'general and specific research projects' for the department and for its various territorial administrations, including such issues as the effects of policy on conditions in the External Territories, the practices, procedures and developmental programs in those administrations, and the maintenance of 'a general statistical and information service' for the department.[14]

That the new title entailed a return to something resembling Rose's earlier task of dealing with the Northern Territory's postwar development, and in particular with indigenous issues, is apparent from his own recollections of that time. Hasluck, he soon became aware, was eager to impose a policy bearing the new label 'assimilation', though in reality it was not much different from the approach advocated by Elkin and applied by the conservative government on the eve of war. The intention was that the Aboriginal population of the Northern Territory should be assimilated to the white population, quite ignoring the reality, as Rose put it, that they 'might want to adhere to their own culture and way of life'. Hasluck, in Rose's view, 'missed the point completely that this was also straightout racist policy'.[15]

As a public servant it was not his place to object to the minister's wishes; indeed he was asked to play a role in applying the policy in the Northern Territory. Eager to avoid censure in international forums, above all the United Nations, Hasluck was careful to ensure that the policy did not appear racist, and that meant creating at least the illusion that Commonwealth legislation did not specifically target Aborigines. When Rose was consulted on the matter, he pointed out that the war years had proved a watershed for indigenous people. Previously large numbers of them had lived in isolation from the organs of the state, but during the war that isolation had largely been broken down. Most now lived in sedentary groups in regular contact with state representatives, including the police. Consequently the vast majority of Aborigines could now be named and identified. Should the government wish to do so, it would be possible to bring Aborigines under new legislation without defining them separately as 'Aborigines'. The persons to whom legislation was to apply could simply be named in the *Northern Territory Gazette*, neatly sidestepping suggestions that 'Aborigines' collectively were the objects of government policy.[16]

This new legislation Hasluck had in mind was the Welfare Ordinance, and he accepted the advice from Rose that the best way to apply the new law was via gazetting. Rose was instructed to prepare a kind of layperson's draft of the legislation, 'incorporating all or most of the discriminating provisions of the previous Aboriginal Ordinance but [. . .] only to apply to individuals who were named in the gazette and who were to be known as "wards of the State" or for short "wards"'. The challenge was to apply non-racial criteria to determine who was a 'ward'. Two such criteria were ultimately adopted: the social conditions under which the persons lived, and their ability to manage their own affairs. These criteria allowed a wide interpretation, but in practice they were to be applied only to Aborigines. The challenge, however, was more difficult than Hasluck envisaged, as became evident when the NT's Legislative Council rejected the first version of the Bill. One of its members attacked it with words to the effect, as Rose remembered, that 'Hitler in his wildest dreams could never have imagined, could never have conjured up such legislation'.[17]

It was in that year, 1951, that Rose unwittingly gave ASIO a reason to sharpen its focus on him. A position advertised in the *Commonwealth Gazette* caught his eye in late June. It was located within the Department of District Services and Native Affairs in the Papua and New Guinea Administration, and it was for an anthropologist. Rose, as he stated in his application, considered himself an ideal candidate: 'I am fit for tropical service having already lived in the tropics for five years during which time my health was uniformly excellent – two days sick leave, if I remember rightly with dengue fever. I am virtually teetotal and would probably be completely teetotal in Papua and New Guinea as I was in Northern Australia. I am a moderately heavy smoker.'[18]

The arrival of his application in Port Moresby prompted ASIO's regional director in New Guinea to solicit an assessment from Canberra. Rose, he thought, 'might constitute a security risk'.[19] Canberra did not hesitate to voice its reservations: in 1947 Rose had been reported to be the CPA's 'official anthropologist', and he had associated with the known communists Alec Jolly and Jim Hill.[20] Rose was not offered the job.

The ramifications of the check did not stop there. Questions were raised as to whether Rose was a security risk in his existing job. Michael Thwaites, an Oxford graduate and Melbourne University English lecturer recruited by Spry, flagged the issue in November 1951. His memorandum to ASIO's regional director in the ACT requested, 'Would you please ascertain whether any of the information which ROSE would have access to in his present position, is classified as Top Secret. Of course, any such research information would be useful to a potential enemy, but for the purpose of assessing the priority of work, I would like to be informed of its nature and official grading'.[21]

When a detailed answer to this request was finally received, there appeared cause for concern. The Assistant Secretary of Research and

Development in the Department of Territories, J.E. Willoughby, was interviewed by an ASIO officer, who learned that Rose's duties related largely to the Northern Territory and that it was proposed to appoint him Officer-in-Charge of Mining, Secondary Industries, Fisheries and Forestry. In that capacity he would be intimately involved in work concerning the Rum Jungle uranium deposit. Though Willoughby indicated he believed Rose to be 'absolutely loyal', the department sought ASIO's advice on how to proceed with Rose.[22]

While ASIO headquarters addressed that conundrum, it received a report that did little to help Rose's cause. An ASIO informant reported on a party that took place at a private home in Canberra and was attended by a number of people of interest to ASIO, including Fred Rose. Among the other guests were Don Baker, a lecturer at Canberra University College, and Bruce Yuill of the Trades and Labour Council. There was reportedly a conversation on the topic of the CPA's weekly publication *Tribune* and of communism generally. During that discussion Rose had suggested 'that a person selling this newspaper may be blackballed. He also enquired if it was known whether any members of the "Gestapo" purchased it'. After Rose had excused himself to return to visitors staying at Froggatt Street, conversation turned to him. The evening's host offered the view that Fred 'was a very smart fellow and "reeking" with brains'. That in itself was hardly revelation, though the informant's ears pricked up at the announcement that soon followed, namely that John Burton was due back in town and would be hosting a party at his home in two or three weeks.[23]

When the security assessment of Rose was concluded, that party was mentioned, as were Rose's contacts with Jim Hill, Alec Jolly and even Katharine Prichard. The outcome was that Rose was assessed to be 'a security risk in a position which involves access to secret information'.[24] Rose's department responded by reducing his exposure to sensitive material. Rose was not informed, but he soon realised it – files that would earlier have crossed his desk now passed through other channels, and certain tasks were excluded from his duties.[25]

In a small place like Canberra in the early 1950s it was no easy task for

ASIO to operate without its subjects becoming aware they were targets. It was common knowledge that ASIO officers recorded the car registrations of people attending parties hosted by ALP activists or suspected members of the CPA. As one historian has noted, this operation 'was particularly conspicuous at night because the ASIO vehicle had one constantly inoperable headlight'.[26] Moreover, 'it was known whose telephone was currently being tapped by ASIO because of the informal network of friendships in which telephone technicians who connected the tapping equipment mixed'.[27] Yet there was a sinister dimension as well. Early in 1952 a Sydney comrade staying with the Roses issued a chilling warning: 'Watch out! The [failed] referendum was only an incident in the struggle, important, but an incident. What Menzies' next move will be is anyone's guess. While he stayed at the legal level we knew roughly what he was up to but now – watch out! You bloody intellectuals in Canberra have been living in a fools' paradise!'[28] Whoever it was, that comrade had a point. On 3 June 1953 Rose's security rating was upgraded from 'Category C' to '"RISK" with access to "Top Secret"'.[29]

Into this atmosphere of intrigue stepped Peter Worsley. Like Rose he was an Englishman with a Cambridge anthropological training and had travelled to the Antipodes with the intention of doing fieldwork. Worsley's intended destination was New Guinea; Canberra was to be simply a necessary stepping stone on the way there. As far as he and his wife Sheila were concerned, the shorter the stay in Canberra the better. Canberra for him was still 'the vision of a garden city by an American urban planner, but unfortunately it hadn't been built yet'.[30] He would have lengthier dealings than anticipated with the Department of Territories where Rose worked, but it was politics that brought the two communists together. In time he achieved the rare and dubious distinction of having Paul Hasluck keep his personal file in a locked safe in the ministerial office.[31]

It is an indication of the extent to which the CPA was under siege that Worsley had to follow a clandestine process to make contact with fellow communists. Through the research he undertook at the ANU in preparation for his New Guinea fieldwork, he became familiar with the historian Eric

Fry. In the research room he got to talking with Fry about Marx, and it soon became clear that both of them were Marxists: 'And we became good friends. And that tiny community of underground communists cleaved together and got to know each other.'[32]

ASIO kept tabs on them as best it could, well aware that it needed to track not only the CPA's members but others who did not formally belong and keenly avoided any suspicion that they might. A consequence of the big security drive in the CPA masterminded some time earlier by Wally Clayton was that some of the comrades were still underground.[33] Gleaning what information it could, ASIO reached the conclusion that there was a Party cell at the ANU, comprising all of five members. When issues requiring wider attention arose, one of the group, usually the historian Bob Gollan, would travel to Sydney to meet with the CPA's secretariat there.[34]

If ASIO's observations were accurate, then the CPA enjoyed wider support outside the university, where its members took both their politics and their socialising seriously. A report by an unnamed ASIO mole conveys the genial atmosphere that prevailed at one CPA gathering in Canberra, held in the home of Bob and Mavis Michell. Fred Rose and the Worsleys were among the twenty-six who attended. The special guest that evening was Audrey Blake from Sydney. She gave an address, fielded some questions and engaged in discussion. Supper followed, and then 'some music selections from Burl Ives and Reedy River'.[35] Years later Peter Worsley reminisced that those CPA meetings held in suburban Canberra offered 'a tremendous social life [. . .] we used to drink vast amounts of beer and sing bush ballads all night long'.[36]

Fred Rose occupied centrestage in Worsley's memories. His first impression of Rose was that despite his English background and Cambridge education he appeared very Australian, indeed '1000 percent Australian [. . .] a dinky di Aussie'.[37] As a scientist, though, Rose 'had a very methodical mind', and Worsley soon became well versed in how Rose had applied that methodical mind to his kinship studies on Groote Eylandt.

It was ASIO that stymied Worsley's New Guinea plans. Spry thought it appropriate for ASIO to be accorded a role in the recruitment of staff to both the ANU and the older Canberra University College, and indeed evidence suggests that an informal liaison between ASIO and the ANU led in effect to a vetting of university staff.[38] Technically Worsley was not a staff member but a research student wishing to undertake fieldwork for his PhD. Nonetheless, his arrival at the ANU came to the notice of Spry, who lamented that Worsley had arrived at the ANU at all. 'I am sure', he wrote to Menzies, 'that you will readily appreciate the inadvisability of employing, in any University, lecturers who are likely to infect students with subversive doctrines'.[39]

ASIO had not managed to prevent Worsley's arrival, but it certainly had a say in his work. It refused to issue him with the required security clearance to visit New Guinea. So when Worsley went to collect his permit from the Department of External Affairs, having already bought his supplies for an extended stay in the Central Highlands, he was stunned by the news that he had been denied entry. No explanation was provided.[40]

ASIO's actions seem to have their origin in information supplied by MI5. The issue became public when raised in parliament, forcing the Minister for Territories, Paul Hasluck, to defend the ban. Hasluck responded that 'a great deal of mischief could be done to natives', pointing out that the cause lay with Worsley's political affiliations. Worsley would not let that statement pass unchallenged and called on Hasluck to repeat it without the protection of parliamentary privilege. His intention in New Guinea in any case, he insisted, was to study kinship structures, not administration policy.[41]

With no avenue of appeal, Worsley faced the desperate prospect of unemployment far from home. Fred Rose came to his rescue, suggesting that Worsley apply to work on Groote Eylandt, and lining up Fred Gray to act as the Worsleys' host – without tipping off Gray that his prospective guests were communists.[42] When that was approved, Rose provided Worsley with all his data, so the latter could supplement work Rose had started years earlier. Worsley did his fieldwork on Groote from December 1952 to September 1953, and then submitted his thesis to the ANU in June 1954. In it he duly thanked his supervisors W.E.H. (Bill) Stanner, at that time Reader in Anthropology at the ANU, and S.F. (Siegfried or Fred) Nadel, the Austrian-born anthropologist, who from 1950 held the first chair of anthropology at the ANU. It was probably out of political savvy that Worsley chose not to acknowledge his indebtedness to Fred Rose.[43]

Worsley was one of many academics whose careers were shaped by ASIO, often in quite obscure ways. Another was Manning Clark. Born in the same year as Rose, Clark too worked for a time in Melbourne, having been appointed by Ian Milner to a lectureship at the University of Melbourne.[44] Like Rose, Clark made the trek north to Canberra, in his case to become Professor of History at Canberra University College. And like Rose, he attracted attention from ASIO, on whose advice Clark's duties in teaching cadets in the Department of External Affairs were withdrawn in 1953.[45] Compared with Rose's communism, Clark's political views were quirkily iconoclastic, yet the two men kept some similar company. For several months in 1950, when Jim Hill was on a London posting, Clark and his growing family occupied Hill's cottage at 41 Froggatt Street, a few houses down from the Roses.[46]

For Fred Rose, things went from bad to worse. His department could not sack him, but ASIO managed to conjure a cunning way to get rid of him. The body that became the agent of ASIO's will was the Public Service Board, which staged discussions with Rose's department head Cecil Lambert. The outcome was that 'due to the exigencies of work in ROSE's particular section' certain jobs were to be declared redundant. Rose's would be one of them. Officially ASIO was to have had no role in this; information on Rose's impending fate was passed 'to the R.D. [Regional Director] A.C.T. "off records" because of the manner in which they intended transferring ROSE from the Department'.[47] Technically this was not a sacking but a transfer, for Rose was to be offered a new position. In all likelihood, as ASIO well knew, it was one Rose would reject. After seventeen years his days as a Commonwealth public servant were numbered.

14. King Island

The middle of the year 1953 created the perfect storm in Fred Rose's life, buffeting him personally, professionally and politically. He battened down the hatches as best he could, but he would not emerge unscathed.

In his personal life the big development was the decision that Edith would leave Australia with the three Rose daughters: Sonja, by now aged ten, Ruth aged seven and Nita, not yet a year old. They would visit Fred's family in England and then proceed to Germany and to Edith's family, who eagerly anticipated catching up with the long absent Edith and meeting her three daughters for the first time. The eldest of the children, twelve-year-old Kim, would stay with Fred and continue his schooling in Australia.

ASIO got wind of the impending departure and followed preparations closely. On 17 June 1953 Kim, Sonja and Ruth flew from Canberra to Sydney and took a bus to the airline office in the city. There they were met by a woman described as being roughly forty years of age, 'about 5'6", medium to solid build, black hair, sallow complexion, dressed in grey dress, full length fur coat, black shoes, no hat'. The party made its way to Circular Quay and from there by ferry to Manly.[1]

The woman with the sallow complexion was Kay – Kathleen – Phillips, an attractive, well-heeled Irish-born widow some years Rose's senior.[2] She had two children,[3] and according to information made available to ASIO she and Rose had known each other as youngsters in London.[4] She was later reported as an active member of the Canberra Committee of the Australian Convention for Peace and War and subsequently the Canberra Peace Group.[5]

Rose, Edith and baby Nita followed by train, attracting no less interest from ASIO. Rose was aware that a seemingly ubiquitous agent named

MacDonald travelled on the same train. Such, by now, was his sensitivity to ASIO's attentions that he speculated that the family's compartment might be bugged, so they limited their conversations to the mundane. In Sydney, Kay Phillips' Manly flat was burgled while the Roses stayed there. Fred seems to have been the target, since the only objects removed were his jacket and wallet. Both were subsequently found in the garage attached to the flat, the money still in the wallet. At about the same time, the Roses' house in Canberra was broken into. In this case, too, nothing of value was removed, for Rose a clear pointer to the handiwork of 'the Gestapo'.[6]

It was on his first day back at work after farewelling Edith and the girls in Sydney on 19 June that Rose was informed that his job was being abolished. The alternative offered him was a position in the Bureau of Census and Statistics. He could not be entirely surprised; the writing had been on the wall for some time in large, luminous letters. As he contemplated career options, he settled on a curious choice – he would become a farmer.[7]

It was a radical departure from all his previous employment and inevitably triggers questions about his motivation. That Rose was consumed by a passion for both anthropology and politics is clear; he was also imbued with a sense of mission that had carried him to this point, so why would he abandon all he had achieved now? Obviously he feared unemployment, but he had influential contacts in Canberra to whom he could have appealed. Was there something sinister he feared in Canberra? Did he suspect that the attention being directed to him by ASIO would not stop at the loss of his job? What is clear, at least, is that Rose's decision for a radical change of career and a new life far from Canberra was made neither on a whim nor in haste. As a first step, instead of simply throwing in the towel in Canberra, he took his accumulated long-service leave. He would use that time to explore the possibility of acquiring a dairy farm on King Island in Bass Strait.

ASIO knew this, but struggled to understand it. Canberra might have been small, but it at least had a network of communists who would serve Rose's social and political needs. King Island, in contrast, could offer only isolation. Why would someone like Fred Rose, who through his working life had relied on his very substantial intellect, turn to the back-breaking work of farming? And what exactly was the role of Kay Phillips in all this? It soon became apparent that she had moved into 25 Froggatt Street with her children. By the latter part of 1953, it was noted, she was certainly thinking of Rose's house as her home; perhaps, ASIO speculated, she was now Rose's 'de facto wife'.[8] The plot thickened further when it emerged that she would provide much of the capital for Rose's efforts to purchase a property. So was she a housekeeper, a business partner, a lover, a political activist, or perhaps some combination of all those things? ASIO was determined to find out.

To invest in a farm was a major commitment. In late July important information arrived to help Rose make his decision. It was a set of charts of the island, supplied to him by the Lands and Survey Department in Hobart. What intrigued ASIO was why of all places Rose had focused on King Island. It occurred to them that his real interest was not genteel country retirement or farming but the island's mine, which supplied tungsten to other countries of the British Commonwealth and the United States.[9] These suspicions were eventually given public expression when a Sydney *Sun* article headed 'Red Nest in Vital Mine' reported: 'What is believed to be a plot by communists to disrupt production of scheelite ore, an important material in defence production, is being investigated by Commonwealth Security officers. Security is closely watching what has been described as "a small nest of communists" on King Island in Bass Strait.'[10]

All indications are that Rose's genuine intention was to succeed as a farmer. At least that is the impression conveyed in his correspondence with Edith in Berlin, as he prepared her for the likelihood that she and the girls would not be returning to their Canberra home but to an isolated farm and life on the land. Farming, he enthused, would give him 'a certain independence which is quite impossible under the public service'. And yet his move should not be construed as a flight from politics. On the contrary, there was 'as much if not more political work to be done in the Australian rural areas as elsewhere'. As for the property Rose already had in mind, he did his best to talk it up. The homestead was in poor repair, he conceded, but at over sixteen squares it was large, 'with sufficient room for three adults and six children without getting under each other's feet'.[11] The plan, then, was that the Rose and the Phillips family would share a kind of communal venture. Edith's feelings on the subject are not recorded.

Others were concocting similar plans in the second half of 1953. One of them was Don Kelly, a mechanic who had spent some time working on John Burton's rural property at Weetangera outside Canberra. Like Rose, Kelly was looking for a fresh start. Rose knew the Kelly family as neighbours at 33 Froggatt Street; they were often seen at Jim Hill's place in the same street.[12] Pater familias John Henry Kelly was an agronomist and senior public servant. Rose knew a lot about the pastoral industry in the Northern Territory, the topic of an historical essay he published in 1954, but Kelly Senior trumped him with his Australia-wide knowledge.[13] Indeed, as Rose reported to Edith, Kelly Senior held a sanguine view of the future of cattle farming on King Island, largely on the basis of the anticipated construction of an abattoir. On the strength of that advice, Don Kelly opted for a soldier settlement block and expected to move to the island in early 1954. Even John Burton, Rose told Edith, was thinking of moving there.[14]

All of this was followed with interested cynicism by ASIO, whose officers assumed that a dangerous communist cell was being formed, as the mainlanders joined forces with the island's small band of blue-collar workers. One of them, William Bell, was pithily derided in one ASIO report as a 'waterside worker and troublemaker'.[15] Through the second half of 1953 Rose was making multiple trips to the island, but not for political reasons. Not only was he still scouting for a property, he also wanted to gain invaluable farming experience, and did so working as a rouseabout on a farm just outside Currie.[16]

When Kay Phillips provided the best part of the funds to purchase a property, ASIO's curiosity was piqued. In September the director-general prepared a 'Top Secret and Personal' memorandum on Rose for the Prime Minister.[17] In the same month ASIO set up an observation post in a residence in Froggatt Street to observe all the comings, goings and goings-on at number 25. In 'Operation Traveller' two field officers kept a discreet eye on the house, even when Kay Phillips was there alone.[18]

On 7 November, when Rose was on one of his trips to King Island, Kay

Phillips hosted a party attended by some twenty-five people. It followed the annual reception at the Soviet Embassy to commemorate the anniversary of the Bolshevik Revolution. Among the guests were, the ASIO officers outside noted, 'well-known Party officials and well-known Party members'.[19] If there had been any doubts about Phillips' politics, they were soon dispelled.

When Rose returned to Canberra about a week later, ASIO followed him all the way. A clandestine party observed his arrival in Melbourne en route from King Island. Two officers were allocated to provide a photographic record, while no fewer than three took on the task of surveillance. It was no wonder their report did not want for trivia. They watched him as he stepped on to the tarmac in Melbourne, 'dressed in fawn slacks, short leather belted jacket (brown), no hat, carrying a type of haversack ... untidy in appearance and ... with a slovenly gait'. He took a bus to town, then a taxi to a private residence in Hawthorn. He was kept under surveillance that evening until lights went out. But ASIO was back on the job by 8.15 the next morning.[20]

By December Rose was ready to leave Canberra for good. On King Island he settled on a block and a price. It was a 938-acre property some eight kilometres from Currie, and it would earn the vendor £5250, secured first with a deposit of ten per cent provided as a cheque by Rose; the balance was paid with two separate cheques drawn by Kay Phillips, and one more drawn by Rose.[21] This bold new co-sponsored venture was given the name 'Philrose'.

There was some suspicion, at least on ASIO's part, that a third party might have been involved in the acquisition – the CPA. In February 1954 it was reported that Rose's friend Bob Gollan had claimed that Rose 'had been instructed to buy an estate on King Island at the approximate cost of £10,000 ... The Party are interested in the proposition to the point of helping with the financing of it, if necessary'. The purchase, the report speculated, 'would be the first of a series of such purchases right around Australia. GOLLAN [...] hinted strongly that the purchasing had something to do with the tying-up of illegality throughout Australia'.[22] Could it be, fearing the worst in the event of the re-election of the Menzies government in May 1954, the Party was preparing for another bout of illegality by investing in a network of properties that might help its members go underground and carry on their activities there?

Rose moved permanently to Philrose in January of 1954.[23] For the first three months he was absorbed in knocking the property into shape, deprived of even his ersatz family, and with not much of a political network to sustain him either. His CPA membership was transferred to Melbourne, from where literature was posted to him. The best he could do on the island was to make the acquaintance in Currie of an 'old comrade', a building worker, and some militant waterside workers. But that was the extent of his adoptive bucolic idyll's revolutionary class.[24]

Kay, her two children and Kim Rose joined him at the end of March, though Kim's presence was temporary. He was sent to Launceston High School, boarding with wartime family friends the Gardiners, who had moved there from Melbourne. On 28 March 1954 Rose tendered his letter of resignation from the public service.[25] With that, he was officially a farmer. And if the shift to Bass Strait rendered him a no less enigmatic figure, ASIO and its political masters could at least rest assured that he was in no position to pass on secrets to the enemy.

Nonetheless, a bang about to be heard in Canberra would soon reverberate around the world. Its cause was not an Australian communist but a Soviet diplomat by the name of Vladimir Petrov. After months of cajoling and seduction by ASIO, by 1954 Petrov was about to defect. He crossed his Rubicon on 3 April, without, apparently, having told his wife Evdokia. Her defection took place under more dramatic circumstances more than two weeks later. Claiming that Petrov had been kidnapped by Australian authorities, the Soviets sent two couriers to escort Evdokia back to Moscow. In the milling throngs at Mascot she was hustled aboard a Moscow-bound aircraft, one of her fashionable red shoes irretrievably lost in the scrum. Wracked with indecision, somewhere between Sydney and Darwin she reached the decision to follow her husband's lead in accepting an offer of asylum. As the aircraft in which she was travelling was being refuelled in Darwin, ASIO officials separated her from her couriers and formally offered her asylum. After speaking by telephone with her husband, she accepted the offer. She and Vladimir would deliver to ASIO and the conservative government of the day a cache of information about communist espionage activity in Australia.[26] What neither the Petrovs nor ASIO could know was that in a secret Soviet trial they had been sentenced to death *in absentia*; plans were being made for KGB assassins to hunt them down.[27]

It was just a matter of time before the shock waves from those events reached Fred Rose on King Island. From there he learned of the defections, of the sensational espionage claims that flowed from them, and of the establishment of a royal commission to investigate those claims. With an election looming the following month, Menzies' calling of a commission was no surprise, since it was clear that the conservative government would milk the Petrov Affair for all it was worth. On 14 May, Rose wrote to Edith in Berlin with a grim foreboding. Should the Menzies government be returned in two weeks, 'rabid reaction would be let loose and I may be persecuted to some degree and it would not be wise to have the girls back here'.[28]

Just before the election Manning Clark's former student and now colleague and friend Don Baker came to visit Rose.[29] The two would certainly have discussed the Royal Commission on Espionage, the first sessions of which had been held in Canberra. Baker had been spotted there twice in the public gallery, on one occasion in the company of Clark.[30] With Menzies' electoral victory sealed, Baker and Rose might well have pondered what consequences the return of the conservatives would bring. Rose might have sought some consolation in the thought that his decision to leave Canberra had been vindicated. And perhaps the thought flashed across Don Baker's mind that he, too, might join the ranks of the farming fraternity.

Rose's brief career as a farmer came crashing down late one July afternoon, just before dusk. He was returning to Philrose in his Landrover with timber for a cow yard. He was filthy. When the timber was half unloaded, he noticed two figures appear at the front gate. They were not regular visitors, he surmised, because they would normally drive their vehicle through the gate up to the house. 'These must be new chums', he concluded. Indeed, they were.[31]

In Rose's recollection one was an enormous man of perhaps 300 pounds, his face betraying 'an addiction to the bottle'. It was the other, smaller man who addressed him, 'You're Fred Rose, aren't you?' which Rose confirmed. They identified themselves by the names Leo Carter and Jack Gilmour and as officers in the Department of the Attorney-General, but answerable only to the Prime Minister. They asked Rose if he knew of the Petrov commission, and when he replied that he did, they informed him that they had come to subpoena him as a witness. They delivered a document, asking him to sign it to acknowledge receipt, and went on to explain the cause of the commission's interest in him. A young woman by the name of June Barnett, an officer in the Department of External Affairs, had claimed that Rose had introduced her to a member of the CPA, who had attempted to persuade her to act as a source of information. When Rose refused to comment on the allegation, he was handed a copy of Barnett's statement. When he read it, he had no doubt that it stemmed from June Barnett, a visitor to his Canberra home on numerous occasions. Asked if he might keep a copy of the statement, the officers refused, whereupon Rose dismissed their request that he immediately make a statement for the record. Any statements to be made, he told the officers, would be made before the commission, and only after he had consulted a lawyer.[32]

Carter and Gilmour did not readily give in, resorting to a range of tactics to elicit a revealing comment from Rose. 'You're looking for a loan from the bank, aren't you? [. . .] What would your mother and father think of you being involved in this dirty little espionage affair? [. . .] Was your wife involved in this business too?' Rose let all that pass, as he turned his mind to devising a way to elude the interlopers before booking a passage to Melbourne and facing questions in a more formal setting. When they suggested they speak with him the next day, he invented a reason why he could not. Escorting them from the property, he faced one last question, 'Do you know Walter Seddon Clayton?' Rose did know Clayton, though had never to that point learned his middle name. He answered honestly, 'Walter Seddon Clayton? Yes, I think I've met him.'[33]

These, at least, are Rose's recollections of that fateful encounter, published fourteen years later. There is another record of the event – that provided by Messrs Gilmour and Carter. In its basic details it accords with Rose's account but offers a quite different perspective on Rose's reaction to the unwelcome surprise. Central to the conversation, as the officers reported it, was June Barnett. They told Rose that Petrov had identified Barnett as a person in whom the Soviets were interested. In their account, as in Rose's, he did not dispute knowing her. Then they put it to him that it was clear he was working either directly or indirectly with the Soviets, to which Rose responded 'that he would like to think over the matter and asked could he contact us later if he wanted to. He was obviously upset at the time. It was agreed that he could ring us at the King Island Hotel if he wished to do so before we left on Friday'.[34]

The officers' report covers the next day as well, when Rose was observed shopping in Currie and visiting the post office. They spoke to him, suggesting 'that he should disclose whether it was his idea of arranging the meeting between Miss BARNETT and the Communist official from Sydney, or whether somebody else suggested the proposition to him'. On this occasion, too, and then with further pressing on his links with Wally Clayton, Rose chose to remain silent. When the officers returned to Philrose next morning, they found neither Rose nor Kay Phillips there, only her children. Rose had already flown the coop.[35]

The last interviews the ASIO men conducted on the island were with the local constables, who said that to their knowledge Rose had not been politically active; they believed Rose was pursuing a legitimate farming enterprise. Moreover, he was just contemplating the purchase of twenty-four cows to get his dairy going and planned to fatten cattle on the property. The new abattoir was already in operation. Rose, they concluded, had been well advised on the future possibilities of the cattle and dairy industry on the island.[36] The ASIO officers' report nonetheless closed enigmatically, as if they sensed Rose had teetered tantalisingly on the brink of a major revelation. He had left them in no doubt, they wrote, 'that if we had been in a position to offer him some consideration regarding his future protection he would have told a story which would be of considerable interest to our Organisation'.[37]

As Carter and Gilmour pondered Rose's vanishing act, he was already back in Melbourne. Careful to avoid further contact with the 'wallopers', Rose had made a pre-dawn trek through ti-tree scrub to the airport, where he cadged a lift to Melbourne from the pilot of a freight plane. Once in Melbourne he was 'in smoke', making contact with a comrade at the railway goods yard so as to send a message to Party headquarters. By that evening he had what he wanted – a long chat with the Queensland barrister Max Julius, also a comrade.

15. Nemesis

To the world outside the Soviet Embassy in Canberra, the Siberian *bon vivant* Vladimir Petrov was a humble third secretary; in reality he was an agent of the Ministerstvo Vnutrennikh Del (MVD, the Soviet Ministry of Internal Affairs). His wife Evdokia had trained in 1933 in the Soviet Special Department (Spets-Otdel), created to handle both civilian and military signals intelligence.[1] In the embassy she, too, was much more than the clerical assistant she appeared to be.[2]

In the Petrovs' time there were two branches of Soviet espionage. While the MVD covered the civilian realm, military espionage was the remit of the GRU, the Glavnoye Razvedyvatel'noye Upravleniye. Both branches were successful in gathering intelligence in Australia during and after the war.[3] As an officer of the MVD, indeed as its so-called Resident in Australia, Vladimir Petrov's brief from the time of his arrival in 1951 was to keep a close eye on expatriate Russians and to maintain, if possible even expand, an intelligence network. That would be no easy task, since by then Western agencies had discovered leaks and had largely plugged them. The heyday of Soviet espionage in Australia was already over, even if the political fallout was still being felt.[4]

When Petrov defected in April 1954, he was the most senior Soviet defector since the Second World War[5] and handed over a cache of information on ciphers and agent networks, plus the names of around 600 KGB officers working as diplomats across the world.[6] These documents offered intriguing insight into the way in which the Soviets had conducted their espionage activities in Australia. No mention was found of Fred Rose, whom, as far as can be ascertained, neither Vladimir nor Evdokia Petrov ever met. It was nothing the Petrovs revealed that led to Rose having a subpoena hand-delivered to his farm on King Island. Rather, Rose's nemesis on this occasion was an Australian public servant, a young woman named June Barnett. ASIO had been interested in her, too, for quite some time.

June Hyett Barnett was born in Melbourne in 1920, the daughter of Frederick Oswald and Elizabeth Barnett of Balywn. In 1938 she commenced a commerce degree at the University of Melbourne, transferring in 1940 to science. In 1942 she enlisted in the RAAF, attaining the rank of flight officer before her discharge at the end of the war, at which time she returned to university to complete a Bachelor of Arts degree. In 1947 she applied successfully for a position as staff cadet in the diplomatic service of the Department of External Affairs. As part of her cadetship she undertook the diplomatic course, which entailed studies at Canberra University College. These she completed in December 1949, before taking up a post as Third Class Under-Secretary in Canberra.[7]

Some of the finer details of her background drew ASIO's attention. For a practising Methodist pursuing a career in accountancy, Barnett's father, Frederick lived a colourful existence. He was deeply passionate about the abolition of slums in Melbourne and the welfare of children. When the Housing Commission of Victoria was set up in 1938, he was its vice-chairman for a decade.[8] The reasons he came to ASIO's notice lay somewhere quite different. It appeared that he actively supported 'suspect' organisations, including 'Australia–Soviet House' in Melbourne, of which he was the auditor. In March 1949 he was relieved of his appointment with the Victorian Housing Commission because of his outspoken criticism of it. Further investigations revealed that he was a good friend, indeed a patron, of the Youth Action for Peace Congress.[9]

His daughter's politics followed a similar course. During the war, it was learned, she distributed 'communistic literature' among other members of the RAAF.[10] Her sister Betty was married to E. Ralph Blunden, who in 1934 had stood as a communist candidate in municipal elections.[11] This was enough to set ASIO thinking that it had been 'highly undesirable' that June Barnett had entered the public service in the first place.[12]

Surely enough, in Canberra June Barnett continued to keep interesting company. On 27 May 1950 she was observed spending the morning with Brian Fitzpatrick, who was visiting Canberra.[13] Another report places her among a group attending a University College review in late July 1950. She and those with her were observed after the performance. When an ASIO officer later that night passed by the home of Manning Clark, June Barnett's distinctive MG sports car was parked outside. After midnight she had still not returned home.[14] ASIO thought it noteworthy, though it was not entirely mysterious. Barnett would have known Clark from her studies at Canberra University College; she may even have known him at the University of Melbourne some years earlier.

Her cadetship completed, Barnett took a position in the United Nations section of the Department of External Affairs. In 1951 her name came up for an overseas posting. A security check was carried out, more rigorous than the checks that had allowed her into the RAAF and then the Department of External Affairs. In making this request of ASIO, Assistant Secretary of the Department of External Affairs J.C.G. Kevin confided that he was 'not entirely happy with Miss BARNETT's political views'.[15] ASIO's assessment produced similar misgivings, noting her association with 'recorded' individuals like Clark and Fitzpatrick, not to mention members of her own family. Accordingly she was declared too great a security risk to undertake an overseas posting.[16]

The ruling was confirmed at the beginning of August 1951 by Charles Spry,[17] and the secretary of Barnett's department was informed of the adverse finding.[18] Barnett was stuck in Canberra, at least until March 1953, when she was invited to an unusual interview in a suite at the Hotel Canberra. Her interviewers were two senior ASIO officers. Another officer from her section, her immediate boss Ric Throssell, was interviewed separately the same day. What both were told was that there were 'certain doubts' about their 'Security Status', and that they were being given the opportunity to resolve those doubts.[19]

ASIO's account has it that Barnett appeared nervous on the day of the interview. She appeared at the hotel at the appointed time of 9.30. 'Her appearance was not impressive. Her hair and her clothes were untidy and she was without make-up; she appeared more mannish than feminine. She seemed to be rather apprehensive during the interview.'[20] The officers had come from Melbourne, she was told, 'to give her the opportunity of explaining certain actions of hers in the past'. She was informed that if she did not wish to talk about anything then she was at liberty to say so, but it soon became evident that she was prepared to get a lot off her chest. She confirmed that she had been a member of the CPA, having joined when she worked in the RAAF's education service in Perth. She admitted to attending 'cottage lectures' at the Nedlands home of the university lecturer Sid Williams. In 1944 she was deployed to Melbourne, where she transferred her CPA membership to the Camberwell Branch. She claimed that after her return to study she lost interest in the CPA and allowed her membership to lapse. Her father was 'a strong Christian socialist', and she had come to that view herself. Her brother had been a CPA member but had left the Party, and she thought her brother-in-law, too, 'had given it away'.[21]

The line of questioning shifted to Canberra and the more recent past. She had not joined the CPA in Canberra when she came to the capital in 1948, she insisted. But when asked whether she knew any communists in Canberra, she freely admitted, 'Yes, a family who are Communists were very kind to me soon after I came to the Department. I was only a young girl and they looked after me very well and I am very grateful to them.'[22] The ASIO officers immediately suspected that the 'kind' family was the Roses, well known to have opened their home to lonely public servants seeking a life outside work. On this point, however, Barnett was evasive: 'I suppose you know who I am referring to but I would rather not tell you their names. They were very good to me and I would rather not tell you who they are unless I have to.'[23]

A new topic was broached, and the conversation ran like this:

Q: Miss BARNETT, you realize with the position you hold in the Department and with your background, that you may have been noted down as a person who might be approached to give information about your Department?

A: No, I have not considered that.

Q: Do you know that the usual approach made by Russian Intelligence has in most cases been through the Party?

A: No, I did not know that.

Q: Have you not read the report of the Canadian Spy Trial or any of the other Spy Trials?

A: I have heard of them but I have not studied them.

Q: Well it is pretty clear from these reports that the person who is usually picked to work for them is a person like you who has either been a member of the Party or has attended study groups.

A: I didn't know that. [24]

The reference to the Canadian and other spy trials could only have unsettled Barnett. The Canadian trial stemmed from the September 1945 defection of Igor Gouzenko, a Ukrainian cipher clerk in the Soviet Embassy in Ottawa. He took with him 109 documents relating to Soviet espionage in the West. A commission of inquiry to investigate espionage in Canada ensued, and eventually eighteen people were convicted. Coincidentally, among those jailed was another Fred Rose, the only communist Member of Parliament in the Canadian House of Commons. After serving over four years in prison, the Lublin-born Rose returned to his homeland behind the Iron Curtain, forever protesting his innocence.[25]

More chilling for Barnett would have been the implicit reference under the heading 'other Spy Trials' to the convictions of Julius and Ethel Rosenberg. The two American citizens were convicted in August 1950 of espionage. A cloud still hangs over Ethel's precise role, but Julius had passed on information about the American development of the atomic bomb. Both husband and wife were sentenced to death. As June Barnett was being interviewed by ASIO officers, the Rosenbergs were on death row.

Perhaps it was these thinly veiled references that prompted Barnett's candour. Asked whether she might at some point have been approached, Barnett conceded that something along those lines had happened, though she had attached no importance to it at the time:

Soon after I joined the Department in 1950 I was taken with another girl, by another officer of the Department, to a party in Canberra, at the home of the people I mentioned earlier where I met them for the first time. I became friendly with the man and his wife and visited them quite often. I had told them I was a member of the Party (as I have said) and he seemed very anxious to discuss Communism with me but I told him I was no longer interested.

One night this man asked me to meet a member of the Party from Sydney who wanted to talk to me. I was not very keen about it, but as this man wanted me to see him I said I would. I met this man from Sydney and he asked me would I tell him things that happened in the Department. I said that I was no longer interested in the Party and would not do that for him, and I have not seen him since.[26]

Barnett could remember neither the man's name nor what he looked like, only that he 'took me for a walk round the block and asked me then, and when I told him that I was not in any way interested the matter was dropped straight away. I didn't attach any importance to it until you have mentioned these things to me. It was three years ago and it was night-time and really I have no idea what he was like'.[27] She did, however, remember that the officer from her department who had taken her and one other 'ultra conservative' woman with an interest in anthropology to the party was George Legge.[28] The mention of Legge might well have made the interviewing officers' pulses quicken, because George Legge was the cousin of Jack Legge, a known CPA member and acquaintance of Wally Clayton.[29]

Pressed once more on the identities of the dinner-party hosts, Barnett showed signs of cracking, not divulging names but issuing a clue: 'They live in Turner if that is any help to you.' The ASIO officers would not let it rest at that and pressed her on the need to convince them of her loyalty. The best proof of that would be for her to give them the names. She had, after all, taken an oath of allegiance; it was her duty to tell them. Finally, she relented: 'His name is Fred ROSE.'[30] In the next breath she assured them that she was no longer in touch with the Roses. It was about twelve months since she had seen them: 'I got sick of them discussing my music and my art along Marxist lines and I dropped out and have not seen much of them since.'[31] But there was no taking back her identification of her hosts, and a chain of events was set in motion which, in time, would reach around the world.

Barnett's candour did her no harm. The security assessment recorded a few weeks later gave her the benefit of the doubt when she affirmed that she had put her communist past behind her. The newly formed opinion was that she was 'a loyal subject' and that she did 'not constitute a security risk'.[32] The same conclusion was reached about Ric Throssell after his interview, Spry going so far as to write to Minister for External Affairs Richard Casey with the advice that Throssell 'is not, and never has been, a member of the Communist Party or any of its subsidiary organizations, and that he is neither a Communist nor pro Russian in outlook'.[33] The rapidity with which Spry's views on Barnett and Throssell had moved from doubt to bold assertions of blamelessness appears almost disarming. Was the man who controlled Australian counter-espionage so bright-eyed as to take at face value their protestations of loyalty? Or had some kind of deal been struck that would revive the professional prospects of both Barnett and Throssell at a time when their careers appeared to have stalled? And if that was the case, what might they have been expected to offer in return?

On 18 June 1953 Barnett was interviewed again by ASIO, this time in Melbourne. She retold the story of being asked by Rose to meet a 'Party man' from Sydney who 'wanted to have a talk with her'. Against her sister's advice, she explained, she went ahead and saw the man, but had no recollection of what his name might have been, or whether even a name was mentioned. The man, she recalled, had come to the door of the Roses' house without entering; they had then walked down the street 'where he very vaguely asked her to furnish information from External Affairs'. She had refused the request, she said, whereupon they had returned to the house and he had departed. As for his appearance, she recalled that he was not particularly tall, was wearing a hat but no glasses, and was perhaps 35 to 40 years of age. When shown photographs of a number of men, including Wally Clayton, she could not identify any of them.[34]

This second meeting had helped to clarify a couple of points. The 'ultra conservative' with an interest in anthropology with whom Barnett had gone to the Roses' home was Elizabeth Warren. That first visit, on the invitation of George Legge, had been early in 1948, not 1950.[35] Barnett regretted mentioning George Legge's name at all, insisting he was 'a very friendly bloke' and as far as she knew not a communist. But she still had no name for the 'Party man'.[36]

Well may Barnett have made some effort to remember faces and names. In line with Spry's assessment, since the March interview she had received her security clearance. Her diplomatic career was back on track. And on 29 June 1953, just over a week after her Melbourne interview, she was appointed Third Secretary in the Australian High Commissioner's Office in Wellington.[37]

Perhaps it was a matter of coincidence, but just as June Barnett was being interviewed in Melbourne, Fred Rose was dealing with security issues of his own. It was at this time that he was in Sydney farewelling Edith and the girls. Kay Phillips' Manly flat in which he stayed was burgled, as was his Canberra home. All of it, he was convinced, was the work of ASIO. And unlike June Barnett's, Rose's public service career was about to come to a screeching halt. It was on the day after Barnett's Melbourne interview – 19 June – that ASIO's regional director in Canberra had a chat with the Public Service Board about transferring Rose to the Census Office.[38]

ASIO was active on other fronts at that time. One of its operatives, a Macquarie Street medical practitioner Michael Bialoguski, had for a couple of years been working hard to cultivate a relationship with Vladimir Petrov, supplying him with whisky and women and holding out the prospect that they might even go into business together, implicitly dangling before him the prospect of defection. Petrov was taken in by Bialoguski's feigned leftist leanings, which manifested in, among other things, membership of the 'Save the Rosenbergs Committee'.[39] Their relationship had become so close that on the evening of 19 June 1953, while Fred Rose was in Manly, Petrov was spending the night in the guestroom of Bialoguski's harbour-view apartment in Point Piper. As Petrov slept the deep sleep of a man who had been plied heavily with whisky, Bialoguski was in the nearby lavatory, copying onto a roll of toilet paper the contents of documents he had removed from Petrov's pockets. So rich were the pickings, including a list of some forty names of Australians and a variety of notes, that the last of them was recorded on the cardboard.[40]

Both Barnett's testimony to ASIO during the day of 18 June 1953 and the documents filched from the drunken Petrov's pockets the following night would have their roles to play at the royal commission a year later. Before that came to pass, a news item reminded all concerned just how high the stakes were in international espionage. Condemned spies Ethel and Julius Rosenberg were put to death by the electric chair at sundown of 19 June 1953 in the Sing Sing Correctional Facility in Ossining, New York State. Julius, eyewitness reports revealed, had died after the first shock, but the normal course of three shocks had not killed Ethel. When unstrapped her heart was still beating, so two further shocks were applied. After all that, it was noted, smoke was rising from her head.[41]

When the ASIO officers Carter and Gilmour paid their unwelcome visit to King Island, Fred Rose may have been surprised that the name of June Barnett appeared on the papers he was served. Could he have had an inkling that his former house guest would implicate him in a spy ring? And while ASIO might have been pleased that in mid-1953 June Barnett had given them at least *something* to pin on Rose, they might also have lamented that it was not much. Apart from Barnett's recollection that Rose had introduced her to a man from the Party on some undetermined date in 1950, there was no proof. But with Petrov's defection in April 1954, June Barnett, by now ensconced in Wellington, suddenly became interesting again.

Among the documents Petrov handed to ASIO on his defection was a list in the handwriting of Valentin Sadovnikov, a former resident MVD officer in Australia, and headed 'Contacts K'. 'K' was taken to be the abbreviation for 'Klod', Wally Clayton's cryptonym. Among the eleven contacts on the list was one without a codename, without even an abbreviation, but with a description: 'Member of the Communist Party, girl, having finished the school of the Department of External Affairs, and will go over to work in the Department of External Affairs.'[42] It was vague, but it matched June Barnett. And it was enough for at least one ASIO officer to conclude that the Soviets 'had given her case considerable study and that she was of great interest to them'.[43]

ASIO flew her to Sydney to interview her again. She appeared composed, and not at all surprised to be met on arrival by ASIO officers, but she declined their offer of help with accommodation – she would be staying with the Reverend Keith Dowding in Woollahra.[44] Her choice of lodging with a pious Christian family in leafy Woollahra could not be taken as evidence that she had abandoned the left-wing sympathies she had acquired in her youth. On the contrary, the politics of Keith Dowding, whose son Peter would become Labor premier of Western Australia, were a reminder that, as in her own father's case, many Christians had aligned themselves with the left. Dowding was an alumnus of the University of Melbourne; after the death of his first wife he married a Jewish widow, Marjorie Lazarus, in 1951. Their manse at St Columba's became a meeting point for a number of prominent politicians of the left, among them Doc Evatt. In 1953 Dowding was expelled from the RSL for his 'alleged communist leanings'. June Barnett was not the only one to turn to him for assistance in these turbulent times. Dowding also appointed himself 'spiritual adviser' to Alan Dalziel, the devout Christian and Evatt staffer who, like June Barnett, would soon find himself testifying before the Royal Commission on Espionage.[45]

On the afternoon of 24 June 1954 Ron Richards and Jack Gilmour conducted an extensive interview with Barnett at a safe house in Sydney to confirm the details of what she had said a year earlier, and try to match it with what they had since gleaned from Petrov. Richards, one of very few who had been indoctrinated into Venona and what it revealed about 'The Case',[46] was above all interested in Barnett's meeting with the mysterious visitor to the Rose residence in 1950. It was clear that he had Rose in his sights, pressing Barnett on the question of whether she believed Rose had carefully planned his approach to her. She answered:

I suppose I do now. At the time I just thought it was Fred being enthusiastic and fanatical and that he did know me and my moods. He is or was very enthusiastic.
Mr Richards: About Communism?
Miss Barnett: Yes – or left wing thought.
Mr Richards: He is a fanatic?
Miss Barnett: Everything he did was connected with it – the people he had in his house, his music, his art – everything was related to it.[47]

Richards was like a dog with a bone, and further interviews followed the next day and beyond. But Barnett in essence merely repeated what she had said earlier; her description of the mystery visitor to 25 Froggatt Street remained vague, and, most frustratingly, she could not remember his name.[48] If the aim was to pin a crime on Fred Rose, as it no doubt was, then there was still no smoking gun.

ASIO tried a couple of other ploys. Carter and Gilmour questioned the Petrovs about June Barnett, but neither had even heard her name.[49] They tried to catch Fred Rose off-guard on King Island, hoping, presumably, that their surprise appearance might provoke him into an indiscretion. That, too, had come to nothing. The last hope was that, hauled before a royal commission, Rose might at last crack.

16. The Petrov Commission

With a federal election looming on 29 May, the timing of the Petrov defection could hardly have suited Menzies better. The polls had been giving him and his government little cause for optimism, but the dramatic revelations of espionage activity and of dire threats to national security posed by allegedly treacherous elements on the other side of politics helped the conservative cause. What better way to capitalise on those revelations than to conjure in full public view the spectre of world communism as it set its sights on Australia? And what better way to discredit the alternative government than to depict it as not merely weak-kneed and vacillating in the face of a grave danger, but perhaps even in cahoots with it?

The idea of a royal commission had been raised as early as 10 February, when it was becoming increasingly likely to ASIO – who duly told Menzies – that Petrov was about to jump.[1] It was discussed by Menzies and Spry on 4 April, the day after the defection; both were enthusiastic. Both, too, would have been aware of the Canadian precedent of the commission established in the wake of the Gouzenko defection. Its report had brought great benefits to both conservative politics and to counter-intelligence, benefits that Menzies and Spry could only wish upon themselves. 'We thought', Spry recalled many years later, 'that by having the commission we would awaken Australians "that it can happen here".'[2]

The strategy was not without risk. If Petrov had inflated the value of the intelligence he would provide in exchange for the £5000 ASIO offered him,[3] then the government would be left with egg on its face, its re-election prospects dashed. Menzies waited wisely as ASIO translated and assessed its intelligence haul. Petrov, it was established, brought with him three kinds of documents. There were the Moscow letters, photographic prints of letters written to him by the MVD Moscow Centre in 1952, when he was chief of the MVD espionage section. Then there was a series of miscellaneous documents, also in Russian and designated the 'G' series. One of them, G.2, was Sadovnikov's 'Contacts K' list. Then there were two documents in English, labelled 'H' and 'J', shortly to become the subjects of considerable controversy. One was a series of personality reports on Australian journalists written by Evatt's press secretary Fergan O'Sullivan and given to the former MVD resident in Canberra Ivan Pakhomov. The other was a carbon copy of a document written by the journalist Rupert Lockwood in the Soviet Embassy, also consisting of reports on personalities in Australia.[4] Translation alone did not solve all the mysteries of the documents. The authenticity of document J in particular was to become a bone of contention, but ASIO had good reason to be satisfied. As a supplement to the information gleaned from the Venona decrypts – a source about which only a tiny elite could know – they were priceless.

On 13 April Menzies broke the news to his Cabinet colleagues. They learned for the first time that Petrov, holed up in a safe house in Sydney, had defected. The drama around Evdokia was still to unfold. Cabinet was not just amenable to Menzies' proposal for a royal commission, it also supported an immediate change to the *Royal Commissions Act* so that witnesses could be compelled to attend.[5] This did not bode well for Fred Rose on King Island.

On the evening of 13 April Menzies intoned before parliament that the 'unpleasant duty' had befallen him to tell the House, and with it the world, of both the Petrov defection and his decision to hold a royal commission into espionage in Australia. He did not intend to reveal the names of those mentioned in Petrov's documents, but announced they would be placed under surveillance until the commission was formed, as Menzies trusted, without delay. Unhappily, so Menzies advised, this would mean that the commission would commence its work before the coming election.[6] Opposition leader, Evatt, in contrast, was sincere in his unhappiness; he had little choice but to declare his support.

Heading the formally titled 'Royal Commission on Espionage' were three Supreme Court judges: the chair Mr Justice Thomas Langer Owen from New South Wales, Mr Justice George Coutts Ligertwood from South Australia, and Mr Justice Rosslyn Philp of Queensland. Victor Windeyer QC, a well-known member of the Sydney bar and former militia officer once considered to head ASIO,[7] was appointed counsel assisting the commission. On 3 May, the day before Menzies launched his re-election campaign, the commission's major appointments and terms of reference were announced. A few days later it was determined that the commission would be held openly. This meant, in effect, that anyone mentioned in Petrov's documents, guilty or otherwise, would be required to give evidence in public.[8]

With these arrangements in place, it was possible to commence the public hearings before the election. The venue for the first of them was Canberra's Albert Hall, hastily equipped with the accoutrement and gravitas of a courtroom, with generous provision for the expected large media contingent. Proceedings commenced with two-and-a-half days of opening remarks by counsel assisting Windeyer, who on the one hand affirmed the value of an open inquiry in a matter of such seriousness, while also offering reassurance that this would be no McCarthyist witch-hunt, and that no one would be named until investigations had proceeded. He held out the tantalising prospect that with the aid of the material provided by Petrov he would be able to reveal the existence of a 'spy ring' in Australia.[9]

In the unfolding drama played out before the election and the months that followed, Fred Rose had little more than a cameo role, but it would be enough to besmirch his name forever. At first he could at best follow developments from distant King Island, where Don Baker delivered him the news of the Canberra sittings.

After the return of the Menzies government at the 29 May elections, sittings shifted to the High Court in Melbourne, where the first witnesses, including Vladimir Petrov, appeared. Rose prepared for his appearance by consulting Max Julius. Born in Brisbane, Julius was the seventh and youngest child of a Hungarian Rumanian Jewish family; he had joined the CPA as early as 1936 and, despite the antagonism directed at him from the Queensland legal fraternity, made a name for himself at the bar, where he devoted himself to the cause of defending 'an endless procession of impecunious clients'.[10] When Rose met him, he had just stood as a CPA candidate in the recently concluded federal elections. He failed then, just as, more famously, he would fail in 1961, when he stood again in the seat of Moreton. On that occasion, ironically, it was Julius's preferences to the Liberal candidate Jim Killen that won Killen the seat and saved the Menzies government.[11]

Julius had form in defending the interests of the CPA. He had appeared as counsel for the defence at the royal commission into the CPA held in Victoria in 1949–50, and he had provided legal support for the challenge to the Communist Party Dissolution Bill in 1950–51. His enthusiasm for Aboriginal rights might have made him all the more eager to lend his help to Rose. Julius thought he saw some logic in the summons served on Rose. As Rose was physically isolated on King Island and had perhaps drifted away from the Party, ASIO might, he speculated, have reckoned Rose would be easier to crack. Rose had come through that ordeal intact, but Julius warned that worse was to come. The fact that his wife and daughters were living in a socialist country would not help. 'You're really a sitting duck for them!' was his frank assessment.[12] Between them, Julius and Rose decided that when placed in the witness box, Rose would play the injured and innocent intellectual; he would refuse to answer any but the preliminary questions.[13]

And so it played out on 21 July. Before completing his oath, Rose signalled his intentions: he wished to make a statement. The chairman prevailed upon him to complete the oath, and then Windeyer's assistant George Pape managed to elicit a few answers to basic questions concerning Rose's identity. But when asked whether he had joined the Commonwealth public service, Rose returned more forcefully to his desire to make a statement. He was told that he should first answer the question, which he did, at which point the chair asked him what it was he wished to say. Rose answered, 'I wish to say this: although completely innocent, in order to protect my acquaintances, my friends and myself, my conscience tells me this – that I shall answer no further questions.'[14]

Rose's appeal to the dictates of his conscience might have represented a point of high drama; what followed soon descended into farce. Despite Rose's statement, Pape continued to put questions to him, and Rose steadfastly refused answers. The frustration of the three commissioners leaps from the pages of the official transcript. When Owen demanded to know the ground for his continued refusal, Rose, the erstwhile theatre buff, channeled Thomas More: 'My conscience is the ground' – soliciting the unsympathetic rebuke from the chair, 'We are not concerned with your conscience.' There followed fifteen questions on June Barnett, each greeted with silence.[15]

In the end the commissioners Windeyer and Pape gave in. Owen told Rose he could leave, only to find that Rose was not prepared to end the bout by withdrawing meekly to his corner. He wanted to make a further statement. The chair made his position clear: 'You will make no statement, since you refused to answer questions.' Rose withdrew, but Julius took up the cudgels in his absence, pressing the case for Rose to be permitted to make a statement. In the end it was agreed that Julius would present a written statement to the commission, which he did. Owen read it to himself, labelled it 'propaganda' and declined formal receipt. It therefore is not recorded in the official proceedings, though Rose happily made it available to the media. It read:

> *Although innocent of any wrongdoing, my conscience dictates to me that I must decline to answer any questions both for the protection of myself and my friends and acquaintances. The setting up of a Commission to enquire into alleged breaches of the law is contrary to all traditions of true democracy, and as an Englishman I am well aware that proceedings such as these would not be tolerated in my home country.[16]*

The statement went on to cite the example of the 'notorious McCarthy tribunal' in the United States, which had subverted the principle of trial by jury and been used to 'smear' liberals and progressives with lies and rumours. Rose claimed he was following advice given by Albert Einstein, who suggested that intellectuals should go to gaol rather than submit themselves to interrogation. Were he to participate in the commission, he would be acting against his 'ardent desire for peaceful relations between Australia and the Soviet Union and People's China'.[17]

Back in Canberra, his former comrades were taking a close interest in Rose's performance, and they were not disappointed. A CPA branch meeting was held on 5 August, and the president, Bob Gollan, passed on journalist Rex Chiplin's praise for Rose's courage under fire. Before his arrival in Melbourne Rose had been concerned, according to Chiplin, that he would have to 'carry the baby', but then he had behaved well and had made a good statement. The branch members resolved to send Rose a telegram of congratulations.[18]

The government viewed Rose's intransigence less favourably, indeed it passed a revised *Royal Commission on Espionage Act* so as to clarify and sharpen the commission's powers.[19] Justice Owen now had the power to sentence recalcitrant witnesses on the spot. For his next appearance Rose would need a new strategy.

By then the commission was sitting in Sydney. For Rose, there was one other major difference: June Barnett had been summonsed and would give evidence. That was on the morning of 25 October, and Rose was among the interested spectators. The line of questioning delved into her history, her membership of the CPA, her loyalty to Australia, her role in the Department of External Affairs. And then, inevitably, it arrived at Fred Rose.

Asked if she had 'got quite friendly with him', she answered in the affirmative. She described his politics as 'fairly far left', though he did not, she claimed, tell her that he was a member of the CPA.[20] And then came the question about that fateful visit to 25 Froggatt Street in 1950, at which point all the details of her earlier statements – and all their vagueness – were laid before the commission. Yes, she had been invited to the Roses to visit and to meet 'a Communist Party official from Sydney'. But she could not recall whether the invitation had been issued in person or by telephone, she could not say any more specifically than that it was 'around about Easter', and she had no clear recollection of whether Rose had said what the purpose of the invitation might be.[21]

As for the man from Sydney, she could not recall whether she had been introduced to him at all, let alone what his name was or how he was dressed. Owen tried to jog her memory: 'Does the name "Walter" convey anything to you?' It did not. Handed two photographs of the elusive Wally Clayton, her response was as it had ever been. She did not know whether this was the man with whom she had walked around the block in Canberra four years earlier.[22] It was a curious failure; thin-faced and balding as reported in ASIO's records, Wally Clayton – if that is who it was – might well have proved more memorable.[23]

Julius would not treat her with kid gloves in cross-examination, establishing that over a number of years she was a frequent lunch and dinner guest at the Roses', that she found 'a good deal of intellectual pleasure' in their company, and that they were indeed 'firm friends'. Then came his most important question: 'During the whole of the time that you maintained this friendship with Mr. Rose and Mrs. Rose, Mr. Rose never suggested to you that you should pass him any information that might come into your possession?' Her answer was an unambiguous no.[24] A few questions later Julius went in for the kill: 'I am putting it that this lady, whose evidence is of the vaguest nature, is prepared, or was prepared, to make a statement implicating someone who was a close friend in the hope that firstly it would lead to her advancement, or assist in her advancement, in the Department.'[25]

In the absence of Wally Clayton, who despite the best efforts of ASIO remained the commission's most notable absentee, there was little more to be done with Barnett. Further questions were asked, but no progress made. In the end the commissioners might well have wondered how it was that a person who allegedly rebuffed the single attempt to elicit information from her would appear on a Soviet contact list, but to that puzzle, too, there was no answer.

Having sat through all that, Rose appeared the same day, well aware that he could not play a dead bat as in Melbourne. On the contrary, with Julius he had come up with a daring new strategy. He was open, almost expansive in his answers, confirming that he had known Barnett in

Canberra and was aware that she had been a communist. He volunteered that he was a member of the CPA, but he denied, even on being asked the question multiple times, that he had invited Barnett to come to his house to meet a Communist Party official.[26] And then he, too, went on the attack, implying that Barnett had concocted the story of the stroll around the block for career purposes. 'The point is', he said, 'that the pimp, the perjurer, and the liar can get a long way in the Public Service providing he plays along with people such as Security.'[27]

He must have expected the question about Wally Clayton. Yes, he had known him since about 1948 or 1950, he was not sure when. Clayton came to Canberra three or four times a year, and he used to call on the Roses to leave literature and collect moneys and dues. Rose, after all, as he now conceded, had been treasurer of the Canberra branch of the CPA.[28] There was nothing untoward in that. Unlike Barnett, he was readily able to identify Clayton when shown a photograph.[29]

The line of questioning shifted to his links with the Soviet Embassy. He had been there, he said, when in 1946 he inquired about the whereabouts of his father-in-law Richard Linde. But in answers to questions about Sadovnikov, Pakhomov and Mikheyev, he said he knew none of them. Pape delved even deeper into the past, wondering whether the work he had co-authored with Jolly had been provided to the Soviets. But that was back in 1942, before there was a Soviet Embassy in Canberra, and Rose claimed he had no role in sending the manuscript to the Soviet Union. He was not about to dob in Katharine Prichard.[30]

Then the issue of Rose's loyalty was raised. Philp asked him if he had a greater loyalty to the Communist Party than to Australia. Rose saw no question of choice, 'As a Communist I have a very great loyalty to Australia. I am primarily an Australian'. And when asked if he would consider it wrong to pass 'any special information' to the Communist Party if he knew it would be sent to the Soviet Union, he answered neither 'Yes' nor 'No'. The point was, he said, that the Communist Party did not work like that: 'Your proposition is purely hypothetical and probably would not exist in fact.' Asked point-blank – twice – if he had ever given special information to any official of the Communist Party, he answered on both occasions: 'No; never.'[31]

Rose had parried every attack with growing confidence. It was now time for him and Julius to implement the dénouement they had concocted. Julius adroitly picked up a line of questioning about Rose's access to information in the public service. He wondered whether a good deal of it might have been confidential. 'Oh yes', Rose said, 'a very solid amount of confidential stuff passed through my hands'. Julius asked about Rum Jungle. 'Yes, I actually handled the security of Rum Jungle – the issuing of passes.' Owen unwittingly became a participant in the scheme to embarrass Rose's enemies: 'Up to when was that going on?' 'Probably to about the end of 1952', Rose told him.[32] Windeyer tried to shut down the line of questioning, but Julius pursued it until the day's proceedings were adjourned.[33]

The US Embassy in Canberra had long been interested in Rum Jungle's security,[34] and before the day was out its first secretary was on the phone to ASIO. He wanted information about Rose's assertions regarding security at Rum Jungle. The Americans 'felt that the cable advice on this matter overseas would have a serious and detrimental effect, and they desire to inform Washington of the true position'.[35] ASIO sprang into action, assuring the Americans that Rose had misrepresented the situation.[36] None of this, though, could change the headline run the next morning by the *Sydney Morning Herald*: 'Red "Handled Secret Material".'[37]

Rose's appearance the next day did not extend beyond the first hour. Julius used it to discredit Barnett. The G.2 document mentioned a 'girl' who was a member of the CPA. Had Barnett not testified that she had left the Party? Pape, on the other side, made much of Rose's connections to East Germany. Asked whether his father-in-law was a communist, Rose answered that he was not: 'I think actually, if he has half political leanings, it would be towards the Quakers.'[38] With that, Rose's detractors had nowhere else to go, and Rose was dismissed.

All that remained to be done for now to tidy up the utterly inconclusive Rose/Barnett sideshow was to repair the damage that Rose and Julius had done the previous afternoon. Rose's former boss, Secretary of the

Department of Territories Cecil Lambert, was called before the commission on 27 October to issue assurances that Rum Jungle's security had never been compromised; Rose had only ever forwarded passes, not issued them.[39] The commissioners no doubt listened politely, but the intended audience was the Americans, sceptical as ever of Australia's trustworthiness in matters of security.

As during Rose's Melbourne session, ASIO monitored Rose's former comrades' response to his Sydney performance.[40] It had somehow gained access to comments made by Rose when he visited his Sydney friends Rita and Jimmy Kelly soon after the ordeal. He reportedly claimed that he had indeed met Clayton at his Froggatt Street home at the time mentioned by Barnett. There was a large crowd present 'and people were being introduced on the front verandah, at the front door and even at the front gate, and it is obvious that BARTLETT [sic] was introduced to CLAYTON during hurried introductions at the front gate'.[41]

It would be months before all the evidence was heard and the commissioners' report prepared. In Rose's absence his name would be mentioned several times by a number of his acquaintances. Pamela Beasley, the anthropology graduate whose sister was married to John Burton, was called before the commission, having appeared on G.2 as a K contact under the cryptonym 'Sister of B's wife' – B was understood to be John Burton. She said she knew Rose but had nothing to divulge.[42] Rex Chiplin said he knew Rose, indeed had stayed several times at Froggatt Street,[43] while the CSIRO radio astronomer Wilbur Norman Christensen also conceded a social relationship with Rose.[44] Ric Throssell recalled meeting him socially several times in Canberra;[45] his wife Dorothy was 'friendly' with Rose.[46] As for Jim Hill, he could hardly pretend he did not know him well; after all, he lived just a hundred yards or so away for years.[47] But there was nothing untoward, let alone sinister, in any of this. If anything, it merely confirmed the bleeding obvious – Fred Rose was an affable man with many friends in left-wing circles. Some were on Wally Clayton's contact list – but not Rose. Whether or not he was a spy was at that point still anyone's guess.

As for the 'spymaster' Wally Clayton, to the surprise of many, after months of being on ASIO's 'wanted' list, he finally turned up at the commission and blithely wondered what all the fuss was about. His appearance was announced in the press in advance. He claimed that he had been slandered and wished to correct the record. 'Health reasons' had hitherto kept him away, though he was well aware that his attendance was sought. On the subject of Fred Rose, he admitted knowing him and conceded that he had stayed with him in Canberra on one or two occasions.[48] As for the allegations made by June Barnett, he not only denied being in Canberra at all in 1950, he claimed to have no memory whatsoever of her.[49]

The last act was played out on 18 March 1955. June Barnett was back in the witness box. She had previously said that she felt she would be able to recognise the man who had strolled around Turner with her if she saw him. Confronted, finally, with the real Wally Clayton, the best she could manage was, 'I can only say it could be and it could not be'.[50] Her own ordeal over, she was seen being whisked away from the commission in a car driven by the Reverend Dowding.[51]

Soon she was back at work in Wellington, most of her diplomatic career still ahead of her. And when she was not on an overseas posting, she lived in leafy Yarralumla. She had had a house designed there by the architect couple Heather Sutherland and Malcolm Moir, and she lived there for the rest of her life with her partner Kay Keightley.[52]

For Rose, in contrast, there could be no return to his pre-commission life. As he sat out the final months of hearings in Sydney and awaited the findings, Philrose fell into disrepair. ASIO learned that Kay Phillips 'proposed leaving the property there as she had gone "troppo" due to the loneliness'.[53] Rose found lodging with a sympathetic host in Sydney's Vaucluse and set about finding work to support Kim and himself.

When it finally appeared, the commissioners' report could offer Rose little solace. He was, they wrote, 'one of the most unsatisfactory witnesses called before us. At our sittings in Melbourne he refused to answer any questions and the evidence he gave in Sydney was so full of prevarications and evasions that, on critical matters, no reliance could be placed on it'.[54]

They smeared his reputation in other ways too. His home, they concluded, 'was a meeting place for persons of Communistic or "progressive" views'. They found it suspicious that he 'saw a great deal of CLAYTON' – hardly a fair summary of Rose's statement that he might have seen Clayton three or four times a year.[55] And on the question of whose version of events to believe in relation to that night back in 1950, the commissioners opted unambiguously for the patchy evidence of Barnett: 'In spite of the denials of Rose and Clayton, and in spite of Miss Barnett's failure to identity Clayton positively, we are satisfied on the whole of the evidence, and particularly having regard to the description of Miss Barnett appearing under the heading "Contacts K", that, on the probabilities, Clayton was the person who interviewed her in April 1950 and that he did attempt to suborn her as an officer of the Department of External Affairs.'[56]

It could have been much worse for Rose. No criminal charges were laid against him. Indeed, for all the commission's efforts over many months, and for all ASIO's feverish activities before and during the hearings, not a single witness faced prosecution. His former life shattered, Rose was at least now free to attempt to construct a new one.

17. On the Hook

Was Fred Rose a spy? The full truth of the matter might never be known. In March 1956, in the wake of the royal commission, even Director-General of ASIO Charles Spry noted that 'there is no positive proof that Rose has actively engaged in espionage'. On the other hand, he added, it 'appears to me extremely likely that he did so'.[1] When the commission had concluded, Spry spent some time trying to find out if he had put the right man in the witness stand.

Over the years that followed, ASIO conducted interviews with a man by the name of Tim White, who knew Rose in Canberra. Like many public servants, White lived for a time in hostel accommodation and gladly accepted the Roses' invitation to expand his social horizons at Froggatt Street. He was, as he put it, 'one of some hundreds who visited his house for a meal and social discussions'.[2] In 1958 White said that he was aware from conversations with Rose that the latter received visits from Wally Clayton, with whom he probably had 'some irregular association'. Rose, he said, 'was secretive and a lot of the things he did he kept to himself. He didn't give any indication to anyone that I knew of, that he was engaged in illegal activity'.[3]

In 1960 ASIO interviewed Mabel Lincoln, whose background was not so different from June Barnett's. Some time after her arrival in Canberra in 1949 she, too, joined the stream of visitors to the Rose household. Fred, she reminisced, was 'a devoted Communist and an intellectual person with an easy carefree manner, fond of entertaining and of company – particularly female company – charming, open-hearted and generous, and ... a keen debater of politics without any attempt to force his own political views'. As for Edith, Lincoln judged her to be a 'quiet and morose yet friendly type of person who rarely entered into political discussions but when "roused or baited" she undoubtedly revealed her training, knowledge and support of Communism'. During regular visits over a period of two to three years 'she saw no evidence of any organized meetings or political discussions, nor was she ever asked by ROSE or any person whom she met at ROSE's home to either supply any information concerning her employment or carry out any assignment'. As for the spying allegations, she could only say, 'I felt for a long time that perhaps Fred ROSE may have been wrongly accused'.[4]

And then there was the Roses' old friend Bob Michell. He too 'talked' in 1960, by which time he had distanced himself from the CPA. His views on Rose, too, were ambivalent. On the one hand he said, 'My reaction to the Commission was a hell of a lot of bull. Fred gave no indication at the meetings or to anyone I knew of what he was doing'. On the other hand, Michell pondered, 'I would not have been very surprised if Fred could have done the things he is said to have done. If Fred was concerned he concealed it very well. I don't think he was concerned ... I still have great doubts about Fred'.[5]

Unavailable to anyone but a very select few in 1954 and 1955, though crucial in bringing about the commission in the first place, were the top-secret Venona decrypts. The one that mattered most in the Rose case, dated 16 May 1948, was among the last cables between Canberra and Moscow to be decrypted. It was a message from Moscow to Semyen Makarov, at that time the MVD resident in Canberra. Bearing the heading 'Questions To Be Put To "C" about Persons Selected for Future Work', it was intercepted and, in time, partially decrypted. The masters in Moscow made the request that 'K' (Wally Clayton) be called on to recommend which of his 'old sources' ('Professor' or 'Tourist'?) should be taken on, since 'C' (or actually 'K', that is either 'Claude' or 'Klod') was not finding new leads.[6] The implication was that both 'Professor' and 'Tourist' were not new to the game of passing on information, since they were described as 'old sources'.[7]

'Tourist' was Jim Hill, but who was this 'Professor'? In the version of the decrypt made in 1967, the cryptanalyst provided a key to unlock the cryptonyms. For 'Professor' the analyst suggested, 'Unidentified covername. First occurrence'.[8] Seven years later, in 1974, American intelligence was still pondering the intercept, because at that time it came up with a slightly expanded decrypt. In the key to the codenames an analyst had now recorded next to 'Professor' the words 'Possibly Frederick George Godfrey Rose'.[9] The version of this particular decrypt currently appearing on the National Security Agency website – the one made in 1967 – does not suggest that 'Professor' was Fred Rose.[10] The Americans, it seems, are not at all sure who 'Professor' was. And when the CIA is asked if it has a record of Frederick George Godfrey Rose, the answer is that it 'can neither confirm nor deny the existence or nonexistence' of such records.[11] The British intelligence agency MI5 gives the same, unhelpful answer that it applies the principle of 'neither confirm nor deny' in the interests of protecting national security.[12]

One man who could have put this conundrum to rest was 'Klod', Wally Clayton. He gave little away when he finally appeared before the commission, but in 1996, aged 90, he received a visit from the academic Desmond Ball, armed with Venona transcripts. Deeply aware of his mortality – he would die the next year – Clayton confessed his role as spymaster, quipping that 'Klod' was an awful cover-name.[13]

With the aid of Clayton's confession, and of unprecedented access to ASIO archives, Ball pieced together a plausible explanation of how the Soviet spy network functioned. The spymaster was Wally Clayton, his role to gather intelligence from his contacts in Canberra and Sydney and to pass it on to the Soviets, typically via the TASS representative in Sydney, where Clayton was based. The TASS representative, in reality an MVD operative, for most of the period in question (1943–50) was Feodor Nosov. He would then pass the material to MVD operatives in the Canberra embassy, and they would send it to Moscow. Anything sent by cablegram was encrypted first.[14]

Clayton needed a collection point in Canberra so that he could gather intelligence when he drove down from Sydney. For a long time after the war the collection point was a flat in the Myuna complex on Northbourne Avenue in Braddon. The flat belonged to Elfrida Newbigin (later Morcom). For a time after the war it was rented by Doris Beeby, the Canberra correspondent for the *Tribune*. Sometimes she staged CPA branch meetings in the flat.[15] From 1947 Ric Throssell took on not only the flat but also the associated duties of receiving intelligence, collecting it and passing it on to Clayton. His new wife Dorothy came to share both the flat and the nefarious obligations that came with it.[16]

Later, according to Ball's thesis, it was Fred Rose who took on the role of Clayton's Canberra contact, and 25 Froggatt Street became the collection point for intelligence. That is most likely to have been from February 1949, when the Throssells moved out of the Myuna flats,[17] Throssell having been posted to Rio de Janeiro.[18] Certainly by 1951 ASIO was more than a little interested in Rose's home, as it was one of the premises nominated for searching under Communist Party Dissolution legislation.[19] The beauty of the arrangement was this: if anyone had asked awkward questions about what might have brought Clayton to that address, a ready explanation was at hand. Clayton was a member of the CPA visiting from Sydney to deliver copies of the *Tribune* and collect Party dues. Fred Rose was the treasurer of the Canberra branch of the CPA, so it was his role to pass on those dues and to receive and distribute the latest issue of the *Tribune*. Plausible deniability of anything untoward was guaranteed.[20]

The story meshes with Rose's testimony before the commission that Wally Clayton would visit him two, three or even four times a year; Rose would hand over Party subscriptions or other 'donations'.[21] This in itself was news to ASIO, which had been curiously inept in tracking their putative master-spy's movements from his Sydney base in Mosman; the most they pinned on the man they called 'Pop' was a speeding fine, and they were strangely ignorant of his connection with Rose. Despite the surveillance resources committed to Clayton, Rose does not appear among those with whom he was observed.[22] Rose, too, was watched like a hawk, and was known to associate with communists, suspected communists and fellow travellers. But when ASIO put together a list of over eighty such associates, Clayton was not one of them.[23]

If 25 Froggatt Street was an intelligence collection point, it would not have been for long. By late 1948 the Soviets knew of Venona and so knew their agents were under suspicion.[24] The key players who had handed on useful information in the immediate aftermath of war were now gone. Ian Milner had taken up a United Nations posting in New York as early as 1946.[25] Jim Hill, under grave suspicion because of Venona decrypts from 1948, was sent to London at the beginning of 1950, where in June he faced a grilling from MI5 interrogator Jim Skardon and the sure knowledge that the game was up.[26] Dorothy Jordan had left the public service in 1947.[27] And while Throssell remained in the public service, care was taken that nothing of importance ever crossed his desk, with the result that in Moscow Central he came to be regarded as redundant.[28]

Beyond June Barnett's unsubstantiated claims, there is one other piece of evidence to suggest that Fred Rose played a part in attempts to recruit young officers in the Department of External Affairs as sources of intelligence. It is in the recollections of the late Coral Bell, who, like June Barnett, had been a cadet in the Department of External Affairs. After her training at Canberra University College she took a position in the UN section of the department. She recalls in her unpublished memoirs that she knew Fred Rose when he was in Post-war Reconstruction, housed in the building where she worked – the West Block. Commonly staff would take their lunch to eat on the lawns outside the building. She recalls having lunch in the company of 'three agreeable young men, Jim Hill, Ric Throssell, and Fred Rose'. Fred was an anthropologist who worked nearby, 'a great charmer who always seemed to be at everyone's parties'.[29] He was 'mildly flirtatious', indeed Bell was not aware at the time that Rose was married.[30] She knew him to be a communist, 'but no-one held that against him. Lots of people were in those days'.[31] Nonetheless, she seems to have been at least a little taken aback by a suggestion put to her by Ric Throssell at one of the lunch gatherings: 'Some of us think that the Soviet Union ought to see these documents.'[32] What was meant by 'these documents' were British Foreign Office dispatches and telegrams, officially called Foreign Office prints – confidential material rather than secret, but potentially useful to Soviet intelligence.[33]

It was Throssell who put the proposal, not Rose, and on hearing the proposition Bell assumed that he was joking, 'laughed merrily, and said something to the effect that it sounded like a splendid way to get oneself in jail'.[34] Bell had studied under the philosopher John Anderson at Sydney University and, like Anderson, was firmly anti-Marxist in her views – unusual in a department where, as she recalls, Burton had surrounded himself with perhaps six or seven left-wing people.[35] She surmises that Throssell might have told Burton of her 'frivolous' response. In any case, she was removed from the UN section, headed at the time by Burton, to the South-east Asia division.[36]

As neither the CIA nor MI5 will confirm or deny a knowledge of Fred Rose's activities, clues from outside Australia are sparse. One was located on the other side of the Iron Curtain. Rose's father-in-law Richard Linde once reported to the GDR's State Secretariat of Higher Education that over the years Rose had passed on to the Communist Party 'valuable information from areas to which he had access'.[37] Whether 'valuable' here equated to 'secret' is not at all clear; Linde might have been referring to Rose's anthropological work for the Party. In any case, some years later, when Rose was settled in East Berlin, the East German authorities undertook their own assessment of his security status. In doing so they lodged queries with Soviet security and military intelligence agencies. The Soviet response was unambiguous. Rose was not known to them. Moreover, Rose was not mentioned in any way 'in connection with the traitor Petrov'.[38]

Whatever the merits of the case against him, the royal commission profoundly affected Rose's life. It left psychological scars that never fully healed. Rose had known for a long time that he was being closely watched, his phone tapped, his movements recorded, his house searched. After each of his two trying appearances before the commission his name and image were splashed across the press. From that time on, Rose found it increasingly difficult to clear his mind of the possibility that he was being watched, that hostile forces were out to 'get him'. The episode of the commission and of the events that had led to it triggered a proclivity to paranoia that would stay with him.

With the sale of the King Island farm, ASIO reported in August 1955 that Kay Phillips was living in Edithvale in Victoria.[39] Little is known of what Rose felt about the demise of his relationship with Kay or the collapse of their shared farming venture. In a manner fitting with his 'compartmentalising' tendency, Rose seems to have managed to put that to one side and dedicate himself to making a new life. In any case, he had soon made alternative living arrangements.

His host at 22 Clarke Street in affluent Vaucluse was Rosine Guiterman. Her daughter was married to the scientist – and communist – John Williamson (Jack) Legge. Rosine was shortly to become a founding member of the Aboriginal–Australian Fellowship.[40] With her late husband David she had established quite a record of offering sanctuary to the needy. Together the couple had helped hundreds of German Jewish refugees settle in Sydney before the war.[41] Among them were Emil and Hannah Witton, refugees from Hitler's Germany, who saw Rosine Guiterman as a 'guardian angel'. Victims of racial prejudice themselves, they went on to become vociferous advocates of Aboriginal rights.[42]

Rose had to find a new life, and a new job. He had not shied away from the heavy physical labour that farming had demanded, and he now sought out more of it – as a Sydney wharfie.[43] Later he explained his radical career change in quite abstract terms. When he had lived and worked in Canberra, he had been regarded in the Party as a 'bloody intellectual', confined to the margins of the class warfare being waged in the bigger cities. He had been isolated and vulnerable, an easy target for the forces of reaction, as the royal commission had shown. In Melbourne and Sydney, in contrast, there was strength and safety in numbers.[44] Employment as a wharfie and membership of the Waterside Workers Federation, the communist-controlled WWF, filled a pressing need at a challenging time.

From March 1955 Rose was formally a rank-and-file member of the WWF; in the parlance of his new trade, he was 'on the hook'.[45] The steel hook was the standard tool of the wharfie, used to grab, lift and drag bags of produce. For Rose it symbolised his membership of a kind of proletarian collective; he kept it with pride for the rest of his life.

The conditions under which the men worked, as Rose would soon discover, were onerous in the extreme. On one occasion his gang was unloading soda ash, which in its raw state could be harmful to the airways. For this reason the members of his gang were given masks to tie over their mouths and noses, and they received extra 'dirt money' to compensate for the unpleasant work. Rose noticed that the bags of soda ash were being deposited in a shed, where three Aborigines, who were not wharfies and wore neither footwear nor gloves, let alone masks, were transferring the bags to waiting trucks. During 'smoko' the gang leaders discussed the situation, deciding that if the Aborigines were not issued with boots and masks, the boat would not be unloaded. This message was conveyed by the delegate, the representative of the various gangs, to the supervisor, who answered, 'What the bloody Abos do is none of the wharfies' business!' The wharfies remained adamant, however, and not another bag of soda ash was extracted from the hold until the Aborigines had their boots and masks.[46]

This was the kind of solidarity that deeply impressed Rose. He was surprised to learn that of the 5000 or so wharfies in Sydney, only about 150 were Party members, yet he found a sense of common purpose among them. None asked him about his background, although all knew him to be a communist and bought the *Tribune* from him. Party comrades or not, all possessed an acute awareness of the presence of the class enemy, who appeared in two forms. There was the employers' representative, the foreman, and the police, for whom Rose had already developed an instinctive contempt. It had become common practice for policemen to wait outside the wharf, intercept wharfies on their way home and search them for pilfered goods. The first time Rose was frisked, he felt angry and humiliated; he understood better than ever the wharfies' hostility to the long arm of the law.[47]

By the 1950s the waterfront had taken over from the coalfields as the prime site of industrial disputation in Australia.[48] The fractious atmosphere owed much to the structural imbalances of the industry. Demand for labour could fluctuate wildly depending on shipping activity. It was in the interests of the major stevedores, virtually all of which were owned and controlled by the shipping lines, to have at their disposal a large pool of casual labour alongside a small body of permanents for maximum flexibility. In the old 'bull' system, the foremen would make a daily selection from a congregated throng on the wharf, favouring the strongest and fittest, and leaving the weakest and suspected militants to cool their heels. In more recent times the wharfies had managed to force a transition to the system of rostered gangs that Rose came to know, but the stevedores hankered still for the old system, which gave them control over who worked and when.

The WWF confronted the constant challenge of resisting the resurrection of the 'bull' system, and did so with success. Even the majority non-communist membership of the WWF – and there were even staunchly anti-communist 'groupers' in the union[49] – acknowledged the achievements of the communist leaders' group and continued to vote for them. As one journalist put it in 1951, the wharfies saw communists as 'the sharpest sword with which to hack their way to gains'.[50] The most admired of those leaders was Jim Healy. The Manchester-born son of Irish parents, Healy had volunteered while still underage for service in the Great War, was wounded several times, and then in 1925 emigrated to Queensland, where he eventually became a wharfie.[51] By the end of the decade he was branch president of the WWF in Mackay. With union sponsorship he undertook a study tour of the Soviet Union in 1934 and was persuaded on his return to join the CPA.[52] By 1937 he was elected General Secretary of the WWF, in which capacity he steered it through the war and into the troubled waters of the postwar period.

While some of his opponents developed a grudging respect for the charismatic Healy, Menzies was not one of them. The antagonism stretched back at least as far as 1937–38, when Healy had led campaigns supporting the Sydney wharfies' bans on loading scrap metal for Japan and the Port Kembla men's bans on loading pig iron, also destined for Japan. When 'Pig Iron' Bob Menzies became Prime Minister in December 1949, 'Big Jim' was still a communist, still General Secretary of the WWF and still a thorn in Menzies' side. He participated actively in the campaign to defeat the ban of the CPA in 1951, and in the mid-1950s he was fighting tooth and nail Menzies' efforts to break the WWF's monopoly on the supply of wharf labour.[53]

After Fred Gray and Alec Jolly, Jim Healy was added to the list of Rose's English-born Australian mentors. From Healy he would learn many things, but above all the importance of solidarity for the working-class cause. The admiration for Healy's sharp mind must have rested on some level of mutuality, because as the Official Board of Inquiry into the Stevedoring Industry approached, the WWF engaged Rose as a research officer. His job was 'to ferret out facts and figures for Jim Healy'. He soon found that there were few facts and figures that Healy's impressive intellect did not already have at its disposal. Rose came to refer to himself as Healy's official bag-carrier. A typical request from Healy might run along the lines: 'Fred, we're leaving for Melbourne this evening! Dig out what you can on the increase in sling-loads over the past five years. We need the information for tomorrow's session.' Rose would set to work and discuss his findings with Healy on the flight to Melbourne and late into the night at their hotel. When the inquiry was in session, he sat back and admired Healy in action, running proverbial rings around the 'bright committee boys' of the kind Rose had known in his public service days.[54]

Admirable, too, was Healy's capacity to get on with all types. During the inquiry he was fully engaged in the cut and thrust of debate with the stevedores' representatives. When the heat of those daily battles subsided, Healy would retire from the committee room to the local pub, where he would have a beer with the ship owner's attorney. As Healy's bag-carrier Rose tagged along, but he later claimed he could raise little enthusiasm for drinking with a Queen's Counsel. The QC in question was John Kerr.[55]

While Healy could employ a disarming friendliness to his advantage, he also had a full arsenal of industrial weapons at his disposal when required. From January 1956 the wharfies staged a nation-wide strike to restore privileges which, they believed, had been whittled away over the years. It engendered much vitriol from the Menzies government and from the press, so that the WWF had to struggle hard to garner support among other sections of the working classes. Their discipline, in Rose's view, was exemplary. The ship owners dared not break the picket lines or attempt to employ scab labour; no wharfie would rat on his mates.[56]

163

By now Rose's days in the WWF were numbered, yet he knew that the experience had been crucial for his development. He was no longer a 'bloody intellectual'; his beliefs not simply a matter of rational choice. Those fifteen months had deepened and strengthened his devotion to the cause. His communism was now firmly anchored in social engagement, and it would not be shaken.

18. Germany

At the height of the Cold War the German Democratic Republic was no easy place to visit, let alone seek permanent residency. It declared itself an independent state in October 1949, a few months after its Western neighbour, and lived a tenuous existence in the following years. Its government was deeply suspicious of the West and its representatives, and permanently indebted to the Soviet Union's commitment to maintaining an anti-capitalist bulwark.

The shakiness of the new state had much to do with its brittle material foundations. While the United States had poured Marshall Aid into the Western zones of occupation, the Soviet Union extracted reparations in kind as partial compensation for a war which had cost millions of Soviet lives and wreaked untold damage. Entire factories in the Soviet zone were packed up and shipped east, resources diverted and capitalist enterprises shut down to make way for communism. Whether it would work, even Stalin doubted. 'Communism fits Germany as a saddle fits a cow', he once quipped to a Polish politician.[1]

Stalin's paranoia shaped the early years of the GDR's development. Communist forces, it was clear from the start, would rule the roost. Even before the end of hostilities in 1945, the Soviets smuggled into occupied territory groups of German communists who had spent their exile years in the Soviet Union. They would provide the loyal vanguard for the establishment of a deferential postwar order. Prominent among these 'Muscovites' was Walter Ulbricht, who famously instructed his own acolytes: 'It has to look democratic, but we need to have everything under control.'[2]

From the West it did not even look democratic. The Soviet expectation that the defeat of fascism, combined with the devastation of war, would conjure a great breadth and depth of support for communism among the German population soon proved illusory. The German Communist Party, the KPD, had no hope of achieving majority support, so it was merged with the Social Democratic Party, the SPD, to form the Socialist Unity Party (Sozialistische Einheitspartei Deutschlands, or SED), destined to be the ruling party. Any hopes that the SED might provide a means to realise a distinctively German version of socialism were dashed. With the descent of the Iron Curtain, the SED was transformed into a 'party of the new type'. For all intents and purposes, that meant a party of the Stalinist type – highly centralised and authoritarian, its leading figures marching in lockstep with the Kremlin.

Stalin died in March 1953, triggering outpourings of sincere grief in some quarters and sighs of relief in others. Within the walls of the Kremlin a jockeying for positions led to the emergence of the reformer Nikita Khrushchev. His position secured by early 1956, Khrushchev famously excoriated Stalin in his 'Secret Speech' to the 20th Congress of the Communist Party of the Soviet Union. The once great hero of the Motherland was condemned for his authoritarian ways and his 'cult of personality'. Bit by bit, much of the Stalinist legacy was dismantled.

In the GDR it was different. Soon after Stalin's demise the East German communists faced a crisis at home. On 17 June 1953 discontent among Berlin building workers triggered uprisings against communist rule throughout the GDR. The very people who should have been its most fervent supporters were calling into question the regime's legitimacy. The official response was to blame Western *agents provocateurs* and to call Soviet forces onto the streets to quell the uprising. This was no time to tinker with the leadership. Ulbricht kept his job and, far from renouncing Stalinism, took measures to ensure that any further hint of opposition was stifled.

Edith, Sonja, Ruth and Nita Rose arrived in the GDR at the worst possible time. In July 1953 they stayed in England, making or re-making acquaintances with Fred's parents and sister. But Edith was eager to get to Germany, which she had not seen since before the war, and to meet with her parents and two sisters, about whom she had been anxious for so long.

The family situation had changed dramatically. Her parents had divorced, and Edith's father Richard Linde had remarried in 1946, at the age of 65. His second wife, Else, had been employed as a gardener at the Lindes' stately residence at Hohen Neuendorf and so was already known to Edith. The couple had two children, a girl and a boy, close in age to the younger Rose children. Still a resident of Hohen Neuendorf, albeit at a new address, Richard Linde resumed his career as a patent lawyer, working initially with the Soviet military administration.[3]

The ideological foundation of the GDR was 'antifascism'. Having hidden Jews and POWs in his house in Hohen Neuendorf, Linde was well-credentialled at a time when antifascism was still a broad church. His behaviour at the moment of liberation had enhanced his standing. As the Red Army closed in on Hohen Neuendorf, so the story went, Linde negotiated a peaceful settlement, free of bloodshed. In recognition of his achievements, the Red Army attached a sign to the front gate of his home: 'To Russian and Polish soldiers and officers: Please to not interfere with the owner of this building, because he helped hide people, Soviet prisoners of war and also Jews. 23.04.45.'[4]

Linde had every prospect of becoming a pillar of the new order, of contributing to the creation of what he and countless others hoped would be a new and better Germany. He joined the resurrected Social Democratic Party of Germany at the end of the war, then the Socialist Unity Party, the SED, on its establishment in 1946.[5] It is some indication of his standing at the time that he was asked to draft a new patent law. With the founding of the GDR in 1949 he continued his patent work, setting up an office in central East Berlin. In 1951 he and his new family moved to new lodgings in Kleinmachnow south-west of Berlin, attached administratively to Potsdam.

On arrival in Berlin, Edith and the children made their way to her sister Ruth's house in Dahlem, West Berlin – in the American sector. Ruth had married a fellow-sculptor, Bernhard Heiliger. At this time there was no Berlin Wall. There were customs controls at the inter-sector boundaries, but there was nothing to stop Edith and the girls crossing into the Soviet sector to visit Richard Linde at his office in the Mauerstrasse, little more than a stone's throw from Checkpoint Charlie. Not only could Edith visit her father there, her mother also worked in the office, as did the familiar figure of Luise Neumann. Edith knew Luise as her father's secretary before the war; now she lived in the district of Wedding in the West, travelling each day across the sector boundary to work for Linde, who was making the much longer trip from Kleinmachnow. In October Edith moved into her father's house with her daughters, until separate accommodation was found.

After the excitement of connecting and reconnecting, life seemed to settle into a more stable routine. The two older daughters attended school, while Nita was put into a crèche, and Edith looked for work to support herself and the children. They all lived comfortably together in a flat, not at all sure if and when they would be returning to Australia. By May of 1954 Fred on the other side of the world, fearing imminent persecution, was advising that they should stay where they were until matters settled in Australia.[6]

But then a large hurdle was placed before them. Prior to leaving Australia, Edith had been furnished with a letter of recommendation from the CPA, giving its blessing for her departure. She duly handed the letter to the relevant authorities on her arrival in the GDR. In time suspicions arose, and the authenticity of the letter was questioned.[7] In mid-1954, when Edith had finally found a job in Potsdam, she was told that she was required to leave the GDR. For her that meant shifting across the Iron Curtain into the city's West, and tolerating accommodation arrangements resembling those of a fugitive. Sometimes she stayed (illegally) in her father's office in the East, on other occasions she lived in Luise Neumann's apartment in the French sector. The existing hardship of separation from husband and son on the other side of the world was compounded. What began as an inconvenience experienced over days and then weeks turned into a nightmare to be endured for months, with no end in sight.

As a bizarre consolation, the three girls were permitted to stay in the East, so they moved back into the Linde residence in Kleinmachnow.

On weekends Edith would travel from West Berlin to her father's office to be reunited with her children, who had made the journey in from Kleinmachnow. Sonja and Ruth innocently adapted to what seemed to them an extended 'holiday' in Germany. With baby Nita they became part of a new blended family consisting of their grandfather, his wife and their two children. At school Sonja and Ruth were immersed in a new language and were struck initially by the atmosphere of liberality that prevailed there.[8] They were shocked one day, however, by their grandfather's reaction to their playful piano rendition of 'God Save the Queen'. It had been a regular part of their school routine in Canberra, but 'Sir Richard' warned the girls never to play the anthem in his house again.[9]

Though school attendance imposed order on their lives, the girls were conscious that they had entered a world quite different from that of their early years. Ruth began one of her regular letters to her father: 'Dear Daddy, I hope I am not too late in sending a letter. I am typing this letter in the usual place, Sir Richard's Office. The weather is getting colder here but I suppose it is hot in Australia, is it? Many buildings are knocked over near here, and there are many spaces where buildings have been.'[10]

Frustrated by East German paranoia and intransigence, Edith pinned her hopes of reuniting her family on her husband. But Fred was also subject to forces largely beyond his control. As long as the royal commission ran, Party discipline demanded that he remain in the country. The last thing the CPA wanted was for the conservative press to jump to conclusions about Rose, should he head overseas. When the furore around the commission was finished, the report written, and the CPA's blessing finally given, then the Rose family could make plans. Their centrepiece, Edith hoped, was that Kim and Fred would join the rest of the family in East Germany, where Fred would become an academic anthropologist.

This was an idea with quite a history. Its most tenacious advocate for many years was Richard Linde, long eager to bring his daughter and her family to the 'new' Germany. As early as 1947 he raised the prospect with Fred, pointing out that mutual acquaintances had already returned home from their Australian exile. Why should Edith and her family not join them? He promised, 'Very shortly I shall make contact with the fellows who control lectureships at the Berlin University. Social Anthropology is a field that is not properly covered as yet, I assume. So there is a favourable prospect for Jagara'.[11]

Rose was not averse to the idea of an academic career, indeed he had made some effort to pursue one. There had been those early postwar applications for jobs at the ANU and in Aberystwyth. Then in 1949 he had lodged an application for a research fellowship in anthropology at the ANU, only to have it culled in the first round. He could not blame Elkin, since on this occasion resistance came from Fred Nadel, a former student of Malinowski at the London School of Economics about to take up the ANU's inaugural chair in anthropology. His view of Rose was damning: 'He is probably a crank, but certainly a poor anthropologist, inadequately trained (in spite of his Cambridge degree) and intellectually arrested.'[12] Dismissed by the discipline's powerbrokers, Rose's chances of getting a job in Australia were bleak.

The GDR, in contrast, appeared promising, especially when his father-in-law flattered him that there was 'a decided inclination' to invite him. More ominously, though, Linde passed on the sober assessment that obstacles had emerged in matters of 'passports, visa, and the route of access to this place'.[13] Linde was a realist, but even he must have been dismayed at the glacial pace of progress. He sought again and again to employ his good standing as leverage with both the Soviet 'friends' and local heavyweights. He boldly targetted senior government figures, to whom he passed Rose's qualifications and samples of his anthropological work. He pulled strings to smuggle into East Berlin via Switzerland Rose's huge Groote Eylandt manuscript. He turned to the influential 'Muscovite' Anton Ackermann, a member of the SED's powerful Central Committee, singing Rose's praises as an anthropologist.[14] And when all that failed, he turned to Minister for Education Paul Wandel, restating with undiluted vigour the case to offer Rose a university appointment. In this instance, as in all before it, the response was polite indifference.[15] Having reached a point of dejection after several years of trying, he broke Rose the bad news. 'I did everything

I considered useful in order to force your case. Unfortunately, the red tape disease is very virulent in this new state.'[16]

Edith's wretched situation in Berlin prompted her father to take up Fred's case afresh two years later. His dark mood was barely concealed in a letter he fired off to the very top – the Politburo – reminding its members that in over four years his letter to Ackermann about 'the exceptionally gifted Australian anthropologist Frederick Rose' still awaited a reply.[17] Edith tried a new tack in mid-1955, writing to the GDR's Ministry of External Affairs to request asylum for herself as a matter of urgency.[18] Once again it was the cold voice of East German bureaucracy that recited to her the letter of the law – only whole families could be granted asylum.[19]

In Australia Fred Rose was kept aware of Edith's plight by his father-in-law, whose letters were conveying a growing urgency. Linde pleaded with Rose to ensure that his 'friends' in the CPA did everything in their power to allow him to leave Australia. Otherwise, he warned, 'you are fully aware of the fact that the (illegal) position of Edith is hardly any longer bearable'.[20] Rose resolved that the only way to break the stalemate was to force the issue. With no job to go to, and Edith living the life of a fugitive, he would travel to the GDR anyway and hope for the best.

Even as he prepared his departure, Rose remained a person of interest for ASIO. It soon got wind that something was afoot. Kim, who for a time had been doing odd jobs around CPA headquarters in Market Street, departed ahead of his father. Funds were short after the failure of his farming venture, so once again Fred appealed to his long-suffering mother for Kim's fare. After the scandal of their son's appearance before the Petrov commission, which had made front-page news in London's *Times*,[21] the Roses' disillusionment was palpable. Frances complied with her son's request, but wrote: 'Dear Fred, Your letter and politics sadden me. I quite understand the position ... My only reason for doing this is to have your family reunited. Love [squeezed in] Mother.'[22]

A passage was booked for Kim to sail to England on SS *Strathmore* in February 1956. He had just turned fifteen, yet ASIO thought that he, too, warranted close surveillance.[23] Its officers learned that a guardian, a

Reverend Brother Phelan, had been appointed to keep an eye on Kim on the voyage. On the day of departure they observed that Fred, Kay Phillips and her daughter were present on the wharf to farewell Kim. 'As the ship was leaving', an officer recorded, 'ROSE Senior was seen to exchange clenched-fist salutes with his son'.[24]

ASIO did not leave it at that. It established contact with Brother Phelan and informed him that it 'had a certain interest in this young man because of the past subversive activities of his father'. Asked to observe and report on his charge, Phelan 'promised to do his best', and proceeded to pass on what information he could as *Strathmore* docked in Melbourne, Adelaide and Fremantle.[25] Just to be sure that Kim did not fan revolutionary flames in Colombo, ASIO's Director General wrote to Ceylon's Director of Public Security informing him of the lad's impending arrival.[26]

Fred Rose left Australia aboard the *Castel Felice* the following month, with the full blessing of the CPA. He had been concerned that the tardiness of his acceptance of the 'Stalin Criticism' might have impacted on his standing in the Party and perhaps even threatened his departure. But a thirty-three-page letter written to Laurie Aarons in April 1955 setting out his final position had forestalled that threat.[27] The CPA's Secretary General Lance Sharkey furnished him with the requisite letter of recommendation to present to his East German comrades. Sharkey extolled in particular Rose's appearance before the royal commission, where he had 'conducted himself with Communist courage and forthrightness'. He closed his encomium with the words that really mattered, 'The Communist Party of Australia has given Comrade Rose permission to go overseas and he leaves the Party in good standing'.[28]

The timing of Rose's departure was determined by an invitation he had been given to attend a peace congress in Venice, both as a representative of the wharfies and an anthropologist who had worked among Aborigines. To help defray his travel costs a hat was passed among his workmates, who were reminded that Rose had 'made many sacrifices for the working class movement'.[29] The highlight of an otherwise uneventful voyage was the chance to renew an acquaintance in Colombo with his old Cambridge friend Pieter Keuneman, since 1948 General Secretary of the Ceylon Communist Party.[30]

At the last moment the venue for the peace conference was shifted to Stockholm, so Rose's arrival in Genoa was followed by a long train journey through Switzerland, West Germany and Denmark to Sweden. It was there he first met Jessie Street, sometimes known as 'Red Jessie', another of the Australian delegates. They established their mutual interest in Aboriginal issues, and in the months and years that followed that first encounter they swapped correspondence and information to promote their common cause.[31]

After the conference Rose made his way to West Berlin, where he was reunited with Edith. Together they crossed the inter-sector boundary to catch up with the girls at Richard Linde's office in the East. Only Kim, stranded with his grandparents in England, was missing. A plaintive letter greeted Rose on his arrival: 'Dear Dad, I am glad that you have arrived at Berlin. Do you have any idea when I will be going over? Auntie Edie and I went along to British Europe Airways yesterday and got a timetable that comes into operation in two weeks time. I am not sure whether there is a direct service operating to Berlin at the moment but in two weeks time there will be. The fare is 21 pounds single so I will have to get some money from Nana & Pop . . .'[32]

For Fred Rose, a card-carrying communist since 1942, that arrival in Berlin was a poignant moment – his first glimpse of life behind the Iron Curtain. In due course he would write a letter for *Tribune* readers in Australia, extolling the new Germany that had risen Phoenix-like from the ashes of the old: 'Who was it who said, "I have seen the future and it works", when he visited the Soviet Union in the 1920s? . . . That is exactly how I feel . . . It was one of the most astonishing experiences of my life.'[33]

There was more than a touch of hyperbole in this, because in reality not all was running smoothly. Rose began to experience the Kafkaesque workings of the East German bureaucracy at first hand. He turned to one of his father-in-law's old sparring partners, Günter Harig in the Ministry for Higher Education, announcing his presence and an eagerness to place his knowledge in the service of Marxist anthropology.[34] The response was no different from that received by Linde – inertia. So despondent had Rose become by early June that he fired a broadside in the form of a three-page memorandum, with copies to the SED's Central Committee and to Harig's office. Lamenting the inordinate slowness of the process to make an academic appointment, he demanded a decision – one way or the other.[35]

It worked, and an offer was made. At first it was all quite tenuous: from June to August he held a research position at the Humboldt University, a lectureship would follow in September.[36] The road to that humble post had proved tortuous, but it had finally come to fruition, and, in time, the Chair would come too. Both Edith and Fred would forgive the state its intransigence. As good communists, they understood that the security and wellbeing of the collective must have priority over the wishes of individuals.

Edith's father was not so easily appeased. When push had come to shove, his antifascist credentials had counted for little, and his continuing Freemason links only heightened suspicions. The passing of years had highlighted the differences between his essentially humanitarian and cosmopolitan worldview and that of his political masters. He resisted pressure to join the GDR's Chamber of Lawyers, a step that would have deprived him of control over his choice of clients and endangered his treasured links with the world outside the GDR. The final straw came in 1958. Articles he wrote on patent law were rejected for publication, and a request to travel to West Germany to undertake a much needed health retreat was knocked back. Never one to bow to injustice, Richard Linde exercised his own will and departed the GDR for the West, leaving his family behind. A report the Stasi received some time later indicated that he feared he might soon be arrested if he remained in the GDR.[37] In advance of his departure he had quietly arranged his affairs to ensure that, materially at least, his family would want for nothing. At the age of seventy-eight, he would attempt one more beginning.

19. Professor

For Fred Rose, taking up a position as an academic anthropologist in the GDR was both an enticing and a daunting prospect. It was enticing because Germany could claim a rich tradition of anthropological endeavour, a tradition intimately linked with the city of Berlin. And it was daunting, because the German tradition was quite different from the British one with which he was familiar. Moreover, it was expressed in a language of which he possessed at best a smattering.

In Germany, as elsewhere, the origins of the discipline of anthropology lay in the Enlightenment and in the vast ambition of knowing, documenting and categorising the world in its entirety, from its most basic elements through to all living things, including human beings. This ambition bore fruit in the German states before Germany became a colonial heavyweight, indeed even before there was a united Germany.

Various German cities in different states vied with each other to collect and display vast ethnographic collections, pilfered, bought or traded from all over the world. Berlin, Frankfurt am Main, Munich, Dresden, Bremen and Leipzig all established ethnographic museums boasting exhibitions that claimed to introduce their visitors to the cultural and physical traits of the world's peoples. Not only the state but German private interests, too, fed a seemingly insatiable appetite for knowledge of the wider world.

Such was the level of sophistication achieved in German anthropology that it divided into a number of sub-disciplines. The German term *Anthropologie* corresponds roughly to the English 'physical anthropology'. Its practitioners came typically from backgrounds in biology, anatomy or human physiology; they were interested primarily in the physical characteristics of humankind and how they varied over place and time.

As for other forms of anthropological study, above all social and cultural, these could be covered in German by the term *Ethnologie*. In the nineteenth century the tendency was to divide non-physical anthropology into two sub-disciplines, namely *Volkskunde* and *Völkerkunde*. *Volkskunde* – sometimes translated as 'folklore studies' – was understood to mean the study of one's own people. As practised in Fred Rose's time at the Humboldt University, it might be translated as German, or even European, ethnology. Fred Rose was not a practitioner of *Volkskunde* but of *Völkerkunde*, that is, he was devoted to the understanding of peoples in the world beyond Europe.

All German variations on the theme of anthropology benefitted from political developments in the last part of the nineteenth century. German unification in 1871 was a boon for *Volkskunde*. Though the existence of such an entity as a German *Volk* was long established in cultural terms before Bismarck's time, unification created the German *Volk* as a political phenomenon. Bismarck's achievement had been to bring together populations of varying backgrounds and historical experiences. *Volkskunde* could be accorded an integrative function, bestowing a sense of shared identity on those who were held to belong to the Reich, finding common roots and characteristics, and promoting a sense of national coherence and purpose.

By the middle of the 1880s Germany was flexing its imperial muscles, opting to join other European powers in the scramble to lay claim to far-flung regions of the world. *Völkerkunde* might have been well established before 1871, but the *Kaiserreich* delivered a new dimension, converting the discipline into a kind of handmaiden of empire. Knowledge of the peoples over whom Germany ruled, according to the discipline's new *raison d'être*, would allow the benefits of a higher form of civilisation to be imparted with greater ease.

That is not to say that German anthropological endeavour always followed the flag. Indeed, Australia came to occupy a special place for reasons that had little to do with politics. Since the time of Johann Gottfried Herder, German *Völkerkunde* had taken to drawing a distinction between *Kulturvölker* and *Naturvölker*.[1] The former term was used to designate those peoples to whom a level of cultural development was ascribed, and that meant above all Europeans. *Naturvölker*, in contrast, exhibited no such development; they lived in a primitive state of harmony with nature. Their close study was warranted, according to the thinking of the day, because people living in the most natural state offered insight into the very essence of what it meant to be human. Australia, it was widely believed, provided a rare opportunity to study a *Naturvolk*. As Lewis Henry Morgan had put it, Australian Aboriginal societies 'represent the condition of mankind in savagery better than it is elsewhere represented on the earth – a condition now rapidly passing away'.[2]

The rise of the German Empire cemented Berlin's place as the focal point of German anthropology. The most influential anthropologists of the day were active there, both in the university and in the Museum für Völkerkunde, which by the 1890s was sagging under the weight of its massive collections. The most renowned of the scholars was the medical doctor Rudolf Virchow, a Prussian polymath who pioneered the kind of anthropological study that conceived of the discipline as a branch of the natural sciences in immediate proximity to biology. The most enduring of Virchow's legacies was his foundation of the Society for Anthropology, Ethnology and Ancient History in 1869. His co-founder was Adolf Bastian, who at the same time established the leading journal of German anthropology, the *Zeitschrift für Ethnologie*, and went on to direct Berlin's Museum für Völkerkunde. Bastian became the first dedicated academic anthropologist in Germany; his assistant director at the museum, Felix von Luschan, went on to claim the university's first chair in anthropology.

That was in 1909, in the first decade of a century that would bring fresh challenges to German anthropology. Some of them were related to the world far beyond academe. Defeat in the Great War deprived Germany of its empire; the very purpose of anthropology was now called into question.

Other challenges came from within. More and more scholars were drawn to the 'science' of race. They conceived of the world as divided into superior and inferior races; their features, it was argued, were biologically predetermined and therefore immutable. The health of any race demanded that miscegenation be avoided at all costs. For many anthropologists, it was the 'hygiene' of the *Volk* that counted above all else.

The Third Reich delivered the discipline's nadir. Hitler's obsession with the virtues of the German *Volk* meant that there was a secure place for *Volkskunde* in the universities and outside them. Nazi Germany's imperial visions also sponsored an interest in *Völkerkunde*. The putative origins of the Aryan race were sought through expeditions that led far beyond Europe, while closer to home the Aryans' arch enemies, the Jews, were slated for extinction. During the twelve years of the Third Reich, anthropology, while still presented as a 'science', was degraded and abused to the point where all scholarly integrity was forfeited. At best it lent racism 'an aura of professional credibility'.[3]

At the end of the Third Reich there were those who thought that anthropology could – indeed should – never recover. The discipline, they believed, was fundamentally flawed; at its core lay a persistent and unyielding anti-humanism.[4] Such voices were plainly heard in the founding years of the German Democratic Republic, which was by self-definition an 'anti-imperialist' state. What use, then, could it have for a discipline that had bound itself so tightly to the imperialist project? If the Nazi obsession with the *Volk* had brought death and misery to untold millions, how could one justify preserving *Volkskunde*? Equally, in a state sworn to the dictates of Marxism's universalising claims, what place could there be for *Völkerkunde*, the study of distinct peoples?

There were serious practical problems to be addressed as well. American money had funded the foundation of a new university in the American sector, the Free University of Berlin. Anthropology would gain a foothold there and offer an alternative to the offerings of the older institution, located in the Soviet zone, and in 1949 renamed the Humboldt University. The old and centrally located Museum für Völkerkunde had been damaged by Allied bombs; in 1961 the building was destroyed altogether. For safekeeping its precious contents had been evacuated during the war to a storage facility in the West Berlin district of Dahlem; at war's end they were shared as war booty among the victors. A large part of the collection taken by the Western Allies was returned to the city and deposited in a new anthropological museum in Dahlem. East Berlin was not so lucky. Soviet booty was taken to the Soviet Union; when eventually 55,000 artefacts were returned, their new repository was the museum in Leipzig, not East Berlin, which had to make do without a museum of *Völkerkunde*.[5]

If anthropology were to be revived in the Soviet sector, the availability of staff would be a problem. Many anthropologists were so tainted by their association with Nazism that employment in the Soviet zone was out of the question. Of those who remained uncompromised, a number were attracted by the relative riches of the university landscape in the Western zones, which began to blossom after the injection of Marshall Aid.

There were two universities in the Soviet zone – later the GDR – where anthropology was re-established, albeit in ways calculated to signal a radical break with the past. At the university in Leipzig, in 1953 rebranded the Karl Marx University, a new Institute for Ethnology was created and Julius Lips appointed to the chair. With Lips's death in 1950 his wife Eva took on the role; both had spent the Nazi years in American exile. The university continued to teach and research in the field of anthropology through to the end of the GDR, often working closely with the nearby Museum für Völkerkunde zu Leipzig, which, with its Australian and many other collections, had survived the war intact.[6]

Then there was the Humboldt University in Berlin, the traditional centre of German anthropology. In the postwar order, the main figure to attempt to reconnect with the university's Humboldtian humanist legacy was Wolfgang Steinitz. Hailing from an intellectual Jewish upper-middle-class background, Steinitz had become a Marxist in the 1920s and managed to complete his PhD in Berlin in his specialist area of Finno–Ugrian languages in 1932. After the war he returned to Berlin from Swedish exile and set about creating a unified Institut für Völkerkunde und deutsche Volkskunde in 1952.[7] While his own field was *Volkskunde*, Steinitz insisted that *Volkskunde* and *Völkerkunde* be taught within the same institutional framework, and in unity. Resurrected versions of the disciplines should bind peoples together rather than divide them. After overseeing the resurrection of anthropology at the university, however, Steinitz moved sideways into the Academy of the Sciences.[8]

This, then, was the institutional landscape into which Fred Rose was cast when he was finally granted an academic post at the Humboldt University. His place of work was not the imposing structure on East Berlin's main boulevard, Unter den Linden, but rather a modest building in the Friedenstrasse in the nearby district of Friedrichshain. In visible ways the location was connected to Germany's horrific recent past. It was directly opposite Berlin's oldest public park, the Volkspark Friedrichshain. During the war massive flak towers and bunkers were set up there, so that it became a target of Allied bombing raids, which razed much of it. After the war a plan was devised to transport rubble from the devastated city and form it into two artificial mountains in the park.

The building had once housed a Jewish kindergarten, which from 1940 had served as emergency accommodation for needy elderly members of the Jewish community. The last rabbi of the Lippmann-Tauss Synagogue, Dr Felix Singermann, had also worked here, bravely advocating the rights of his co-religionists, until he, his wife and their six children were rounded up by Nazis in 1942 and murdered.[9]

After Rose's initial, tenuous appointment, efforts were made to upgrade his status to a permanent lectureship with the ultimate goal of a chair. The problem was his academic status. He did not have a doctorate. In June 1936 he had graduated with a BA from Cambridge. Such were the peculiarities of the Oxbridge system that the mere passage of time and the payment of a fee entitled him to the degree of MA in February 1940. In Germany a doctorate was typically the minimum requirement for academic employment. To gain a permanent post and ultimately to occupy a chair, Rose would require what was known as a *Habilitation*, a kind of second doctorate. How could he acquire a second doctorate if he did not yet have his first?

At a faculty meeting on 19 September 1956 a discussion took place on whether to set aside the formal requirement that a candidate for *Habilitation* should already possess a doctorate. It was decided that the condition need not be imposed if it could be shown that the candidate's written work was of exceptional scholarly quality. To establish whether this might be the case, it was resolved that Rose's study of kinship on Groote Eylandt should be assessed by an expert. If positive, the assessment might also serve as an examiner's report.[10]

The expert called upon was Sigrid Westphal-Hellbusch, chosen primarily because she had written her own doctoral thesis on Australia. Politically, she was an unusual choice, not just because she had moved west to take up a chair at the Free University, but because she was not a Marxist. Moreover, in the Nazi period Westphal-Hellbusch had studied in Berlin and worked at the city's Museum für Völkerkunde.[11] Her considered opinion was that Rose's ethnographic work was 'very good' if judged at the level of a doctoral thesis, but in her view it did not meet the requirements of a *Habilitation*. It left too many questions about the nature of the kinship under examination unposed and unanswered.[12]

Happily for Rose, the lukewarm assessment did not block his *Habilitation*, and his thesis was sent to three examiners anyway. The two internal examiners reached the conclusion that despite certain misgivings Rose's work was worthy of a *Habilitation*.[13] The external examiner, Peter Worsley, might have seemed a safe bet, especially when Rose wrote to request a sympathetic and speedy judgement.[14] Worsley, by now lecturing in sociology at the University of Hull, owed much to Rose, not least his thesis topic and the opportunity to do fieldwork on Groote Eylandt. On the other hand, as an intellectual Worsley was fiercely independent and given to speaking his mind. His report opened with words of high praise: 'This work seems to me of first-class quality. It is a major contribution to Australian kinship studies, and has implications of importance for the general theory of kinship.' Nonetheless, Worsley picked up on some points of weakness. Above all, he was not convinced that Rose had entirely abandoned his indebtedness to Engels' foregrounding of biological factors and his ideas on group marriage. In Rose's thesis, he claimed, there was 'a ghost which I thought had long been exorcised by him, that of biologistic reductionism, the explanation of social facts in terms of human physiology'.[15]

Those reservations were no reason to refuse Rose his *Habilitation*, but the tortuous German system required that he clear two more hurdles. The first was to hold a *Habilitation* lecture, which he did on the topic 'The Foundations and Development of the Northern Territory Native Welfare Ordinance of 1953'. He knew the topic inside out and faced little prospect of contradiction from his audience. More intimidating would have been the prospect of delivering his presentation in German, his script having been faithfully translated by Edith, but that trial, too, was successfully negotiated. The final step was a public colloquium held at the end of January 1959. But it was little more than a formality, an opportunity for some back slapping among colleagues. The degree was conferred, and Rose was at long last a professor.[16]

A pleasing by-product of that process was that his thesis was recommended for publication by the prestigious Akademie-Verlag. It would appear in its original English, complete with the most distinctive feature of Rose's methodology, namely its 221 portrait-style photographs and the same number of tables representing the classificatory terms of Groote Eylandt Aborigines. Only minor changes were made to the text, among them the addition of a dedication, 'To the Australian working class who alone can ensure the full emancipation of the Australian aborigines'.[17] In 1960 the book appeared under the title *Classification of Kin, Age Structure and Marriage Amongst the Groote Eylandt Aborigines: A Study in Method and a Theory of Australian Kinship*. It was then, and remained, Rose's *magnum opus*, the outcome of fieldwork performed in the most trying of circumstances and of mental labour which had stretched over many years.

The published form gave Elkin no reason to like it more than when it was a manuscript, and he studiously avoided it. Then, as always, Rose had numerous detractors in the anthropological fraternity who did not deign to read his work.[18] For his own part, Rose would not resile from his conviction that the old structural functionalist approach to kinship studies had had its day. His heretical finding was that 'the classificatory system of relationship of a tribe is always in a state of flux and is constantly changing'. The data he adduced were the first to demonstrate that, in his words, the Groote Eylandt relationship system could not be ascribed any 'formalised structure'.[19]

Kinship organisation, then, was unsuited as a basis for ethnographic investigations. Instead, in a terminology that pinned his scholarly colours to the mast, he insisted that 'the social organisation of any people is part of the superstructure raised on and ultimately determined by the mode of production ... [that is] the forces of production in conjunction with the relations of production'.[20]

Reviews of the book ranged from the positive to the mixed. The Cambridge anthropologist Meyer Fortes, although critical of what he described as some 'bizarre hypotheses' regarding gerontocracy, concluded that Rose's study had described institutions and practices 'that are more authentically traditional than is the case with most studies of Australian aboriginal societies of the past half century'.[21] Similarly, in the pages of *American Anthropologist*, Jane Goodale was 'strongly disposed to view Rose's book as a major contribution to the theory of Australian social structure and kinship'.[22] The European doyen of structuralism, Claude Lévi-Strauss, generously penned a personal note to Rose assuring him, 'As far as I know your inquiry into the age structure, associated with a set of marriage rules and kinship systems is something quite new'.[23] But the most ardent of Rose's champions was the Dutch anthropologist Patrick de Josselin de Jong, who extolled *Classification of Kin* as a 'remarkable' book with far-reaching implications. Rose's work was 'not only a new contribution to kinship studies, but marks a new approach to them'.[24]

There were disappointments as well. In *Nature* the structuralist anthropologist Rodney Needham panned the book as 'defective' and 'eccentric', its ethnography as 'slight and unsatisfactory'.[25] What disappointed Rose much more, however, was the absence of any discussion of his work in Australia. He suspected the long arm of Elkin. More surprising was the deafening silence that emanated from the Soviet Union. Surely the Soviets of all people should have acknowledged the achievement of a Marxist like Rose, who had gone to some effort to absorb the lessons of the 'Stalin Criticism'?

George Rose had lived long enough (he died in 1957) to experience the shame of his son's exposure as a communist, an alleged spy and then resident of the GDR, and would have found no grounds for redemption in the publication of Fred's great book. But Frances Rose abandoned for a moment her disapproval of her son's politics to pen him a congratulatory letter. The book was the outcome, as Frances was well aware, of two of Fred's defining characteristics, ambition and the capacity for hard work. 'Altho the book is well above my head', she conceded, 'I am very proud of you'.[26]

His future as an academic was at last secure, and Rose took to the performance of intellectual labour with the same dedication he had shown in his previous jobs. There were challenges that were not easily overcome: the sheer distance from Australia, the difficulty of communicating in a language whose sounds and grammar he would never master, and the difficulty of accessing much of the literature in his field. At one point he even turned to his Aunt Edie in England with the request that she send him a copy of Lowie's *History of Ethnological Theory*.[27] None of this, though, would be allowed to thwart him in his firm ambition to become *the* Marxist anthropologist of Aboriginal Australia. Before long he was delivering conference papers in various parts of Europe. At the conference of the International Union of Anthropological and Ethnological Science held in Paris in 1960 he distinguished himself with a bold resolution urging the Australian government to support fieldwork among the few remaining Australian Aborigines living traditionally.[28]

Less welcome for him were the administrative corollaries of his professorial status, including terms as institute director. Though he performed all such duties with energy and a determination that anthropology would flourish in the East German academic landscape, he always felt more at home in front of his students. He possessed no formal training as a teacher, yet as his former students attest, he soon gained the reputation of an engaging, animated and sympathetic instructor. His manner both in the classroom and outside it was open and what the Germans call *locker* – relaxed – appreciated by students accustomed to a disciplined formality and rigidity in higher education. The GDR might have understood itself as a radical departure in German history, yet in academe the tradition of the imposing *Ordinarius*, the infallible professor, still maintained its foothold. Rose, however, was its antithesis. Temperamentally, he was what a professor at a university founded on the ideal of equality should have been, and the students instinctively understood this.

It suited Rose that the teaching spaces and classes were small, encouraging familiarity and rapport. His failure to master the tongue-twisting sounds and convoluted grammar of the German language was a source of some humour among his protégés, yet Rose used the atmosphere produced in this way to his advantage. For some time he relied heavily on Edith's translations, but as his confidence grew, he strayed from the prepared script and launched himself into German sentences of his own creation. Where he became stranded in the middle of them, the students would come to his aid, attaching a grammatically correct conclusion to the diffidently formed beginning. Then he would engage the students with the verbal challenge, '*Stimmst Du mit? Stimmst Du mit?*' – 'Do you agree?' – hoping to provoke a response. In reality it proved to be simply useful well-intended and jocularly received nonsense.

In another way, too, he cleverly capitalised on his awkwardness in German, constructing for himself the character of a typical Australian, intimately familiar with the linguistic and behavioural idioms of what the Germans called 'the fifth continent'. That made him a novelty, a subject of curiosity, and Rose understood how to harness the curiosity he provoked in his students for dramatic pedagogical advantage. His manner was genial, even gregarious; his passion for his discipline infectious.[29]

In the social circles that formed around work and family Rose was invariably a welcome guest, just as he had been in Australia. He wore his status as a professor lightly, setting others quickly at ease as he regaled them with lively and exotic yarns of his life among the Aborigines. For his eager East German audience, tales of his experiences in Australia were tantamount to a travelogue from another planet. Confined in their real world travels to the modest delights of the communist bloc, many responded with a sense of wonderment to Rose's accounts of a universe they could never witness themselves. For them he was not just the dedicated, groundbreaking scientist but the intrepid explorer, adapting with ease to the numerous hardships that accompanied life in the Australian outback. That, at least, was the persona Fred Rose projected.

University life in the GDR was not all intellectual labour. A feature of the East German university curriculum, and not just in anthropology, was the integration of components of physical labour undertaken in local communities. Universities were not to be ivory towers, their denizens removed from the daily struggles of the workers. Staff and students should not work with their minds alone but roll up their sleeves and experience firsthand the world of manual labourers. Such work was nothing new to Rose; he had done his stints as both a farmer and a wharfie in Australia, and in the GDR he did not shirk days of digging brown coal or helping with the harvest.[30]

His greatest love, nonetheless, remained research. Teaching, administrative and other duties aside, his tenured post brought with it the entitlement to apply for sabbatical leave to do fieldwork. And the only kind of fieldwork that attracted him was in Australia. That, however, as he would soon learn at great cost, would not be easy.

20. Angas Downs

Newly established as a professor of anthropology, the last thing Rose expected to be doing during his first period of research leave was waiting at café tables and manning a petrol pump on a cattle station in Australia's Red Centre. But that was what his visit to Australia in 1962 entailed. It was a visit that Rose, having carefully considered the directions his research might now take, had imagined quite differently. It was also a visit that would never have taken place if certain Australians in positions of power had had their way.

Rose envisaged returning to Australia to continue his fieldwork almost as soon as he arrived in the GDR. On New Year's Eve 1956 he wrote to his old friend Fred Gray on Groote: 'I hope that when the political situation clears somewhat in Australia I shall be able to do some more field work in the north: clearly this would not be practical till the Australian people empties my "mate" Mr. Menzies out onto the rubbish dump.'[1] Gray was by no means discouraging, although his days on the island were numbered. Bad health, he told Rose in early 1958, would soon see him retire to the mainland, and his Umbakumba settlement would be taken over by the Church Mission Society.[2]

By 1962 Fred Gray was no longer on Groote Eylandt, the CMS had taken over Umbakumba, and Menzies was still in office. If Rose were to do fieldwork in a country whose government viewed him with undiluted suspicion, he would need to tread carefully. Moreover, the anti-communist paranoia, which had driven Rose out of Australia in the first place, was as strong as ever. Fanned by international tensions over Cuba, it had even reached the placid shores of Groote Eylandt. From Angurugu the Reverend R.B. Dent wrote to Harry Giese, the Director of Welfare in Darwin, to express his concern at communist infiltration among Aborigines. 'There is quite enough evidence', Dent complained, 'to see that the communists are active among our people'. He singled out the pernicious influence in Darwin of Brian Manning and his Aboriginal 'sidekick' Davis Daniels, fomenting discontent by telling Aborigines that white people were not 'giving them a fair go'. Dent knew, however, how to counter this threat, assuring Giese of the quality of the 'excellent literature especially designed for Aboriginal people' that had been provided to him by the 'Christian Anti Communist Crusade'.[3] Giese concurred; he too was 'extremely disturbed about these influences and particularly in relation to the attempt which is being made to develop in the Aborigines the attitude that they are being unjustly treated and that the remedy is in their own hands'.[4]

Rose's plans were ambitious. He not only wanted to revisit Groote but also to test his theories of social evolution in other Aboriginal communities where traditional social structures survived. In 1962 that would be no easy task. According to one survey, whilst there were an estimated 7352 'nomads' in the Northern Territory in 1938, by 1960 there were just 400.[5] Was it already too late? In the age of assimilation, the very purpose of which was to undermine traditional culture, the chances of still encountering systemic gerontocracy or polygyny were next to nil. As the responsible minister at that time, Paul Hasluck, expressed it, 'no apology . . . should be made for promoting the benefits of civilization above all other possibilities. The only future for Aborigines could be along the pathways to civilized ways of life'.[6]

Professor or not, Rose was still *persona non grata* to the Menzies government. The easiest solution would have been to deny Rose entry to the country. Advice provided to ASIO by the Department of Immigration suggested that the Migration Act included the authority to deny entry to any person, regardless of citizenship. However, there was a snag, because 'in regard to British subjects, this would be most difficult to carry into effect as the holder of a British passport could arrive at the first port in Australia without the knowledge of the Immigration Department'. Rose, it was known, possessed a British passport.[7]

Unable to keep him out of the country, ASIO and the government contemplated ways of preventing him from doing research once he arrived. It was not just that the suspicions about Rose's role in Soviet espionage had never dissipated; there was also a fear that he might exploit his research activity to tarnish Australia's international reputation. In ASIO's view it was 'highly probable ROSE's research will be used for propaganda purposes by the C.P. of A.'. Its recommendation to block any research activity was to be conveyed not just to the Commonwealth government but to state governments as well, all of which were to be advised of the 'facts' of the Rose case and of the recommendation to refuse assistance.[8]

Eager not to provoke any action against him, Rose flew metaphorically under the radar. For fear that his mail would be intercepted, he did not mention his travel plans to his Australian friends. Not until after his arrival at Kingsford Smith Airport in March 1962 did he announce his presence – by heading straight to the wharves, where he felt certain of a warm reception.[9] Jim Healy had died the previous year, but another prominent communist in the WWF, Stan Moran, welcomed him with, 'I thought you were teaching the Fräuleins something about the Aborigines. What are you doing here?'[10] Within a short time he had re-issued Rose's so-called medal, his union card, using his old number – 4919. Even if Rose did not wish to go back 'on the hook', he had ready access to the wharves and the wharfies.[11]

He then looked up other old friends, among them the historian Eric Fry, who recalled that Rose just 'blew in' and was still the same 'cheery, bright, talkative bloke'.[12] Rose made his base in Sydney, courtesy of accommodation offered by friends Frank and Pat Graham in Waverley. From there he explored his fieldwork options, with each step becoming more aware of the scale of the hurdles before him.

One of them was money. He had arrived with just over £50 on him. East Germany suffered a severe shortage of Western currency, and this was the minimum amount the Australian government required of visitors arriving to ensure that they would not become a liability.[13] To conduct research over months, he would need a lot more.

Another was Paul Hasluck, Rose's former boss and, in 1962, still

Minister for Territories. He had not forgotten Rose, indeed he had received correspondence from him and a copy of *Classification of Kin*.[14] In late March, Hasluck received another letter from Rose, this time with a proposal for fieldwork among the Pintubi and Walbiri people, followed a few days later by a personal call.[15] Rose was met politely enough, but Hasluck's response was that he would need to discuss the proposal with his advisers. When after three weeks no word had arrived, Rose wrote again to Hasluck, pressing him for a response. Several more letters written over the following weeks similarly went unanswered. Hasluck had adopted a simple but effective tactic – he was stalling.[16]

Rose had already endeavoured to prepare the ground for his confrontation with Hasluck. On 24 March he swallowed his pride and dashed off a friendly letter requesting an informal meeting with his old adversary A.P. Elkin. He enclosed ten copies of a research submission, a proposed budget, and a copy of an enthusiastic letter from the American anthropologist Richard B. Lee, congratulating Rose on his book.[17] Elkin at least dignified Rose's letter with a reply, albeit in a condescending tone. He frostily suggested that 'Mr' Rose should consult the work on the Walbiri by Mervyn Meggitt, Lester Hiatt and Donald Thomson before he would agree to meet with him. A curt handwritten line was added to his secretary's typed letter – Elkin's grudging acknowledgement of Lee's positive assessment, 'very hurriedly read'.[18]

Anticipating the failure of the research application, Rose shrewdly decided to enlist the services of 'Red' Jessie Street, whom he had befriended in Stockholm.[19] For some time he had been assisting Street with material for her presentation on Aborigines to the United Nations, and now he called in the favour. Enclosing a copy of his application, Rose presumptuously wrote: 'The question is whether I (or perhaps you) should send a copy to Hasluck or not. Another question is whether it would be worth your while speaking to Elkin on my behalf. We can discuss this when I see you.'[20] This placed Street, the wife of former Chief Justice of the Supreme Court of New South Wales Kenneth Street, in an awkward position, but she agreed to make representation to Hasluck on Rose's behalf. The minister was now in a tricky position. Street's politics were well known, but she enjoyed an elevated social standing. To rebuff her would risk provoking bad publicity.

When ASIO was called upon for advice, Charles Spry suggested that Street 'be advised that the Commonwealth Government will only consider ROSE's application through an application from ROSE himself'. He feared that otherwise Street would be armed with a 'propaganda weapon', which she would undoubtedly 'use to the maximum through the various Communist frontal organizations with which she is connected'.[21] In due course Street got a mealy-mouthed reply, Hasluck following ASIO's suggestion to the letter. Rose was to make a 'direct approach on this matter giving specific information regarding his wishes and proposals'.[22]

The body to which Rose submitted his application was the nascent Australian Institute of Aboriginal Studies (AIAS). It was the mercurial Liberal MP W.C. (Bill) Wentworth who had proposed the idea of the institute back in 1959; through Kim Beazley Senior the ALP had given its support.[23] After a sub-committee of Cabinet considered the proposal in 1960, an ANU working party investigated setting up the organisation. In 1962 the formal founding of AIAS by an Act of Parliament was still a couple of years away, but with the assistance of the ANU and an Interim Council (without a single indigenous member),[24] the institute was already grappling with its brief of recording the 'language, song, art, material culture, ceremonial life and social structure before those traditions perished in the face of European ways'.[25] Fred Rose was well aware it could disperse research funding to meet that brief.

In principle, at least, AIAS would make decisions on the funding of applications on purely scholarly grounds. Yet ASIO files reveal egregious political interference from a very high level in the consideration of Rose's application. The Secretary of the Prime Minister's Department Jack Bunting expressed the view that Rose's application 'and similar ones must be blocked diplomatically with no loopholes and no comeback by ROSE for any reason or for any other job with the Institute'. When the institute was set up, he claimed, 'Cabinet was rather fearful that some of the long-haired boys might use this for what they might call objective material of use either consciously or unconsciously by the Communists'.[26] Just how an application such as Rose's might be 'blocked diplomatically' was not clear, but it would be a sensitive matter to have a decision reached by a committee of scholars overturned by a political authority or – even more delicately – by the Director-General of ASIO.[27]

Rose was well attuned to the possibility of political interference, and presumably for that reason sought a meeting with the economist Sir John Crawford, at that time Director of the Research School of Pacific Studies at the ANU and later Vice-Chancellor. The meeting was arranged for 11 am on 5 April. At 9.30 am on the day in question, Crawford rang the regional director of ASIO in Canberra to solicit advice. What should Rose be told? How should any request be treated? Crawford was told that ASIO had already given advice to the Secretary of the Department of Territories on this matter, and it would be wise to speak with him. Crawford indicated he would do so, but not until after he had met with Rose.[28]

Rose was in ASIO's sights once more. A photograph in ASIO's files records an encounter between Rose and Manning Clark on that very day. Grainy and slightly offset, it was plainly taken surreptitiously; the photographer is unnamed. Clark, with trademark headwear and hands in pockets, looks toward the photographer, perhaps suspecting that something is afoot. Rose is dressed formally and carries a briefcase, possibly on his way to the meeting with Crawford. Perhaps purely by chance Rose had come across Clark, now on staff at the ANU after it had absorbed Canberra University College a couple of years earlier. And perhaps he had used the opportunity to solicit some last-minute advice before his crucial meeting. ASIO's caption for the photograph, in any case, merely records the names of the subjects, the date, and location – Ellery Crescent ACT.[29]

Soon after meeting with Rose, Crawford called back to let ASIO know what had transpired. Rose did indeed intend to apply for a grant, and Crawford had no issue with Rose doing so, since from the university's viewpoint Rose's project 'was a desirable one and on its merits, the project has a strong chance of support'. The decision would be made by a panel of experts, likely to be chaired, Crawford said, by Professor Elkin.[30] Elkin might have retired several years earlier, but he was still pulling strings.

Rose's application, unsurprisingly, was not supported. A memorandum sent to the Prime Minister at the end of April reported the rejection, listing among the reasons, 'There are real doubts about whether Rose would be making a genuine partial [sic!] enquiry and would not just be seeking to adjust the facts to his (Morganite-Marxist) theories'.[31] Menzies was further advised that he 'should not show any knowledge of the fact of rejection' but rather 'to offer, if you think it necessary, to seek information from the Institute'.[32]

Without a permit, with dwindling funds and time slipping away, Rose was in trouble. Moreover, the AIAS rejection of the funding request furnished a grateful Hasluck with grounds to refuse Rose access to Aboriginal communities. Rose prevailed on fellow-scholars and politicians to coax a long overdue decision from Hasluck, but it was all in vain.[33]

Rose had no choice but to reconceive his plans radically in the hope of salvaging something from his visit. The Commonwealth government controlled access to Aboriginal settlements in the Northern Territory, so Rose's new strategy was to leave the government out of the equation. If Rose conducted his research on private land, there was nothing Hasluck could do to stop him. The source of this new idea was Bill Harney, now working as a tourist guide in Alice Springs. He suggested that Rose travel to Angas Downs station, owned by Arthur Liddle, who in Harney's estimation would be sympathetic to Rose's project. Harney wrote, 'You will like him and his wife who, once they know you will give you a lot of information. They are both half-castes and were born in the area. The place is about 190 miles west of Alice Springs'.[34]

It was not what Rose had imagined, and it was not ideal. This was not a place to study Aboriginal communities in anything resembling a traditional form.[35] On the other hand, Angas Downs had the potential to offer invaluable insights into the disruption caused by the arrival of Europeans. In spending time there, Rose could turn his anthropological gaze to the processes of change that arose from the destruction of traditional society and the imposition of a capitalist economic system.[36]

Only after Rose committed to the Angas Downs project did the wisdom of Harney's compromise solution become apparent. In August Rose received the long-awaited answer from Hasluck. Rose's application had been refused on the grounds that the Aborigines on the settlements and reserves were being 'overworked by scientists'.[37] As it turned out, it was not just the best but the last piece of advice Harney gave Rose. Illness meant he had left his beloved Territory before Rose got there; he died in Queensland at the end of the year.[38] By that time Rose, having scanned the Sydney Public Library for information on the Loritja people, had been at Angas Downs for several weeks.[39] He had made the last stage of his journey there by bus from Alice Springs in early July. At that time tourist buses on their way to what was generally called 'Ayers Rock' – today's Uluru – would often stop at Angas Downs. There the tourists received a meal in the dining room and the opportunity to purchase locally made wooden artworks. While the tourists dined, purchased their artefacts and moved on, Rose stayed.[40]

In doing so he had successfully shaken ASIO from his tail. Hasluck's man in Darwin, Harry Giese, assured ASIO that all welfare officers had been warned that Rose might enter a reserve surreptitiously.[41] Eventually a welfare officer on a tour of duty did come across Rose at Angas Downs, but Rose fobbed him off with the fiction that he had formal approval to carry out kinship surveys and would 'be there for some considerable time'.[42]

The last bit at least was true. Rose stayed until October, during which time he developed a firm friendship with Arthur Liddle. Liddle's family history was inseparable from the history of the station. His Scottish-born grandfather Thomas Liddle had arrived in Australia in 1851 and settled in Angaston in South Australia, where his son William was born. William eventually moved to Central Australia, working for a time in the post office in Alice Springs, where he met Mary, the daughter of an Aranda woman and a white man. In 1930 Liddle pursued a change of career, taking up a pastoral lease at Angas Downs, named for the town of his birth. William and Mary's fourth child Arthur, born in 1918, began working on the station in 1938. In 1945 he and his brother Milton bought the station and ran it together. A couple of years later Arthur married Bess, the daughter of Johnson Breadon of Middleton Ponds and an Aboriginal woman of the Loritja people.[43] Arthur bought out his brother in 1956, so that by the time of Rose's visit Arthur and Bess were the sole proprietors of a station now running cattle rather than sheep, and struggling to make ends meet during a severe drought.[44]

The station was a massive 1244 square miles, with spinifex and mulga as far as the eye could see, but in a drought even a property of that size could not carry more than about 550 head of cattle.[45] When a pastoral inspector from the Lands and Survey Branch of the NT Administration in Darwin turned up in late July, he painted a bleak picture. Very little developmental work had been done, 'perhaps understandable in view of the financial circumstances brought about by the drought, while it is doubtful if any maintenance work has been attempted'. Most of the water sources were 'a depressing sight with tumbled down yards and slack fences. Some of the mills are complaining from lack of oil'.[46] It was all the more important, then, that the station picked up as much tourist traffic as it could. The effect, as Rose observed, was to draw the Aborigines 'willy-nilly into a money economy'.[47]

The harshness of the times underscores the Liddles' generosity. They set Rose up in an unlined corrugated-iron shed about nine feet square and with a concrete floor. The furniture consisted of a camp bed, table and chair. Stored under the bed were several boxes of gelignite, persuading Rose to confine his smoking to the outdoors. In time, though, he forgot the gelignite was there, and it became customary for him to roll cigarettes for Aborigines visiting him in his humble abode.[48] Rose would have been hard pressed to pay even a token sum for the lodging and board. Instead he and Arthur came to a 'gentlemen's agreement' that when Liddle was working cattle or in Alice Springs, Rose would look after the station's petrol pump. It did not entail much work, since there were never more than about six cars seeking petrol on any day. Later in his stay there were occasions when Rose was left in charge of the entire homestead, preparing three-course meals for thirty or so tourists at a time, managing the store and arranging the distribution of rations and pensions to the Aborigines.[49]

He still found time to devote to fieldwork and, thanks to the Liddles, sufficient funds. As Harney had anticipated, Rose needed to pay the Aborigines to participate in his study. They had become accustomed to charging passing tourists for taking their photos. While Rose had needed to reconceptualise his project, the central methodological component of his work – photographing his subjects – remained as it had been on Groote Eylandt more than two decades earlier. 'Each click of the camera', Harney had advised, 'costs two shillings'.[50]

A small number of Aborigines lived in the homestead enclosure, but the majority lived in the nearby camp. Over half were 'permanents', though this did not necessarily mean that they were there the whole time. Occasionally they camped at waterholes or soaks. Most insisted that their 'countries' lay far away to the west, in some instances as far as the Warburton Ranges. The 'non-permanents', who arrived individually or in small groups, would make Angas Downs a stopping place on their way to or from Ayers Rock or a mission station.[51]

Though the Liddles were Loritja speakers, most of the people in the Angas Downs area were Pitjantjatjara. Indeed, the station lay at the north-eastern extremity of the 'Pit' lands extending into South Australia. Further to the north, on land that included the Hermannsburg mission, was the territory of the Aranda.[52] There were many signs that the region and its population were in a state of profound change. A small number of Aboriginal workers were employed in the pastoral industry; Liddle paid them ten shillings for a day's work.[53] As station manager, he was also responsible for handing out government pensions and child endowment money. Aboriginal women now dug for food with iron rods, not with their traditional digging sticks, while the men hunted with rifles as well as spears.[54] Boomerangs, once used for hunting, were now made purely for sale to the tourists along with a few shields and nulla-nullas.[55] The tools used to manufacture these 'commodities' were all of European origin.[56]

The social impacts were wide reaching. Rose observed that with the introduction of white man's flour and animal transport, there was no need for Aboriginal women to form themselves into 'gathering' collectives. Their once active lives had become passive.[57] The greatest change, however, was that on Angas Downs station polygyny and, to a lesser extent, gerontocracy, had virtually disappeared. To Rose it was a clear illustration of the Marxist dictum that 'the economic factor was decisive and the relations of production rapidly changed, if not directly in step with the means of production, at least not far behind'.[58]

The book which emerged from Rose's 1962 visit to Australia was *The Wind of Change in Central Australia*. Like its predecessor *The Classification of Kin*, it was stocked with photographs and tabular data, its language that of the empiricist, accurate and dispassionate, and the argument was supported with a surfeit of meticulously recorded evidence. And, like its predecessor, it was generally well received. The Sydney-trained anthropologist Mervyn Meggitt found that Rose's account of the Angas Downs situation 'rang true' and praised Rose's admirable 'flexibility of mind [which] is as valuable as a head full of models'.[59] One of the most fascinating parts of Rose's book proved to be his observations in the anecdotal 'Notes from Diary July–October 1962'.[60] Of all his work, this probably came closest to the Malinowskian model of ethnographic writing he had come to admire many years previously.

Elkin was reserved in his judgment of the book. Managing to insert into his review several references to his own work, he commended the study as a 'very useful document on culture change', but he derided Rose's central thesis and stated emphatically that the Aborigines had remained 'hunters' and 'collectors', who had simply adopted a response that Elkin labelled 'intelligent parasitism'. There was nothing, he insisted, that was 'ideological' or 'airy-fairy' about their situation, but what could one expect from 'a Marxian materialist and a member of the Humboldt University of East Berlin?'[61]

Considered in the context of his life's work, *The Wind of Change* can be seen as a cutting of the apron strings that still connected Rose with British social anthropology. His fieldwork had given him insights into the struggles faced by Aborigines as they adapted to the imposition of a capitalist economic order. As a Marxist he did not wish to wind back the clock; the arrival of capitalism was as inevitable as its eventual defeat. But Rose wanted to help shield Aborigines from the harsh wind, and in doing so recognised the importance of the land. The Aborigines' relationship with it was not primarily spiritual but economic; without it, their future had no economic foundation. More than ever before, Rose's scholarship and his activism were converging.

21. By Any Other Name

On the last page of his never completed memoirs, dictated on Boxing Day 1990, Rose touched once more on the issue that would never leave him – the accusation levelled at him decades earlier that he was a spy: 'If anyone had asked why I said that I would not act as a spy I would have explained that in 1935 I was caught attempting to smuggle money out of Nazi Germany for Jews and my conclusion from that experience was that I did not possess the necessary attributes and personality that would have enabled me to act either as a smuggler or as a spy. From that date I have never attempted either to smuggle or to spy.' That did not mean that he could not admire people who did engage in espionage – he expressed 'great admiration for the modus operandi of such people as Kim Philby' – but such activity was unsuited to his own temperament and talents.[1]

One cannot take his words at face value. Rose's innate ability to compartmentalise his life provided him with one of the key attributes of a successful spy.[2] He had the capacity to deceive, to appear as something other than he was, and to hide the truth even from those close to him. Added to his personal charm and unwavering devotion to the communist cause, these qualities presented him with a potent gift. And Rose's Stasi file, well over 2000 pages of it, reveals that it was a gift he used willingly for a very long time.

By the time the Stasi (the popularly abbreviated form of the Ministerium für Staatssicherheit, the Ministry for State Security[3]) became interested in Fred Rose, it was an organisation set firmly on a course of expansion. It had not always been so. In the early days of the GDR it was of a modest scale, assuming security tasks previously performed by the Soviets in their occupation zone.[4] Not surprisingly, then, when it was founded in 1950 the Stasi was deeply indebted to Soviet security agencies and a legacy stretching back to 1917 and Felix Dzerzhinsky's Cheka.

The year 1953 delivered a massive blow to the GDR's ruling caste and, before long, a change of course for the Stasi. A stern lesson was drawn from the 17 June uprisings: the Stasi had not met its task of identifying sources of discontent within the state and tracking the alleged activities of Western agents bent on the destruction of the GDR. Its head, Wilhelm Zaisser, was sacked and unceremoniously dumped from the SED. The new leaders, initially Ernst Wollweber, and then from 1957 the formidable Erich Mielke, were sworn to ensure there would be no repeat of 17 June 1953.

In time Mielke presided over the creation of a behemoth, which by the end of the GDR had swollen to the size of 91,000 full-time employees.[5] It developed an insatiable appetite for the gathering of information about the GDR's own citizens. By the time the Berlin Wall fell, the Stasi had created 111 kilometres of documents, including some 39 million file cards, 1.4 million photographs and 34,000 sound and film recordings.[6] All this information, its officers persuaded themselves, would enable the Stasi to pursue its noble goal of being the GDR's 'sword and shield'. In both its longevity (forty years) and its level of penetration (there were some 55 Stasi full-time personnel for every 10,000 GDR citizens) the Stasi was unique in the twentieth century.[7]

Its size and multi-functionality dictated that the Stasi would be an administratively complex entity, divided geographically into fifteen regional administrations and 209 district offices.[8] It was also divided for most of its existence into some 20 main departments or directorates with different areas of responsibility.

If one of these directorates formed an élite, it was the HVA. It was a distinctive feature of East German security that this agency, responsible for foreign espionage, was located alongside the organs of domestic surveillance. HVA stood for Hauptverwaltung Aufklärung, Foreign Espionage Directorate. Its head was the tall, urbane Markus Wolf, regarded in some quarters as the greatest spymaster of the Cold War era, and not without reason. He could count among his triumphs the planting of a spy on the personal staff of West German Chancellor Willy Brandt.

Fred Rose never met Markus Wolf, and yet their lives did intersect. Wolf's HVA began to show an interest in recruiting Rose as early as 1963. After the building of the Berlin Wall in 1961 the Stasi was particularly interested in foreigners living in East Berlin, and the Roses came to its attention. What the HVA would have found particularly appealing about Fred Rose was that he was one of relatively few who, with his British passport, could readily pass through the Wall to West Berlin, to West Germany, or even to more distant regions of the capitalist world. He had the potential to establish connections that other agents could barely contemplate. Nonetheless, in this as in all other cases, the HVA pursued the possibility of recruiting him with caution. More than any other directorate, the HVA had to be utterly convinced not only of the political reliability of its agents but also of their suitability for the task it had in mind.

The first step was to delve into Rose's background and his circumstances. His personnel file from the Humboldt was the obvious place to start, and it proved auspicious. An extract from it gathered by the Stasi in May 1963 showed that in the few years since Rose's arrival in the GDR he had become deeply committed to the cause, not only joining the SED but taking on a leadership role in its university branch.[9] In his teaching, it was observed, he had gained the confidence of the students, 'went with them to experience work in the brown coal mines and is making an even greater impact on them politically'.[10] At home in the district of Kleinmachnow, too, there was nothing that might have given rise to concerns about him or those around him. 'The reputation of all members of the family', the Stasi concluded, 'can be described as without blemish; they are setting a good example. They have good contacts with comrades and progressive artists in Kleinmachnow'.[11] The one exception to all this was that five years earlier Rose's father-in-law had become *republikflüchtig*, that is, he had moved to the West, but seemingly with little impact on the regard in which the rest of the family was held.

By the time it planned its approach to him, the Stasi was aware that during the working week Rose lodged with a Frau Zimmerman, who lived adjacent to his institute, thus avoiding a lengthy daily commute. That by itself was of no concern to the Stasi; quite the contrary, it made their job easier. They could readily arrange a meeting with Rose alone, keeping the rest of the family in the dark.

Their plan of approach envisaged informing Rose that the task the Stasi had in mind for him was the seemingly innocent one of meeting with visitors to the GDR and helping to look after them during their stay.[12] His charm, intelligence and wit were the perfect traits for such an ambassadorial role. This, in the language of the Stasi, was the *Legende*, the 'fiction' to be put to Rose in order to win his cooperation. Their own *Legende*, used on Rose and countless others, entailed introducing themselves not as Stasi agents but as emissaries of the Ministry of the Interior.[13] It was a tactic not unlike that used by ASIO officers in Australia, who would customarily introduce themselves as members of the Attorney-General's Department.

That first contact, arranged by telephone and made when two agents turned up at Rose's workplace, went smoothly. Rose enquired whether they had called at his weekday abode, for Frau Zimmermann had expressed some anxiety as a result of two unexpected visitors making enquiries about him. Rose then requested that the officers speak in hushed tones, for otherwise their conversation might be heard in the library next door. It was a sign, the Stasi officers concluded, that Rose knew very well that the conversation he was about to have was of a confidential nature.[14]

That first meeting was viewed as a success. It was agreed that others would follow, always with the same two agents, every few weeks. The meetings would take place either at work or at Rose's rented room. Rose, it was decided, would not submit written reports, since he could hardly ask Edith to correct his faulty German in these clandestine texts, but the officers would prepare a summary for their records. Dates for the meetings were set in advance, but Rose was free to contact the officers to arrange a meeting ahead of schedule, which he sometimes did. Both sides were free to raise points of interest; Rose's candour was to be encouraged.

At these early meetings the handlers set Rose a number of simple intelligence-gathering tasks. They soon established that the 'candidate' carried them out efficiently; moreover, he distinguished himself with an astonishing capacity to invent explanations for his behaviour. They recognised that he could be of value to them in reporting on people and circumstances in the university; potentially he could recruit others to work for the Stasi.[15] The frankness of his assessments impressed them.[16]

What pleased them less was that it became evident that he had been indiscreet. To work for the Stasi required on the one hand total transparency in meetings with the handlers but on the other absolute discipline in maintaining the conspiracy, even in relation to one's own family. It became known to his handlers that Rose had revealed to Edith that he had received a visit from officers purporting to be from the Ministry of the Interior. But as Fred was not entirely convinced at the time that they were who they claimed to be, he mentioned the incident to Edith. Edith passed that information on to a contact in Potsdam, from where it made its way to the Stasi in Berlin.[17] The officers were unimpressed – were Rose to be formally recruited, he would need to prove he could be trusted with secrets. It was resolved, nonetheless, that the best strategy was to be frank with him, to remove any doubt about their identity, and that meant revealing the stark truth. They were from the Stasi, they told him, not the Ministry of the Interior. Rose calmly accepted this revelation and then, following the officers' advice, proceeded to cover his earlier indiscretion.[18] He told Edith that the curious meeting he had mentioned earlier had turned out to be an innocuous and inconsequential visit from Ministry of the Interior officers. And he assured the Stasi agents that he was now sworn to absolute secrecy, even in the company of his wife.[19] The Stasi, too, through its Potsdam office did what it could to throw Edith off the scent, telling her that the Ministry of Interior had indeed paid her husband a visit, but was not interested in pursuing the relationship any further.[20]

There are signs that from Rose's viewpoint the relationship with the Stasi was one which held the prospect of mutual benefits. He would not have been alone among the Stasi's recruits in believing that collaboration might bring with it a certain kind of leverage. Over the following months he raised issues of concern to him, presumably with a tacit understanding that his cooperation might help to have some of those concerns addressed. One of them was the question of finding a publisher for his work, another related to his accommodation. In the longer term he did not wish to live away from his family in Kleinmachnow, but it was no easy matter to find a sufficiently large apartment in central Berlin for the whole family. And then there was his burdensome administrative role at university. He was not happy, he told his handlers, with directing an institute devoted in large part to German *Volkskunde*. His area was *Völkerkunde*, anthropology on a global scale. What would he as foreigner know about German *Volkskunde?*[21]

The Petrov commission, now a decade past, seems to have been a common topic of discussion, though only because Rose repeatedly raised it. His handlers faithfully recorded his references to the scandal and Rose's role in it, but in the end drew the conclusion that he placed too much emphasis on 'certain phenomena connected with the Petrov Affair'.[22] Rose's verbosity on the topic and the Stasi's apparent indifference are fascinating. There is nothing in the record of those discussions to suggest Rose claimed he had played a role in an Australian spy ring. Had he done so, surely he would have boasted of it to the Stasi? What better way could there have been for him to convince the Stasi of his devotion to the cause and his suitability as a collaborator? In any case, the Stasi had already learned from the Soviets that Rose was not known to them.[23]

Tantalisingly, on the other hand, the Stasi records also show that Rose deliberately stopped short of telling them *everything* he knew about the events in Australia. At a meeting with his handlers in early March 1964 the topic of the Petrov Affair was raised once more. Rose told his visitors that he had sworn to remain silent on a number of details and would keep his word. The officers noted, 'He cannot tell us everything, because he had given his word to the Communist Party of Australia and he had to remain silent'.[24]

Rose also discussed his colleagues at the Humboldt in meetings with his handlers. Rose, it became clear, had a dim view of one colleague, whose attitude to her work and the quality of her research in his view left much to be desired.[25] What he did not know, but was soon noted by the Stasi, was that that colleague had herself been engaged by the Stasi to make contacts in the West and be active there.[26] Of another colleague Rose had a much higher opinion, so high indeed as to recommend him as a potential recruit to the Stasi.[27]

The Stasi came to the view that Rose possessed 'a great confidence' in the organisation; in some regards he even behaved like an old hand. Should a meeting be disturbed by the unexpected arrival of Kim, then Rose would concoct a story to explain his guests' imminent departure. None of this should have surprised. After years of exposure to ASIO's attention, Rose was well-schooled in the arts of evasion and deception. Whatever character weaknesses Rose might have, the Stasi concluded, they could be ironed out with some well devised training. In time and with effort their candidate would learn that his work would be 'supported and guided by the collective'.[28]

In the meantime, as a manifestation of his induction into the world of subterfuge, Rose was given the codename 'Frieden' or 'Fried', presumably chosen from the street in which he lived and worked. Here, too, Rose's ready acceptance of a name for his nefarious alter ego should not have raised the eyebrows of those who conferred it. In Australia, too, he had had to live the double life of the dedicated public servant who also belonged to a persecuted political party teetering permanently on the brink of illegality. To conceal that other self, he had written as 'Alec Jolly' or 'Jagara'. The offer of another name by the Stasi gave him confidence that he was being treated as an equal, that he now truly belonged.

In more practical terms the conferring of a cryptonym meant very little. At this stage Rose was what the Stasi called a *Kontakt-Person*, a contact person, or simply KP. This was a relatively casual arrangement, not a formal recruitment. If all went well, the next step would be to engage Rose as a so-called *Inoffizieller Mitarbeiter*, an unofficial collaborator, or IM. Yet after some eighteen months of meetings and dutiful reporting as a KP, Rose was still not invited to take that next step, and by late 1964 he was feeling slighted. He wanted and expected more. At a meeting with his handlers he described his dealings with them as '*Fummelei*' – fumbling around – and complained he could see no clear purpose in his work for them.[29]

Rose's concern at the lack of progress is revealing. Having welcomed the approach many months earlier, his enthusiasm at the prospect of putting himself at the Stasi's disposal was undimmed. Indeed, he had invested more in the relationship than had his handlers; they were showing no inclination to raise the collaboration to the next level. For Rose, then, this was not simply a matter of keeping his masters happy, of submitting himself to Party discipline, or even of extracting favours for himself and his family. As time passed by, and as his frustration rose, it was becoming much more than that. Rose saw a fully-fledged relationship with the Stasi as an opportunity to contribute to a cause in which he still fervently believed. For Rose, as for many who worked for it, the Stasi was an instrument by which the communist cause could be advanced. Whatever reservations one might have about spying, they were far outweighed by the greater good to be served. Fred Rose needed no persuading that the ends justified the means.

The Stasi's problem, however, was that it was not convinced that in Fred Rose it had the right man, at least not for the task it had in mind. While his commitment and enthusiasm were exemplary, successful work for the HVA would require sensitivity and subtlety in the way Rose dealt with potential informants or recruits. If he were ever to be deployed outside the GDR – the HVA was contemplating some unspecified role in the West – then he would need to be able to cultivate friendships and liaisons not according to his own desires or inclinations but with sights set unflinchingly on extracting intelligence from the most auspicious source. It was not clear that he was temperamentally suited to that brief. Rose could be charming, but he was also forthright in his views, which were widely known. Did Rose possess the essential quality of being able to win the confidence of intelligence targets whose beliefs were quite different from his own? The answer, the HVA decided, was no.

Eager to avoid his discouragement or loss of interest, the handlers arranged a meeting in early 1965 to put their cards on the table. They reassured Rose of their faith in him and the work he was doing, but they also told him they were postponing any deployment in a foreign intelligence gathering role. As a sop, and as a token of the progress he had made, his handlers conferred a new cover-name on him – from this point he was 'Aust'. And as a way of addressing his complaint of a lack of purpose in his work, they identified a set of objectives in the area of counter-intelligence. He was to focus on colleagues, students and any foreigners visiting the GDR. In addition, he should report on his wife Edith and his son Kim.[30] On all counts Rose held no scruples and proceeded to carry out his tasks.

Kim at this time was becoming a matter of some concern, both for Rose and the Stasi. After spending the first fifteen years of his life in Australia, Kim appeared to have adapted well to life in the GDR. He had certainly made a better fist than his father of acquiring the language; his school grades were good, he had formed numerous friendships, and by 1965 he was enrolled for a doctorate in astrophysics in the Academy of Sciences. By that time he lived in an apartment in the district of Pankow with his girlfriend, 'Elke Schmidt'.[31] Suspicion had arisen that both would soon leave the GDR, suspicion that only sharpened when the couple married and 'Elke' became entitled to a British passport.[32] Such a step would reflect poorly on Fred. In an echo of his youthful relations with his own father, Fred's relationship with Kim had deteriorated to such an extent that he had little influence over his son's behaviour. He knew all too well from experience that youthful idealism could be harnessed in the service of generational revolt. While airing his anxieties openly with his handlers, and not uncommonly at meetings that Rose himself initiated, he could at best hope that Kim would choose to stay put.

Rose also reported diligently to the Stasi on his travels overseas. While a KP for the HVA he made one of his fieldwork visits to Australia, whose strategic importance he considered woefully underrated in the GDR.[33] That was not about to change. Later he attended a conference in the United States, certainly of greater interest to the HVA, about which he submitted a detailed report. It was symptomatic of the opinion the HVA had already formed of him that its value 'was not rated highly'.[34]

So it was that in the HVA Rose never climbed above the rank of KP. Ultimately the HVA decided he had no future with them at all. A final report on Rose's work spelled out the reasons. The operational goal of deploying him in a recruiting role had not been reached. There was little doubt that intelligence agencies around the world knew exactly who he was, and no change was to be expected on that front. It was time, so the report concluded, for a change of plan.[35]

Indeed, before the ink was dry on the HVA's final report, a new plan was already being implemented. The area in which Rose had shown the greatest promise was in counter-intelligence on the home front. The Stasi certainly did not want to lose the services of one so clearly willing to serve, so dedicated to the cause, and so untroubled by the pangs of conscience that might have deterred others. Accordingly, Rose was handed over from the HVA to one of the directorates with a domestic focus, Directorate XX. From 1967 Rose had new Stasi handlers, a new role and, before long, a new status.

22. A Modest Proposal

When Fred Rose was approached by the Stasi, he had good reason not to be entirely surprised. Edith had already been approached, and he knew it. The Stasi's reasons for their interest in her were much the same as for him. Edith had a British passport, she had numerous contacts in the West, and after the building of the Berlin Wall she could still travel to the other side. When discreet enquiries were made among authorities and acquaintances, it became clear that Edith was a devoted member of the SED and very involved in political and social activities in Kleinmachnow. Like Fred's, her commitment to the cause was beyond question.[1] The lone blemish of her father's flight to the West was pardonable; in all other respects Edith appeared an exemplary candidate, ripe for an approach.

It came on 6 September 1962. Two officers – Lieutenant Mehlhorn, accompanied by his offsider, Second Lieutenant Wunderlich, both from the Stasi headquarters in nearby Potsdam – turned up on Edith's doorstep in Kleinmachnow's Clara-Zetkin-Strasse at ten in the morning. Unlike her husband's, Edith's visitors immediately identified themselves as officers of the Ministry for State Security. At this time Fred was still in Australia on his Angas Downs trip and not due back until the end of the month. The one other person in the house at the time, presumably Edith's step-mother Else Linde, soon left. Mehlhorn made it clear that for future reference it would be preferable if such meetings took place without involvement from third parties.[2]

The recruitment began with a modest proposal. The officers knew that Edith did translation work, work that was arranged for her by a fellow resident of Kleinmachnow, the Australian Barbara Kaufmann.[3] Perhaps, the officers suggested, Edith might be able to help them with some translation work? The work consisted of a couple of job advertisements from an English newspaper. For an experienced translator like Edith, who possessed an excellent knowledge of English, it was a request she could hardly refuse. In a couple of weeks they would return to collect the finished work.

As agreed they returned on 19 September, and with a more ambitious agenda. Edith was just finishing the translation work, which provided a handy topic for discussion. The first of the advertisements bore the heading 'Commonwealth – Agricultural Office Seeks Scientist for Information Service with Knowledge of at Least One Slavic or an Unusual European Language'. Mehlhorn explained to Edith that the advertised position was clear evidence of an attempt to engage in espionage against the socialist states. Her translation, he assured her, would be of great value to the GDR.[4]

Edith must have been pleased enough with the officers' response for them to take a second, much larger step. Would she, they wondered, be prepared to sign a formal pledge that she would help to preserve the security of her state? Edith raised no objection, and when the text of a pledge was laid before her, she needed no further persuasion. More than that, as Mehlhorn later noted, the process was 'not without a certain excitement'.[5] With her signature, Edith committed herself to becoming what was still widely known at that time as a *Geheimer Informator*, a 'GI', or secret informant. It was the equivalent of what was later more commonly known as an IM. Her pledge stated, 'I am conscious that I must preserve strict silence toward other persons and know that if I breach that silence I will be called to account.' For reasons unknown she received the codename 'Miller'.[6]

For the translation Edith was paid a sum of fifty Marks. It was a token amount that had as much to do with the signing of her name on the pledge as with the rendering into German of the advertisements. She was given further tasks to prove her mettle. One was to prepare a written record of her family connections. It seemed innocent enough at the time – Edith would have had little inkling of the inordinate interest the Stasi would later develop in the Roses. The second task was to write a report about Barbara and Walter Kaufmann. The Kaufmanns, now divorced, were known to Edith because of their Australian connections and because they lived in the neighbourhood. Edith was also to find out what she could about another resident of Kleinmachnow, Fred Wander, though she did not know him personally. Like Walter Kaufmann, Fred Wander, born in Vienna as Fritz Rosenblatt, was a writer of Jewish background who had spent some time in exile in the West, in his case mainly in France. In attempting to get into Switzerland in 1942 he was seized by the Swiss border police and handed to the Gestapo, with the result that he spent the rest of the war in Auschwitz and then Buchenwald.[7] Just what the Stasi thought Edith might turn up about Wander and Kaufmann is not known. The request was perhaps a manifestation of the general lingering suspicion about 'Westerners' or of a nagging unease about the cluster of writers and intellectuals in Kleinmachnow. Possibly, too, it hinted at residual German anti-Semitism.

And then there were a couple of jobs that looked to the world beyond Kleinmachnow. One was a translation, an intercepted Christmas card sent to the US Military Mission. The other was to prepare a report on whatever information Edith could gather about the formal British presence in Berlin.[8] These two tasks would soon cast Edith deep into the murky world of Cold War espionage on both sides of the Iron Curtain.

Two of the key targets of the Stasi's, and now Edith's, interest were the military liaison missions established by the Americans and the British. They were a throwback to the days of Allied wartime collaboration, when it could be easily agreed that the Allies needed to work together to impose a new order on Germany once Nazism had been defeated. It was in that spirit that military missions came into being. And although the cordial relations engendered by shared victory soon descended into the frosty distrust of the Cold War, the missions remained. As the political environment around them changed, their original functions disappeared, and they became irritating thorns in their newly acquired enemies' side.

The full and proper name of the British mission was 'The British Commanders-in-Chief Mission to the Soviet Forces in Germany', or BRIXMIS. It was created in 1946 and lasted until German unification in

1990. Its Soviet equivalent, that is, the Soviet military mission in the British zone of occupation, was called SOXMIS. The concept was extended in the following year to include American and French equivalents.[9]

When two separate German states were founded in 1949, their existence was in effect ignored by the staff of all the military missions. They clung stubbornly to the notion that Germany was still under occupation, and that it was their agreed right to travel through *all* the zones of occupation. Thus the members of the missions would go on 'tours' to collect intelligence, with a special interest in military intelligence.[10] Most of this they did quite overtly, the officers wearing uniforms and driving marked cars, which from West Berlin would head into GDR territory via the border crossing on the Glienicke Bridge, the famed 'bridge of spies' separating Potsdam from West Berlin. But there were covert operations as well, each containing the risk of triggering an incident that might spiral into something altogether more serious.

The British liaison mission was quite large, with thirty-one accredited members, entitled to move into or within what was at first the Soviet occupation zone, then the GDR. Its nominal home was in the Mission House in Potsdam, but its operational centre was on safer ground in West Berlin, in the so-called London Block at the Olympic Stadium complex in Charlottenburg, where the British sector's military government was based.[11] Various Commonwealth governments had military missions here, while senior officers lived in nearby villas. All of this, of course, was of great interest to the Soviets, who were well aware that BRIXMIS operations were keeping close tabs on the disposition of Soviet forces. The Stasi played the Cold War game of observing the observers. The British labelled these Stasi counter-surveillance teams 'Narks'.[12]

Australia, too, had a military mission in Berlin. It grew from a decision made by the War Cabinet as early as March 1945. Cabinet agreed to appoint an 'Australian Military Mission to the Allied Control Council for Germany and Austria' – the Control Council being the body designated to rule occupied Germany and Austria until self-government was restored. By the end of 1945 the mission was up and running. It consisted of one representative of each of the armed forces and a political adviser. The first of those political advisers was J.D.L. Hood, who became head of the mission and eventually Australia's first Ambassador to the Federal Republic of Germany, several hundred kilometres west of Berlin in Bonn. Although it remained nominally a 'military mission', responsibility for it was passed from the Department of Defence to the Department of External Affairs in 1948. And when an Australian Embassy was established on the Rhine, the Australian Military Mission in Berlin was little more than a diplomatic outpost,[13] though quite useful for gathering information on political developments in the city that formed the epicentre of the Cold War.

It was useful, too, for Australians who happened to be living in Berlin, no matter in which sector. With Bonn so far away, the Australian Military Mission was the nearest port of call, at least until the Whitlam government recognised the GDR and established an embassy in East Berlin. The beauty of all this for Edith – and for the Stasi – was that she had, or could readily invent, reasons to cross into West Berlin and visit the British facilities at the Olympic Stadium. Above all there were passport issues that had to be addressed: her own British passport would need to be renewed, and all the Rose children, born in Australia, were entitled to British passports. The mission also acquired a small library, which Edith would frequent. She sought to strike up friendships with the Australian and German staff there. And on top of all that, she still had a sister living in West Berlin; a visit to the other side of the city need not attract undue attention. Having passed through the Wall, Edith could 'snoop around' the Olympic complex, report on the location of the various facilities, in some instances even check inside them. She observed the villas where some of the British officers lived and noted the number plates of the vehicles parked there. It was not exactly high-grade intelligence, but it was valued nonetheless. Edith was, it was noted, the only Stasi IM with access to the Olympic Stadium.[14]

There was one other way in which she could be very useful, one that did not require her immediate presence in her allotted 'operational areas'. She could use her immaculate English and German to elicit information via targeted telephone calls. The Stasi had acquired a copy of the telephone directory of the British Army Headquarters. Edith's job was to try to establish the phone numbers of those working for BRIXMIS and whether, if rung, it was the relevant officer or someone else who might answer. She would travel to West Berlin and seek appropriate public telephone boxes from which to make calls. In the case of a particular British captain she identified herself – in her perfect English – as an Australian citizen attempting to contact the Australian Military Mission. Similarly, in making a call to a major whose wife was known to be Austrian, she identified herself in flawless German as a West German, employing a pseudonym, and claiming to be trying to contact an old friend with a number given her long ago.[15]

Whatever information she found, she would dutifully pass on to her handler at regular meetings. In time, for the sake of preserving secrecy, those meetings were shifted from her Kleinmachnow home to what the Stasi called a 'conspiratorial apartment' codenamed 'Andrea', neutral territory where they could meet without fear of interruption. She received financial compensation for her work, just to cover the expenses incurred and not much more. There were tokens of appreciation, too, such as flowers and chocolates, and although gratefully received, they were hardly the reason Edith performed her allotted tasks. Like Fred, she did her bit for the Stasi because she wanted to, and the Stasi knew it. A report noted, 'The IM entered the arrangement with the MfS out of political conviction. She saw the support of the MfS as a comrade's moral duty'.[16]

In Edith's case, however, there was one thing that troubled her. Fred did not know of the Stasi's approach to her; he had, after all, been on the other side of the world at the time. When Edith voiced her concern about this, the Stasi resolved that he should be told, and so a meeting was set up to enlighten Rose on his wife's clandestine activities. That was as early as February 1963 in the family home at Kleinmachnow. Mehlhorn identified himself to Fred as being from the Ministry for State Security. In revealing to the ignorant husband that he had been working for some time with his wife he offered his apologies, but Rose reportedly expressed no indignation. The conversation was cordial, with Edith characteristically saying little in

Fred's presence, restricting her input to an expression of gratitude that her husband was now properly informed.[17]

In time Fred not only knew what Edith was up to, he became fully involved. By 1971 Edith was using her putative library visits to make arrangements for the Head of the Australian Military Mission, J.H.A. Hoyle, to visit Fred in the East. She would line up cosy tête-à-têtes in such locations as the Hotel Berolina or Café Moskau in central East Berlin.[18] There they might have had the chance to reflect on mutual acquaintances, such as Manning Clark (who taught Hoyle when the latter studied diplomacy at Canberra University College)[19] and, perhaps, June Barnett.[20] For Hoyle, as for the Roses, the Wall was an inconvenience, but it was porous.

In discussing work matters with Edith, Rose knew all too well that his wife was a conduit to the Stasi in Potsdam. Indeed, many of Fred's own materials – letters, reports and so on – appear in Edith's Stasi file, having been faithfully passed on to her handlers. On the other hand, Edith did not formally know that Fred had been recruited; he and the Stasi had gone to some lengths to persuade her that the initial approach made to him had proceeded no further. Yet Edith was not that naïve. She would have known that her husband was just the kind of man they would wish to recruit, and just the kind who would accept. She would not have disapproved. From the point of view of the Stasi, the vows of silence observed among KPs, GIs and IMs, even between husbands and wives, were useful. The reports of one could be used to crosscheck the reliability of the other.

As Edith bore the multiple burdens of housework, caring for grand-children, and then a job at a semiconductor factory in Stahnsdorf, she took every opportunity to do what her handlers asked of her. Her commitment was exemplary, even if her work was less than perfect. She tended to anxiety during operations, at times even withdrawing from them out of fear that her cover might be blown. Temperamentally, it was noted, she was not inclined to show initiative.[21] Her anxiety was discussed with her but never fully resolved, the handler noting with more than a hint of resignation that this character trait 'naturally limits the IM's deployment options'.[22]

With Kim it was different. The approach to Kim in 1966 was prepared in the same way as those to his parents, with a surreptitious delving into his past and present. There was nothing to set alarm bells ringing. The Stasi knew all about his Australian origins, even knew the many addresses where he had lived in Australia. They knew that in the previous year alone Kim had made no fewer than ten trips across the Berlin Wall.[23] In that year, too, as the Stasi well knew, Kim had married 'Elke Schmidt', with whom he had a daughter. And they knew he was working toward his doctorate in the Institute of Pure Mathematics at the Academy of Sciences at Adlershof, though much of the time he chose to work at home. That presented something of a challenge for the Stasi, who wanted to approach Kim alone, not in the presence of his wife.[24]

In May 1966 Kim and 'Elke' were placed under close surveillance. Even before contact, Kim was given the cryptonym 'Nelke' – carnation – as floral as his real name. A first approach was made on 14 October 1966, but it did not run according to the carefully devised plan. The officer chanced upon Kim heading to the academy and offered him a lift. He immediately introduced himself as working for the Stasi. In the putative interest of opacity and trust, he told Kim that his name was Hoffmann, though his real name was Fiedler. Then he painted Kim a dire picture of the numerous security threats confronting the GDR. It was precisely the line of argument that had proved so compelling for both Kim's parents – their homeland was in grave danger; by working for the Stasi they could do their bit to protect it. There was of course no mention of Edith or Fred, but Kim was told that there were already many foreigners like himself who were working to protect the GDR from its sworn enemies. Perhaps, then, the officers proposed, Kim might also consider joining them in defending their state against the 'wheelings and dealings' of Western intelligence agencies? All he would need do was pass on some information.[25]

And that, for now, was it. Kim was reported to have indicated his awareness of foreign activity and of the GDR's need to defend itself. As for the offer, all he would say was that the Stasi 'could surely find better and more useful sources of information than him'.[26] Kim could not warm to the idea of a systematic collaboration.[27]

But the Stasi would not leave it at that, and there were more meetings over the next couple of years. Kim was recorded as a KP, a contact person, but he did nothing more than offer a few titbits, feigning vagueness about names and details. The acid test of his relationship with the Stasi came with an offer to become an IM. Kim refused. His handler got the message: 'Obviously he is bothered by the thought of reporting on his friends to an officer of our organisation.'[28] Further meetings followed, but it was all too apparent that Kim was not interested. At times he failed to show up, and eventually, in 1968, the Stasi abandoned its recruitment efforts altogether.[29]

The problem, as became more evident with the passing of time, was not Kim's indifference but his opposition to the political system that ruled his life. Suspicions of Kim's political unreliability appeared to be confirmed in the wake of the bloody crackdown on the reform movement in neighbouring Czechoslovakia in 1968. The Soviet response to the Prague Spring was brutal, yet it received a ringing endorsement from the GDR government. A Stasi informant among the regular cluster of foreigners and students who gathered in Kim's Pankow apartment reported on the negative responses within the group to the Soviet invasion.[30]

Over the following years the Stasi kept an eye on Kim, noting among other things the failure of his marriage. But by 1973 it decided that Kim would be classified an AP – an '*Archivierte Person*' or 'archived person' – his file added to those who were of no use to the Stasi.[31] By coincidence, it was in the following year that ASIO headquarters in Australia received and approved a request from its South Australian office to destroy the file it had kept on Kim Rose.[32] 'Archived' or 'destroyed', on both sides of the Iron Curtain, Kim was no longer a person of interest.

After being silently committed to the ranks of the APs, things did not go well for Kim Rose. He completed his dissertation and took up a position at the Academy of the Sciences, but in his view it was not appropriate to his qualifications. Increasingly he found solace in drink and in other forms of behaviour that strayed from the straight and narrow path that the authorities, and his parents, desired for him.

Had Kim Rose lived just a short distance to the west, across the Wall, he might well have joined the young demonstrators taking to the streets of West Berlin to vent their anger and frustration on an array of issues. In time he might even have joined the 'long march through the institutions', which brought generational renewal in the Federal Republic. East Germany, however, kept a firm lid on the revolutionary mood of the times. It was no place for people like Kim Rose.

Rose relaxes in the garden of the house at Kleinmachnow, south-west of Berlin. After the building of the Berlin Wall in 1961 he lived closer to work during the week and spent weekends at home with the family. (Rose family collection)

A hidden camera being operated in the service of ASIO records a meeting between Manning Clark and Fred Rose on 5 April 1962. The location is Ellery Crescent on the campus of the Australian National University. (National Archives of Australia, A9626 281)

Housing conditions at Angas Downs as Rose encountered them in 1962. In front of his 'gundi' a man is making items for sale to tourists. (SLNSW, Frederick Rose papers, Box 5)

Arthur Liddle, second from left, with a group of tourists at Angas Downs station. (SLNSW, Frederick Rose papers, Box 5)

Rose with Joe McGinness in Cairns. McGinness had spent some of his early years in Darwin's notorious Kahlin Compound. Later he joined the Waterside Workers Federation and the Cairns Aboriginal and Torres Strait Islander Advancement League. In 1961 he became the first Aboriginal president of the Federal Council for Aboriginal Advancement. (From Frederick Rose, *Australia Revisited*, Berlin: Seven Seas, 1968)

Kim in East Berlin. Approached by the Stasi to act as an informant, his reaction was quite different from that of his parents. (Rose family collection)

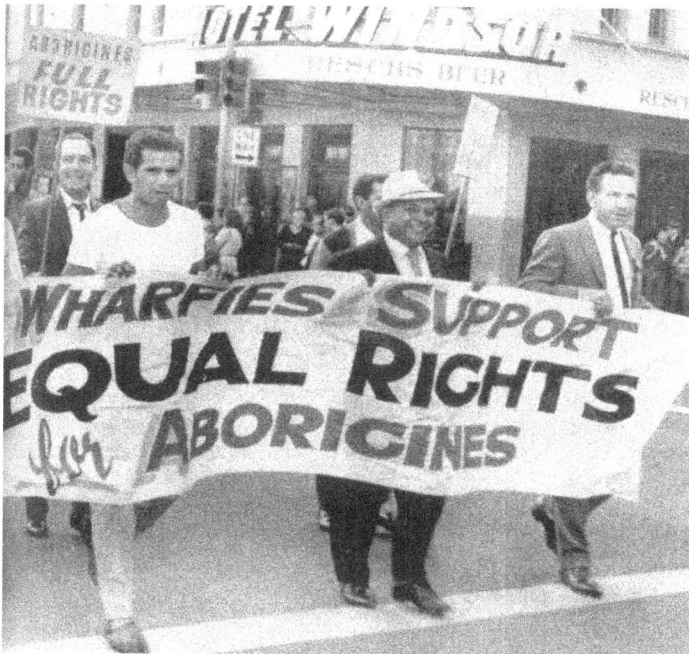

Sydney, May Day 1965, wharfies march in support of Aboriginal rights.
(From Frederick Rose, *Australia Revisited*, Berlin: Seven Seas, 1968)

A photograph taken by Rose records a meeting in July 1965 with Aboriginal poet and activist Kath Walker (later Oodgeroo Noonuccal). (Rose family collection)

In 'Operation Shiver' ASIO captures Rose talking with Eric Aarons outside Communist Party headquarters in Sydney, 21 April 1965. (National Archives of Australia A9626 281)

Rose is interviewed on television in the home of his regular Australian hosts Frank and Pat Graham in Sydney's Waverley. (Rose family collection)

A social gathering in Cremorne during one of Rose's visits to Sydney. Among the guests are Dymphna Cusack and Faith Bandler. (Rose family collection)

Poster for a public address to be held by Rose at Newcastle's Namatjira Room in June 1968. (National Archives of Australia A6119 5027 Vol. 9)

ABORIGINAL STRUGGLE

... THE WAY FORWARD?

Hear ....

PROFESSOR FRED ROSE
SOCIAL ANTHROPOLOGIST
from Humboldt University — Berlin

EXPLAIN THE REASONS IN HIS ADDRESS:

"HISTORICAL ASPECTS OF THE ABORIGINAL STRUGGLE AND ITS IMPORTANCE TODAY"

PROFESSOR ROSE WAS BANNED BY THE FEDERAL GOVERNMENT FROM CONTINUED RESEARCH AMONG ABORIGINALS ON GROOTE EYLANDT

FRIDAY, 28th JUNE, 1968, AT 8.00 P.M.

NAMATJIRA ROOM
UNION STREET, NEWCASTLE

At the home of George and Moira Gibbs in Darwin the night before departing for Wattie Creek (Daguragu). Left to right: two unidentified men, Captain Major's wife Amy, Moira Gibbs, George Gibbs, Captain Major (Lupgna Giari). CPA member George Gibbs was among the most ardent and active supporters of the strike action and land claims of the Gurindji people. Captain Major was a Gurindji man who had led the initial strike action at Newcastle Waters and remained a key figure in the land rights campaign. (Rose family collection)

Rose on the road in Queensland in 1968 with Queensland Labor Senator George Georges. (Rose family collection)

After the Soviet invasion of Czechoslovakia in 1968 the Socialist Party of Australia was formed as a political home for Australian communists who remained loyal to the Soviet Union. Here an SPA contingent, with Hannah Middleton front and centre, marches on May Day 1975. (SLNSW, Frederick Rose papers, Box 7)

The Soviet anthropologist Vladimir Kabo and his second wife Elena Govor in Moscow in 1983. Kabo was one of very few Soviet readers who appreciated Rose's work; Govor translated into Russian Rose's *The Traditional Mode of Production*. Photo by Fred Rose. (Rose family collection)

The Roses return the favour – Vladimir Kabo pictured with Fred Rose on the balcony of the Roses' apartment in the Schulze-Boysen-Strasse. (Rose family collection)

Eric Bogle, with guitar and a young East German guest,
in the Roses' apartment, 14 February 1985.
(Rose family collection)

The last of Rose's lovers, Anke Bornschein, photographed on a beach on the
Baltic coast with Mick Thompson and Ricky Lovegrove-Maher of the touring
Aboriginal band No Fixed Address.
(Gabriele Senft)

Rose approaching his 70th birthday.
(Ingrid Hänse)

23. Australia Revisited

If the wind of change had helped fill Rose's sails during his troubled stay in 1962, by the time of his return in 1965 a veritable gale was blowing. In many parts of the world decolonisation was in full swing; new nation-states were being founded as Britain and other European powers abandoned their formal empires. Where colonialism lingered, its victims were striking back. Leaders of anti-imperialist movements like Che Guevara, Franz Fanon, Nelson Mandela and Ho Chi Minh were becoming household names. The changing mood of the times was felt not just in the imperial peripheries but at their core as well. In the United States a civil rights movement was stridently advocating equality for African Americans; 'black power' was both a slogan and an agenda.

In Australia, Aboriginal activism was gaining a momentum which would prove irreversible. Indigenous Australia would be in a much different place at the end of 1960s than it had been at the beginning. Throughout the states and territories, numerous political and welfare groups were actively promoting indigenous rights, seeking to overturn decades of entrenched disadvantage and prejudice. A new generation of leaders was emerging with the talent, the determination and the confidence to take the cause of Aboriginal rights into the public realm and to prosecute it uncompromisingly.

There were new challenges to confront, too. The discovery of large deposits of uranium, bauxite and other minerals in Arnhem Land attracted the attention of mining companies. In February 1963 Menzies announced that his government would grant leases for companies to mine bauxite on land to be excised from Arnhem Land reserves. He provoked a response delivered six months later in a most unusual form. Leaders of the Yolngu people sent bark petitions to Canberra, where they were tabled in the House of Representatives. These elaborately crafted documents marked a crucial point in the long process of legislative and constitutional reform to recognise indigenous rights.

It soon became apparent just how protracted and keenly contested that process would be. As an awareness of the huge mineral wealth in northern Australia grew, so too did anxiety about indigenous activism, especially when claims of land ownership were being staked. That anxiety was all the more acute when the promotion of Aboriginal rights was allied with forces of the radical left. The Northern Territory Council for Aboriginal Rights (NTCAR) was an outstanding example of the kind of alliance that sent a shudder through conservative ranks. It had emerged from meetings between CPA members Brian Manning and Terry Robinson and interested indigenous people.[1] At a meeting at Lee Point near Darwin late in 1961 a draft constitution was adopted, and NTCAR came into existence with a clear agenda to protect Northern Territory Aborigines from exploitation.

Such alliances between indigenous activism and the left were emerging in other parts of Australia too. In New South Wales the Freedom Ride of February 1965 illustrated the dynamics of the new activism. A group of students from Sydney who had formed the group Student Action for Aborigines (SAFA) toured by bus through the western towns of New South Wales, loudly proclaiming their objections to the egregious segregation and discrimination they witnessed. SAFA was in many ways typical of the activist groups of the day. Charles Perkins, a third year arts student, was its president, but most of its members were not indigenous. Many of the 'freedom riders' were from a consciously leftist political background, among them a number of communists.[2]

The primary vehicle for harnessing the regional, temperamental and ideological variety that marked the movement for Aboriginal rights was the Federal Council for the Advancement of Aboriginal and Torres Strait Islanders (FCAATSI). It was founded – initially as FCAA, the Federal Council for Aboriginal Advancement – when a number of state-based Aboriginal rights and welfare groups convened in Adelaide in early 1958.

The formidable Jessie Street had used her considerable powers of persuasion and organisation to bring together an assortment of groups.[3] It was a sign of those early times that of the twenty-five delegates at that founding convention only four were indigenous.[4]

It was a sign of the times, too, that many of the most influential members of FCAATSI over the years that followed were associated with the political left and were friends or acquaintances of Fred Rose. Some were members of the ALP, among them the left-wing Labor MPs Les Haylen and Gordon Bryant. There were also those who, for longer or shorter periods, were in the CPA. Two of them, Joe McGinness and Faith Bandler, were well known to Rose and had life stories which intersected with or paralleled his in multiple ways.

Like Rose, McGinness, for most of its existence the president of FCAATSI, was a member of the WWF, in his case in Cairns.[5] The son of an Irish father who died young and an Aboriginal woman of the Kungarakan people, McGinness had lived for a time in Darwin's Kahlin Compound and had become acquainted with Xavier Herbert and trepanged with Fred Gray. He cut his activist teeth in Darwin in the mid-1930s. As a wharfie in postwar Cairns he was a central figure in the founding of the Cairns Aborigines and Torres Strait Islanders Advancement League, one of the groups to affiliate with FCAATSI.[6]

Faith Bandler's family history was profoundly shaped by racism. Her father was black-birded from Vanuatu, her mother carried the disadvantages attached to a Scottish–Indian heritage, while her husband Hans, an Austrian Jew, had survived Dachau and Buchenwald to help his wife in her battle for racial equality in Australia.[7] Faith Bandler travelled to East Berlin in 1951 to attend the World Festival of Youth and Students. She was one of a number who took the opportunity to tour other parts of the Eastern bloc, provoking the wrath of Australian authorities and the confiscation of their passports and various possessions on their return to Australia.[8] One of the men who accompanied her behind the Iron Curtain was an Aboriginal man from Dubbo, Ray Peckham, but only after the Aboriginal Welfare Board was pressured by unions into giving him the required permission.[9]

The politics of some key members like Bandler and McGinness, and affiliations with unions such as the WWF, provided the Menzies government with grounds to be wary of FCAATSI. Moreover, FCAATSI's program of reform set alarm bells ringing, as it advocated abandoning assimilation in favour of integration. The great hope of those who supported integration was the maintenance, not the extinction, of distinctive indigenous identities. Moreover Aborigines, FCAATSI's members urged, should receive the same citizen rights as other Australians, the same pay and conditions; all discriminatory legislation – still rife in the states – should be overturned.[10]

A particular focus of FCAATSI advocacy in the middle of the 1960s was a campaign to amend the Australian constitution so as to allow the federal government to make laws that would apply to indigenous Australians, and thus override discriminatory state legislation. It was a campaign the government could not ignore, and Menzies agreed to meet with a delegation of indigenous FCAATSI leaders. After the meeting he magnanimously offered them a round of drinks, prompting Queenslander Kath Walker (later Oodgeroo Noonuccal) to chide him: 'You know, Prime Minister, where I come from, you would be put in jail for this [that is, offering Aborigines alcohol].'[11] Beyond his hospitality, however, Menzies was not prepared to take the step of staging the referendum needed to change the constitution.

One of the government's quandaries was that part of the push for change in indigenous matters came from the most despised of political enemies, the CPA. As in all matters relating to the CPA, the government followed its strategy of soliciting advice from ASIO, which in 1962 furnished it with a report documenting the level of communist penetration in FCAATSI and similar organisations. In the Northern Territory, ASIO revealed, communists George Gibbs and Brian Manning had established the NT Aboriginal Rights Council; in 1959 three persons associated with the CPA were among the elected office-bearers of the NSW Aboriginal Australian Fellowship; in Queensland the State Council for the Advancement of Aboriginal and Torres Strait Islanders was increasing its activities with Communist 'front' organisations; in Victoria the executive of the Council for

Aboriginal Rights in 1962 included three persons with known association with the CPA.[12] In short, the red fingerprints of the CPA were ubiquitous.

In these circumstances ASIO and the government were eager to learn of indigenous leaders inclined to share their anti-communist views. One of them was the SAFA leader Charles Perkins, who was also the driving force behind the Sydney-based Foundation for Aboriginal Affairs (FAA), hailed in 1965 as the only Aboriginal rights organisation of the time to stand outside communist influence.[13] He was to become a regular critic of what he saw as the communist domination of FCAATSI; when he resigned as its vice-president in 1967 he lambasted it as unrepresentative of Aboriginal interests. For Perkins it was not just a matter of wresting control of FCAATSI from whites – one of his targets was Ray Peckham.[14] Having once described communists as 'the cross the aboriginal people have to bear',[15] Perkins went so far as to attempt to form a rival National Aboriginal Affairs Association, which would exclude white activists.[16] He was adopting a strategy in contrast with that of Kath Walker, who had come to share Perkins' anti-communist views but remained in FCAATSI 'to fight the Comrades from within'.[17]

These were the contours of the political landscape that Fred Rose entered via Sydney in April 1965. The changes taking place were not only a cause of great excitement for him, they were the primary subject of his research endeavours. His task, as he put it, was to 'investigate on an Australia-wide basis the Aborigines' struggle for emancipation and equality and particularly the role played by the working class movement'.[18]

It was with some bemusement that shortly after his arrival Rose saw a headline in the *Herald* which proclaimed, 'Man in Petrov spy case now with Reds'. It was filed by a 'Herald Special Representative', who had 'tracked him down to a small bedsitter in a boarding house in the heart of East Berlin near the Karl Marx Allee'.[19] By this time Rose had been living with the 'Reds' for some nine years, and in that time had made a lengthy visit to Australia. It was hardly news. A couple of days later the *Sun* ran a story confirming the 1962 visit. This had been disclosed by 'a Perth friend who wished to remain anonymous'.[20]

The 'Perth friend' was of course Alec Jolly, who had become accustomed to keeping a low profile. He had gained some unwanted attention in August 1951 when his pugilist instincts were awakened in a late-night drunken brawl involving fellow-communist Jim Kelly. Whether as a politician standing for federal parliament, as he had, or as a local GP, as he still was, it was not a good look. The CPA stripped him of his leadership roles; within a couple of years he was reported to have left the Party, though there was no evidence he had discarded his communist views.[21]

Rose had flown under the radar in 1962; the 1965 visit was quite different. This time he *wanted* to be noticed, he knew that circumstances had changed, and so he courted the media. To that end he staged a formal conference in the CPA's Sydney offices, and the press turned up. A decade after his appearance at the royal commission, he had not been forgotten, and tales of spies behind the Iron Curtain made good copy. Rose resolutely refused to pander to that romantic image. He was a victim of a 'frame-up' and of the Australian version of McCarthyism; he had gone to the GDR in order to pursue his anthropological work; he was no 'exile' in the communist bloc, but rather could – and did – travel on both sides of the Iron Curtain as he pleased. As for the purpose of his visit, he announced his intention to undertake a wide-ranging investigation of the contemporary living conditions of Australian Aborigines. 'Australia does not stand very high in the East or the West because of its unjust treatment of Aborigines', he admonished. 'Any moves to improve living conditions for Aborigines, such as the recent bus tour by freedom riders in NSW country towns are a very good thing.'[22]

He spread his media wings into the electronic realm too. As an invited guest on Bob Sanders' television interview program *People* he told his host that 'the Aborigines themselves were taking their own lead in the movement for emancipation'.[23] Asked whether he expected any resistance to his efforts to undertake fieldwork on this visit, he reminded viewers of Hasluck's refusal to give him permission in 1962 but said that this time he did not intend to enter reserves.[24]

ASIO picked up Rose's scent early, alerting 'all available sources' to his presence. It had a good idea of his movements. Rose would again stay with the Grahams in Waverley and then head to Canberra to attend the annual FCAATSI meeting.[25] He was not the only outsider to take an interest in proceedings there. The presence of several Soviet Embassy personnel was noted by ASIO's man on the spot, as were a couple of conversations between Rose and *Pravda* correspondent Yuri Yasnev.[26] The *Pravda* man was also observed speaking with an unidentified female who had earlier been introduced as 'the well known aboriginal poetess' – Kath Walker.[27]

A few days later Rose was back in Sydney visiting CPA headquarters in Day Street, as the handiwork of an ASIO photographer engaged in 'Operation Shiver' reveals.[28] One of the images shows Rose, cigarette dangling from his lip, in conversation with Eric Aarons. Rose spent much time, ASIO noted, with Laurie Aarons[29] and was a guest at a dinner party at Wally Clayton's place in Baulkham Hills.[30] Clearly Rose was revelling in being back in touch with old comrades; ASIO's unnamed informant described him as 'an extremely personable gentleman, intelligent, easy to talk to with a high sense of humour'.[31]

Over the following weeks Rose was on the move, visiting large swathes of eastern and Central Australia, taking opportunities to travel as they presented themselves. By early July he was in the Northern Territory, having travelled there by car via Queensland in the company of Fred Thompson of the Amalgamated Engineering Union; in Darwin he stayed in Nightcliff with fellow communist Bill Donnelly.[32]

Then on one July morning he strolled into Harry Giese's office and asked for a permit to visit Groote Eylandt. Giese, still Director of Welfare, was forthright in his response, 'Fred, you're the last person I'd recommend for a permit'. Rose countered, 'Very well, Harry, if that's the way you feel about it. But if I don't get a permit the Government will probably be placed in an embarrassing position'. Giese understood very well the implicit threat – refusal would trigger union action. A few days later Rose received a message that he could pick up the permit.[33]

In 1965 the prospect of a visit to Groote was every bit as sensitive as it had been in 1962, if not more so. A recent development had changed the course of the island's history. A mine was established near the mission township of Angurugu on the west coast. In his own small way, Rose had played a part in that. As far back as 1941 he had been struck by the heavy black minerals he found on the island. The locals used it as a distinctive black background on their bark paintings. Curious, Rose sent some samples to the Department of Mines in Darwin for identification. A few weeks later he received a reply, indicating that the samples he had sent had been impounded, and that no prospecting or mining was permitted on Aboriginal reserves.[34]

What he had not been told was that the samples were manganese, a substance of great value in steel manufacturing; the addition of it adds both strength and flexibility. By the 1960s moves were afoot to do something with Groote's massive deposits. It was Broken Hill Propriety Limited that saw the potential and commissioned its open-cut mine in 1965; within a short time it was supplying a quarter of the world's needs. If the presence of missionaries and a flying-boat base had chipped away at traditional indigenous lifestyles, the mine delivered a sudden blast. Rose wanted to witness that process of accelerated change at first hand, and ideally would have done so over a period of months. Just a few days would have to suffice.

Rose flew to Groote on 9 July. He was met on arrival by one of the Northern Territory Administration's welfare officers, who did not let him out of his sight. Rose spent his time photographing artwork and, as ASIO noted, 'displayed an interest in settlement living conditions'.[35] He did not attend the union meetings staged at the mine by his travel companions, the unionists Fred Thompson and Walter Bevan. Moreover, ASIO's contacts in the Welfare Section indicated that Rose 'did not attempt to agitate the native dwellers in any way; however, ROSE did take numerous photographs of life in the Settlement'.[36] On 12 July he was heading back to Darwin with Thompson and Bevan.

By the middle of the following month he was in Sydney, saying his farewells and preparing to depart Australia. As he headed home to Berlin he broke his journey to complete some unfinished business in the Top End. He spent three days visiting his old friend Fred Gray. Having left Groote

Eylandt in 1958, Gray now lived outside Darwin at a place he named 'Little Umbakumba'. ASIO placed the home under surveillance for a time, but there was little to report, as the two Freds reminisced.[37]

The 1965 visit produced a rich published legacy. For a German readership he wrote *Ureinwohner, Känguruhs und Düsenclipper* (Aborigines, Kangaroos and Jetliners), which appeared in 1966.[38] In 1969 there followed *Die Ureinwohner Australiens: Gesellschaft und Kunst* (The Aborigines of Australia: Society and Art), which built in good part on his 1965 tour, including his brief visit to Groote Eylandt.[39] Richly illustrated, the volume allowed Rose the opportunity to express in layperson's terms his views on kinship and to pursue an interest in Aboriginal art which stretched back at least as far as his one and only publication in Elkin's *Oceania* in 1942.[40]

For readers of English, Rose wrote *Australia Revisited: The Aborigine Story from Stone Age to Space Age*. It was an account of Rose's own experiences, ranging from his early days as a meteorologist on Groote Eylandt, through to the royal commission and his months 'on the hook' in Sydney, and ultimately to his visits in the 1960s. If there was a model for it, it was Egon Erwin Kisch's *Australian Landfall*, which not only documented the author's triumph over plodding, bigoted authority but also offered its readers a Marxist reading of Australian history.[41] Three decades later, reviewers of *Australia Revisited* could not miss its tendentious qualities. One of them complained, 'Rose lets fly with some whopping generalisations which he doesn't trouble to back up', but in the next breath lauded his exposition of Aboriginal history and his 'eye for a good story'.[42]

Rose would have felt chuffed at that piece of praise. There was, however, one thing that pleased him more than telling a good story, and that was being the story. By the time his book was being published and read in 1968, he was back in Australia, living a real life drama in which he was once more the main character.

24. 1968

When Rose left Australia in 1965, it was with a sense of optimism – indigenous rights appeared to be heading in the right direction, albeit from a pitifully low base. That optimism was well founded. Within two years, on 27 May 1967, a major milestone was reached. The long-awaited amendment to the constitution was passed in a referendum; the Commonwealth could now make laws relating to indigenous people and include them in the census. It was a moment of triumph to be savoured by FCAATSI members like Faith Bandler, whose unstinting efforts were finally rewarded. Almost ninety per cent of voters supported the change. In a further sign that things were on the move, within a few months the government appointed one of its most passionate advocates of indigenous rights, William C. (Bill) Wentworth, to the new office of Minister in Charge of Aboriginal Affairs.

Not everything, however, was running smoothly. The referendum achievement contrasted starkly with a frustrating lack of progress in two crucial areas: pay equality and land rights. The most eloquent public manifestation of these twin issues occurred at Wave Hill, a remote cattle station in the Northern Territory.

As far back as 1964 the Australian Council of Trade Unions had attempted to negotiate full award conditions for Aboriginal stock workers, but without success. In the following year the Northern Australian Workers Union made its bid with an application to the Arbitration Commission. The NT pastoralists, concerned at the costs they would incur if forced to pay equal wages to the indigenous workers on whom their businesses so heavily depended, hired the QC John Kerr to represent them. The government in Canberra played its part to protect business interests, determining that any award granted would not cover pastoral work performed on Aboriginal missions or settlements. Much to the chagrin of FCAATSI, the commission eventually handed down a compromise ruling, according to which Aboriginal stockmen would receive equal pay, but not until the end of 1968.[1]

The most voluble objections to government intransigence came from a militant group of activists in the Northern Territory who were prepared to match words with deeds. On 1 May 1966 Aboriginal stockmen on Newcastle Waters station went on strike; those on a number of other large stations followed. Most famously, at the Wave Hill station on the Victoria River, owned by the British Vestey's corporation, the Gurindji people staged a walk-off in June 1966 and set up a strike camp near the Wave Hill settlement. Over the following months a number of Darwin wharfies ran supplies to the strike camp. In Sydney, the author and CPA member Frank Hardy organised press conferences to publicise the strikers' cause. Though it had not triggered the strike, FCAATSI ran a national campaign in support of it.[2]

In 1967 the strike action at Wave Hill took on the powerful new dimension of land rights. From a little thing a big thing had grown. In April of that year the Gurindji moved to Wattie Creek, or Daguragu, a site they considered the heart of their land. With Hardy's help they petitioned the Governor-General for the return to their possession of most of the Wave Hill lease. The proposal was rejected by Minister for Territories Ceb Barnes.[3] Wentworth, in contrast, travelled to Wattie Creek and met with the Gurindji elders. The suggestion he then put to Cabinet was to excise a small area from the lease, land that the Gurindji 'can call their own'. All the Gurindji wanted, he thought, was a place where they 'can have a vegetable garden and an orchard'.[4] Even this trivialised expression of the Gurindji's claim was too much for Cabinet, especially Country Party members like Minister for the Interior Peter Nixon. Later Wentworth's own Liberal Party colleague Billy McMahon rubbed salt into the wound, telling him, 'Look, you're more trouble to Australia at the moment than all the communism you imagine you're fighting'.[5]

Wentworth was wedged. He was more sensitive than most of his Cabinet colleagues to the trashing of Australia's international reputation because of a woeful record on Aboriginal rights. And as the most belligerent of Cold Warriors, he was concerned that if his government made no concessions, then the left, and most chillingly in his mind the CPA, would seize the initiative.

The last thing Bill Wentworth wanted was for a communist like Fred Rose to arrive in the country and fan the flames of the Wave Hill brushfire. Yet that was exactly what confronted him. Not one to endure such tribulations passively, he sought advice directly from ASIO. In particular, he requested a report on CPA involvement in indigenous issues and information on particular individuals, including Fred Rose.[6]

The news on Rose was troubling, because it revealed that he had once more turned to AIAS for support. As part of a team Rose had put an application to AIAS under the heading 'Proposal for Social Anthropological Research among Four Tribes of Australian Aborigines'. It was knocked back. Les Hiatt at the University of Sydney then encouraged Rose to put in an application on his own, which he did, only to be knocked back again.[7] But a third, modified attempt was successful, as AIAS informed him on 3 April 1967. There was, however, just one more potential snag: in giving Rose the good news, AIAS told him he would need a permit from the Welfare Branch in the Northern Territory.[8]

The prospect of Fred Rose spending any time at all on Groote Eylandt, let alone a period of six months, provoked the same apprehension as in 1962 and 1965. ASIO was among the most concerned and considered it well within its purview to express a characteristically trenchant opinion, even before Rose's application was approved by the AIAS Advisory Committee. A further visit by Rose

> would be undoubtedly exploited by the [Communist] Party to consolidate and widen its influence in this field. In view of ROSE's past history of involvement in espionage in Australia, his conduct before the Royal Commission on Espionage, his continued strong adherence to communism

and the specious nature of the grounds on which he has apparently applied
for a grant, the payment of Commonwealth funds to him would appear, on
policy grounds, to be reprehensible.[9]

Wentworth sought to resurrect a solution considered as far back as 1962, that is, forbidding Rose entry into the country. He put this suggestion to Minister for Immigration Bill Snedden, only to be told that as a holder of a British passport Rose could not be refused a visa, because he did not need one.[10] Another option might have been to refuse him an entry permit on arrival, but as Snedden pointed out, 'he would challenge this by habeas corpus proceedings and the fact of his being an Australian citizen would certainly be given prominence'.[11] Snedden and Wentworth were united in their desire to ensure that Rose was not given undue prominence – the idea was dropped.

Rose's chances of avoiding the disappointment of 1962 were enhanced by one important difference this time. Back then Spender had eventually been able to point to Rose's failure to get support from AIAS. That did not apply in 1968. And one other factor favoured Rose's chance of gaining access to Groote. AIAS had pre-emptively written to the Northern Territory Administration with the request that Rose's application for access to Aboriginal reserves be considered favourably.[12]

That, in turn, presented a conundrum to the Department of the Interior, responsible for the Northern Territory, which turned to ASIO for advice.[13] Charles Spry was more than happy to oblige, copying his reply to the Attorney-General's Department and the Prime Minister's Department for good measure. Rose should be refused permission. He was a known communist, he had been strongly suspected of involvement in espionage, and both the communist government of East Germany and the CPA would seek to use his visit for propaganda advantage. Spry pointed to the role that the 'Communist writer' Frank Hardy was already playing at Wave Hill. Moreover, he insisted, communist exploitation of the situation 'would cause dismay to a number of Aboriginal leaders who feel that it would hurt their cause. For example, Charles PERKINS in an address at Melbourne University on 16th April 1968, declared that he hoped Communists would keep out of prominent positions in organisations concerned with Aborigines, since, in his view, their presence would be detrimental to Aboriginal interests'.[14]

In the meantime, to garner support in case of resistance, Rose wrote to the ALP's Gordon Bryant and Arthur Calwell on 12 April, informing them that he had received a grant from AIAS and expected to visit soon. He did, however, anticipate a problem in his letter to Bryant: 'It may only be a formal matter getting a permit once the Institute has given its blessing to the project: on the other hand refusal of a permit could be used as a means of preventing my doing the field work. If the latter transpires it would be worth-while asking a question in the House with possible follow-up action.'[15] By the end of the month he had received an encouraging reply from Calwell, pleased to hear of Rose's impending visit and promising to discuss with Bryant 'any action we should take in an effort to help you to get the permit you need to enter the Groote Eylandt Reserve'.[16]

In the end, the question of whether to follow Spry's advice and refuse Rose entry to Groote Eylandt was left to Cabinet. The matter was raised there by the Prime Minister himself – by this time John Gorton – on 9 May 1968. Cabinet noted that AIAS had granted Rose funding for his project 'as an autonomous academic body'. Nonetheless, Cabinet decided that having regard 'to Rose's background' it would refuse him a permit.[17] Rose and AIAS were to be informed immediately. Within a couple of weeks of his planned departure from Europe, Rose received the dreaded blunt cablegram from Harry Giese in Darwin, 'Your application of 12 April for permit to enter Groote Eylandt Reserve has been considered and I have to advise you that no permit for such visit will be issued to you'.[18] It was a severe blow, but Rose resolved to travel to Australia anyway.

Wentworth welcomed Cabinet's decision, yet his problems were far from over. His judgment was that the government could not be seen to be acting purely defensively on indigenous issues; it needed to acknowledge some post-referendum realities and take some initiatives of its own. Within a week of the decision on Rose he put a submission to Cabinet replete with grim forebodings: 'Hesitation in formulating a policy could have quite serious repercussions for us, both internally and internationally. Communists are devoting great efforts to capturing Aboriginal organisations, and unless we have an alternative to offer, they are likely to succeed. They plan to develop an "American Negro injustice" image and to focus the hatred of Asian peoples upon Australia.'[19]

When Rose arrived in Australia on 26 May, the government knew it could not sweep its refusal of a permit under the carpet. Rose went to the press and slammed the permit refusal as 'perfectly absurd' and an example of 'paternalism towards aboriginals'.[20] He told the *Age*: 'I am a Communist. I make no bones about that. But all I wanted to do was study their kinship, marriage and age structure.'[21] The *Sydney Morning Herald* conveyed his flagrant sarcasm: 'What the devil do they think I want to do on Groote Eylandt – start a revolution?'[22] His old friend Fred Gray sprang to his defence in the *Australian*, condemning the exclusion as 'utterly stupid' and adding, 'If I was running Umbakumba settlement today, I would welcome him back as a helper, and so would the Andilyaugwa people'.[23]

Having supported Rose's project, AIAS could hardly escape the controversy, though its council, of which Wentworth was a member, did its best at a meeting on 1 June, where the issue was neatly sidestepped. An ASIO source noted wryly, 'Whether this was intentional or because the Council became (as it usually does – Source Comment) so immersed in the minutiae as to prevent matters of substance cannot be ascertained'.[24]

Not everyone at AIAS was inclined to caution; some sought to shift focus to the larger issue at stake, namely the permit system through which the government controlled access to reserves. The social anthropology section at AIAS registered its objections to the system, as did FCAATSI.[25] Les Hiatt contended that the treatment of Rose 'exemplifies the kind of State tyranny from which such decisions are allegedly preserving us'.[26] Even John Barnes, who held the chair of anthropology at the ANU and was far from Rose politically, expressed his grievances with a system that did not even require the director of welfare to state reasons for refusing entry. He advocated a system 'whereby Aboriginals decide on their visitors and on the extent to which they will co-operate in scientific inquiries'.[27]

In early June the controversy had a generous airing on the floor of both houses of parliament, as the government knew it would. In the Senate the ALP's Jim Cavanagh asked Liberal Senator Malcolm Scott, representing the Minister for the Interior: 'Was Professor Rose refused permission to visit Groote Eylandt because he was a Communist? If there was any other reason, what was it?' Scott's well-rehearsed reply was: 'An application was made by an organisation to bring Professor Rose to Groote Eylandt. Permission was refused by Cabinet because he was a Communist.'[28]

Before doing battle in the House of Representatives, Wentworth again sought advice from a favoured source: ASIO. Deputy Director-General (Operations) Peter Barbour furnished him with information on Rose's visit to Groote Eylandt in 1965 and copies of Rose's recent publications. It was useful ammunition, but his Cabinet colleagues refused to supply him with the weapon that would have assured him the moral victory he craved. As Barbour put it, 'The Minister is hoping that the Government will decide quickly to approve the grant of land to the Gurindji aborigines. If this decision is taken before the ROSE case is raised, the Minister proposes to expand his reply regarding ROSE to embrace the general matter of Communist involvement in aboriginal affairs'.[29]

When Labor's Gordon Bryant went on the attack in the lower house,[30] he sprang the question not on Wentworth but on Minister for the Interior Peter Nixon. Bryant opened with: 'Has Professor Frederick Rose been denied permission to land on Groote Eylandt on a visit sponsored by the Institute of Aboriginal Studies?' He then asked if Nixon knew of Rose's international standing, his many previous visits to the island for research purposes, including as recently as 1965. Why then, he wanted to know, was Rose refused permission on the grounds that his visit would be contrary to the interests of Aborigines? Nixon offered the same straight bat as Scott: 'It is a fact that Professor Rose has been banned from visiting Groote Eylandt. The reason is that Professor Rose is a Communist.'[31]

Now Whitlam took up the cudgels against Wentworth, adopting a slightly different approach by picking up on Wentworth's position at AIAS. 'Is Professor Rose', Whitlam wondered, 'visiting Australia on a grant from the Australian Institute of Aboriginal Studies, on which the honourable gentleman is the representative of this House? I ask the Minister whether he was consulted by the Institute about the grant to the Professor. Was he consulted on the refusal to grant a permit to the Professor to visit Groote Eylandt?' In his answer Wentworth acknowledged his membership of AIAS and its Council but pointed out he was not present when the Rose issue was discussed and the grant awarded. He claimed, however, that the grant was conditional on Rose gaining a permit. Wentworth then made it clear that he fully supported Cabinet's decision not to allow Rose entry to Groote. Whitlam's deputy Lance Barnard joined the fray, 'What are the reasons?' Wentworth was prepared to go a step further than his colleagues. The reason was 'not just because Professor Rose is a Communist'. Rather, he said, it was because Rose 'has a particularly bad record of treachery and of prostituting his position as an anthropologist for the gains of the Communist Party'. Made under parliamentary privilege, they were allegations for which he provided not a shred of evidence.[32]

Sure enough, Rose did not let Wentworth's calumnies pass unanswered and moved quickly to occupy the moral high ground. A lengthy letter in response to Wentworth's allegations was published in the *Australian*. Rose preserved a more temperate and statesman-like tone than his accuser, dismissing the charge of 'scientific prostitution', and pointing out that he was himself a corresponding member of AIAS, a sure indication of the esteem in which his fellow-scientists held him. He expressed regret that the incident had caused AIAS embarrassment, but he reminded readers that it was the government 'that took the first political step by banning me from the Groote Eylandt Reserve because I am a communist'. Then he sought to score points in the area of Wentworth's greatest vulnerability – Australia's international standing. The rest of the world had consigned McCarthyism to the past; the government's actions in banning him, he predicted, 'will sadly dent the image of Australia abroad'.[33]

Rose continued to apply the pressure through mid-June. He shared a stage with Hardy and senior FCAASI member Ray Peckham at a public meeting at the BWIU Hall in Sydney's George Street; the topic was land rights. The refusal of a permit had been a blow, but a welcome by-product was that he was now a *cause célèbre*. In letters back to Berlin he gloated over his *succès de scandale*: 'This time it was a cabinet decision to keep me out of G. Eylandt Reserve. In 1962 it was only a ministerial decision – we're going places!' He had been 'incredibly busy – speaking at meetings, radio and on television ... gave a 30 min television interview on a rabidly anti-communist session of "Meet the Press". You will be pleased that they got as good as they gave!'[34] Channel 7's 'Meet the Press' panel had indeed sought to provoke Rose by picking through the embers of the royal commission and the allegations that Rose had perjured himself. Rose would admit only to being evasive – after all, in Australia 'you don't shelve on your mates'. Challenged to declare whether his loyalty to communism had priority over his loyalty to Australia, he answered – as he had done before the commission – that he saw no conflict between the two. Then the panel avoided all niceties in giving full vent to its prejudices: 'What are you – are you a fair dinkum Anthropologist, with the motives, the purest motives of science, or are you a Communist out to make trouble?' Rose insisted he was in Australia to do scientific work, but, at the same time he was 'not prepared to keep my mouth shut on issues'.[35]

The collapse of the project did however have two serious drawbacks for Rose. He would have to reconceive his research plans, just as in 1962. And once more he fell into the role of mendicant anthropologist, relying heavily on friends and contacts to provide him free or cheap accommodation and travel. He was, as ASIO well knew, operating 'on a shoe-string'.[36] The CPA helpfully kicked in $200,[37] and many others donated in cash or kind to the cause, as Rose cadged lifts over vast distances or set up camp in spare rooms all over the country.

In July he travelled with Queensland ALP Senator George Georges by caravan from Brisbane to Townsville, where they attended a social function of the 'Townsville Inter-Racial Citizens' Committee', hosted by Henry and Margaret Reynolds.[38] From there he made his way to Darwin, where he met up with Fred Gray. Then he was reported to be travelling toward Wave Hill with the purpose, so ASIO suspected, of delivering supplies to the Gurindji.[39]

That much was true. Rose did visit Wattie Creek, from 13 to 14 August, having travelled there with former wharfie and CPA member John Meaney, who was involved in the running of vital supplies to the protesters. ASIO reported that at Wattie Creek Rose took photographs and discussed land rights with the Gurindji.[40] By 16 August he was back at Gray's Little Umbakumba, reportedly contemplating a chartered flight to Groote.[41] One ASIO source claimed that Rose had asked his CPA contacts in Darwin to get him to Groote 'at any price'.[42]

Those suspicions were not far wide of the mark. After his return to Germany, Rose gave a detailed account of his Australian visit to a member of the SED's Central Committee, reporting on his dealings with the CPA. There had indeed been plans to smuggle him on to Groote Eylandt via a chartered plane. He would disappear into the bush and do fieldwork for some four months. Work completed, he would reappear and embarrass the government. The plan was shelved, however, when it was learned that Gorton was planning to visit Groote in early September. The security arrangements ahead of that visit, the CPA had concluded, would make Rose's visit too difficult.[43]

The authorities had taken steps to deal with Rose if he did turn up on Groote. Normally there was no policeman permanently stationed on the island, so a Darwin-based officer, Christopher Crellin, was sent there. His brief, as he recalled many years later, was 'to meet any boats and aircraft that came in, and if this Rose was on any of them I was to arrest him and bring him immediately back to Darwin'.[44] Rose did not show, so Crellin spent a month on the island twiddling his thumbs.

Within days Rose had left the country, though not quietly. He had learned to use the media to his advantage, and the media for their part found the 'Red Professor' a consistent source of provocative copy. Rose issued a statement warning of the possibility of violence on Groote Eylandt because of the increasing resentment among the local population. BHP, with the help of the government, 'was riding roughshod over the cultural heritage of the Aborigines'.[45]

It was 1968, a year of revolution. In the northern spring students and workers in France took to the streets to give voice to a litany of grievances and demands. On the other side of the Iron Curtain Alexander Dubček's government in Prague was embarking on a courageous program of reforms with the avowed aim of giving socialism a human face. In Paris Charles De Gaulle stepped in to restore a conservative order. In Czechoslovakia, in contrast, it was brutal intervention from outside that undid the precious achievements of the Prague Spring. As they had done in the GDR in 1953 and Hungary in 1956, in August of 1968 Soviet forces staged an invasion of Czechoslovakia, issuing a bloody reminder to Czechs where real power over their country lay. The East German leadership prepared to add its troops to the Soviet invasion, only to withdraw them at the last moment when it was recognised that German participation would trigger ugly memories and heighten the sense of outrage.[46]

There is precious little in the record of Fred Rose's life to indicate what he felt about the Soviet invasion. How much credence can be placed in an ASIO report that he was 'dismayed and disillusioned'?[47] Was his conscience in the least troubled by the bloodshed and loss of life, as the hopes of the Prague Spring were crushed under the tracks of Soviet tanks? Asked his views in Darwin, he was prepared only to issue a tight-lipped, 'No comment'.[48] If he did harbour reservations, he concealed them well.

There were many communists of Fred Rose's generation for whom 1968 was the last straw; as the tanks rumbled through Prague, they committed their Party cards to the flames. That was nothing new. Many years earlier British Labour MP Dick Crossman edited a book with the telling title *The God That Failed*. It collected the views of six intellectuals, who wrote both of their belief in communism and their abandonment of it. One of them, the American journalist Louis Fischer, developed the notion of a 'Kronstadt' moment, referring to the brutal Bolshevik suppression of the uprising by sailors in 1921 – and with it the recognition that the noble hopes of the 1917 revolution had been cruelly dashed. Fischer himself needed many years for his 'Kronstadt', but when it came, there could be no going back.[49]

Over decades there were many such moments for communists to question the foundations of their faith. After Kronstadt there were reports of famines and purges in the Soviet Union, there was the Hitler–Stalin Pact, and in 1956 there were both Khrushchev's denunciation of Stalin and the invasion of Hungary. That was the point where Peter Worsley made his break with communism, dashing off a futile plea to Rose not to 'swallow the bloody (and vicious) nonsense put out by Hungary in recent months, though you cannot possibly know the real story where you are'.[50] At each of these points, and at others in between, there were those who chose apostasy, unsure whether to cast their lot in with the other side of politics, or to try to construct some alternative vision of 'the left'. The 1968 invasion was another 'Kronstadt', perhaps even the severest test of the true believers' faith.

Fred Rose was one of those who held firm. Confronted with the harsh reality that the Soviets had thwarted an earnest effort to give socialism a human face, he still saw no reason to recant. By now he was much too heavily invested in communism, politically, intellectually and personally. Unlike 'Westerners' such as Worsley, Rose had made his life behind the Iron Curtain and had proved his loyalty to the system, even to the extent of working with its secret police. For him there could be no going back. Whatever the failings of the socialist states, they pointed the only way to the future, and he was as sure of it as ever.

25. Double Lives

Personally and professionally, marriage was a recurring theme in Fred Rose's life. As Edith's husband he managed to maintain for some four decades the appearance that they led a conventional wedded existence. And as a social anthropologist with a special interest in kinship, the topic of marriage was central to his work. But what did he really want or expect from marriage?

Rose's marriage with Edith had provided an economic and social foundation for raising four children, all of whom distinguished themselves academically, entered marriages of their own and raised children. Throughout that time, and in common with many contemporaries on both sides of the Iron Curtain, Rose was not averse to seeking sexual gratification outside his marriage. Put colloquially, Rose was a dog inclined to stray from the porch, an inclination that stretched back to the time well before his move to the GDR. In the words of a close male friend in the Canberra years, Rose's sexual exploits had earned him the epithet 'the bull of O'Connor'.

Through his fieldwork on Groote Eylandt and in the Kimberley, Rose had discovered that as far as sexual behaviour was concerned, marriage 'rules' did not often match social reality. It was an observation not uncommonly applied to anthropologists themselves, whose covert sexual behaviour at times 'breached law and social convention'.[1] Yet in the 1960s divorce remained rare in the GDR, as it did in Australia, and a veneer of social conformity was preserved.

At some point early in that decade Rose commenced a clandestine affair with 'Petra Vogler'. She was married, had three children, and worked for a bank. Her occupation was not unimportant, because it was one in which workers were warned against pursuing relationships with Western foreigners. When that advice went unheeded, there was a compelling reason to keep both the relationship and then the birth of a child under wraps. The revelation of the affair would have cost 'Vogler' her job, and after her divorce in 1963 she could not afford that. She lived in fear of the Stasi chancing upon her secret, not realising that her paramour was working for the very agency she feared. The circle of the initiated remained small.

Despite the desire for secrecy, the child born in September 1964 was given the name Frederick. Rose helped out with payments to 'Vogler' over a number of years, even when her job took her to Moscow for a time in the 1970s. It was only much later, in 1988, and on the initiative of young Frederick, that Rose's paternity was formally acknowledged.[2]

Edith seems to have been similarly unaware of the romance that developed between Rose and one of his postgraduate students. The affair lasted at least a decade. The first, fleeting encounter was one frosty evening in Berlin in early 1963, when Rose, recently returned from Angas Downs, picked up a distinctive London accent among the babble of voices at a gathering in an Unter den Linden apartment. The speaker was a young Englishwoman named Hannah Middleton. She had been brought to the Humboldt to teach English through an arrangement made by Diana Loeser, the English wife of the Humboldt philosopher Franz Georg Loeser. Through her work in support of Paul Robeson Diana had been in contact with Hannah's mother Peggy Middleton, a left-wing Labour politician who served both on the Greater London Council and, from 1960 to 1961, as Mayor of Greenwich. Both women had been outraged by the shabby treatment of the activist and singer Robeson, whose passport had been revoked by American authorities. Subsequently Hannah was invited to teach English at the Humboldt University and to experience 'real existing socialism' at first hand.[3]

When the invitation arrived from the Humboldt, Hannah was enrolled in African Studies at the University of London. Living in Berlin was a brief but invaluable experience, so that after graduating with an Honours Degree from London she took the opportunity to return to the Humboldt to teach 'English Language and Institutions'.[4]

In 1968 she became a postgraduate student in anthropology. Her co-supervisor with Fred Rose was Rose's historian colleague, confidant and fluent English speaker Ernst Hoffmann. For Rose the involvement of Hoffmann could ease his anxieties about Middleton's shaky grounding in Marxist theory. In a letter to Hoffmann, Rose conceded that 'like all English comrades – myself included – [Hannah's] theoretical understanding of Marxism is not good'.[5] Her 'one-on-one' tutorials with Hoffmann on Marxist materialism were gruelling sessions conducted at Hoffmann's home. Even with her mentor's sympathy and support Hannah would at times be reduced to tears as she grappled with the complexities of *Das Kapital*. The kindly Frau Hoffmann would often provide a box of tissues with morning tea.[6]

Eventually the relationship between Rose and Middleton crossed the line into a full-blown romance. When he headed to Australia in 1968, she took a study break in England, where he wrote to her: 'Dearest Hannah, writing to you in England I can at least explain myself fairly openly: so let me just say that I love you deeply – can you imagine how I have missed you these last few weeks? It has been hellish.'[7]

Back in Berlin, their relationship continued and intensified, and the prospect of a shared future in Australia was raised. But in the northern summer of 1969 doubts appeared and, in time, were given full voice. Rose felt that his commitment to Middleton was not being reciprocated. He played the jilted lover; plans to move to Australia together 'were no longer real'. What Middleton did when in Australia or England was her own business, but when in Berlin she was not to make him a 'cuckold'.[8]

His plans for a fully-fledged relationship with Middleton thwarted, Rose sketched an alternative scenario for her consideration – an affair. They would meet as lovers perhaps a couple of times a week. After all, he had other duties with his children along with his university and political work. It would, he conceded, not be ideal for her. Eventually she would finish her degree and presumably leave the GDR, with 'neither a husband nor the immediate prospect of one', while he would remain behind. His attitude to her might change, but for now that seemed the best possibility. He thought it important to be frank: 'I am not holding this possibility out to you like one holds a carrot in front of a donkey for I think you should make your decision on the basis of the bleakest possibilities one can conjure up. Nevertheless I think it must be clear to you that if a committed affair is to develop in the future, it must be based on an uncommitted affair now.' Of course, he could not assume that Hannah would accept such conditions. If that were the case, he closed melodramatically, 'I hope that you will remember me, at least as the lover who taught you to appreciate your own sex and the meaning of an orgasm as the highest sexual experience'.[9]

In 1970 Middleton was in Australia for several months doing fieldwork, largely among the Gurindji.[10] Rose was an assiduous mentor, facilitating her travels, connecting her with a network of scholars and activists, and offering her guidance as she assembled her data and developed her ideas. In 1972 she submitted her thesis to the Humboldt, its title 'The Land Rights and Civil Rights Campaign of the Gurindji at Wattie Creek'. In due course she received a distinction for it.[11] Back in Berlin, the oral defence of her thesis went without a hitch, enhanced perhaps by her mother's generous gift of an elegant black dress bought in London and worn with fashionably high boots. Celebrations followed with the popping of corks and toasting with Russian champagne.[12] With that Rose's formal relationship with Middleton as her supervisor came to an end, though the ties between them, both professional and personal, would remain.

Edith might not have known of the relationship with Hannah, but the Stasi certainly did – because Rose told them. His role in the Stasi had changed as he had been passed on from the HVA to Directorate XX, devoted to counter-intelligence. Apart from a new handler and a new meeting place, for Rose it was largely business as usual.[13] The transfer appears to have had no impact on Rose's attitude to the Stasi or his willingness to report on everything, including his private life. And that meant that his new handler, Lieutenant Neumann, was well informed about the vicissitudes of Rose's love life. At times he would even offer advice.

At a meeting in April 1969, Rose mentioned he had been contacted by a scholar from India by the name of 'Sanjay Gupta'. In the previous month 'Gupta' had written to Rose from Munich, where he was attached to the Institut zur Erforschung der UdSSR, the Institute for the Study of the USSR. A postcard followed at Easter. In it 'Gupta' suggested that he could meet Rose any day at the Friedrichstrasse, one of the crossing points for Westerners entering East Berlin. Rose saw little benefit in pursuing the contact with 'Gupta', but the Stasi thought otherwise, and Rose was instructed accordingly.

Rose obeyed and arranged to meet with 'Gupta' for coffee. 'Gupta', he learned, was a visiting professor of anthropology at the University of Munich, while also attached to the Institute for the Study of the USSR. He had done postgraduate work at the Humboldt, but had abandoned his study in 1967. Since then he had worked in the United States and been an adviser to UNESCO in Paris. As for the institute in Munich, Rose gleaned that it was funded largely with American money, was dedicated to research on the Soviet Union, and counted among its members a number of Soviet émigrés. What Rose could not work out, however, was what 'Gupta' *really* wanted in the GDR.[14]

The Stasi had good reason to be interested in Munich and its institute. The Bavarian capital had become a centre of *Ostforschung*, the research into the lands to Germany's east, and not just since the war. It was a discipline which, like anthropology, had compromised itself shamelessly under the Nazis but was revived with American help during the Cold War. Munich was an obvious choice, because Bavaria was home to large numbers of Eastern Europeans, including ethnic Germans, driven west after Germany's defeat in 1945. What united this diverse group was an abiding interest in their homelands and a visceral hatred of communism. Those were characteristics they shared with the American forces, which had occupied Bavaria in 1945 and stayed.

The Institute for the Study of the USSR was founded in 1950 with a brief to disseminate information about the Soviet Union; it had an active publishing arm and a richly stocked library, made affordable by the generous financial support of the CIA until 1972, when a changing political climate brought about the closure of the institute.[15] Its scholarly interests ranged across a number of disciplines; Stasi sources suggested that CIA agents used the institute to prepare for operations behind the Iron Curtain.[16]

There were other reasons for the Stasi to be interested in Munich. It was the home of two Western propaganda services, so-called 'freedom radios', set up to influence public opinion in Eastern Europe by transmitting anti-communist content into the communist bloc. Radio Free Europe and Radio Liberty had a precedent in the radio service set up in the American sector of Berlin right after the war. RIAS (Radio in the American Sector) became in effect a surrogate information service for East Germans, who otherwise relied on Soviet-controlled sources of news and commentary.[17] Radio Free Europe and Radio Liberty observed a clear division of labour. While Radio Free Europe had been founded by the US-based National Committee for a Free Europe and had a broad brief to influence public opinion in the Soviet satellite states, Radio Liberty was targeted at the Soviet Union itself. The more disaffected its listeners were, the more likely they were to tune in.

Unsurprisingly, then, Radio Liberty had a symbiotic relationship with the Institute for the Study of the USSR. It performed the charade of enjoying private support for its operations but in reality was funded by the CIA.[18] Radio Liberty's base, set up with the help of a number of former officers from Hitler's Ministry of the Eastern Territories, was in the former administration block at the Oberwiesenfeld airport.[19]

When Fred Rose was despatched to Munich by the Stasi in 1969, the Cold War was undergoing a thaw, and that had consequences for both the 'freedom radios'. In that year West Germans elected a coalition government headed by the Social Democrat Willy Brandt, determined to promote better relations with the GDR and the rest of the Eastern bloc via his *Ostpolitik*. Internationally the talk was not of war but *détente*. Radio Liberty and Radio Free Europe were regarded by many as Cold War dinosaurs, their mere existence an unhelpful provocation. Some within the Brandt government favoured shutting the stations down; across the Atlantic, Senator J. William Fulbright promoted a similar course.[20] As it happened, it was only the Institute for the Study of the USSR that was axed in 1972. The 'freedom radios' survived and in the Reagan presidency experienced a revival in funding and activity. Their supporters would boast they did more than their share in bringing down the Soviet monolith. But when Fred Rose was active in Munich, the radios were following a 'softly, softly' approach, and their existence was tenuous.

The Stasi was not the only intelligence agency keen to sniff around Munich and compromise radio operations. A couple of murders of Radio Liberty staff in Munich in the 1950s have been put down to the KGB. Over the years a number of Soviet agents managed to infiltrate the organisation and report to Moscow on the inner workings of what they viewed as a haven of neo-Nazi activity. The most damaging was probably Oleg Tumanov, who managed to infiltrate both radios. Not until 1986 did he unexpectedly disappear from Munich and turn up in Moscow. Before then he met regularly with his control agent in East Berlin.[21]

Fred Rose was not in that league. His initial targets, 'Sanjay Gupta' and the Institute for the Study of the USSR, were small. 'Gupta' had provoked puzzlement in the Stasi's Directorate II, where it was thought he might have been recruited by the CIA. That would explain his approach to Rose, who, so the thinking ran, might have got him a lectureship at the Humboldt and, with it, cover for CIA-sponsored operations behind the Iron Curtain. When 'Gupta' had studied in Berlin earlier, he had aroused suspicions among foreign students that he was a spy. Even Indians in East Berlin, the Stasi ascertained, were reserved in their attitudes to him.[22]

In his dealings with 'Gupta', Rose was to create the impression that his interest was solely academic. Nonetheless, he was instructed not to share that interest with his Humboldt colleagues. As he planned a visit to 'Gupta' in Munich, he created a 'legend' to deceive them. They were given to understand that he was travelling to Paris to hold discussions with Claude Lévi-Strauss and André Leroi-Gourhan. Rose did travel to Paris, but just for a day, before making his way to the Bavarian capital.[23] It was June 1969. All the visa arrangements had been made by the Stasi, who covered his expenses.

Rose stayed with 'Gupta' in the latter's Munich apartment, a detailed description of which he would later provide to his handlers. 'Gupta' appeared vague and evasive, but Rose at least extracted from him that his main research interests related to minority problems and religion in the USSR. Rose also learned that 'Gupta' was well connected; among his American acquaintances he counted Ted Kennedy, with whom he had studied at Harvard. At the institute Rose spoke with some eight to ten individuals, among them two visiting American professors. He noted, too, that 'Gupta' shared an office with the Soviet dissident Lev Tolstoy, who had allegedly worked for the State Department.[24]

Back in Berlin Rose supplied the Stasi with a detailed report. His handlers at Directorate XX handed it on to Directorate II, which had a special interest in Munich.[25] So satisfied were they that in October they proposed to elevate Rose to a higher level. No longer would he be simply KP 'Aust'. If he were to agree, he would be formally engaged by the Stasi as an IM, an unofficial collaborator. It was not a salaried position, but it was a clear step-up from the role of KP. Rose accepted. His formal engagement as an IM took place on 6 November. Rose told his hosts he had already learned much from them, and that 'as a communist it was a matter of course that he would do everything to support the Ministry for State Security'. The occasion was toasted with champagne. Asked, however, to sign a formal pledge of commitment, Rose refused. Such a signature was superfluous, he explained; his word alone was a guarantee he could be trusted.[26]

Further visits to Munich followed, allowing Rose to expand his range of contacts there. In 1970 he made the acquaintance of visiting American scholar David Nissman, who had a particular interest in Kurdish minorities in the USSR.[27] That contact augured well, because Nissman's primary duties were with Radio Liberty, and Rose was able to gain access to the Radio Liberty base.[28]

West Berlin, too, lay in Rose's 'operational area'. His handlers hoped he could establish contacts in the anthropological museum and at the Free University.[29] In addition, like Edith, he could pursue contacts with Australian and British diplomatic personnel in West Berlin, whether by visiting them on the other side of the Wall or hosting them in the East.

In the 1970s Rose's field of activity extended across the Atlantic. The anthropologist Arnold Pilling of Wayne State University extended an invitation to discuss mutual interests. Where Rose was an acknowledged expert on Groote Eylandt, Pilling had an extensive knowledge of the Tiwi Islands.[30] In transit in New York, Rose spent a couple of hours in private discussion with fellow communists Hyman Lumer and Margrit Pittman.[31] In Detroit, by contrast, his appearances were in public view. The first, on 21 May, was as guest speaker at a lunch hosted by the District Area Council on World Affairs. Among a mixed audience was Stewart Dow of the Dow Chemical Corporation, the manufacturer, as Rose noted, of napalm. Rose addressed some of the pressing issues of the day – the Vietnam War, student protests, the political situation in the Middle East, the need for better political and economic relations between East and West.[32] For the second of his performances the following evening he struck a more scholarly note, explaining to an audience of about 150 the application of historical materialism to anthropology.[33] On his way back to the GDR he made stops once more in New York, and then Montreal, where he met with Canadian communists.[34]

These travels were no doubt of some personal and professional advantage for Rose, but they offered slim pickings for his spymasters. If anything, the experience merely confirmed what the HVA had long known. Rose's reputation as a devoted communist went before him; the likelihood that interlocutors of another political persuasion might take him into their confidence was next to nil. Probably the most useful information Rose was ever able to feed the Stasi was gathered not in the capitalist West but in his own backyard. His most revealing sources were his colleagues, his friends, his family, and even Rose himself.

26. Anthropologist

Kim had given his parents the greatest cause for concern, but signs were emerging that his siblings also were deviating from their parents' expectations. Sonja, the eldest of the Rose daughters, had always thought of the GDR as a provisional home; now she and her family were preparing to move to the West. Even the youngest child, Nita, who at the age of eighteen would be able to claim a passport of her own, seemed likely to pack her bags and leave.

These prospects sent a cold shiver down Fred Rose's spine, and yet even as he candidly discussed his children's suspected *Wanderlust* with the Stasi, he was developing itchy feet of his own. In his case, the urge to leave did not spring from political disaffection or loss of faith in the 'system'. Rather, the problem was his job. For Rose the academic anthropologist, there was much to lament about the state of his profession, and it was not in his nature to suffer in silence.

To the wall of the Humboldt University's main building is attached in large letters an aphorism penned by a much admired former student, Karl Marx. It reads: 'The philosophers have only interpreted the world in various ways; the point is to change it.'[1] Rose took this piece of wisdom as an injunction. As a scholar he wanted to make a difference outside the cloistered world of academe. All forms of intellectual endeavour in his view had to be devoted to the task of changing the world for the better. Anthropology should be no different; the labour of its practitioners needed to be harnessed in the service of the greater good.

The issue for Rose was not that he lacked institutional support. His university, after all, had allowed him to take regular sabbaticals; his books and articles found publishers and readerships. Rather, as an activist as much as an academic, he agonised over whether all of this was really making a tangible difference to people's lives. As the end of the 1960s approached, Rose's frustrations with the state of his discipline, and with his own place in it, were growing to a point where something had to give.

Just what he thought anthropology could achieve was well encapsulated in a presentation he gave in 1962 to a conference hosted by his institute. 'Bourgeois' anthropologists, in their rejection or simply ignorance of the laws of social development, had at best acted as apologists for the imperialists' self-styled 'civilising' mission. Socialist *Völkerkunde*, in contrast, had two main goals. The first of these was to investigate social developments in pre-capitalist conditions, and the second was to work collaboratively with other 'historical' sciences to promote an understanding of politics and liberation movements around the world.[2]

Rose's frank assessment several years later was that neither of these goals was being met. After a period of grumbling to his Stasi handlers about political and administrative inertia in the university, his disgruntlement eventually hardened into the conviction that East German *Völkerkunde* suffered from systemic flaws requiring urgent attention. In October 1967 Rose composed a memorandum on the subject of his discipline's problems and sent it to Kurt Hager, the member of the powerful Politburo of the SED's Central Committee with responsibility for matters of education. He was also a 'Westerner', a Spanish Civil War veteran who had spent most of the war years in a British internment camp.[3] Perhaps he could be persuaded to pull some strings for the Englishman Rose?

The thrust of Rose's argument to Hager was that anthropology was not being used effectively as a weapon in the struggle against imperialism. Quite the contrary: the truth was that the discipline was small and poorly resourced; its presence in the university system confined to just two universities, where quotas on the student intakes were pitifully small. *Völkerkunde* was falling far short of the grand vision Rose had for it.[4]

Hager's thoughts are not recorded, but Rose was at least afforded the opportunity to present his case in person at a meeting held in early 1968. Among those present to hear him were his Humboldt colleagues, along with representatives of the Ministry for Higher Education and the Central Committee.[5] The outcome appears to have been a good deal of nodding agreement. Who could argue against the idea that East German anthropology should flourish and make an impact outside the walls of the university? Beyond that, however, nothing much changed.[6]

When Rose returned from Australia later that year, things had hardly improved. The reform of the GDR's higher education system meant that at the Humboldt *Völkerkunde* and *Volkskunde* joined prehistory and history as separate disciplines in a School of History. As a Marxist Rose had no objection to the notion that anthropology was an historical science, but in this instance the effects of the restructuring were, in his view at least, cosmetic.

In all likelihood, the primary cause of anthropology's malaise in the GDR was not that the relevant authorities were antithetical to it. Rather, they were indifferent and ultimately prepared to let it languish. *Völkerkunde* was locked in an arm wrestle for scarce resources with its neighbouring discipline *Volkskunde*, and *Volkskunde* had gained the upper hand. It had the advantage that it could attract larger numbers of students, who could readily do fieldwork in various parts of the GDR, and who had good prospects of employment in the multitude of regional museums operating around the country. In contrast *Völkerkunde* and its students laboured under the GDR's international isolation. Only in a few states of Africa and the Middle East could students and academics do their fieldwork; employment options in the GDR were few and far between. For all the good intentions that had accompanied the discipline's revival after the war, the reality was that *Völkerkunde* in the GDR was descending into an 'Orchideenwissenschaft', an 'orchid' science, a colourful embellishment to an academic establishment whose priorities lay elsewhere.

Rose's despair grew, and when he turned to Hager again in 1971, he made a barefaced threat: 'Over the years here in the GDR I have become increasingly frustrated politically and now in my 57th year I feel that, with ten or at most fifteen years political activity in front of me, I would be more effective in Australia and as a consequence I have decided to return to

Australia at the end of the present semester.'[7] His ultimatum delivered, he proceeded to detail those frustrations at great length.[8]

When nothing changed, he repeated his demand the following year, this time in a longer and shriller form. By now he occupied a stronger bargaining position, and for reasons that lay largely outside the GDR. One of his most heartfelt grievances was that his own work had gone largely unacknowledged in the communist bloc. That oversight was particularly egregious in the Soviet Union, where, in Rose's view, Sergei Tolstov had taken a dim view of Rose from the beginning and had authored a conspiracy of silence to 'kill' him.[9]

What had strengthened Rose's claims by 1972 was that the dreaded Tolstov had retired, and there were signs that Rose was starting to receive some long overdue recognition. In 1966, Daniel Tumarkin at the Institute of Ethnography of the USSR Academy of Sciences in Moscow had written to Rose to tell him he proposed writing a short article about him for the *Soviet Historical Encyclopeaedia*.[10] When published in 1969, the relevant entry described Rose as a 'Marxist ethnographer', an epithet Rose could only take as high praise.[11] More pleasingly, the leading Soviet expert on Australian ethnography, Vladimir Kabo, had just months earlier written a complimentary assessment of Rose's work as an afterword to the Soviet edition of Rose's *Ureinwohner, Känguruhs und Düsenclipper*.[12] Thirteen years of silence after the issuing of Tolstov's 'veto' had been broken.[13]

The gist of this latest memorandum was clear. Rose was an important, internationally recognised scholar; the Soviets now valued his work highly. His departure to the capitalist West would be a source of great embarrassment to the GDR. The question which now needed to be asked, Rose decided, was, 'Can the GDR allow itself to let Rose go?' He was even so audacious as to itemise the conditions under which he might be prepared to reconsider. First he would need to be released from his duties at the university. That would mean taking a position at the Academy of Sciences, where he could devote himself entirely to his research on hominisation. The move would have to be arranged for him by others and presented as a *fait accompli*. Indeed, he warned, if his plan were agreed to in principle but nothing done to realise it, then he would travel to Australia in the new year and not return.[14]

On the very eve of that planned visit to Australia, in May of 1973, Rose reiterated his ultimatum to his colleague Ernst Hoffmann. There had been no response to previous ultimata, so he urged Hoffmann to prosecute his case for him, and he was full of advice on how best to do that. Rose's reading of the situation was probably accurate. Those in positions of power were not antithetical to him; they simply did not care enough about him and his scholarly endeavours. His best hope was to present them with irrefutable proof of his scientific standing and of the potential value of his proposed work. That would mean neutralising the potentially damaging influence of his rival in the Academy of the Sciences, Irmgard Sellnow. If she were consulted, Rose assumed, his chances of joining her in the Academy were small. Sellnow, he complained to Hoffmann, 'has absolutely no idea of what my work actually contains and less idea of its significance'. For Sellnow the Rose approach was tantamount to sociology; she abhorred his use of statistics, while he complained that the importance of his work for earliest history 'goes completely over her head'.[15] To circumvent her influence, Rose advised, Hoffmann had to play the international card: 'There is a political obligation – whether a moral obligation is hardly relevant – for the scientists in the GDR to give me the same recognition as is accorded me outside the GDR.'[16] He closed in typically forthright style: 'Personally, I am sick and tired of my "case" not being resolved. It has been under discussion as far as I am concerned, or not under discussion whichever way you look at it, for over two years now – ich habe die Nase voll! [I am sick of it].'[17]

The truth was that even if the East German authorities had been prepared to throw more resources at anthropology, they could not have made Fred Rose entirely happy. His repeated threats were symptomatic of Rose's deeper conundrum. Both as an anthropologist and as an activist, he needed to be in Australia. From the other side of the world there was precious little he could do to intervene effectively in Australian politics, especially in the area that was dearest to him, indigenous rights. Just at the time when Aboriginal activism was reaching an apogee in the late 60s and early 70s, Rose was sorely conscious that for most of those crucial years he must observe things from afar. On his visits he would need first to catch up on the state of play before investing his energies in the cause. Frustration was inevitable.

His anthropological pursuits suffered from the tyranny of distance as much as from the political manoeuvrings that thwarted him when he got to Australia. His sabbaticals did not afford him the same possibilities that he had had three decades earlier. The time spent at Angas Downs in 1962 had been a pragmatic compromise, forcing him to shift his line of inquiry away from traditional forms of kinship to the impacts of exposure to a capitalist economy. Fellow anthropologists in the West confronted similar challenges, but they were better positioned to generate new interests, formulate new lines of inquiry, adopt different theoretical perspectives and exchange fresh ideas among themselves. At the Humboldt, Rose was only too aware of his intellectual isolation.

It was not surprising then that much of the work he published in the 1960s and 1970s revisited issues that can be traced back to his early fieldwork on Groote Eylandt. First and foremost he was interested in Aboriginal marriage and kinship, and he was not alone in this. The quest to codify 'authentic' marriage rules had almost totally preoccupied a generation of anthropologists, yet time and again the rules had proved elusive.[18] Rose for his part continued to apply a rigorous and unwavering Marxist analysis. In books, journal articles and conference papers, he enlarged on the same theme. The notion that ideal schemes or notions of kinship explained social structures was just plain wrong. 'Blood relationships', whether real or fictive, were also wide of the mark.[19] As Rose saw it, kinship systems in Aboriginal society, as in any society, were expressions or 'codifications' of economic relations or, to put it in plain Marxist terms, of the 'economic base'.[20]

On Groote Eylandt he, like many other early European visitors, had been struck by the existence of what he called polygynous gerontocracy. At any one time, though most marriages were monogamous, there was a significant minority of polygynous marriages.[21] Older Groote Eylandt men,

Rose had observed in 1938/39 and again in 1941, were commonly married to several women of various ages. Even though polygyny was on the decline during the period of his fieldwork on Groote, he had analysed it closely in *Classification of Kin* and returned to it many times. For him polygyny and gerontocracy went hand-in-hand, they were 'reciprocally dependent'.[22] They also made economic sense. The older men, who were experienced hunters, were at the peak of their economic productivity and were able to sustain a number of wives. As for the women, it was of benefit to them that during their child-bearing and child-rearing years they were able to draw on the assistance of co-wives.

By viewing Groote Eylandt society through a materialist lens, Rose was able to identify what he regarded as 'bias' and misconceptions in the observations made by Westerners, especially in matters of sex and marriage. For him Aboriginal marriage systems were not fundamentally about sex; where conflict occurred it was not driven by sexual jealousy, as Westerners were inclined to believe it must be. Marriage was essentially a reciprocal economic relationship, 'the man primarily providing the meat and the woman the vegetable foodstuffs for themselves and her children'.[23] Consequently, as Rose explained, 'The desire to monopolise the women – or the "jealousy" of the male – is not the origin of the aggregation by a man of a group of co-wives about himself, but rather the reverse, that the aggregation of the co-wives had its origin in "economic" factors and was the origin of this supposed "jealousy" of the male'.[24]

The views Rose adopted by applying a materialist interpretation of Groote Eylandt data were not set in stone. One of the distinctive contributions to the study of polygyny was his work on age, and in particular the age differences between husbands and wives. Where once he had claimed that a man was at his productive peak at the age of forty-two, data gathered by Merv Meggitt in his studies of the Walbiri persuaded Rose to revise his figure down to twenty-six.[25] Data on women, too, caused him to rethink his models. While a woman's biological productivity reached a peak in her mid-20s, her maximum economic productivity might be reached much later, presumably in part when she was free of the burden of looking after offspring.[26] Reaching the peak of productivity in food gathering when she was past that burden, at around the age of forty-five, also seemed to explain why wife-stealing of older women was regarded 'considerably more seriously'.[27]

Rose insisted that his ideas about Aboriginal society were relevant beyond Groote. His view was that the polygynous-gerontocratic society he had observed on the island was in essence repeated in hunter-gatherer societies all over Australia. Indeed, he wanted to argue that that had been the case for tens of thousands of years. It was a case not easily proven, because by the 1960s – and that was his own experience at Angas Downs – polygynous gerontocracy had virtually disappeared in Australia. In one regard that tended to support Rose's argument – take away the economic base, and the social organisation on which it depends soon disappears. But not all Rose's critics would accept his universalising claims, and not all were convinced that the economic base was the sole determinant of social forms.

Another idea Rose developed at some length over a period of decades concerned the 'local group'. All over Australia, he contended, the 'local group' was the basic unit of Aboriginal society. In its prolix, scholarly form the correct term was the 'patrilineal land-owning local group'. For Rose the 'land-owning' element was pivotal, and was one of the reasons he preferred it to 'clan' or the older term 'gens', though both conveyed essentially the same concept of a unilineal aggregate of relatives.[28]

In the Australian context the local group might number anything from ten to a hundred men, woman and children, averaging about forty. It was self-sustaining and able to feed itself from the land it owned (typically something in the region of 400 square miles).[29] The right to use the land was passed down through the generations. That did not mean, however, that the group had exclusive use of the land it owned. Rather, it entered into a kind of association with other such local groups, with which there were complex sets of rights, reciprocities and obligations. Some of those entailed, for example, one group allowing another access to its land and the resources on it.

Marriage was generally considered to be exogamous by the anthropological establishment of the period,[30] which meant that the male members of a local group, while remaining with the group, would marry women from another group. At the time of marriage the female would move to the land, and join the land-owning group of the male, so that the group was essentially 'patrilocal'.[31] However exogamy was not always the norm, as Rose had discovered during his Groote Eylandt fieldwork, a fact which made him concur with Stalin's insistence that Marxism was a sociological rather than a biological science.[32] The resulting classificatory relationships established among land-owning groups could thus be aggregated into what Rose would describe as 'an extraordinarily complicated network linking groups and individuals throughout society'.[33]

For this complex association of local groups, perhaps ten to fifteen of them, and perhaps with a total population of some 400,[34] Rose however resisted the use of the term 'tribe', because in his view that had a particular kind of political connotation. In Australia there was no central political authority in such an association. At most one might speak of a 'dialectical' or 'linguistic tribe', but that was as far as it went.[35] The example he knew best was Groote Eylandt, where he had identified eleven land-owning groups. Collectively the people of the island came to be known as the Anindilyakwa, but there was no form of centralised political authority. And although the insularity of the groups was distinctive, Rose believed that the pattern he observed there could prevail all over the country.[36]

In all of this, both collectively and individually, the local groups' economic relationship to the land was crucial. Rose had come to the view that it was this understanding of the economic importance of the land that was the most crucial of the insights that he and other anthropologists had gained.[37] There was no doubt in his mind that all across Australia a sophisticated system of land ownership existed before colonisation. It was based on the land-owning group's economic relationship to the land, and not, as some tended to believe, on some kind of religious or totemic connection. That is not to say that such connections did not exist, but they were secondary to the economic relationship and determined by it. Of course, in the wake of dispossession the spiritual connection might have been all that was left, a kind of relic or remnant. For Rose, however, to see only these remnants or relics of a former state of society – he sometimes referred to them as 'survivals' – would mislead. What was crucial was to understand the economic base on which any society was built. Only then could current ills be properly diagnosed and strategies to address them formulated.

Aboriginal land ownership was the point where Rose's scholarship and his activism intersected. For most of the 1960s he followed the Australian debates and controversies from afar, wading in as deeply as he could during his visits. While the conservative government clung to power in the early 1970s, and for as long as it would not accede to activists' demands, Wattie Creek remained a focal point of the land rights campaign. By 1972, however, there were clear signs that political momentum in Australia was finally shifting. There seemed every chance that after twenty-three years in the political wilderness a Labor government would win power, a government more sympathetic to Aboriginal demands than any before. For Fred Rose this was all the more reason to pack his bags once more and return to the Antipodes, at the very least for a visit.

27. The Whitlam Years

From the moment of its birth in October 1949, the GDR was an unloved child. It grew up in a stern, single-parent household alongside a number of siblings with similarly ambivalent feelings toward their authoritarian Soviet father. That the siblings got along as well as they did had more to do with necessity than mutual attraction, let alone love. Understandably, then, what the GDR craved over the first decades of its existence was friendship outside the family, but that proved extraordinarily elusive. Even as late as 1970 there were just 29 states that formally recognised the GDR, and they were a motley bunch. There were all the eastern bloc neighbours, of course, and a collection of Middle Eastern states attracted by the GDR's vociferous anti-Zionism. Beyond that, there was pitifully little, and the West was eager to keep it that way.

In its dealings with the wider world, the Federal Republic of Germany imposed the so-called Hallstein Doctrine. In practice this meant that it would sever all ties with any state that extended diplomatic recognition to the GDR. Such was the economic, political and military clout of the Federal Republic that few countries chose to provoke its ire by recognising its eastern neighbour. Officially, the Federal Republic's view was that the GDR was not a state but had always remained merely a zone under Soviet occupation. It expected its international friends to treat the GDR accordingly.

Australia was as firmly integrated into the Western bloc as the GDR was into the East; there was little room for international manoeuvre. Indeed, under the twenty-three years of the conservative government of Menzies and his successors, Australia went to some lengths to demonstrate to its allies its anti-communist *bona fides*. The shabby treatment of Fred Rose during his visits to Australia was just one minor manifestation of that. On a higher level, Australia was careful not to offend its allies' sensibilities, which meant never calling the GDR the GDR, and never having any contact at a ministerial level, since that might be construed as *de facto* recognition.[1]

However, by the end of the 1960s a thaw was setting in, and there were signs that a relationship which had not extended beyond a small volume of trade conducted in an almost clandestine manner was about to develop into something more substantial. Economic necessity was the driver of change. The communist bloc craved access to Western products. Australia was bracing for British accession to the European Economic Community. Crucially, too, there were signs in the Federal Republic of Germany that the days of the Hallstein Doctrine might be numbered.

For as long as the conservatives were in power in Australia, diplomatic recognition of the GDR appeared unlikely, but behind the scenes quiet steps were being taken in that direction. The establishment of an East German trade office was prepared by Canberra bureaucrats. A representative of the GDR's foreign ministry came to visit, and although a meeting with members of the government was out of the question, he nonetheless secured an audience with ACTU leader Bob Hawke, whom he described as 'a progressive left-wing Social Democrat who influences decisively the policies of the ALP, and whose activities are watched closely by the mass media'.[2]

By late 1972 there were signals from Bonn that the Hallstein Doctine would soon be revoked. The last impediment to mutual recognition was the Australian government, and it was soon to face an electorate craving change. On 2 December 1972, the day of the election, an East German delegation arrived in Australia and made it clear that the main item on its agenda was the normalisation of relations between the two states. With Whitlam's success, this was accomplished before the year was out.

Among those keen to congratulate Whitlam on his elevation to the prime ministership was Fred Rose. As an 'expatriate Australian' he offered both warm congratulations and gratuitous advice. He was not, he said, 'suggesting that you endeavour to introduce socialism into Australia but I do suggest that you recognize the realities of international political life'.

Rose's prediction was that when the so-called 'Basic Treaty' between the two Germanys was ratified, there would be a 'flood of recognition of the German Democratic Republic by western countries'.[3] He was right.

On 6 December the GDR delegation met with senior Australian bureaucrats in Canberra, sealing a deal over lunch at the Lakeside Hotel. The Australians had even started thinking about a location for an embassy in East Berlin.[4] A week later another meeting took place, this time in the Rex Hotel, to nail down details of the announcements of mutual recognition.[5] Both sides would wait until the Basic Treaty was signed on 21 December. That courtesy observed, Australia's self-appointed Foreign Minister Gough Whitlam announced the good news.[6]

The paradox was that at this time the CPA had never been in such a parlous state. Through the 1960s it had navigated the treacherous currents of bitter sectarianism. Ted Hill broke away in 1964 to form a pro-Beijing Communist Party of Australia (Marxist–Leninist).[7] That was nothing compared to the ructions triggered by the Soviet invasion of Czechoslovakia in August 1968. Leading CPA figures Laurie Aarons and Rose's longstanding friend Bill Brown, who had once worked in unison, now engaged in a series of bitter denunciations, which opened cracks in the rump party.[8] The powerful group led by Aarons came to the view that the CPA had to break its formal allegiance to the Soviet Union.[9] For Bill Brown's group, that was unthinkable, so they severed ties with the CPA to form the resolutely pro-Soviet, and therefore pro-GDR, Socialist Party of Australia (SPA).

Fred Rose was an SPA man, though not a member. Nonetheless, the whole issue did not make things easy for him, because among the many friends and contacts he still had in the labour movement in Australia, there were considerable numbers on both sides of an ugly divide. The oddest case was perhaps that of his old friends and his Australian hosts Frank and Pat Graham. Frank was now in the SPA, while Pat remained in the CPA.[10]

At least in the ALP things were cheerier, as Whitlam set about implementing his ambitious reform agenda. Rose applauded his early initiatives in foreign policy, but it was Aboriginal affairs that mattered most. The early signs were encouraging, as Whitlam allocated Rose's longstanding friend Gordon Bryant to the Aboriginal Affairs portfolio. There was every expectation, and not just from Rose, that Bryant would drive a vigorous program of reform – all the more reason for Rose to get to Australia, not just to observe but to contribute to the changes already underway.

The groundwork for the first of Rose's two visits to Australia during the Whitlam years was laid well in advance. Now, at last, he was visiting as a resident not of a loathed pariah state but of a fully acknowledged member of the international community. In theory at least, that should have impacted on the way Rose would be treated as an East German visitor to Australia.

In expectation of doing fieldwork in northern Australia, Rose applied for the appropriate permit to enter a reserve even *before* he applied for funding from AIAS. That application was sent to the Director of Welfare in the NT as early as August 1972, with the request that he be permitted to do fieldwork in the period March to October 1973.[11] But by the time his AIAS application was due for submission, he still had no reply. When he received word of a favourable outcome from AIAS, Darwin was still silent. This was not what Rose had envisaged under Labor.

What he did not appreciate at first was that under Whitlam the process of issuing permits had changed. The decision was now up to the local communities in which the proposed visits were to take place, which meant in Rose's case the Aboriginal communities on Groote Eylandt. In mid-April 1973, when Rose was already in England en route to Australia, he got the bad news. Without giving reasons, the chairman of the Combined Aboriginal Communities told Rose he was not welcome on Groote.[12]

Without the permit Rose could not access funding. Gordon Bryant advised that as the people on the island did not want him to visit that year, the best thing would be to remain in Europe 'and await the outcome of the islanders' further deliberations'. A number of the Aboriginal communities, he warned, were 'disaster areas' as a result of 'the inadequacies and misdirected programs of the past'.[13] Even from the other side of the world Rose could smell a rat. The advice to stay away from Groote was a sign 'that the "powers that be" – Giese and his boys and his CMS supporters in Darwin and at the GE mission – have, as I suggested they might do, "manipulated" the Chairman of the combined Aboriginal Council or got him to sign a document that I am persona non grata'.[14]

Rose flew to Australia anyway, arriving on 10 June. Gordon Bryant would, he assumed, be 'without doubt prepared to support me personally'.[15] After a stay in Sydney, where he renewed his union contacts, Rose made his way to Canberra. His old mate the historian Eric Fry, still a member of the CPA, was by this time Dean of the Faculty of Arts at the ANU. The Frys invited Rose to a dinner, attended also by two of the staff from the new GDR embassy.[16]

Although he had friends in high places, Rose's prospects of getting to Groote remained bleak. He flew to Darwin anyway, only to receive a telegram from Groote to the effect that his presence there was not desired. Pressing Bryant to grant him permission at least to fly to Groote and photograph the ruins of the flying-boat base, he was again knocked back. Bryant's hands were tied. The best that the minister could offer was the proverbial turning of a blind eye should Rose proceed with his plan anyway. That, it was clear, was the only option available, and so Rose took it.[17]

Once more he tapped into his union connections. The Groote Eylandt Mining Company (or GEMCO, a subsidiary of BHP) had by now established a large manganese mine on the west coast of the island, not far from the mission station at Angurugu. At any time there was a substantial population of blue-collar workers in the company town of Alyangula. When Rose flew to the island on 17 August, it was with the connivance of Darwin comrades who declared him an auxiliary organiser of the Federated Miscellaneous Workers' Union. If white authorities sought to eject him, industrial action would ensue. What Rose had not reckoned with was the extent to which the 'enemy' had developed the capacity 'to bribe and to manipulate' some of the indigenous leaders on the island. Thus it transpired that Rose was soon sent back to Darwin by local Aborigines. With no prospect of doing any useful fieldwork in the Territory, Rose headed to Canberra, where he would unburden his frustration on the minister.

Bryant was prepared to listen, but also to talk. He gave Rose to understand that he was having problems of his own.[18]

In fact, Bryant was experiencing more than just a few irritations in his portfolio; his days as Minister for Aboriginal Affairs were numbered. Whitlam had taken the view that Bryant had been running his ministry as a personal fiefdom, appointing family and friends to positions in his office and department. There was, Whitlam at one point confided to then Governor-General Sir Paul Hasluck, 'no worse minister than Gordon Bryant'.[19] In a Cabinet reshuffle in October 1973, while Fred Rose was still in the country, Bryant's ministry was handed to Jim Cavanagh. The rap across Bryant's knuckles was delivered in the form of his appointment as Minister for the Capital Territory.

Relieved of any obligation to protect his friend's position, Rose now gave full vent to his anger, firing off letters to both the *Age* and the *Australian*. Neither was published. Although Queensland senator George Georges was typically sympathetic, sympathy alone did not help much.[20] Privately, too, Rose harboured resentments. In his view the support that communists had given Aborigines in their struggle for basic rights had not been adequately acknowledged. The trenchantly anti-communist element of Aboriginal activism, keenly cultivated by Wentworth in his days as minister, maintained its views and its influence into the Whitlam years. Rose's deep suspicion was that Aboriginal activism had been hijacked by elements determined to ensure that communism did not gain a foothold in the movement. The defining characteristics of those elements, in Rose's view, were black chauvinism, leftist radicalism and even traces of anarchism. Altogether unhealthy and unpropitious, too, was a tendency within the movement to distance itself from the white working class.[21] A process of 'class differentiation' was underway, in which the establishment cultivated the emergence of a black middle class out of touch with the needs of their black brothers. As a consequence the solidarity among those exploited by capitalism was being eroded, to the detriment of the great majority of Aboriginal Australians.[22]

The second of Rose's visits to Australia during the Whitlam years began a week before Christmas 1974. Its preparation was auspicious. Hannah Middleton now had a lectureship in sociology at the University of New South Wales. The Whitlam government had been re-elected in May of that year; it appeared that it still had time to implement its ambitious reform program. And Rose himself benefited from the extra funding that Whitlam was investing in the arts. He had received a grant from the Literature Board, a forerunner of the Australia Council, to support his travel and research.

It was not the first time Rose had requested such a grant. In the pre-Whitlam era, in 1972, he had applied for a similar grant from what was then the Commonwealth Literary Fund. He must have known that for political reasons alone his application had the odds stacked against it. Four years earlier Frank Hardy had been recommended for such an award by the Fund's advisory board, only to have the decision overturned by Bill Snedden on the grounds of Hardy's communism, though Hardy was by this time veering toward renegade status.[23] For his 1972 attempt Rose had made contact with Peter Ryan at Melbourne University Press, the prospective publisher of the book Rose proposed on his early Groote Eylandt experiences. Ryan, who was to distinguish himself many years later by trashing Manning Clark's reputation after Clark had died, was encouraging. He advised Rose to write to the Fund's chair Geoffrey Blainey, which Rose duly did. The submission, which listed Dymphna Cusack and Nugget Coombs as referees, failed.[24]

Under Whitlam matters were different. The Literature Board took over the functions of the Commonwealth Literary Fund and received a generous injection of funds. Rose's fresh application was much like the last; the intended outcome a book published by Ryan at MUP. The grant enabled him to do archival work in Canberra, Melbourne and Brisbane. As it turned out, he did not have time to finish the book during his stay, but he undertook to deliver a completed manuscript by the end of 1975.[25]

Events in East Germany had also facilitated this second visit so soon after the first. The ultimata he had been delivering to Kurt Hager and others had finally achieved their goal. A way was found to avoid the embarrassment of Rose's departure to the West, though not by offering him a position with the Academy of the Sciences. Instead, he was given a research post at the Museum für Völkerkunde in Leipzig. It meant incurring a substantial decrease from his professorial salary at the Humboldt, but for Rose it was never about the money. The financial loss was more than compensated by the freedom he gained from the administrative tasks, the teaching duties and the petty politicking in Berlin. Moreover the Leipzig position was regulated by an individual contract, an *Einzelvertrag*, which enabled him to take on whatever research interests he chose without a supervisor breathing down his neck. It would also allow him to pursue his interests in Australia.

As ever, some of them were political, and in principle the Leipzig post should have helped Rose expand his activism in Australia. From the other side of the world and behind the Iron Curtain, it had been difficult enough just to keep in touch with Australian politics, let alone make a sustained and meaningful intervention in them. That had long been a source of frustration for a man so committed to the concept that his work should make a difference. There was all the more reason, then, to make his voice heard in Australia now that there was finally a government that might listen.

There were those inextricably linked scholarly interests, too, to advance. Apart from the work promised to MUP under the working title 'Ripples in the Gulf', he planned a second manuscript on the history and politics of Aboriginal Australia. It would be a kind of sequel to the CPA's 1967 policy statement on indigenous issues, updated in accordance with the requirements of the SPA, the breakaway party to which Rose now owed his allegiance.[26]

Hannah Middleton had similar intentions, indeed she had been working on such a book since taking up her job at UNSW. When Rose arrived in Australia, Middleton was in London on holiday, but she had left her manuscript for him to read, which he did immediately. Middleton was now a mature academic, intellectually and emotionally independent. Rose, on the other hand, found it difficult to retreat from his mentoring role. He not only suggested revisions to the manuscript, but when it was completed he arranged for it to be printed in the GDR. The book finally appeared in May 1977 under the title *But Now We Want the Land Back* and with the publishing moniker New Age Publishers. It staked the bold claim to be 'the first Marxist analysis of the history and present-day situation of the Australian Aborigines' and to provide 'essential reading for anyone committed to justice and equality for the Aboriginal people of Australia'.[27] Middleton was listed as the sole author, while Rose's thinking on Aboriginal land rights at the time found expression in his book *Australien und seine Einwohner: Ihre Geschichte und Gegenwart* (Australia and its inhabitants: their history and present).[28]

In a lecture Rose delivered to the Young Socialist League on 16 March he revisited another of his favourite topics, 'The Petrov Conspiracy'. Through two decades it had been an issue with a brooding presence in Rose's psyche and had fundamentally shaped his life. Prompted or otherwise, it was a common subject of conversation, and he was discovering that in Australia, too, there was a renewed interest in the episode. Gough Whitlam's son Nicholas had just published a book on the topic, which contained a photograph of Rose. The line Rose took in his public utterances was that the scandal had been a conspiracy concocted by conservative and capitalist interests, a cunningly sophisticated example of anti-Soviet propaganda.[29]

Indigenous politics, too, were never far from his mind, yet for all the initial enthusiasm, his final assessment of the Whitlam era was deeply ambivalent. On the one hand, things had clearly changed; in rhetoric, policy and practice, the Whitlam government invested in Aboriginal issues like no government before it. One event above all others lent that process symbolic weight. The passing of the *Aboriginal Land Fund Act* of 1974 finally enabled the Gurindji people to purchase a large pastoral lease of some 3000 square kilometres, while Vesteys acquired a lease to what remained of the original Wave Hill station.[30] In August of the following year Whitlam travelled to Wattie Creek, where he famously poured Gurindji soil into the hand of Vincent Lingiari. As he did so he made a brief and simple speech, written by Nugget Coombs: 'Vincent Lingiari, I solemnly hand to you these deeds as proof in Australian law that these lands belong to the Gurindji people, and I put into your hands part of the earth as a sign that this land will be the possession of you and your children forever.'[31]

Fred Rose was among those not convinced that this simple act had laid the land rights issue to rest. His own experiences on Groote Eylandt, and the sacking of his mate Gordon Bryant, suggested that not all was as it should be and that promises remained unmet. Worse than that, it seemed to him that the blocking of progress had come about through the government's own connivance and prevarication. A case in point was the much vaunted National Aboriginal Consultative Committee, in Rose's eyes a toothless tiger, little more than a forum for discussion, imposing no other obligation on whites than to listen politely.

Another was the Aboriginal Land Rights Commission, also known as the Woodward Royal Commission after its chair, Justice Edward Woodward. Set up by Whitlam on the basis of a pre-election promise in 1972 to investigate Aboriginal land rights in the Northern Territory, the commission seemed to offer much. Woodward recommended that Aboriginal reserve lands should be returned to their Aboriginal inhabitants and that Aborigines had a claim to other vacant crown land if they could demonstrate a connection to it. Aboriginal land councils should be set up to administer that land and regulate access to it by mining or tourism concerns. In effect, mining could proceed on Aboriginal land only with the express approval of the traditional owners, who would be entitled to royalty payments. That principle would not, however, apply to existing projects on Aboriginal reserves, and that included GEMCO's manganese mine on Groote Eylandt.[32] As it happened, the Whitlam government was ejected from office before the land rights legislation flowing from Woodward's commission could be enacted. It was left to the Fraser government to reintroduce a bill, which was not signed into law until December 1976.

None of this went far enough in Fred Rose's view. For him it was the economic dimension of the land rights issue that was crucial. The pseudo-scientific blather of 'bourgeois' anthropologists and others about the Aborigines' 'spiritual' connection to the land was an irrelevance. To return the land to the Aborigines, and not the right to exploit its economic potential, was at best a limited victory, at worst an unconscionable surrender to capitalist mining interests.[33] Rose argued that the solution lay neither in imposing on Aborigines a Western model of private land ownership nor in granting them the capacity to dispose of it. Rather, what he thought they really wanted and would benefit them most was a permanent form of ownership without the option of selling. In his view they understood all too well that a capitalist form of private ownership would inevitably mean that land would pass into the hands of wealthy white people. His warning was clear: 'What the colonist achieved with violence in the past, the mining company would seek to achieve today by more sophisticated legal means.'[34]

With that, though, he was already back in the GDR, and little more than an observer from afar, rather than a participant in the events that really moved him.

28. Leipzig

To a research anthropologist, even one whose specialist interest was in distant Australia, Leipzig had a lot to offer. At the Museum für Völkerkunde Fred Rose had ready access to the kind of ethnographic collection long lost to East Berlin. It was impressive for its size and range, its provenance covering all corners of the globe. Founded in 1869, just before German unification, the Leipzig museum counted among its benefactors Heinrich Schliemann, the 'discoverer' of ancient Troy. Tragically the building that housed it on the edge of the city centre was badly damaged in World War II, a fifth of the collection lost forever. But the GDR authorities rebuilt and re-opened the museum, and it became, with the museum in Dresden, one of the country's showcase ethnographic institutions.

For its Australian collection the Leipzig museum had to thank one remarkable woman in particular, Amalie Dietrich. The Saxon-born naturalist had been charged by the Hamburg merchant J.C. Godeffroy with collecting for his private museum, which she did in exemplary fashion for almost a decade from 1863, primarily in the mosquito-infested heat of tropical Queensland. While much of her attention was devoted to flora and fauna – among her achievements was the dissection of a 6.7 metre crocodile at the Fitzroy River – she also evinced a keen ethnographic eye.[1] When the vicissitudes of the German economy propelled the Hamburgers to part with the fruits of Dietrich's labours, it was Leipzig that benefitted.

For Fred Rose the Leipzig years from 1974 were a time of a freedom unparalleled in his working life. By the terms of his contract, he was answerable neither to the museum's director at that time, Wolfgang König, nor to König's successor Lothar Stein. The work did not even bind him to the museum, with the result that he shared his time between Berlin and Leipzig. If there was any lingering disgruntlement that he had not gained the long hoped-for post with the Academy of the Sciences, it did not show. He soon made friends with his new colleagues at the museum, where he played the role of the 'dinkum' Australian, donning his corked hat on festive occasions and regaling all those who would listen with tales of adventure Down Under.

Distance from Edith was no drawback. In 1972 Edith had finally left the house in Kleinmachnow. She and Fred moved into an apartment in Berlin's inner-eastern district of Lichtenberg. Like all their living arrangements, in Australia as in Germany, it was modest bordering on spartan – Fred and Edith had never attached importance to material comforts. In this case the place they were allocated was quite new, an archetypal East German *Plattenbau* dwelling in the Schulze-Boysen-Strasse. The address was named after a Nazi-era resistance hero, in Fred's case an apposite one. Harro Schulze-Boysen, just a few years older than Rose, came from a conservative family background but threw in his lot during the Third Reich with the left-wing resistance group Red Orchestra. It cost him his life when the Gestapo discovered that Schulze-Boysen was sending sensitive military intelligence to the Soviets.

Cohabitation did little for Fred and Edith's failing marriage, which Fred took as the subject of a letter he wrote to Edith in November 1974, on the eve of a visit to Australia. He claimed that he did not wish the letter to provoke rancour or accusations of blame, but the truth was that for at least a decade they had had no sexual relations, yet neither had raised the issue for discussion. Over that time, he said, 'our marriage has de facto not existed', and now it needed to be discussed.[2] The reason they had stayed together, he suggested, was because it seemed in the children's best interests, though with the benefit of hindsight that seemed a dubious logic. Had he returned to Australia, as he intended until the middle of 1973, then Edith would probably have remained in the GDR; in effect they would have separated. Now that he had resolved to remain in the GDR, the question of their relationship could no longer be swept under the carpet. Things had to change, and, as he put it with reasoned egocentricity, 'the effectiveness of my intellectual work (and this includes both scientific and political work) depends very largely on "normal" or at least reasonable sex-relations, which, as you are well aware, just do not exist between us'. Divorce, he insisted, was the only option.[3]

He tried to soften the blow. Their social relations, he envisaged, would continue as before. As their sexual relations had in any case already come to an end, little would change. Financially he would continue to pay his part for the joint household.[4] As for the formal legal requirements, he had already made enquiries and established two possibilities. They could proceed either through an East German or an Australian court. The latter would require little to be done. As he understood the situation after the Whitlam government's changes to family law, the prolonged absence of sexual relations alone would suffice to secure a divorce. The East German option would require Edith to support her husband's application. This was the cheaper and easier alternative, the one he preferred, but Edith would have to cooperate.[5]

He also informed Edith that in the interests of transparency he would provide copies of the letter to Sonja and Ruth. Nita and Kim, on the other hand, need not yet be told; the latter in any case had become in his view something of an 'outsider' to the family. What he did not divulge to Edith was that a copy of the letter was also given to the Stasi, so that it would be aware of the situation in the Rose family.[6]

In reality the 'frankness' of Rose's proposal to his wife was itself a mask. There was another reason he wanted a quick divorce, one on which the Stasi, but not Edith, was well informed. Rose was pursuing yet another extra-marital relationship. At first he had not been candid about it with his handler. But, as was its way, the Stasi found out. The woman in question was Gudrun M. Born in 1944, she was nearly three decades his junior. When Rose met her she had recently ceased working as an interpreter. The Stasi's fear was that she was planning to flee the GDR to study in the West, possibly Paris. Its blunt assessment of the relationship was that it would go nowhere. The IM, the handler noted, 'is some 30 years older than M. and has already had numerous extra-marital relationships with younger female persons. The IM currently assumes that he exercises a great influence on M. and can prevent her from taking ill-considered steps. It has to be taken into account that the IM appears to be in the thrall of M. and wants to divorce his wife so that he can move in with her'.[7]

While Rose was trying to assure his handler that he had the situation under control, and that he would restore his young lover's faith in socialism, the handler was appropriately incredulous. He knew Rose's proclivities and weaknesses all too well: 'Based on the IM's past experiences of such relationships one must conclude that after a certain time the female persons extract themselves from the IM's influence and the IM's interest also evaporates.' The instruction given Rose was to keep his handler informed of Gudrun M.'s intentions. It was also impressed on him that his relationship with her posed a number of dangers for him.[8] Whether it was because he heeded the Stasi's dire warnings or for other reasons, Rose did not move in with M., and the relationship seems to have run its course.

What is not clear is whether the Stasi might also have known of yet another lover, who in Rose's later correspondence goes simply by the name Ingrid F. There are few traces of her, except that Rose by his own admission pursued a relationship with her in the period 1973 to 1975. The liaison, and with it the thoughts of marriage, fell apart when Ingrid's manic depression manifested itself with growing severity.[9]

The divorce from Edith proceeded, but at a leisurely pace; it was finally granted on 30 March 1976. Fred again considered a permanent move to Australia and a rekindling of the relationship with Hannah Middleton, but she felt more ambivalent about that prospect than he, with the result that that idea, too, came to nought.[10] Rose's consoling words to Edith that their divorce would change very little proved more accurate than he had hoped. There was by now little stigma attached to it, as on both sides of the Iron Curtain divorce rates climbed.[11] In any case, those who had no more than a fleeting acquaintance with the Roses would have had little inkling that they were no longer a married couple. Fred had no reason to leave the marital apartment. Some of the time, in any case, he was in Leipzig. When in Berlin, one of the rooms in the apartment served as his bedroom and office, where he banged away as furiously as ever at his typewriter. In time he and Edith would even be able to share the luxury of their own telephone, another reason to stay put.

In Rose's relationship with the Stasi, too, the status quo was preserved, at least for a time. All the signs were that he performed his work as keenly as ever, and the Stasi took the trouble to acknowledge his devotion. On the 25th anniversary of the founding of the GDR in 1974 he was awarded a silver medal 'For Loyal Service'.[12] Of course, a Stasi medal was not the sort of thing to pin on one's chest and wear in public, but it might well have added a spring to his step. After Rose had openly contemplated a permanent move to Australia, there was a desire to make him feel at home in the GDR, and how better to express it?

Rose's IM activity had been boosted by a flurry of diplomatic activity. After Whitlam extended formal recognition at the end of 1972, the GDR was serviced for a time from the existing Australian Embassy in Warsaw. Then a provisional embassy was installed in Tschaikowski Strasse in the district of Niederschönhausen, until a new embassy was built in the Grabbeallee in Pankow. The new ambassador was Malcolm Morris, the man who had once lived at Rose's old address in Canberra, and who would accompany the Roses and the Whitlams on their night at the opera in 1976. Morris had commenced his Berlin tenure in December 1975, just weeks after the unceremonious unseating back in Australia of the man who had created the job.

The Stasi did its homework on Morris. An unnamed source – it may well have been Rose – engaged in a detailed conversation with the Australian diplomat Phillip Peters in early 1976 to find out more about the new ambassador. Peters had done his bit in Canberra in 1972 to clinch the deal which assured the mutual diplomatic recognition of Australia and the GDR. Having also served stints at the Australian Military Mission in West Berlin and the embassy in Bonn, he had been sent to East Berlin to set up the new embassy in preparation for the new ambassador's arrival and had an accurate idea of who his new boss was. Morris appeared a wise choice. He had spent four years in Vienna, which meant he spoke good German, but he boasted other German credentials as well. In the last year of the war he had been attached as a British liaison officer to Soviet forces on the Eastern Front. More specifically, he was placed with the staff of the Red Army's Marshal Konstantin Rokossovsky, whose forces on the Second Belorussian Front were tasked with pushing across northern Germany to link up with Field Marshal Bernard Montgomery's British forces. Morris's brief had been to ensure the transfer of British – including Australian – POWs liberated by the Soviets into British hands. His other job was to ensure that when the Red Army and Montgomery's forces met, they did not shoot at one another.[13] With that experience behind him, Morris knew Germany and the Soviets well, and he had proved he could keep a cool head.

Rose became familiar with Morris and the embassy, largely because he saw it as his job to report on both to the Stasi. Visits to Morris and the embassy's library enabled him to put together a detailed plan of the building, which he passed to his handlers. He attended functions as an invited guest – he was, after all, the most prominent of the 'Australians' living in the GDR. But Rose was doubly useful in this kind of role. As the holder of a British passport he also paid visits to the British embassy on Unter den Linden, passing on to his handlers plans of the layout of that building too.[14]

Then there were the diplomatic representatives on the other side of the Berlin Wall. In 1974 the Australian Military Mission was relocated from the Olympic complex to central West Berlin; the Deputy Head of Mission who now ran it, Kieran Desmond, was also designated a consul general. He had a deputy, 'Heidi Manne', a freshly minted University of Melbourne law graduate in her first posting. She would go on to become UNHCR Assistant High Commissioner, but in 1974 her career was just beginning, and she was happy to broaden her horizons by agreeing to visit Fred Rose on the eastern side of the Wall. The designated meeting place was the Café Moskau, but as it was full at the nominated time, Rose invited 'Manne' to his apartment in the Schulze-Boysen-Strasse. He told his handler later that she had not been keen on the idea, but when he assured her 'that he would not compromise her either as diplomat or as a woman', she agreed. From the apartment she could see a complex of modern high-rise buildings in nearby Normannenstrasse. She asked Rose what it was, but it was clear to him that she was already well aware of what nefarious operations were performed there – it was Stasi headquarters. In the end, she might well have extracted just as much information from him as he did from her.[15] And dutifully she reported her 'contact with communist personnel' to her superiors.[16]

In the Stasi's view much that Rose did was exemplary, and it said so.[17] But there were problems. He had limited expert knowledge of issues relating to embassies and their security. His German was flawed; there was a string of personal problems stemming from his vexed relations with his son and his lovers.[18] Rose, the handler believed, was inclined to overestimate his attractiveness to young women; the relationship strains that inevitably arose came with a great psychological cost.[19] Directorate XX decided to drop him. In May 1977 he was moved sideways into Directorate II, dedicated to counter-intelligence, and to a new handler, Lieutenant Beyer.[20] Rose would do the same kinds of things he had done earlier, and with as much relish.

Edith's role also changed, for a number of reasons. The main one was that in June 1973 she took on a job as a translator working for the Allgemeiner Deutscher Nachrichtendienst, the ADN, which was the GDR's state-run news agency.[21] It was quite a privileged position, as workers had access to information received by the agency, before it was censored and disseminated – or not – through the East German press. But it came with a disadvantage that impacted on Edith's role as an IM. ADN workers' travel freedoms were restricted, even for a time after they left the service. Edith was as willing as ever to do as requested in her West Berlin 'operational area', but even as a holder of a foreign passport she was restricted to just one visit across the Wall per year.[22]

Accordingly the Stasi changed her status. From 1975 she was designated an IMK, a particular kind of IM. Her role was in counter-intelligence, and her specific brief was to snoop around for any suspicion of conspiratorial activity that might pose a security threat.[23] Her field of operations was now east of the Berlin Wall, which meant that she, like Fred, reported on activities in the newly established British and Australian embassies.

For Edith, as for Fred, a highlight in this period would have been the night at the opera with the Whitlams in the summer of 1976. The Roses' companions might have suspected that Fred would pass on the contents of their discussion to the Stasi, but were perhaps less inclined to impugn the meekly mannered Edith with such base motives. Nonetheless, at Edith's next meeting with her handler, she too reported on the course of that evening at the opera, recalling that she and Fred had been greeted at the entrance to the opera house by Roger Pescott. Morris, she noted, always sat at some distance from Whitlam, who throughout the evening was seated close to Fred; the two were engaged in lively conversation.[24]

In the reports that Fred and Edith filed on matters closer to home, the downward spiral of their only son's life was a disquieting leitmotif. Tensions arose at his workplace in the Academy of the Sciences and remained unresolved. Kim was accused of being unpunctual; it was suspected he drank heavily. For his part Kim was offended by the requirement that as a Westerner he was refused access to the academy's computer centre.[25] Nonetheless, it came as a shock when he was sacked from his job at the beginning of 1977, charged with breaching work discipline and 'dismissed with immediate effect'.[26] It was difficult to escape the conclusion that the charge was little more than a pretext to end his career, and that the Stasi was behind it. Like all intelligence agencies, the Stasi had a long memory; in all likelihood it had neither forgotten nor forgiven Kim's rebuff several years earlier.

In the GDR everyone was guaranteed work, and from that time Kim was able to make do with a range of part-time jobs while he spent more time mixing with what passed in the GDR for a bohemian set. Fred offered to help Kim financially if he would seek treatment for his drinking problem. He also devised a plan for Kim to stay with Nita, who was studying psychology, in the hope that she might be able to extract him from his malaise. In the end, none of this bore fruit, but every stage of Kim's tragic downward spiral was faithfully reported to the Stasi.

Then there was Sonja, who for a long time had been working toward a future elsewhere. A nadir was reached in the mid-1970s, when the Stasi shared with Edith the suspicion that her daughter and son-in-law were working for the British.[27] Edith obediently undertook to test the claim. The Stasi had Sonja's apartment bugged. Edith's role was to visit her daughter and son-in-law and engage them in conversation. Whether Edith knew of the bugging was unclear; she could in any case be relied on to deliver accurate renditions of the conversations.[28]

Fred was no different. In 1979 Sonja did move West with her husband and children, initially to West Germany. When her father crossed the border to visit her, as he did on a number of occasions, Sonja asked him to deliver letters for her on his return to East Berlin. He could easily put East German stamps on them when he returned home. Rose agreed, and suggested that to avoid difficulties on re-entering the GDR, the letters should remain unsealed until he had crossed the border. Before sealing, stamping and posting them, as he had promised, he photographed them and handed the full collection of photos to the Stasi.[29]

Edith's relationship with the Stasi took yet another turn, mainly because of her divorce. It was her much more genial husband who cultivated the relationships with the diplomats, the visiting dignitaries and sundry others. Divorce meant that Edith's capacity to cultivate such relations atrophied. In 1978 the Stasi formally ceased its relationship with IMK 'Miller'.[30] In the language of the Stasi, Edith, like Kim before her, was 'archived'.[31] At least for now.

While one door was shutting for Edith, another opened for Fred. Once more it was Eros who was beckoning him inside. His new lover, 'Anna Wittmann', was barely in her twenties, some forty-five years younger than Rose. He first met her when, fresh from school, she commenced working at the museum in Leipzig. A shared fascination with Australia meant their paths crossed intellectually. As they collaborated on an article on Oenpelli painting, Rose was flattered to learn that 'Anna' had read his books while still a school student, and that despite her youth she was herself the author of a children's book on Australian and Oceanic myths of Australia and Oceania.[32]

There were many echoes of Rose's earlier relationships with young women. Like Hannah Middleton, 'Anna' was highly intelligent and passionately committed to her subject. Intellectually she allowed herself to be guided by Rose deep into the arcane world of Australian Aboriginal culture, but she was an intellectual sparring partner as well as an acolyte. Further co-publications followed, and, in time, so too did sex.

Unfailingly the scientist, Rose brought his knowledge and analytical mind to bear in evaluating his blossoming romance. He had observed relationships with such yawning age gaps in Aboriginal Australia; he had read of gerontocracies prevailing in many different periods in numerous parts of the world. And while he was acutely aware that the gap measured in decades between 'Anna' and himself would inevitably be viewed with abhorrence in some quarters on both sides of the Iron Curtain, rationally he persuaded himself that it *could* work, because in other places and times it *had*. And though he had not himself had sexual relations with Aborigines, he had observed them closely enough to know that both men and women 'until ripe old age virtually until they were ready to die led a full and regular sex life'.[33]

As if the pursuit of this unconventional relationship alone did not raise enough eyebrows, in 1983 it became evident that 'Anna' was pregnant. In early July she gave birth to a baby boy. Rose was not married to 'Anna' but did not hesitate in offering regular maintenance payments. The Stasi, as ever, knew all about it and fully shared his assumption that he was the father of yet another 'Frederick'.[34]

29. The Unravelling

As Rose approached the conventional retirement age of 65 in 1980, his academic colleagues and friends felt it was time to honour his achievements. To this end, Ken Maddock from Macquarie University and David Turner from the University of Toronto decided to assemble a volume of essays. In its conception, the editors insisted, this was to be no ordinary *Festschrift*. Contributors were 'free to disagree and to criticize'; the collection should be 'an assessment of the importance and fertility' of Rose's work.[1] The papers were collected, edited and sent off to AIATSIS to be reviewed for publication. And that is where it ended.[2]

Peter Worsley, Rose's long-time friend and anthropological protégé, was approached to write the preface and an essay. Worsley by now had a chair in sociology at the University of Manchester, had become a bestselling author, noted among many other achievements for introducing the term 'Third World' into English.[3] Politically he and Rose had grown apart, but the bonds of friendship had not been broken. They had remained regular correspondents, and Worsley was happy to meet the request to contribute to the *Festschrift*. Putting the history of communism into perspective after the Soviet repressions of 1956 and 1968, in his draft preface Worsley harked back to his more idealistic Canberra days:

> It is worth recalling that despite our (partial) illusions about the USSR my comrades in Canberra were singularly humane and decent people, dedicated to improving the lot of their fellow men, and commonly pleasant and creative personalities. This is not to excuse bad faith, or to justify the adoption of unacceptable means in pursuit of noble ends. Nearly all of them, a little later, were to walk out of the communist Party precisely

because they did believe in socialist values. But neither did they relapse into that other bad faith: the denunciation of 'the God that failed' and the concomitant renunciation of any effort to overcome exploitation and inequality.[4]

Rose was shell-shocked. With a stroke of the pen, Worsley had insinuated that by remaining a card-carrying communist Rose had abandoned his 'socialist values'. To make things worse, elements of the chapter Worsley submitted also touched a raw nerve. Rose could not believe his old Marxist comrade could use the term 'East Germany' instead of 'German Democratic Republic'. 'Such a cheap political jibe', Rose grumbled in a draft letter to Worsley, 'might be appropriate in a political pamphlet, but it defeats its own purpose in a *Festschrift*, which after all, is a scientific work, or at least, is assumed to be'.[5] Incredulous that a scholar of Worsley's standing and integrity might have resorted to such a tactic, Rose wondered if a third party had injected these offensive 'insertions' into Worsley's article?[6]

Rose agonised long and hard over how to approach the matter, consulting with colleagues in Berlin and Leipzig and registering his objections with Turner and Maddock.[7] He decided that the thing to do was to travel to Manchester and discuss the problem with Worsley in person.[8]

It was to no avail. When Rose was back in Berlin, Worsley wrote to inform him that he would not be making the changes Rose had requested. More than that, he expanded on the differences that had opened up between them:

Litvinov once said that peace was indivisible; well, so is freedom of thought and expression. There's too ready a tendency to dump overboard rights won over centuries of struggle as being 'merely' bourgeois ... any socialism which is worthy of the name ought to expand them and extend them. The failure to do so is why 3000 people a day are leaving Cuba – and they're not all criminals and bourgeois intellectuals. I fully realize that I would have to take a pragmatic position if I lived elsewhere. But I don't so I won't.[9]

Rose's rejoinder was no less passionate:

The concept of freedom expressed in your letter coming from a self-designated Marxist is quite frankly most extraordinary as is the typical open-ended so-called 'freedom' propaganda which is pumped out 24 hours a day over the BBC and 24 hours a day over the Voice of America. Granted, in the way it is presented it has a seductive appeal, but I am astonished that you as a Marxist should fall for it! . . . Objectively you are taking the same position as those who persecuted you (and me) in the 1950s.[10]

It was never sent. Labelled 'Draft – Not Used', it was stored in Rose's folder as a reminder of the gulf that was widening between erstwhile comrades.

Without Rose's explicit endorsement, the *Festschrift* could not proceed. Rose mulled over it at great length, and the more he mulled, the more he convinced himself that some nefarious forces were at play. To get to the bottom of them, he arranged to meet with Turner, who was travelling in Europe. Their *tête-a-tête*, staged aboard a train travelling across Holland, did nothing to allay Rose's fears.[11] He began to suspect 'a classic case of CIA activity, stretching across several continents . . . designed apparently for the sole purpose of corrupting me'.[12]

And there the matter stayed, Rose never expressing the required approval of the *Festschrift*, leaving Turner and Maddock perplexed and unable to proceed with publication, and in all likelihood mystified at Rose's attitude. His conspiracy theory received another frank airing when he was interviewed on the ABC by Robyn Williams. The interview offered Rose the opportunity for the kind of theatrically provocative performance he craved, and he was determined to make the most of it. As so often in the past, stretching back as far as the royal commission, the role he chose for himself was that of the aggrieved party. He told his host,

I knew about this Festschrift probably about 1980 and, at that time I was being groomed as I was before 1954 for the Petrov Affair. I was being groomed in a rather similar way and this Festschrift actually turned out to be flattery which was probably organised, or at least taken into the hands of the CIA in order to exert flattery on me, possibly in an attempt to turn me into a dissident. That is a tactic of the CIA in order to encourage dissidents from (scientists in) the socialist countries.[13]

An incredulous Williams had gone to the trouble of contacting the prospective publisher, AIAS, to find out why, against Rose's putative expectations, the book had not appeared. The answer, he told his listeners, was that a standard assessment process had been followed and fears expressed 'that it would be a very technical book and would be hard to sell'. For Williams it was all an academic 'storm in a tea-cup'; the moral he drew from the story was 'that people in the eastern bloc are worried about being tempted to become dissidents'.[14]

Williams' throwaway line misjudged Rose, who was certainly no prospective dissident, but it points to a deeper truth. While the performance might have had clear echoes of 1954, this time there was a crucial difference. Back then there was very good reason for him to believe that there were forces out to 'get him'. There were. But in 1983 Rose's theory that the CIA had concocted an elaborate plot to embarrass him was not just implausible but completely deluded.

The truth was that in the intervening decades Rose had succumbed to a form of Cold War-induced paranoia. In his private and professional life, he could not shake the idea that he was being watched, that somewhere, somehow, a plot was being hatched targeted quite specifically at *him*. Visions of the CIA lurking in the background, the trip to Manchester to confront Worsley, the strange meeting with David Turner on a train in Holland, the interview with an incredulous Robyn Williams – all were indications of a man who felt himself permanently in a state of siege.

The origins of Rose's paranoia might be traced back as far as 1935, to that prison-cell in Mainz, and the horrible realisation that the Gestapo had taken more than a passing interest in him. Later it was shaped by the unflinching attention directed to him by ASIO: the surveillance of his home, tailing by agents, interception of his mail and tapping of his phone, leading finally to his implication in the Petrov scandal and the glare of the public spotlight during the royal commission. How could any individual emerge unscathed from all of that?

It did not stop there. Issued the invitation to participate in the murky world of espionage, Rose had accepted it and for many years reported on family, friends, colleagues and strangers with no sign of compunction or regret. So when he posed himself the question, as by now he perpetually did, whether some sinister agency might be following his every move, seeking to snare him in some kind of trap, he habitually answered in the affirmative. It was entirely feasible, he believed, that someone might be trying to do exactly that. After all, that was what he did; it was the world in which he had chosen to live.

The truth about the whole *Festschrift* episode was potentially more discomfitting for Rose than the paranoid delusions he conjured. While he grasped every opportunity to present his views on politics and anthropology to whatever public he could muster, there were ever fewer listening. And all the signs indicate that by the 1980s neither the CIA nor ASIO thought him worthy of attention, let alone of an elaborate plot to embarrass him.

The Williams interview was conducted in 1983, eight years after Rose's previous visit to Australia. By this time Sonja had moved from West Germany to Australia with her sons. While her initial move West had caused Rose embarrassment, the relocation to Australia brought tangible benefits – he now had cheap, guaranteed accommodation in Canberra. On the political front, too, things had changed. Rose's absence coincided with the Fraser years. The return of Labor under Hawke, however, was no cause for celebration. Indeed there was an eerie echo of 1954 and the Petrov Affair. Soon after Rose's return a Soviet diplomat, Valery Ivanov, was expelled by the 'Israeli sympathizer' Hawke, 'obviously at the behest of Australia's USA masters'. The accusation was that Ivanov was a KGB agent who had compromised David Combe, a former national secretary of the ALP.[15] As in the time of Petrov, the government would soon respond to the exposure of a spy by staging a commission of inquiry, which concluded that Combe had indeed been a Soviet target.

Rose was once more exploring the possibility that he might move permanently to Australia. But what would he live on? The answer seemed simple. He had worked for seventeen years as a Commonwealth public servant and paid his taxes; he was entitled to an old age pension. Canberra's bureaucracy begged to differ. It argued that Rose did not qualify for a pension because he was not a 'permanent resident within the meaning of the Social Security Act'. Rose found this line of argument spurious in the extreme and convinced himself that yet another conspiracy was at play.[16] It was an argument he could not win, but it dragged on for a number of years, until an astonished Sonja received a phone call from Gough Whitlam to ask her to tell her father that he could no longer help him, as he had been out of the law business for too long.[17] Rose would not live out his final years in Australia.

For four months at the end of 1986 and early 1987 Rose visited again, spending most of his time in Canberra but making trips to Brisbane, Sydney, Melbourne and Adelaide. ASIO, it appears, either did not know of the visit or had decided that the septuagenarian did not warrant attention.[18] The Stasi for its part was still prepared to hear what he had to say on his return. Where earlier he had bemoaned Hawke's unprincipled compromises with big business, the Murdoch press and the US military, he now identified the emergence of a 'New Right' in Australian politics. He based his assessment on his own exposure to the media, pausing to praise the relative independence of the *Canberra Times*, but also on conversations he had had. Among his interlocutors were the Sydney economic historians Ken Buckley and Ted Wheelwright, as well as Nugget Coombs, whom Rose had known since 1947, and who was still deeply engaged in Aboriginal issues. Rose reported that Coombs, too, found the political situation in Australia 'thoroughly reactionary'. In their discussion of the plight of the Aborigines, Rose detected in Coombs's comments 'almost a trace of pessimism'.[19]

Though she still lived with him, Edith had no place in Fred's plans to return permanently to Australia. However Rose's new 'family', 'Anna Wittmann' and her baby Frederick did. A first step was to enable 'Anna' to visit Australia, so that she could experience at first hand the country about which she knew so much.

Rose sought to wield whatever influence he could to make that happen. As a corresponding member of AIAS he decided to shake that tree first, writing to John Mulvaney in supplication, only to be told that his request 'would not receive high priority'.[20] Rose then turned to Manning

Clark's wife Dymphna, who had a longstanding interest in Germany. Her father, the Belgian-born Augustin Lodewyckx, had been Australia's foremost Germanist, and Dymphna herself had travelled extensively in Germany. Recent travels there with son Axel had allowed her to renew her acquaintance with Rose and to meet the prodigious 'Wittmann', who showed the Australians around Leipzig. Perhaps, Rose suggested, Dymphna might be able to wangle something like a visiting fellowship. In terms uncannily reminiscent of those he had used to describe Hannah Middleton years earlier – he added that 'Wittmann' was 'hardly a "women's libber" although she is no man's fool'. And cryptically he noted that she had had a child by a 'boyfriend who did not want it so she diced him and had the child'. [21] Rose's supplications worked. In March 1986 word arrived that 'Wittmann' would receive a visiting fellowship in the Research School of Pacific Studies at the ANU for four months in the following year. [22]

Her stay in Australia did not serve the relationship well. Immediately on her return to Germany Rose noticed a coolness toward him. He was convinced that she was infatuated with another man. The relationship descended into a litany of accusations and counter-accusations. Rose wondered whether he really was the biological father of Frederick, or whether perhaps a young German boyfriend had done more than merely hover in the background. The visit to Australia, he learned, had brought 'Wittmann' into contact with a filmmaker; her relationship with him was revived when he toured Germany. Rose began to feel used and betrayed. [23]

His strategy to deal with the painful unravelling of a six-year relationship was to write what he called 'dialogues'. Their purpose was to subject the course of the relationship to scientific analysis. Though he was 'furious', he eventually chose to regard the relationship as 'an intellectual challenge to investigate. What I did was to assemble the available data I had, analyse it and then to draw conclusions from my analysis. I knew that this was the only way to get you – as we say in English – out of my system so that I would eventually bear you no resentment'. [24] Yet he did not remove her entirely from his 'system'. Out of fear of what 'Wittmann' might do with his private papers if he deposited them in the museum in Leipzig, he resolved that for the sake of posterity everything should be handed to the State Library of New South Wales. The maintenance he had paid over the duration of their 'common-law' relationship became the focus of ongoing and unseemly haggling.[25]

There was one other person whom Rose helped travel to Australia, and that was the Soviet anthropologist Vladimir Kabo. Born to Jewish parents in Moscow in 1925, Kabo had fought in the Red Army and participated in the battle for Berlin. After the war he fell foul of authorities and was sent to the Gulag. In the twilight years of Stalinism, it was not easy to be a Russian Jew.[26]

If there was one advantage to be derived from his Gulag years, it was that Kabo mixed there with some of his country's best minds – a consequence of Stalin's purge of intellectuals.[27] Kabo developed a particular interest in anthropology, and when he read the work of the Australian-born Marxist archaeologist V. Gordon Childe, a fascination was triggered and never fully sated. Released from the Gulag in the post-Stalin era, Kabo worked in the Leningrad division of the Institute of Ethnography, part of the Soviet Union's Academy of Sciences. Later, in 1976, he moved to the Moscow division. Despite his acknowledged expertise on matters Australian, Kabo was never among those chosen for antipodean fieldwork. It may well have been a kind of postponed punishment for Kabo's bold denunciation of the informant whose treachery had condemned him to five miserable years in a logging camp.[28]

Kabo's knowledge of Australia was formed from his voracious reading of whatever literature he could lay his hands on, and that included the works of Fred Rose. What Rose did not know for nearly a decade was that in the early 1960s Kabo had written a review of *Classification of Kin* for the journal *Soviet Ethnography*, only to have it rejected. The anonymous negative assessments accused Kabo 'of not slandering Rose's book outright, of calling him a marxist although many Soviet ethnographers disagree with him'.[29] Kabo did, however, manage to publish a glowing afterword to the Soviet edition of Rose's *Ureinwohner, Känguruhs und Düsenclipper*,[30] as well as the foreword to Rose's last book, *The Traditional Mode of Production of the Australian Aborigines.* Moreover, it was Kabo's second wife Elena Govor who translated that book, going to some trouble to tone down the starkly Marxist terminology for a glasnost-era readership.[31]

In his memoirs Kabo recalls his first contact with Rose in East Berlin. He was 'tall, thin and with reddish hair, his bright eyes looking at me benevolently and a little ironically, a cigar in his mouth. "Hello, Professor Rose", I said. "What's all this?" he exclaimed, shifting the cigar from one corner of his mouth to the other. "No Professors. We'll address each other as we would in Australia: I'm Fred and you're Vladimir." '[32]

Beyond the personal warmth, there was also a fundamental scholarly agreement at play. The doyen of Soviet anthropology, Sergei Tolstov, had clung tenaciously to the view, drawn from Engels and before him Morgan, that all societies passed through the same stages of development.[33] Quite independently Rose and Kabo reached a different view and argued that the case of Australia, where there was no evidence that there had even been a stage of 'group marriage', proved Morgan and Engels wrong.[34]

Kabo, like Rose, was an uncompromising empiricist and in the 1980s still suffered under Soviet anthropology's procrustean favouring of 'politically correct' theory over evidence.[35] The rise of Mikhail Gorbachev gave fresh hope not only that this might change, but that Kabo might finally be able to visit the country which he had known only from afar. Fred Rose not only suggested Kabo apply for an AIAS grant but helped him fill in the paperwork.[36] Through the efforts of others, too, Kabo's dream became a reality in August 1990, when he and Elena arrived in Canberra and, for the first time, encountered Aboriginal Australians.[37]

Visits aside, it was Rose who remained behind the Iron Curtain, though he maintained contact with Kabo, using him as a sounding board as Rose tried to work through some complex ideas which occupied him through the years of his formal retirement. He was interested in hominisation, that is, the creation and development of humankind, indeed he had been intermittently for a very long time. As early as 1956, Rose had written to Childe for advice on the latest publications on the subject,[38] and in 1978 he attended a conference in Paris on the topic 'Hunters and Gatherers' and became re-enthused.[39] Now in formal retirement, he devoted much of his intellectual labour to it. In time he assembled an ambitious manuscript he hoped would become his *magnum opus*.[40]

Rose aimed to offer a compelling alternative to the master narrative of human development that Morgan had posited a century earlier in *Ancient Society*.[41] In superseding Morgan, Rose wished to demonstrate that humans had evolved both *biologically and socially* through changes in the tools used to hunt prey. He attached special importance to the change from the use of the jabbing spear to the long throwing spear. This development necessitated a dramatic evolutionary change in posture, while it also raised the capacity to acquire protein by hunting relatively large animals. The hunter's expanded economic productivity had profound consequences for the group's survival prospects and for the ways in which it organised itself.[42]

To Rose's mind there was a strong argument for a coherent materialist explanation for the development of human society from its pre-human origins. Marxist theory, and Marxist theory alone, could 'embrace the vast period of the *Menschwerdung* [hominisation]', that is, the millennia over which 'Homo became sapiens'.[43] Not only was Rose affirming his faith in Marxism decades after his conversion to it, he was expanding the realm of its applicability. In doing so he evinced 'no false modesty' about his writings on Australian Aborigines, for he genuinely thought that this new work on the social/biological development of Homo would put all those earlier achievements 'right in the shade'.[44] It would become the famous endpoint to the historic mission he had envisaged as young graduate in anthropology at Cambridge University in 1936, and it would earn him a place in the history of science alongside the likes of Darwin and Marx himself. His manuscript was, in his words, 'potential scientific dynamite'.[45]

It was never published. New East European data on the population of the Upper Palaeolithic period had 'put the skids under [his] neat Marxist theory'.[46] It was also out of step with the contemporary academic/political directions in the GDR, especially those of his politically influential colleagues Irmgard Sellnow and Joachim Herrmann.[47] He managed to include sections of it in the last of his books, *The Traditional Mode of*

Production, but most of it would not see the published light of day.[48] With more than a hint of resignation he wrote to Peter Worsley that he would 'try another tack' and embark on writing his autobiography.[49]

Any thoughts that he might live out his last years in quiet contemplation and nostalgia were rudely interrupted by the march of history. In March 1985, days before Rose's 70th birthday, the Soviet gerontocracy finally came to an end when Mikhail Gorbachev took the reins of power in Moscow and embarked on an ambitious program of reform. Though Gorbachev could not guess it, he had set the Soviet Union on a course of change he could not control and which would lead to its collapse.

The GDR's gerontocracy, in contrast, clung with serene naivety to a policy of 'business as usual'. The sophistication of its security apparatus surely meant that any hint of rebelliousness would be nipped in the bud. Both Fred and Edith Rose would of course do their bit to ensure that in the GDR things would stay as they were. Edith, by now in retirement from her 'day job', was called back into service for the Stasi five years after being 'archived' in 1978. She was once more 'Miller', but now her approaches to unsuspecting targets were by telephone, not in person.[50] Fred had taken no break. When Malcolm Morris retired as ambassador, Rose cultivated links with his successor, John McCredie, at least until 1986, when the Australian government decided that the embassy in East Berlin was no longer worth the cost and shut it down.[51]

Rose's obliviousness to the profundity of the changes taking place around him is well illustrated by the arrival of another in the long line of visitors from Australia. It was 1985, the beginning of the first Gorbachev year, and the visitor was the singer Eric Bogle, attending a 'Festival of the Political Song' in East Berlin. Fred was a fan, and when he got wind of Bogle's presence in East Berlin he invited him to pay a visit to his apartment in the Schulze-Boysen-Strasse – with his guitar. Edith at the time was visiting family and friends in Australia, but Rose encouraged a host of mainly younger enthusiasts to attend as well.[52]

It all went well enough. Rose reported later that there had been much singing on that evening. Just about every guest brought along an instrument. But there were some serious political discussions as well, in part arising from the puzzlement Bogle expressed at the very existence of the Berlin Wall. In his Stasi report Rose underlined the visitor's 'very limited knowledge of the problems'.[53] Bogle, for his part, remembers a quite curious evening featuring an unusually frank exchange of views:

Fred invited us back to his small flat in East Berlin after a concert there, and a few of his students came along as well. Perhaps because of Fred's status in East Germany at the time, for once we didn't have a 'minder' present, who was usually a shifty looking party member with a party badge conspicuously displayed on their lapel, or shirt or whatever . . . so for once people could speak freely. From the window of Fred's flat we could see a portion of the Berlin wall, and I asked Fred's students why they thought it was there. They spouted the usual guff about keeping Western infiltrators from sullying their Communist paradise, but as the wine took hold they also said it was there to stop people like them from betraying the revolution. As future members of the middle class, i.e. doctors, lawyers, bankers etc. etc. they knew they were more likely to flee to the fleshpots of the West rather than the working class, who, with free education, transport, cheap beer etc would more likely stick by the status quo. To hear these young people describing themselves as possible future traitors to their country was quite disturbing. From memory, Fred said little, but when he did I think he took something of a devil's advocate role, which teachers and lecturers invariably do. I remember that he asked me very few, if any, questions regarding Australia. I got the impression that he was still a dedicated socialist but that the reality of East Germany had blunted his idealism a little . . .

Before I left I asked all those present when if ever they could envisage a day when the wall would come down. All the students there said it would never come down in their lifetime, but I can't remember if Fred felt the same. So more than a little pissed and more than a little depressed I left . . .[54]

30. Annus Horribilis

Rose's *annus horribilis*, 1989, began auspiciously enough – he had met another young woman who would soon become his lover. He was in his seventy-fourth year; Anke was twenty-five. She was a librarian, and her workplace, as convenience would have it, was adjacent to a U-Bahn station often used by Rose. Their point of mutual intellectual interest was not so much her job but her passion. Outside work she was active in the 'Support Group for Native Peoples'. The group's main concern was the treatment of Native Americans, but it extended to indigenous peoples all over the world. One of the annual highlights was participation in the Festival of Political Song, the event that had brought Eric Bogle to Berlin in 1985. In 1988 there was a special focus on Australian Aborigines, who were mourning the 200th anniversary of European settlement of their lands. The Aboriginal band No Fixed Address was invited to the GDR. Anke Bornschein was chosen to accompany the band on its tour and to tend to an exhibition that accompanied the musicians. Faced with the task of learning more about Australia and its first people, she turned to the works of Fred Rose. With the help of some mutual friends, just before Christmas 1988 she met the author himself.[1]

The love that subsequently blossomed, as he told her in a letter, 'was quite indecent (*unsittlich*) according to the prevailing mores of the society in which we live'.[2] That was nothing new for Rose; it presented him with the same dilemmas posed by previous relationships, and was a case of *déjà vu* in other ways as well. Like those other lovers, Bornschein was intelligent and politically engaged. She became involved in collecting signatures for a petition in response to Aboriginal deaths in custody.[3]

In the first half of 1989, Rose flew as planned to Australia. Having just met Bornschein, he departed with a heavy heart, but the two corresponded. Not for the first time there was talk of marriage, Rose making a proposal, as he put it, 'like a drowning man clutching at a straw', and there was astonishment when he was not rebuffed.[4] In the end there would be no marriage, yet the trajectory of this relationship was unlike previous ones. It waxed rather than waned, and ultimately it was ended only by Rose's death, until which time Bornschein had almost daily contact with him, negotiating the awkward fact that he still lived with his former wife.

The visit to Australia that year, which mercifully offered some respite from the bouts of bronchitis triggered by the Berlin winters, was Rose's last. He stayed with his daughter and grandchildren and dropped in on old friends. His new romance aside, another cause for celebration was the publication two years earlier of his book *The Traditional Mode of Production of the Australian Aborigines*, and, even better, a very favourable review. Humphrey McQueen had devoted some time to it on ABC Radio's Science Show.[5] At last, Rose might well have thought, there was someone who really *got* what he had been writing about for decades.

But Rose had no reason to be happy with the state of Australian politics. Unremitting sectarianism had condemned the radical left to the very edges of the body politic. As for the mainstream, the Hawke government was still in office, but it seemed to Rose to be doing precious little for its working-class constituency. First there was the 'accord', an agreement that was 'unashamedly class collaborationist'. Then there was the sidelining of Bill Hayden, replaced as foreign minister by the 'more amenable' Gareth Evans, while Hayden was 'kicked upstairs' to the sinecure of the governor-generalship. The career charting the steepest ascent was that of Treasurer Paul Keating, 'a relatively young man with aspirations to be a future Prime Minister'.[6] Outside government, developments were equally disturbing. The media were firmly in the hands of an affluent few like Rupert Murdoch and Alan Bond, 'associated with multinationals clearly aligned with US-imperialism'.[7] Among the distortions they presented as daily media fare were vast exaggerations of the economic difficulties being faced by the socialist states. These were 'blown-up out of all proportion and used as evidence by the monopoly media that socialism does not work'.[8]

A series of crises awaited Rose on his return to Berlin. The first concerned Kim. At about 7 pm on the evening of 18 June, Edith went in search of Kim at the apartment he shared with his partner. She wanted to check his condition, as he had been unwell for some weeks. Just two days earlier he had recorded a temperature of 39 and blood in his urine but had refused to see a doctor. When Edith entered his bedroom and spoke to him, he did not respond – he was dead. When a doctor arrived it was confirmed that there had been no foul play; he had died 'not in the presence of other persons'.[9] It seems that he had been reading a novel up to a short time before his death. As he had steadfastly refused treatment, the autopsy was in effect also the diagnosis of Kim's condition. He had died of cancer of the oesophagus, which had metastasised into his lungs. For reasons only he could know, he had chosen to do nothing but let things take their painful course.

He was just forty-eight. It had been a long journey from the Kimberley, where he was born and after which he was named, to East Berlin. His last years traced an inexorable slide into wretchedness. Openly or in silence, many wondered what trajectory his life might have taken had he not followed his family behind the Iron Curtain. As it happened, he died just as he was on the brink of becoming a grandfather. Shortly after his death, his first daughter returned from her studies in Budapest and gave birth to a son, almost to the minute that her father's ashes were interred.[10]

Friends came from near and far to attend the funeral, held at the end of July. Confronted with the stuff of every parent's nightmare, Fred Rose did not trust himself to speak extemporaneously; he had written some words and hoped to keep a steady voice as he delivered them. It was the eulogy of a grieving father, an atheist and an erudite scholar, steeped in the knowledge of humankind's ways of life and of death over millennia. In the ancient world, he told his fellow mourners, only the deaths of the very old or the very young were regarded as natural. Those who died in the prime of life were the victims of some malevolent force in human or other form. In the funeral oration the patriarch would exhort those gathered to exact revenge. Should he, Rose, do the same? And if so, on whom or what should revenge be exacted? And how, he wondered, should the suffering of those the dead leave behind be alleviated? Whether relief was sought in religion or other means, the grief was real. Once again it was the anthropologist speaking, positing an historical division in the labour of loss. For women the pain was more acute than for men, and it was Edith, he acknowledged, 'who has been hit hardest and should receive the greatest solace in her present grief'.[11]

As for himself, he confessed to finding it hard to express his feelings without appearing 'cold and distant'. Wisely he reached for words sent from London by an old family friend, Douggie Moncrieff. They seemed to capture best the whole family's heartache:

> *Everyone was fond of Kim, for so much of his life felt desperately anxious about him. A self-confident, brilliant brain – and frustration – was what we saw. Kim was as much a victim of Europe's stupid war as my comrades who died in battle. A victim of politics and war. It is important for all of us to remember this now – because, all of us, his parents, his sisters, his other relatives and friends, will be desperately thinking of something extra that we could have said or done – as if we each could have done something more to help Kim – who would not accept much help anyway. . . . All I can say now is what I have said before: the barriers were too high for us to climb because they were made not just by individuals and by families, but by whole crumbling civilizations.*[12]

Rose quoted lines from Keats, having learned that in the last months of his life Kim grappled not only with theoretical physics but the works of Shakespeare and the Romantics. Then, finally, came the Australian connection and some lines from Mary Gilmore, who on the death of her own son had written:

> *Hold no longer grief . . .*
> *Grief fills no barns*
> *Its ploughs rust at the door.*[13]

Rose wanted to move on, but the events of the months that followed offered no solace. The entire Eastern bloc was in deep trouble, the GDR included. Without the opportunity to change their government at the ballot box, East Germans began voting with their feet. When Hungary opened its border to Austria in August, a hole was torn in the Iron Curtain, and East Germans were among those who passed through it. Others gathered in the West German embassies in Prague and Warsaw and refused to return to their homeland. Eventually the East German government was forced to an embarrassing compromise. The stubborn traitors were loaded onto trains and, in sealed carriages, transported across the GDR to the West and new lives.

Others agitated for reform from within. They did not want to discard socialism but to give it the 'human face' of the kind that Alexander Dubček had wanted in Prague in 1968. Discontent had been brewing in what existed of a civil society in the GDR, and now it came to the boil. 'We are the people', proclaimed ever-growing numbers of protestors who gathered through autumn in places like Leipzig, Dresden and Berlin. As they took their message onto the streets, the gerontocrats contemplated a 'Chinese solution', that is, a military intervention on the model of Beijing's Tienanmen Square in June 1989. They knew, however, that they would need to do so without the blessing of Mikhail Gorbachev. Visiting East Germany to cast an unintended pall over the celebrations of the state's 40th anniversary, he proclaimed ominously: 'History punishes those who come too late.'[14] With that it was clear that there would be no rumbling of Soviet tanks through the streets of Berlin and elsewhere as in 1953. Erich Honecker was replaced by Egon Krenz, but no amount of shuffling of deckchairs would help. Monitored, suppressed, intimidated and patronised for four decades, East Germany's disaffected found their voice, unified in their conviction that the government had to go.[15]

As a final indignity, an element of farce accompanied the fall of the Berlin Wall. At a press conference held on the evening of 9 November, a weary senior government figure, Günter Schabowski, fumbled an answer to a tangential question posed by an Italian journalist. It concerned a new travel law passed three days earlier. Exceeding his brief, Schabowski announced new regulations on so-called 'permanent emigration'. Reading from a briefing intended for the following day, he said that special conditions would no longer be required for applications to the police for private travel. And asked when those new regulations would apply, he answered, 'As far as I know, this is immediate, without delay'. As word of that announcement spread, the first timid, halting breaches of the Berlin Wall took place. By the time the evening was out, the trickle had become a flood. The border guards, as incredulous as those who queued before them, flung open the gates and let history run its course.[16]

Just how it might run was unknown at that moment. Most of the East German proponents of change envisaged the creation of a new kind of state, one to replace the Stalinist-style of politics that had survived into the Honecker era with a new form of socialism. Some favoured a 'third way', a hybrid that combined the best features of communism and capitalism. Even as those options were being contemplated, history moved on. In the public gatherings of the post-Wall period, the slogan 'We are the people' was replaced with 'We are one people'. The future of East Germany was no longer a matter for East Germans to resolve. Almost before the achievements of early November's popular revolution had been digested, unification was placed on the agenda. From that moment any thought of salvaging socialism was a pipedream.

For someone like Fred Rose, who had devoted his life since 1942 to the communist cause, all this was difficult to fathom; Germany's 'liberal' revolution of 1989 surely had no place in a state where socialism had won the day decades earlier. He could at best observe the accelerating changes with a combination of bafflement and alarm. For a time a provisional government took the reins of power until elections could be held in March 1990. Controversially the Stasi was not disbanded during the interregnum, provoking a good deal of anger among the many who counted themselves among the organisation's victims. That anger spilled over into violence on 15 January, when protestors stormed the Stasi headquarters in Berlin, aware that Stasi officers had set about the task of destroying 180 kilometres of files and 17 million index cards. With that intervention the shredders fell silent, and the many tens of thousands like Fred and Edith Rose who had pledged their support for the Stasi had reason to be concerned. In time, the ninety-five per cent of files left intact would yield their secrets.[17]

Whatever battles might be fought to shape a new age, Rose would play little part in them. His abhorrence at the resurrection of capitalism in his GDR was absolute; his predictions of the changes it would ring were dire. Intellectually he was as acute as ever, but physically he was under siege, his health ill equipped to engage in the rearguard battles he had not foreseen. In mind and body, Fred Rose was a man of the twentieth century, not the new age dawning.

He would, of course, happily give his views to anyone who asked, as the Australian journalist Richard Carleton did in the summer of 1990. By that time German unification was not just a foregone conclusion, it had been scheduled for 3 October. Carleton arrived in Berlin with a crew from *60 Minutes*, collecting footage and recording interviews for a story on the impending creation of a New Germany.[18]

Carleton sought out Rose and Walter Kaufmann as 'Australians' who could offer insights into the GDR's collapse and predictions of what unification might bring. There was nothing rueful or contrite in Rose's demeanour; outwardly, at least, his wit and humour were fully intact. He was filmed in his apartment with Edith, at a demonstration, strolling through the Soviet war memorial at Treptow, and beside a length of the Berlin Wall, even as it was being attacked with chisels, pieces chipped off and prepared for sale. No sooner had capitalism triumphed than communism's history was being commodified.

Carleton's voiceover delivered the backstory. Rose had left Australia in 1956 after his involvement in the Petrov Affair, about which he professed no bitterness at all. 'Probably the best thing that ever happened to me', Rose chuckled. He had elected to live 'East of the Wall', so the voiceover said. Actually, there was no Berlin Wall when Rose arrived in the GDR, but no mind. The camera now captured Rose 'wandering amidst its ruins'. Furthermore, Carleton intoned, 'to add insult to injury, this dedicated communist must now watch as the vultures of capitalism seek profit from the very rubble itself'.[19]

Rose did not dispute that he remained a dedicated communist. And although not everything had been perfect in the GDR, there had been 'many, many positive features'. Reminded by Carleton of the reality of 'all the terrible things here – phone taps, the police following you, all that kind of stuff', Rose conceded little: 'I know that, but don't you realise ASIO was on my back with telephone being tapped, mail being gone through, people following me on the plane and so on and so forth from 1950 onwards.' Rose would not take a backward step. Asked whether he was a stubborn old man, he concurred good-humouredly, giving full vent to the Australian vernacular he still mastered: 'I am a stubborn old bastard. Of course I am.'[20]

In other ways, too, Rose was taking stock. A small fire in the apartment in the Schulze-Boysen-Strasse, full to the brim with an accretion of possessions collected by Edith and Fred over long lives on two continents, prompted him to attempt to impose some order. The task of bundling together papers in preparation for deposit in Sydney's Mitchell Library was approached with renewed vigour. And as he sorted through them, he continued to work away at a manuscript he had provisionally titled 'Memoirs of an Unapologetic Anthropologist'.[21]

This, too, could be added to his legacy. Typically he interrogated with scientific acuity the motivation for such a task. 'Perhaps', he pondered, the scientific memoirist 'feels that his contemporaries have not or insufficiently appreciated his contribution to their common science and have not given his work the attention and respect which he thinks are its due'.[22] In reality, there was no 'perhaps'. Rose was convinced that due recognition had been denied him, but it was not too late to change all that.

By now the completion of his memoirs was a race against time. The acrid smoke caused by the fire could not easily be dispelled. It hung in the air, stirring his smoker's lungs into fits of wheezing and coughing. And a problem with a more ancient genesis, one he recalled in the memoirs he was composing, was a heart murmur, diagnosed when he was a child. It had no consequences at the time, but tests suggested that it was the cause of a mild heart attack suffered during his last visit to Australia.[23] Long accustomed to standing as he typed, the swelling of his ankles caused by his failing heart obliged him to stay seated now as he pounded his typewriter. Eventually he gave up typing and spoke his recollections into a recorder. The last of those recordings was made on 26 December 1990. After that the decline in his health was rapid and terminal. It was not another bout of bronchitis but a failing heart that demanded admission to hospital in early January. By 14 January he was dead.

Epilogue

If Fred Rose had had his way, his ashes would have been flushed down the lavatory. Instead he was laid to rest in an unmarked grave in the Baumschulenweg cemetery, in soil that just a few months earlier had been part of the GDR, itself now consigned to the graveyard of history. The funeral was the most intimate of affairs, attended only by Edith, Sonja, Nita, Ruth and her husband Rainer. Weeks later a wake was staged; family and friends, old colleagues and students, pressed into the apartment in the Schulze-Boysen-Strasse to mourn, reminisce, and take stock.

In other parts of the world, too, Rose was remembered. In his original homeland, England, Peter Worsley honoured Rose, 'the quintessential stereotype of an earthy, irreverent, iconoclastic, and above all revolutionary Aussie', with a generous obituary in the *Guardian*.[1] He lamented the passing of a 'marvellous, dynamic personality', who, as he put it with characteristic acuity, was 'both persecuted and paranoid'. Rose was not the only left-wing intellectual of his time to be persecuted, as Worsley knew only too well, but 'for sheer duration of victimisation' it was Rose who held the record.[2] In the first of Rose's adoptive homelands, Australia, an article in the *Sun Herald* called attention to his demise under the heading 'Petrov Spy Dies in Germany'.[3] It placed a picture of Rose, 'one of the most outspoken and radical anthropologists of his time' and self-proclaimed 'spy who never was', side-by-side with one of his erstwhile shadows, Vladimir Petrov.

A couple of months later a commemorative ceremony was held in the BWIU Hall in Sydney's Kent Street. The firmest of Rose's allies over many decades, Pat Graham, helped organise it and was master of ceremonies. Among the speakers was Kevin Cook, director of the Tranby Aboriginal College, who in speaking on behalf of Aboriginal people lauded the principle that had guided Rose's research. Rose, he said, 'would not take it away and hide it. He'd give it to the people so they could use it for their betterment, for the Aboriginal people'.[4] Graham also secured the services of Ken Maddock to give the 'academic' address. Maddock reflected then, and in an obituary he published later, on Rose's scholarly career, but he acknowledged that there was an awful lot more to Rose's life than academe, as the attentive faces assembled before him proved. The occasion had the character of a gathering of the 'vestiges of the Old Left', as if it was much more than Fred Rose's demise that was being lamented.[5]

On that day, and on many others in that year, the left had much to bemoan. By coincidence Rose's old friend and supporter Gordon Bryant died on the same day as Rose. The life of Ian Milner, like Rose's, lived in the shadow of suspicions of treachery and espionage, also came to an end in 1991, in Prague. And a mutual acquaintance of both Milner and Rose, Manning Clark, died in May. Clark had been born not just in the same year but the same month as Rose. In death the two were far apart; Clark was the public face of Australian history, Rose barely a footnote to it.

The memoirs to which he had dedicated himself through many of his last weeks remained unfinished. Like so many of the sources that plotted his life, Rose's draft memoirs were unreliable. They showed how it was that he was guided from his parents' cosy, conservative world, via Cambridge, a Nazi jail and the miseries of Black Australia to his ideological home on the left of the political spectrum. Only communism, he came to believe as a young man, could offer all of humankind the chance of a decent and dignified future.

Rose was one of countless young men and women who saw in the Soviet Union the great beacon of hope for humankind, but few were so unwaveringly devoted to the cause as he. For many it was a dramatic and unexpected event – the signing of the Hitler–Stalin Pact, the invasion of Hungary, or the brutal crushing of the Prague Spring – which persuaded them to toss away their Party badges. For others it was the sustained exposure to life in the eastern bloc that forced a radical rethink. The journalist Rex Chiplin, having served a stint as the *Tribune*'s Moscow correspondent, reportedly took a taxi directly from Mascot airport to the CPA's Sydney headquarters, flung his Party membership card down on the table and shouted at a comrade, 'If that's socialism, you can shove it up your arse!'[6]

Rose, too, experienced the harder edges of life in 'real existing socialism'. When once he met Ken Maddock in a train station in Utrecht in the mid-70s, he exclaimed volubly, 'Actually, it's a bit of a bugger living behind the Iron Curtain. They control you from A to Z'.[7] When he considered returning to Australia, however, it was not because his faith in communism had waned. He had invested much too heavily in it for that to happen. Emotionally, communism had given him a family to replace the one he had left behind so many years before in London. Intellectually, Marxism satisfied Rose's scientific mind; it offered a coherent, logical way of understanding the world around him. More than that, it gave him a purpose for being in it. How could he abandon it?

Rose's unfinished memoirs break off at the point where he was reflecting on the Petrov Affair. His looming death would prevent him finishing his life's story, but this was not a bad place to stop. One way or another, Rose's life after 1954, in Australia and in Germany, was lived in the shadow of Petrov. His reputation smeared, he had no chance of returning to the anonymity and security of his pre-Petrov existence. It was a fate shared by many others, but the impact on him, and on the members of his family, was inordinately large. For better or for worse, everything about his life – his career, relationships, home, even his personality – was profoundly and irreversibly affected. In the years and then decades that followed the Petrov episode, Rose repeatedly drew attention to it, seeking even to exploit his notoriety for political advantage or publicity, cementing it as the pivotal moment in his life's story.

In another way, the very inconclusiveness of Rose's memoirs is eerily apposite. This was no life half-lived, but there was much about it that found no fitting conclusion, that was left up in the air, its potential untested or unrealised. The incomplete memoirs would join the recollections of his meteorologist days on Groote Eylandt, the *Festschrift* prepared in his honour, and his 800-page hominisation manuscript as works that for one reason or another did not find their publishers and were consigned to oblivion.

In his glowing review of Rose's *Traditional Mode of Production*, Humphrey McQueen casually pondered what might have been if Fred Rose had taken a chair in anthropology at the ANU.[8] There would have been no career behind the Iron Curtain, but he would have performed more fieldwork in Australia, his work would have been received more widely, and his political voice more forceful. Rose did not harbour regrets or speculate on what might have been, and that was wise. Over its course his life had presented him with fundamental, life-changing choices, and in the end, in bleaker moments, he might have wondered whether he had chosen well. Conditioned though they were by circumstances beyond his control, in every instance his decisions were made by him and him alone. He chose to join the CPA and to do what he could to further its cause, to swap the life of a Canberra public servant for that of a farmer, wharfie, and academic. It was Fred Rose who chose to seek his happiness outside the bonds of marriage. And when the Stasi arrived at his doorstep, it was Fred Rose who signed for that most Faustian of bargains – and kept it.

For each decision good reasons could be found, the relevant factors isolated and interrogated, the pros and cons weighed. The cumulative result of those choices, however, was to place him in a position far removed from that he had envisaged as a bright young man, leaving the shores of England to make a great name for himself in anthropology. He had been pressed, and had pressed himself, into a corner where he swung as hard as ever, generated as much sound and fury as he could, but ultimately was barely noticed.

Could things be any different in death? Would stories of the time and lives of Fred Rose reach out beyond the grave to speak to another age? The implacable atheist Rose might have laughed off such a notion. But the indelible Australian in him might have pondered the fate of that archetypal rebel, the jolly swagman, and hoped that a ghost may be heard.

Notes

Prologue

1   Roger Pescott, 'Why Kerr never told Whitlam of his intention to dismiss him', *Sydney Morning Herald*, 6 September 2012. Available online at http://www.smh.com.au/opinion/politics/why-kerr-never-told-whitlam-of-his-intention-to-dismiss-him-20120905-25env.html#ixzz2TntWGFzT, accessed 23 July 2012.

2   Rose's report on that evening is located at BStU AIM 5163/91 Bd. II/2, 391–95.

1 | War Child

1   Frederick George Godfrey Rose, 'Memoirs', 12, SLNSW, Frederick Rose Papers, Box 1.

2   Ibid., 8–10.

3   Ibid., 5.

4   Ibid., 8–9.

5   Ibid.

6   Ibid., 10.

7   Ibid., 5–8.

8   Ibid., 17.

9   Ibid., 19.

10 Ibid.

11 Ibid.

12 Ibid. 16.

13 Ibid.

14 Gerald R. Shutt, 'Letter of Reference', 7 May 1933, SLNSW, Frederick Rose Papers, Box 17.

15 Ibid., 20.

16 Ibid.

17 Ibid., 21.

18 Rose, 'Memoirs', 19.

2 | Red Cambridge

1   John Simkin, 'Kenneth Sinclair Loutit', www.spartacus.schoolnet.co.uk/TUloutit.htm, accessed 8 September 2010.

2   Miranda Carter, *Anthony Blunt: His lives*, London: Macmillan, 2001, 121.

3   Eric Hobsbawm, *Interesting Times: A twentieth-century life*, London: Allen Lane, 2002, 100.

4   H. Gustav Klaus, 'Heinemann, Margot Claire (1913–1992)', *Oxford Dictionary of National Biography*, Oxford University Press, 2004, http://www.oxforddnb.com/view/article/39546, accessed 27 Nov 2013.

5   Rose, 'Memoirs', 22, SLNSW, Frederick Rose Papers, Box 1.

6   Ibid., 24.

7   Ibid., 27.

8   Born Hedwig Magdalena Simon (1916–2004) on January 6, 1916 in Vienna to Else Reis and the economist and banker Hans Simon, she studied moral science at Vienna until her studies were interrupted by the anti-Semitism of the 1930s which drove her family to leave Austria. She continued her studies at Newnham College in Cambridge graduating with First Class Honours in 1939, yet as a woman, she was excluded under university rules from the award of her degree. See B. Skanthakumar, 'Hedi Stadlen (Keuneman) 1916–2004: Indefatigable Political Activist', *Sunday Observer*, 11 July 2004, www.rootsweb.ancestry.com/~lkawgw/hkeuneman.htm, accessed 1 June 2014.

9   Rose, 'Memoirs', 3, 14. Oskar Spate (1911–2000) the influential Cambridge geographer retired as professor in the School of Pacific Studies at the ANU in December 1976.

10 Ibid., 22.

11 For information on Fritz Loewe we are deeply indebted to Ursula Rack. See also Mark Richmond, 'Loewe, Fritz Philipp (1895–1974)', *Australian Dictionary of Biography*, National Centre of Biography, Australian National University, adb.anu.edu.au/biography/loewe-fritz-philipp-10850/text19255, accessed 20 February 2012. See also the obituary for Fritz Loewe by Michael Piggott in the June 1974 issue of the *Melbourne University Gazette*.

12 Rose, 'Memoirs', 29.

13 Ibid., 29–30.

14 The British journalist John Peet, who, like Fred Rose, chose to live for several decades in the GDR, was the son of Quaker parents and attended a Quaker school in Saffron Walden. Like Rose, he also cycled through Nazi Germany. Peet published his memoirs as, *The Long Engagement: Memoirs of a Cold War legend*, London: Fourth Estate, 1989.

15 Rose, 'Memoirs', 33–34.

16 Ibid., 34.

17 'Auszug aus der Parteiakte des Genossen und der Genossin Rose', Berlin, 27 May 1963, BStU AIM 5163/91 Teil I/1, 75.

18 Rose, 'Memoirs', 28, 35.

19 Ibid., 38.

20 Ibid., 40.

21 Ibid., 35.

22 Julian Huxley, A.C. Haddon, and A.M. Saunders, *We Europeans: A survey of racial problems*, London: J. Cape, 1935.

23 Rose, 'Memoirs', 41.

24 Ibid., 42; on the function of academic anthropology in Britain see Frederik Barth, 'The Rise of Anthropology in Britain', in Frederik Barth, Andre Gingrich, Robert Parkin, and Sydel Silverman, *One Discipline Four Ways: British, German, French, and American anthropology*, Chicago: University of Chicago Press, 2005, 26.

25 Barth, 'The Rise of Anthropology in Britain', 3.

26 Rose, 'Memoirs', 42.

27 Bronisław Malinowski, *Argonauts of the Western Pacific: An account of native enterprise and adventure in the archipelagoes of Melanesian New Guinea*, London: Routledge, 1922.

28 Rose, 'Memoirs', 42.

29 Malinowski's earlier book: *The Family Amongst the Australian Aborigines: A sociological study*, London: University of London Press, 1913, was never mentioned during his course and Rose claims he did not read it until after he migrated to Australia. See Rose, 'Memoirs', 42.

30 Rose, 'Memoirs', 42.

31 Ibid.

32 When Kim Philby graduated in 1933, Maurice Dobb, an economics tutor at Cambridge gave him an introduction to a legal communist group in Paris, 'almost certainly Münzenberg's *World Committee for the Relief of Victims of German Fascism*'. He possibly did not realise that he had begun Philby's recruitment as a Soviet agent. See Christopher Andrews and Oleg Gordievsky, *KGB: The inside story of its foreign relations from Lenin to Gorbachev*, London: Hodder & Stoughton, 1990, 156.

33 In some interpretations the Cambridge Four should in fact be the Cambridge Five, whereby the identity of the Fifth Man – sometimes identified as John Cairncross – remains a matter of dispute, and there may have been a 'fluctuating membership'. Ibid., 168.

3 | Australia: First Contact

1 Anne Ikoku (niece of Fred Rose), telephone conversation with Valerie Munt, York, April 2012.

2 Frederick Rose 'Memoirs', 50, SLNSW, Frederick Rose Papers, Box 1.

3 Rose, 'Memoirs', 48.

4 Simon Bracegirdle, *My Lucky Life*, Brisbane: the author, 1997, 50–52. The communist Mark Bracegirdle, Simon's brother, later became involved in Ceylon's campaign for independence.

5 Ibid.

6 Rose, 'Memoirs', 55–56.

7 Ibid., 56.

8 Ibid., 48–50.

9 See Lewis Henry Morgan, *Ancient Society or Researches in the Lines of Human Progress from Savagery through Barbarism to Civilization*, New York: Henry Holt, 1877.

10 D.J. Mulvaney and J.H. Calaby, *'So Much That is New': Baldwin Spencer 1860–1929, a biography*, Melbourne: Melbourne University Press,1985, 95.

11 'Flawed in its theory, through its limited range of informants and by his linguistic deficiencies', Spencer and Gillen's work did not stand the test of time, however they left a wealth of personal field research. See especially Mulvaney and Calaby, *'So Much That is New'*, 385.

12 Carl Strehlow, *Die Aranda- und Loritja-Stämme in Zentral-Australien*, Frankfurt a.M.: Städtisches Völker-Museum, Frankfurt, 1907–20.

13 Sir James Frazer *The Golden Bough: A study in magic and religion*, London: Macmillan, 1890. Initially published in two volumes, ultimately it grew to twelve.

14 A.R. Radcliffe-Browne, *The Social Organization of the Australian Tribes*, Melbourne: Macmillan, 1930.

15 Sven Lindquist, *Terra Nullius: A journey through no one's land*, London: Granta Books, 2007, 114–116.

16 Ian Hogbin, 'Radcliffe-Brown, Alfred Reginald (1881–1955)', *Australian Dictionary of Biography*, National Centre of Biography, Australian National University, adb. anu.edu.au/biography/radcliffe-brown-alfred-reginald-8146/text14233, accessed 1 November 2012.

17 Tigger Wise, 'Elkin, Adolphus Peter (1891–1979)', *Australian Dictionary of Biography*, National Centre of Biography, Australian National University, adb.anu.edu.au/ biography/elkin-adolphus-peter-10109/text17845, accessed 1 November 2012.

18 Robin Fox, *Kinship and Marriage: An anthropological perspective*, Harmondsworth: Penguin, 1967, 10.

19 Rose, 'Memoirs', 48.

20 Ibid. 42.

21 John Joyce, 'The Story of the RAAF Meteorological Service', www.austehc.unimelb. edu.au/fam/0317.html, accessed 12 March 2012.

22 Rose, 'Memoirs', 49.

23 Ibid.

24 News cutting with photo in *Canberra Times*, 14 August 1991, 23, SLNSW, Frederick Rose Papers, Box 17.

25 J.W. Lillywhite, 'My Early Years in the Bureau of Meteorology', 177. www.austehc. unimelb.edu.au/fam/0169.html, accessed 23 July 2013.

26 Obituary of Fritz Loewe: www.bom.gov.au/amm/docs/1974/obituary.pdf, accessed 11 November 2009.

27 Rose, 'Memoirs', 49.

28 Ibid., 55.

29 Howard Morphy, 'Thomson, Donald Finlay Fergusson (1901–1970)', *Australian Dictionary of Biography*, National Centre of Biography, Australian National University, adb.anu.edu.au/biography/thomson-donald-finlay-fergusson-11851/ text21213, accessed 1 November 2012.

30 Rose, 'Memoirs', 50.

31 *Commonwealth Gazette*, 64, 4 (November 1937), 1949.

32 Rose, 'Memoirs', 51.

33 Ibid., 56.

4 | Darwin

1 Frederick George Godfrey Rose, *Australia Revisited: The Aborigine story from stone age to space age*, Berlin: Seven Seas, 1968, 36.

2 Ibid., 36.

3 Ibid., 37.

4 Ibid., 40.

5 Ibid.

6   Stephen Gray, *The Protectors: A journey through Whitefella Past*, Sydney: Allen & Unwin, 2011, 76.

7   Regina Ganter, Julia Martinez and Gary Lee, *Mixed Relations: Asian/Aboriginal contact in North Australia*, Perth: University of Western Australia Press, 2006, 137.

8   Frederick Rose, 'Memoirs', 51, SLNSW, Frederick Rose Papers, Box 1.

9   Gray, *The Protectors*, 76.

10 Rose, *Australia Revisited*, 41.

11 Julia Martínez, 'The End of Indenture? Asian workers in the Australian pearling industry, 1901–1972', *International Labour and Working Class History*, 67 (Spring 2005), 127.

12 Rose, *Australia Revisited*, 42.

13 Ibid.

14 Rose, 'Memoirs', 52.

15 Rose, *Australia Revisited*, 39.

16 Rose, 'Memoirs', 52.

17 Ibid., 55.

18 Ibid.

19 Frances de Groen, *Xavier Herbert: A biography*, Brisbane: UQP, 1998, 103.

20 Ibid., 110–111.

21 Rose, 'Memoirs', 61.

22 Ibid., 58.

23 Geoffrey Gray, *A Cautious Silence: The politics of Australian anthropology*, Canberra: Aboriginal Studies Press, 2007, 17.

24 Rose, 'Memoirs', 50.

25 Ibid., 56.

26 Rose, *Australia Revisited*, 121.

27 Ibid., 132.

28 Ruth Lockwood, 'William Edward (Bill) Harney', in David Carment et al (eds.), *Northern Territory Dictionary of Biography*, revised edition, Darwin: Charles Darwin University Press, 2008, 260; Harney writes that Linda was 'quarter-caste'. See Bill Harney, *North of 23: Ramblings in Northern Australia*, Sydney: Australasian Publishing, 1946, 152.

29 Rose, *Australia Revisited*, 122.

30 Ibid., 123.

31 Ibid.; Lockwood, 'William Edward (Bill) Harney', 260–61.

32 Rose, *Australia Revisited*, 123.

33 Mackey, George William, 'Memoirs including as merchant marine and with the Bureau of Meteorology, 1927–1940', 10. NTRS, 1195 Box PB 215.

34 Mackey, 'Memoirs', 10.

5 | Groote Eylandt

1   Matthew Flinders, *A Voyage to Terra Australis*, volume II, London: G. and W. Nicol, 1814, 172–73.

2   Regina Ganter, *Mixed Relations: Asian/Aboriginal contact in North Australia*, Perth: University of Western Australia Press, 2006, 4.

3   Ibid., 5.

4   Keith Cole, *A History of the Church Missionary Society of Australia*, Melbourne: Church Missionary Historical Publications, 1971, 185.

5   Peter M. Worsley, 'The Changing Social Structure of the Wanindiljaugwa', doctoral dissertation, ANU, June 1954, 18.

6   Ibid., 11.

7   Ibid., 263.

8   Keith Cole, *Fred Gray of Umbakumba: The story of Frederick Harold Gray, the founder of the Umbakumba Aboriginal Settlement on Groote Eylandt*, Bendigo: Keith Cole, 1984, 80.

9   See Philip Jones, Obituary for Norman B. Tindale, at www.anu.edu.au/linguistics/nash/aust/nbt/obituary.html, accessed 24 July 2013.

10 D.J. Mulvaney and J.H. Calaby, *'So Much That Is New': Baldwin Spencer, 1860–1929: A biography*, Melbourne: Melbourne University Press, 366.

11 Keith Cole, *Arnhem Land: Places and People*, Adelaide: Rigby, 1980, 121.

12 Morphy, Howard, 'Thomson, Donald Finlay Fergusson (1901–1970)', *Australian Dictionary of Biography*, National Centre of Biography, Australian National University, adb.anu.edu.au/biography/thomson-donald-finlay-fergusson-11851/text21213, accessed 3 October 2011.

13 Ibid. On Thomson's activities in Arnhem Land see especially Nicolas Peterson, *Donald Thomson in Arnhem Land*, Melbourne: Currey O'Neil, 1983.

14 Keith Cole, 'Gray, Frederick Harold (Fred)', in David Carment et al (eds.), *Northern Territory Dictionary of Biography*, revised edition, Darwin: Charles Darwin University Press, 235.

15 Cole, *Fred Gray of Umbakumba*, 31–33.

16 Ibid., 63.

17 Cited ibid., 63–64.

18 Andrew McMillan, *An Intruder's Guide to East Arnhem Land*, Sydney: Duffy & Snellgrove, 2001, 169–70.

19 Shedden, Secretary, Dept of Defence to Secretary Dept of Interior, 9 June 1938. NAA: F1 38/557 Flying Boat Base in Gulf of Carpentaria 'Little Lagoon' at Groote Eylandt.

20 Cole, *Fred Gray of Umbakumba*, 65.

21 McMillan, *An Intruder's Guide*, 170.

22 Cole, *Fred Gray of Umbakumba*, 71–72.

23 Cited (unsourced) in McMillan, *An Intruder's Guide,*168.

24 McMillan, *An Intruder's Guide*, 166.

25 Cole, *Fred Gray of Umbakumba*, 66–67.

26 Rose, *Australia Revisited*, 123.

27 McMillan, *An Intruder's Guide*, 171.

28 G.A. Jones, 'Constructing an Air Base at Groote', in Rose, 'Ripples in the Gulf', 356. Originally in *Shell House Journal*, 10, 2 (February 1939), 10–13.

29 McMillan, *An Intruder's Guide*, 173.

30 Ibid.
31 Ellen Kettle, 'Cook, Cecil Eveylyn Aufrere' in David Carment et al (eds.), *Northern Territory Dictionary of Biography*, revised edition, Darwin: Charles Darwin University Press, 2008, 109.
32 McMillan, *An Intruder's Guide*, 174.

6 | Island Days

1 Rose, 'Ripples in the Gulf', 58, unpublished manuscript, National Library of Australia, MS 248, Frederick G.G. Rose, 1938/39 Papers: Groote Eylandt.
2 Frances to Fred Rose, 12 July 1938, SLNSW, Frederick Rose Papers, Box 17.
3 George to Fred Rose, 16 September 1938, SLNSW, Frederick Rose Papers, Box 17.
4 Rose, 'Memoirs', 39, SLNSW, Frederick Rose Papers, Box 1.
5 Rose, 'Ripples', 24.
6 Ibid., 130.
7 Ibid.
8 Ibid., 116.
9 Rose, 'Ripples', 134.
10 Rose, 'Working Papers Groote Eylandt', SLNSW, Frederick Rose Papers, Box 17.
11 Rose, 'Memoirs', 61.
12 From Ernest A. Roberts, Society of Friends, 13 May 1938. 13 May, SLNSW, Frederick Rose Papers, Box 17.
13 Edith to Rose, 3–4 August 1938, SLNSW, Frederick Rose Papers, Box 17.
14 Rose to Cecil Cook, 19 July 1938, SLNSW, Frederick Rose Papers, Box 17.
15 Cited in Rose, 'Ripples', 142.
16 Rose, 'Ripples', pp. 142–43.
17 Ibid., 143.
18 Ibid., 319.
19 Ibid., 144.
20 Ibid., 146.
21 Ibid., 341.
22 Ibid, 148.
23 Ibid, 148–49.
24 Rose, 'Memoirs', 62.
25 Rose, 'Ripples', 149.
26 Typed transcript of oral history interview with Fred Gray 1976, NTRS 226, TS 224, 5.
27 Rose, Memoirs, 66.
28 Keith Cole, *Groote-Eylandt Mission: A short history of the CMS Groote-Eylandt Mission 1921–1971*, Melbourne: Church Mission Historical Publications, 1971, 63.
29 Rose, 'Ripples', ii.

7 | Broome

1   Frederick Rose, 'Memoirs', unpublished manuscript, 63, SLNSW, Frederick Rose Papers, Box 1.
2   Rose, *Australia Revisited: The Aborigine story from stone age to space age*, Berlin: Seven Seas, 1968, 50–51.
3   Rose, 'Memoirs', 63.
4   Ibid.
5   Hugh Edwards, *Port of Pearls: A history of Broome*, Adelaide: Rigby, 1983, 124.
6   Cited unsourced in Hugh Edwards, *Port of Pearls*, 109.
7   Rose, 'Memoirs', 66–67.
8   A.P. Elkin to J.A. Carrodus, 4 June 1940, NAA: A659 1944/1/4313, Rose, F G – Anthropological research at Groote Eylandt.
9   Ibid., 52.
10 Ibid.
11 Ibid., 55–56.
12 Ibid, 54–55.
13 Rose, 'Memoirs', 67.
14 Rose, *Australia Revisited*, 54.
15 Public Health Department Personal File. Dr A.T.H. Jolly. State Records Office of WA, 1940/0617.
16 Public Health Department Personal File. Dr A.T.H. Jolly. State Records Office of WA, 1940/0617.
17 Rose, *Australia Revisited*, 53.
18 Lewis Henry Morgan, *Ancient Society*, New York: Henry Holt and Co., 1877.
19 Rose, 'Memoirs', 68.
20 Ibid.
21 See Michele Barrett, 'Introduction', in Friedrich Engels, *The Origin of the Family, Private Property and the State*, Middlesex, Penguin, 1972, 13.
22 Rose, 'Memoirs', 64.
23 Ibid., 69.
24 Ibid.
25 A.R. Radcliffe-Brown, 'The Social Organization of Australian Tribes', *Oceania*, 1, 1–4 (1930–31), 34–63, 206–46, 322–41, 426–56.
26 Rose, 'Memoirs', 69.
27 Draft manuscript A.T.H. Jolly and F.G.G. Rose, 'The Place of the Australian Aboriginal in the Evolution of Society. A Vindication of Lewis Morgan', SA Museum Archives, AA270, F.G.G. Rose.
28 One place to which they sent the paper for comment was the Royal Anthropological Institute, where it was received in April 1941. The nature of any response received is not recorded, but clearly the RAI was not interested in publishing. Information courtesy Geoff Grey.
29 A.T.H. Jolly and F.G.G.Rose, 'The Place of the Australian Aboriginal in the Evolution of Society', *Annals of Eugenics*, 12, 1 (1943), 44–87.
30 Jolly and Rose, 'The Place of the Australian Aboriginal', 45–46.

31 Ibid., 55–67.

32 Ibid., 80.

33 Ibid., 81.

34 F.G.G. Rose and A.T.H. Jolly, 'An Interpretation of the Taboo between Mother and Son in Law', *Man* 42, 5 (1942), 15–16.

35 Ibid.,15.

36 Ibid.

37 Cited in Rose, 'Memoirs', 65.

38 Frederick Rose, 'Tribal Custom: Marriage Law Infringed. Story Behind Mission Murder. To the Editor', *West Australian*, 23 April 1941, 11.

8 | Groote Revisited

1 Ian Langham, *The Building of British Social Anthropology: W.H.R. Rivers and his Cambridge disciples in the development of kinship studies, 1898–1931*, Dordrecht: Holland/Boston: USA; London, England: D. Reidel Publishing Company, 1981, xv.

2 Tigger Wise, *The Self-Made Anthropologist: A life of A.P. Elkin*, Sydney: George Allen & Unwin, 1985, 53–54.

3 Wise, *The Self-Made Anthropologist*, 54.

4 W.H.R. Rivers, cited in Richard Slobodin, *W.H.R. Rivers: Pioneer anthropologist and psychiatrist of the 'Ghost Road'*, Stroud: Sutton Publishing, 1997, 41.

5 E.R. Leach, 'Concerning Trobriand Clans and the Kinship Category "Tabu"', in Jack Goody (ed.), *The Developmental Cycle in Domestic Groups*, Cambridge: Cambridge University Press, 1966, 144; Slobodin, *W.H.R. Rivers*, 112.

6 Peter Worsley, 'The Practice of Politics and the Study of Australian Kinship', in Christine Ward Gailey (ed.), *Dialectical Anthropology: Essays in honour of Stanley Diamond, vol. 2, The politics of culture and creativity*, Gainesville: University of Florida Press, 1992, 25.

7 D.J. Mulvaney and J.H. Calaby, *'So Much That is New': Baldwin Spencer 1860–1929. A biography*, Melbourne: Melbourne University Press, 1985, 39.

8 W.H.R. Rivers, 'A Genealogical Method of Collecting Social and Vital Statistics', *The Journal of the Anthropological Institute of Great Britain and Ireland*, 30 (1900), 74–82.

9 Mulvaney and. Calaby, *'So Much That is New'*, 195.

10 *The Book of Common Prayer of the Church of England*, London: Oxford University Press (n.d), 384.

11 The First Edition of *Notes and Queries on Anthropology* was published in 1874, 'to promote accurate anthropological observation [. . .] and to enable those who are not anthropologists themselves to supply the information which is wanted for the scientific study of anthropology at home'. See *Anthropological Questionnaires – A Note*, www.espace.library.uq.edu.au/eserv/UQ:246310/Qld-heritage-V3-no4-1976-p23, pdf, accessed 21 October 2011.

12 Royal Anthropological Institute of Great Britain and Ireland; British Association for the Advancement of Science *Notes and Queries on Anthropology*, fifth edition, London: The Royal Anthropological Institute, 1929, 66.

13 *Notes and Queries*, 45.

14 See Michel Foucault, *The Order of Things: An archaeology of the human sciences*, London and New York: Routledge, 2002, xxii–xxiii.

15 Anna Grimshaw, *The Ethnographer's Eye: Ways of seeing in anthropology*, Cambridge: Cambridge University Press, 2001, 36.

16 Ibid., 35.

17 Ibid., 36.

18 Rose, *Australia Revisited*, 140.

19 Ibid.

20 Ibid., 142.

21 Ellen Kettle, 'Cook, Cecil Evelyn Aufrere', in David Carment et al. (eds.), *Northern Territory Dictionary of Biography*, revised edition, Darwin: Charles Darwin University Press, 2008, 109.

22 Stephen Gray, *The Protectors: A journey through whitefella past*, Sydney: Allen & Unwin, 2011, 91.

23 Peter Elder, 'The Winds of Change: E.W.P. Chinnery (1887–1972) and F.G.G. Rose (1915–1991) in the Australian Territories', *South Pacific. Journal of Philosophy and Culture*, (2001), 67.

24 Ibid., 68.

25 Ibid., 69.

26 Lyn Anne Riddett, 'Carrodus, Joseph Aloysius (1885–1961)', *Australian Dictionary of Biography*, National Centre of Biography, Australian National University, adb.anu.edu.au/biography/carrodus-joseph-aloysius-9694/text17111, accessed 22 December 2011.

27 Wise, *The Self-Made Anthropologist*, 144.

28 Elder, 'The Winds of Change', 78–79.

29 Frederick Rose 'Memoirs', 72, SLNSW, Frederick Rose Papers, Box 1.

30 Ibid., 73.

31 Ibid., 72.

32 Elizabeth Edwards, 'Performing Science', in A. Herle and S. Rouse (eds.), *Cambridge and the Torres Strait: Centenary Essays on the 1898 Anthropological Expedition*, Cambridge: Cambridge University Press, 1998, 107–108.

33 Frederick G.G. Rose, *Classification of Kin, Age Structure and Marriage amongst the Groote Eylandt Aborigines: A study in method and a theory of Australian kinship*, Berlin: Akademie-Verlag, 1960, 25.

34 Peter Worsley email to authors, 17 July 2011.

35 Rose used a Voigtländer camera with Skopar 1: 4.5, F–7.5 cm lens taking 16 photographs on Kodak 120mm film. The majority of the films were developed at the native settlement at Umbakumba. Rose, *Classification of Kin*, 27.

36 See 'Tabular Data' in Rose, *Classification of Kin*, 247– 467, and photo portraits, 513–572.

37 Rose, *Classification of Kin*, 30.

38 Ibid., 31–32.

39 Ibid., 29.

40 Ibid., 26.

41 Ibid., 31.

42 Rose, 'Memoirs', 72.

43 Letter Rose to Collings, 15 November 1944, NAA: A659/1/1944/1/4314. Cited in Elder, 'The Winds of Change', 79.

44 As contained in a letter Elkin to Carrodus, 14 March 1945, NAA: A659/1/1944/1/4314, cited in Elder, 'The Winds of Change', 79.

45 Letter Elkin to Carrodus, 14 March 1945. Elkin deplored 'the weakness in Rose's arguments and methods' and his 'bad articles', while a note pencilled by the 'secretary' emphasised that 'Mr Chinnery holds similar views to those of Professor Elkin'. Cited in Rose, 'Memoirs', 84.

46 Rose, 'Memoirs', 74.

9 | The War of the Roses

1 Katharine Susannah Prichard to Timofei Rokotov, 1 April 1942, State Library of WA, Prichard Papers, ACC5835A/5, 8–9.

2 Rose, 'Memoirs', 75.

3 Ibid.

4 Hugh Edwards, *Port of Pearls: A history of Broome*, Adelaide: Rigby, 1983, 126–27.

5 Frederick Rose, 'Memoirs', unpublished manuscript, 76, SLNSW, Frederick Rose Papers, Box 1.

6 Ibid., 77.

7 Rose, Frederick George Godfrey, *Australia Revisited: The Aborigine story from stone age to space age*, Berlin: Seven Seas, 1968, 61.

8 Rose, 'Memoirs', 72.

9 Ibid., 77.

10 Richard Legge to British Medical Association Perth, 11 June 1942, State Records Office of WA, 1940/0617, Public Health Department Personal File Dr A.T.H. Jolly.

11 Jolly to Minister of Civil Defence, 27 March 1942, 2–3, State Records Office of WA, 1940/0617, Public Health Department Personal File Dr A.T.H. Jolly.

12 Service record of ATH Jolly, NAA: B883, WX22993.

13 Rose, 'Memoirs', 79.

14 The Party reverted to the acronym CPA in 1951. See David Horner, *The Spy Catchers. Volume I. The Official History of ASIO 1949–1963*, Sydney: Allen & Unwin, 2014, 191. To avoid confusion we use CPA throughout.

15 Alastair Davidson, *The Communist Party of Australia: A short history*, Stanford CA: Hoover Institution Press, 1969, 72–97.

16 Rose, 'Memoirs', 79.

17 Ibid., 88.

18 Kim E. Beazley, *Father of the House: The memoirs of Kim E. Beazley*, Perth: Fremantle Press, 2009, 38.

19 Rose, 'Memoirs', 79.

20 Tom Wright, *A New Deal for Aborigines*, Sydney: Labour Council NSW, 1939; Bob Boughton, 'The Communist Party of Australia's involvement in the Struggle for Aboriginal and Torres Strait Islander People's Rights 1930–1970', in Ray Markey

(ed.), *Labour and Community: Historical essays*, Wollongong: University of Wollongong Press, 2001, 267.

21 Julie Marcus goes so far as to suggest Pink was the 'real author'. See Julie Marcus, *The Indomitable Miss Pink: A life in anthropology*, Sydney: UNSW Press, 2001, 220.

22 Julie Marcus, "Pink, Olive Muriel (1884–1975)', *Australian Dictionary of Biography*, National Centre of Biography, Australian National University, adb.anu.edu.au/biography/pink-olive-muriel-11428/text20365, accessed 19 January 2013; Carole Ferrier, *Jean Devanny: Romantic revolutionary*, Melbourne: MUP, 1999, 163. See also Terry Townsend, *The Aboriginal Struggle and the Left*, Chippendale NSW: Resistance Books, 2008, 21.

23 Rose, 'Memoirs', 79.

24 Ibid., 80.

25 Ibid.

26 Ibid.

27 Richard Linde had been involved in a number of Lodges since 1921. Information courtesy Martina Voigt.

28 Johannes Tuchel (ed.), *Gedenkstätte Stille Helden: Ausstellungskatalog*, Berlin: Allprint Media, 2008, 19–20. Information on Richard Linde kindly provided by Ruth Struwe, Beate Kosmala and Martina Voigt.

29 Rose, 'Memoirs', 81.

30 Ibid.

31 Service record of Heinrich Eggebrecht, NAA: B884 V378376; Prisoner of War/Internee record of Heinrich Eggebrecht, NAA: MP 1103/2 E39361.

32 Birgit Walter, 'Er diktierte jeden Artikel in die Maschine. Zum Tod des Journalisten Klaus Wilczynski', *Berliner Zeitung*, 14 October 2008, www.berliner-zeitung.de/archiv/zum-tod-des-journalisten-klaus-wilczynski-er-diktierte-jeden-artikel-in-die-maschine,10810590,10592924.html, accessed 12 September 2013.

33 Rose, 'Memoirs', 82.

34 Frank Klepner, *Yosl Bergner: Art as a meeting of cultures*, Melbourne: Macmillan, 2004, 36.

35 Bernard Smith, *Noel Counihan: Artist and revolutionary*, Melbourne: Oxford University Press, 1993, 90.

36 Rose, 'Memoirs', 83.

37 Alastair Davidson, *The Communist Party of Australia: A short history*, Stanford CA: Hoover Institution Press, 1969, 83, 98.

38 Ibid., 115.

39 Dorothy Hewett, *Wild Card: An Autobiography 1923–1958*, Melbourne: McPhee Gribble, 1990, 142.

40 Ric Throssell, 'Foreword', in Ric Throssell (ed.), *Wild Weeds and Wind Flowers: The life and letters of Katharine Susannah Prichard*, London: Angus & Robertson, 1975, 226.

41 Throssell, 'Foreword', 251.

10 | Postwar

1 Tigger Wise, *The Self-Made Anthropologist: A life of A.P. Elkin*, Sydney: George Allen & Unwin, 1985, 194.

2 'Personal–Bogen', 1950, SLNSW, Frederick Rose Papers, Box 26. Whether his application failed for that reason, and indeed whether Rose is accurate in recalling a position being available as early as 1946, cannot be substantiated.

3 T. Maelgwyn Davies, Registrar to Rose, 8 March 1946, SLNSW, Frederick Rose Papers, Box 20.

4 Rose, 'Memoirs', 85, SLNSW, Frederick Rose Papers, Box 1.

5 NAA: Agency note on Department of Post-War Reconstruction, recordsearch. NAA:.gov.au/SearchNRetrieve/Interface/DetailsReports/AgencyDetail. aspx?reg_no=CA%2049, accessed 5 March 2012.

6 Rose, 'Memoirs', 86.

7 Ibid., 88.

8 Application of F.G.G.Rose for the Position of Assistant Secretary (Research etc.) Department of Territories, 4 April 1949, NAA: A6119 1007 ROSE, Frederick George Godfrey Rose Vol. 1, 143.

9 Rose, 'Memoirs', 88.

10 *Resolutions of the 14th Congress of the Australian Communist Party*, Sydney: Central Committee of the Australian Communist Party, 1945, 7.

11 'Extracts from file of Frederick George Godfrey Rose', NAA: 6119 1009, ROSE, Frederick George Godfrey, Volume 3, 47.

12 Rose, 'Memoirs', 97.

13 Ibid., 3.

14 Ibid., 55.

15 Robert Gellately, *Lenin, Stalin and Hitler: The age of social catastrophe*, New York: Vintage, 2008, 332.

16 Stalin cited in Amir Weiner, 'Nature and Nurture in a Socialist Utopia: delineating the Soviet socio-ethnic body in the age of socialism', in David L. Hoffman (ed.), *Stalinism*, Oxford: Blackwell, 2003, 269. (authors' emphasis).

17 Frederick Rose, 'Die Familie und die Periodisierung der Urgeschichte. Im Anschluss an Irgmard Sellnow, Grundprinzipien einer Periodisierung der Urgeschichte', *Ethnographisch–Archäologische Zeitschrift*, 9 (1968), 148–155.

18 Eildermann had written, 'Engels as well as Cunow erred on the point that they view human reproduction as the ultimately determining factor in history. The family, like all other forms of relations, insofar as it constitutes the factor determining social development, is a purely economic institution.' Heinrich Eildermann, *Urkommunismus und Urreligion*, Berlin: A. Seehof & Co., 1921, 8.

19 Cited in Tristram Hunt, *The Frock-Coated Communist: The revolutionary life of Friedrich Engels. The life and times of the original champagne socialist*, London: Penguin, 2009, 309–310.

20 See the English translation published as L.A. Leontiev et al., 'Political Economy in the Soviet Union', *Communist Review*, 40–41 (December 1944/January 1945), 381–82, 410–12.

21 Leontiev, 'Political Economy in the Soviet Union', 381–82.

22 In issues 7–8 (1943), 56–78.

23 Leontiev, 'Political Economy in the Soviet Union', 381– 412. The two-part translation was of the 'essential parts' of the 1943 *Pod Znamenem Marxizma* article.

24 Personal correspondence to authors from Victor Williams, 15 December 2008.

25 Rose, 'Lecture notes', SLNSW, Frederick Rose Papers, Box 21.

26 Rose, 'Memoirs', 109.

27 Rose to the Secretariat ACP, 14 May 1955, SLNSW, Frederick Rose Papers, Box 20.

28 Rose, 'Memoirs', 109.

11 | Monty

1 Denise Chapman and Suzy Russell, 'The Responsibilities of Leadership: The Records of Charles P. Mountford', in Martin Thomas and Margo Neale (eds.), *Exploring the Legacy of the 1948 Arnhem Land Expedition*, Canberra: ANU E Press, 2011, 254.

2 Frederick G.G. Rose, 'Memoirs', 88, SLNSW, Frederick Rose Papers, Box 1.

3 Kim Beazley, 'Nation Building or Cold War: Political Settings for the Arnhem Land Expedition', in Thomas and Neale (eds.), *Exploring the Legacy*, 64.

4 Beazley, 'Nation Building or Cold War', 58.

5 Arthur Calwell, Letter to J.J. Dedman, 28 February 1947, NAA: A9816/4, 1947/89, Part 1, NADC, Arnhem Land Expedition, cited in Sally K. May, 'Piecing the History Together: An Overview of the 1948 Arnhem Land Expedition', Thomas and Neale (eds.), *Exploring the Legacy*, 176.

6 National Museum of Australia (NMA), 'The 1948 Expedition. Barks, Birds & Billabongs: Exploring the Legacy of the 1948 American-Australian Scientific Expedition to Arnhem Land. 16–20 November 2009', www.nma.gov.au/history/research/conferences_and_seminars/barks_birds_billabongs/the_1948_expedition, accessed 5 November 2012.

7 'Charles P. Mountford, SA Memory, South Australia: Past and Present for the Future, Arnhem Land, 1948 – the Expedition', State Library of SA, www.samememory.sa.gov.au/site/pagesfor?u=1298, accessed 10 November 2012.

8 Philip Jones, 'Mountford, Charles Pearcy (1890–1976)', *Australian Dictionary of Biography*, National Centre of Biography, Australian National University, http://adb.anu.edu.au/biography/mountford-charles-pearcy-11188/text19941, accessed 4 October 2012.

9 Philip Jones, 'Inside Mountford's Tent: Paint, Politics and Paperwork', in Thomas and Neale (eds.), *Exploring the Legacy*, 42.

10 Jones, 'Inside Mountford's Tent', 35.

11 Geoffrey Gray, *A Cautious Silence: The politics of Australian anthropology*, Canberra, Aboriginal Studies Press, 2007, 192.

12 Rose to Mountford, 24 June 1945, AASEAL Correspondence, vol. 2, 1945–1948 – Applications, 3, SLSA, PRG 1218/17/5, Mountford–Sheard Collection. Cited in Jones, 'Inside Mountford's Tent', 50.

13 Rose, 'Memoirs', 89.

14 'Brief for Mr and Mrs Petrov re Pamela Howard Beasley', 15 September 1954, NAA: A6119 830/Reference copy, Pamela Howard BEASLEY, Part 1, 28.

15 Mickey Dewar, 'Fred Gray and Umbakumba: the 1930s and 1940s', presentation at 'Picturing relations: Groote Eylandt barks symposium', University of Melbourne, 23 September 2006, www.art-museum.unimelb.edu.au/resources.ashx/ events.transcripts/18/PDF/2FF7660C7E20663DE38EF97593485986/ Fred%2BGray%2Band%, accessed 9 May 2012.

16 NMA, 'The 1948 expedition'.

17 Frederick Rose, *Australia Revisited: the Aborigine story from stone age to space age*, Berlin: Seven Seas, 1968,142.

18 Ibid.

19 Ibid.

20 Peter M. Worsley, 'The Changing Social Structure of the Wanindiljaugwa', doctoral dissertation, ANU, June 1954, 2.

21 Worsley, 'The Changing Social Structure', 272.

22 Rose, *Australia Revisited*,144.

23 Ibid., 146–47.

24 Ibid., 148.

25 Ibid., 148–49.

26 Ibid., 149.

27 Ibid., 151.

28 Ibid., 152.

29 Ibid.

30 Rose, 'Memoirs', 89.

31 Charles Mountford, 'The Story of the Expedition', in C.P. Mountford, (ed.) *Records of the American–Australian Scientific Expedition to Arnhem Land. Volume 1: Art, myth and symbolism*, Melbourne: Melbourne University Press, xxiv.

32 Rose, 'Memoirs', 89.

33 Ibid.

12 | A Nest of Traitors

1 Text of 9 March speech in Percy Spender, *Politics and a Man*, Sydney: Collins, 1972, 309. Cited in David Lowe, *Australian Between Empires: The Life of Percy Spender*, London: Pickering and Chatto, 2010, 124–25.

2 Papers of John W. Burton, Biographical Note, nla.gov.au/nla.ms-ms8405, accessed 10 March 2012.

3 ASIO in 1953 included John Wear Burton among Rose's acquaintances in Canberra. See Memorandum for Regional Director NSW from Regional Director ACT, 23 April 1953, NAA: A6119 1007 ROSE, Frederick George Godfrey, Volume 1, 91.

4 Stuart Macintyre, *A Concise History of Australia*, 3rd ed., Cambridge: Cambridge University Press, 2009, 206.

5 Frederick G.G. Rose, 'Memoirs', 88, SLNSW, Frederick Rose Papers, Box 1.

6 Tim Rowse, *Nugget Coombs: A reforming life*, Cambridge: Cambridge University Press, 2002, 160.

7   Cassandra Pybus, *The Devil and James McAuley*, Brisbane: University of Queensland Press, 1999, 60–76.
8   Ibid., 60–62.
9   Tigger Wise, *The Self-Made Anthropologist: A life of A.P. Elkin*, Sydney: George Allen & Unwin, 1985, 161.
10 Rose to Secretary, Department of External Territories, 20 July 1949, NAA: A6119 1007 ROSE, Frederick George Godfrey Volume 1, 151.
11 Christopher Andrew and Oleg Gordievsky, *KGB: The inside story of its foreign operations from Lenin to Gorbachev*, London: Hodder and Stoughton, 1990, 308.
12 Christopher Andrew, *The Defence of the Realm: The authorized history of MI5*, London: Penguin, 2010, 550.
13 Frank Cain, *The Australian Security Intelligence Organisation: An unofficial history*, Melbourne: Spectrum Publications, 1994, 32.
14 Some argue that security concerns were merely a pretext for withholding information. See for example Cain, *The Australian Security Intelligence Organisation*, 34.
15 David Horner, *The Spy Catchers. Volume I. The Official History of ASIO 1949–1963*, Sydney: Allen & Unwin, 2014, 70.
16 National Archives and Records Administration (USA), RG353, Report to the meeting of SANACC–MIC 206/57, 18 May 1948. Underlining in original. Cited in Cain, *The Australian Security Intelligence Organisation*, 40.
17 Memorandum for the President from Rear Admiral R.H. Hillenkoeter, USN, Director of CIA, Washington, 27 Jan. 1948, Truman Papers, Harry S. Truman Library, Independence Missouri, USA. Cited in Cain, *The Australian Security Intelligence Organisation*, 40.
18 Robert Manne, *The Petrov Affair*, rev. ed. Melbourne: Text, 2004, 229.
19 Cain, *The Australian Security Intelligence Organisation*, 44–45.
20 Ibid., 48.
21 Manne, *The Petrov Affair*, 229.
22 Cain, *The Australian Security Intelligence Organisation*, 53.
23 Ibid., 45.
24 Ibid.,17.
25 Ibid., 22.
26 Ibid., 56, 58.
27 David McKnight, *Australia's Spies and Their Secrets*, Sydney: Allen & Unwin, 1994, 41.
28 Andrew, *The Defence of the Realm*, 368.
29 Ibid, 550.
30 Desmond Ball and David Horner, *Breaking the Codes: Australia's KGB network, 1944–1950*, Sydney: Allen & Unwin, 1998, 188–97; Andrew, *The Defence of the Realm*, 550.
31 Ball and Horner, *Breaking the Codes*, 192–93.
32 Ibid., 199.
33 Andrew, *Defence of the Realm*, 372.
34 Desmond Ball, 'The Moles at the Very Heart of Government', *Weekend Australian*, 16–17 April 2011, Inquirer 4.

35 Ibid.
36 This was the phrase coined by External Affairs Minister Richard Casey. See John Knott, 'About Cabinet notebooks', National Archives of Australia, www.naa.gov.au/collection/explore/cabinet/notebooks/events-issues-1952.aspx, accessed 6 November 2013.
37 Ball and Horner, *Breaking the Codes*, 255.
38 Ibid., 257.
39 Ibid., 256.
40 Ibid., 259.
41 Ibid., 260–61.
42 Phillip Deery, 'Cold War Victim or Rhodes Scholar Spy? Revisiting the Case of Ian Milner', *Overland*, 147 (1997), 9–12. If the Venona decrypts still left any room for doubt, it was filled by evidence found at another source. The post-Cold War opening of Czech archives showed in Prague – Milner's adopted homeland – showed that Milner had done his bit for the Communist cause while in Canberra and beyond, including a stint working for the Czech secret service. See Peter Hruby, *Dangerous Dreamers: The Australian anti-democratic left and Czechoslovak agents*, New York, Bloomington: iUniverse, Inc., 2010, 40–48.
43 Denis Lenihan, 'Was Ian Milner a Spy? A Review of the Evidence', *Kotare* (2008), 1–18, ojs.victoria.ac.nz/kotare/article/view/785/594, accessed 29 November 2013.
44 Ball and Horner, *Breaking the Codes*, 262.
45 Ibid., 263.
46 Manne, *The Petrov Affair*, 235.
47 Cain, *The Australian Security Intelligence Organisation*, 137.
48 See Ball and Horner, *Breaking the Codes*, 262–66.
49 McKnight, *Australia's Spies and Their Secrets*, 55.
50 Ball and Horner, *Breaking the Codes*, 270.
51 Ibid., 270.
52 Ibid., 266.
53 Ibid.
54 Ball, 'The Moles at the Very Heart of Government', 4.
55 Ibid., 4.
56 Ball and Horner, *Breaking the Codes*, 246.
57 Ball, 'The Moles at the Very Heart of Government', 4.
58 Though he remained silent for many years, Clayton finally confessed his role to Des Ball in 1996. See Desmond Ball, 'The Spy Who Came Out as Klod', *Australian*, 24 September 2011, 5.
59 Andrew, *The Defence of the Realm*, 373.
60 Ball and Horner, *Breaking the Codes*, 222.
61 McKnight, *Australia's Spies*, 33–35; Ball and Horner, *Breaking the Codes*, 226–27.
62 David McKnight, 'The Moscow-Canberra Cables: How Soviet Intelligence Obtained British Secrets Through the Back Door', *Intelligence and National Security*, 13, 2 (1998), 162.

63 Deputy Director CIS Melbourne to Director CIS Canberra, 6 October 1947, NAA: 6119 1007 ROSE, Frederick George Godfrey, Volume 1, 21.

64 'Extracts from file of Frederick George Godfrey Rose', NAA: 6119 1009, ROSE, Frederick George Godfrey, Volume 3, 45. Numerous organisations voiced their opposition to the range, which would fire weapons across the Central Aboriginal Reserve. Particularly prominent were the Adelaide churchman Charles Duguid, the Labor parliamentarian Doris Blackburn, and the anthropologist Donald Thomson. Elkin for his part was inclined to accept government assurances that Aboriginal interests would be protected. See Bain Attwood, *Rights for Aborigines*, Sydney: Allen & Unwin, 2003, 120–22.

65 'Extracts from file of Frederick George Godfrey Rose', NAA: 6119 1009, ROSE, Frederick George Godfrey, Volume 3, 47.

66 Macintyre, *A Concise History of Australia*, 208.

67 Ball and Horner, *Breaking the Codes*, 264.

68 Coral Bell, 'A Preoccupation with Armageddon', unpublished manuscript, 5.

69 Ball and Horner, *Breaking the Codes*, 229.

13 | The Gathering Storm

1   Frederick G.G. Rose, 'Memoirs,' 108, SLNSW, Frederick Rose Papers, Box 1.

2   Stuart Macintyre, *A Concise History of Australia*, 3rd ed., Cambridge: CUP, 2009, 215; Frank Cain, *The Australian Security Intelligence Organisation: An unofficial history*, Melbourne: Spectrum Publications, 1994, 98–99.

3   Macintyre, *A Concise History*, 216.

4   David Horner, *The Spy Catchers. Volume I. The Official History of ASIO 1949–1963*, Sydney: Allen & Unwin 2014, 191.

5   David McKnight, *Australia's Spies and Their Secrets*, St. Leonards NSW: Allen & Unwin, 1994, 130.

6   Ibid., 131.

7   Ibid., 113.

8   Deputy Director ASIO NSW to Director, Canberra, 'Royal Commission on Espionage. Mr. F. Rose', 22 July 1954, NAA: A6119 1010, ROSE, Frederick George Godfrey, Volume 4, 31.

9   Intelligence Section Eastern Command to Edith Rose, 26 July 1940, NAA: A6119 1007 ROSE, Frederick George Godfrey, Volume 1, 8.

10 Australian Military Forces – 7th Military Disctrict to ISGS Eastern Command, 30 August 1940, NAA: A6119 1007 ROSE, Frederick George Godfrey, Volume 1, 10.

11 Deputy Director CIS Melbourne to Director CIS Canberra, 6 October 1947, NAA: A6119 1007, ROSE, Frederick George Godfrey, Volume 1, 21; 'Extracts from file of Frederick George Godfrey Rose', NAA: 6119 1009, ROSE, Frederick George Godfrey, Volume 3, 47.

12 Extracts from file of Edith Hildegard Ruth Rose nee Linde, NAA: A6119 1009, ROSE, Frederick George Godfrey, Volume 3, 26.

13 NAA: Agency Notes, Department of Territories, recordsearch.NAA:.gov. au/SearchNRetrieve/Interface/DetailsReports/AgencyDetail.aspx?reg_ no=CA%2042, accessed 31 July 2013.

14 Officer in Charge ASIO ACT to Director NSW, 4 July 1951, NAA: A6119 1007, ROSE, Frederick George Godfrey, Volume 1, 42.

15 Frederick G.G. Rose, 'Memoirs', 96, SLNSW, Frederick Rose Papers, Box 1.

16 Ibid., 96–97.

17 Ibid., 97.

18 Frederick Rose, Application for Position of Anthropologist, Public Service of Papua and New Guinea. Undated, NAA: A6119 1007 ROSE, Frederick George Godfrey, Volume 1, 137.

19 Memo, ASIO Regional Director Port Moresby to Regional Director Canberra, 10 October 1951, NAA: A6119 1007, ROSE, Frederick George Godfrey, Volume 1, 50.

20 Memo by ASIO Regional Director ACT, 12 October 1951, NAA: A6119 1007, ROSE, Frederick George Godfrey, Volume 1, 49.

21 Michael Thwaites for Director-General ASIO to Regional Director ACT, 2 November 1951. NAA: A6119 1007, ROSE, Frederick George Godfrey, Volume 1, 51.

22 C Officer to Regional Director ACT, 'Frederick George Godfrey ROSE', 8 April 1952, NAA: A6119 1007, ROSE, Frederick George Godfrey, Volume 1, 163.

23 Non-Gratis, Report No. 140. Report: 16.6.52. ACT. Communist Party of Australia. Robert Alan Patterson McDONNELL and Others. NAA: A6119 1007 ROSE, Frederick George Godfrey Volume 1, 72.

24 Security Assessment of Frederick George Godfrey Rose, NAA: A6119 1007 ROSE, Frederick George Godfrey,Volume 1, 173.

25 Memorandum Regional Director ACT to Headquarters ASIO, 11 June 1953, NAA: A6119 1007 ROSE, Frederick George Godfrey, Volume 1, 194.

26 Cain, *The Australian Security Intelligence Organisation*, 112.

27 Ibid.

28 Rose, 'Memoirs', 99.

29 'Frederick George Godfrey ROSE', NAA: A6119 1009, ROSE, Frederick George Godfrey, Volume 3, 45.

30 Peter Worsley, *An Academic Skating on Thin Ice*, Oxford, New York: Berghahn Books, 2008, 80.

31 Personal communication from Peter Worsley to the authors, 4 February 2013.

32 Martin Thomas, 'Interview with Peter Worsley', 30 December 2010, National Library of Australian, oral history transcript no. nla.oh-6279–0000, 112.

33 ASIO Report No. 138. Organisation of the C.P. of A, Canberra, 25 February 1954, NAA: A6119, 1008, ROSE, Frederick George Godfrey, Volume 2, 195.

34 ASIO Report no. 139, C.P. of A. Activity National University, Canberra, 25 February 1954, NAA: A6119, 1008, ROSE, Frederick George Godfrey, Volume 2, 196. Gollan was married to Daphne Gollan, also an historian and communist. She had been the unwitting catalyst in the sacking by the CSIRO of the Australian physicist Tom Kaiser. While at Oxford University in 1949 Kaiser had joined a peaceful demonstration to hand out pamphlets, written by Daphne Gollan, outside Australia

House in London. The pamphlets criticised Australia's Labor government for gaoling striking coal miners. Next day, the *Sydney Morning Herald* carried the headline: 'Atom Scientist in Red Attack on Chifley Government'. Kaiser was peremptorily sacked from the CSIRO for 'grave indiscretion and breach of discipline'. Ordered to return to Australia and face an enquiry, he was subsequently banned from work in radio, or nuclear physics, in Australia. See Jeanne Wiseman, 'Tom Kaiser – Meteors and Socialism', *Guardian*, 5 August 1998, tomkaiser.tripod.com/guardian_obit. html, accessed 8 August 2012.

35 Report no. 140, C.P. of A. – Secret Meeting in Canberra, 25 February 1954, NAA: A6119, 1008, ROSE, Frederick George Godfrey, Volume 2, 198.

36 Thomas, 'Interview with Peter Worsley', 113.

37 Ibid, 110.

38 McKnight, *Australia's Spies*, 146.

39 Spry to Menzies, 9 April 1952, CRS A6119/64 item 431, fol. 68, cited in McKnight, *Australia's Spies*, 147.

40 Thomas, 'Interview with Peter Worsley', 115.

41 McKnight, *Australia's Spies*, 147.

42 Thomas 'Interview with Peter Worsley', 191.

43 Peter M. Worsley, 'The Changing Social Structure of the Wanindiljaugwa', unpublished PhD thesis, ANU, June 1954.

44 Peter Hruby, *Dangerous Dreamers: The Australian anti-democratic left and Czechoslovak agents*, New York, Bloomington: iUniverse, Inc., 2010, 194.

45 Stephen Holt, *A Short History of Manning Clark*, Sydney: Allen & Unwin, 1999, 87; Mark McKenna, *An Eye for Eternity: The life of Manning Clark*, Melbourne: Miegunyah Press, 2011, 395. McKnight, *Australia's Spies*, 153; Fiona Capp, *Writers Defiled: Security surveillance of Australian authors and intellectuals 1920–1960*, Ringwood, Vic.: McPhee Gribble, 1993, 97.

46 McKenna, *An Eye for Eternity*, 297–98.

47 Memorandum from Headquarters ASIO from Regional Director ACT, 21 April 1953, NAA: A6119 1007, ROSE, Frederick George Godfrey, Volume 1, 83.

14 | King Island

1 ASIO Field Officer Report on Mrs Edith Hildegard Ruth ROSE, 24 June 1953, NAA: A6119 1007, ROSE, Frederick George Godfrey, Volume 1, 218.

2 Valerie Munt, 'Interview with Peter Worsley', London, 2012.

3 Memorandum Regional Director ASIO ACT to ASIO Headquarters, 19 January 1954, NAA: A6119 1904, PHILLIPS, Kathleen, 23.

4 Memorandum Director General ASIO to Regional Director Victoria, 30 August 1956, NAA: A6119 1904, PHILLIPS, Kathleen, 104.

5 Memorandum Regional Director ASIO ACT to ASIO Headquarters, 29 September 1955, NAA: A6119 1904, PHILLIPS, Kathleen, 44.

6 Frederick G.G. Rose, 'Memoirs', 100–101, SLNSW, Frederick Rose Papers.

7 Rose, 'Memoirs', 101.

8 ASIO Report No. 1019, 7 April 1955, NAA: A6119 1904, PHILLIPS, Kathleen, 41.

9   Memorandum from ASIO Regional Director Tasmania for Regional Director ACT, 3 August 1953, NAA: A6119 1007, ROSE, Frederick George Godfrey, Volume 1, 7.

10 'Red Nest in Vital Mine: Security Moves In', *Sun*, 15 September 1954.

11 Rose to Edith, 6 October 1953, Rose family collection.

12 ASIO Director Sydney to Director Canberra, 'J. Kelly', 5 April 1950, NAA: A6119 974, KELLY, Donald Kelly, 3.

13 F.G.G.Rose, 'The Pastoral Industry in the Northern Territory during the Period of Commonwealth Administration 1911–1953', *Historical Studies*, 6, 22 (1954), 150–72; G.P. Walsh, 'Kelly, John Henry (1895–1983)', *Australian Dictionary of Biography*, National Centre of Biography, Australian National University, adb.anu.edu.au/biography/kelly-john-henry-12721/text22939, accessed 1 May 2013.

14 Rose to Edith, 6 October 1953, Rose family collection.

15 'Persons known to have been friends or associates of Frederick George Godfrey Rose', NAA: A6119 1009, ROSE, Frederick George Godfrey, Volume 3, 28.

16 Memorandum for Regional Director ACT from Regional Director Tasmania, 4 February 1954, NAA: A6119 1008, ROSE, Frederick George Godfrey, Volume 2, 166.

17 Director-General ASIO to Regional Director ACT, 21 September 1953, NAA: A6119 1008, ROSE, Frederick George Godfrey, Volume 2, 20.

18 Minute for Operations Officer from ASIO Regional Director ACT, 11 September 1953, NAA: A6119 1007, ROSE, Frederick George Godfrey, Volume 1, 262.

19 Memorandum Director General ASIO to Regional Director Victoria, 30 August 1956, NAA: A6119 1904, PHILLIPS, Kathleen, 104.

20 ASIO report 'Frederick George Godfrey ROSE – A.C.T. Personality', 17 November 1953, NAA: A6119 1012, ROSE, Frederick George Godfrey, Volume 6, 8.

21 Memorandum Regional Director Tasmania to Regional Director ACT, 15 April 1954, NAA: A6119 1008, ROSE, Frederick George Godfrey, Volume 2, 269.

22 'Frederick George Godfrey ROSE', NAA: A6119 1009 ROSE, Frederick George Godfrey, Volume 3, 36.

23 Rose, *Australia Revisited: The Aborigine story from stone age to space age*, Berlin: Seven Seas, 1968, 75.

24 Ibid.

25 Rose to Secretary Department of Territories 28 March 1954, NAA: A6119 1008, ROSE, Frederick George Godfrey, Volume 2, 238.

26 Desmond Ball and David Horner, *Breaking the Codes: Australia's KGB network*, Sydney: Allen & Unwin, 1998, 320–21. Apart from insights into 'The Case', the Petrovs also provided valuable information on the defection of the Cambridge spy Donald McLean. See Christopher Andrew, *The Defence of the Realm: The authorized history of MI5*, London: Penguin, 2010, 623.

27 Christopher Andrew and Vasili Mitrokhin, *The Mitrokhin Archive II: The KGB and the world*, London: Penguin, 2006 28.

28 Rose to Edith, 14 May 1954, Rose family collection.

29 Memorandum for Regional Director Canberra ACT. Subject: Royal Commission on Espionage. Donald William Archdall Baker, 9 June 1954, NAA: A6119 1010, ROSE, Frederick George Godfrey, Volume 4, 7–9.

30 Case Summary. Subject: DWA Baker, NAA: A6119 861, BAKER, Donald William Archdell [sic] Part 2, 65.

31 Rose, *Australia Revisited*, 77.

32 Ibid., 78–80.

33 Ibid., 81–82.

34 Deputy Director-General (Operations), Frederick George Godfrey ROSE. Service of Summons to Appear at Royal Commission, Melbourne, on 20 July, 1954, NAA: A6119/79 1010, ROSE, Frederick George Godfrey, Volume 4, 24.

35 Ibid., 23.

36 Ibid., 22.

37 Ibid., 21.

15 | Nemesis

1 Christopher Andrew and Oleg Gordievsky, *KGB: The inside story of its foreign operations from Lenin to Gorbachev*, London: Hodder & Stoughton, 1990, 135–36.

2 David Horner, *The Spy Catchers. Volume I. The official history of ASIO 1949–1963*, Sydney: Allen & Unwin, 2014, 320.

3 Nicholas Whitlam and John Stubbs, *Nest of Traitors: The Petrov affair*, Brisbane: Jacaranda, 1974, 107; Desmond Ball and David Horner, *Breaking the Codes: Australia's KGB network, 1944–1950*, Sydney: Allen & Unwin, 1998, 122–24; 144–45.

4 On the impact of Venona especially on Soviet espionage see especially Christopher Andrew, *The Defence of the Realm: The authorized history of MI5*, London: Penguin, 2010, 1508.

5 Christopher Andrew, Christopher and Vasili Mitrokhin, *The Mitrokhin Archive II: The KGB and the world*, London: Penguin, 2006, 28.

6 Ben Macyntyre, *A Spy Among Friends: Kim Philby and the great betrayal*, London; New Delhi; New York; Sydney: Bloomsbury, 2014, 185.

7 ASIO Report 'BARNETT, June Hyett', 20 April 1950, NAA: A6119 733, BARNETT, June Hyett, Volume 1, 13.

8 E.W. Russell, 'Barnett, Frederick Oswald (1883–1972)', *Australian Dictionary of Biography*, National Centre of Biography, Australian National University, adb.anu.edu.au/biography/barnett-frederick-oswald-5138/text8599, accessed 6 August 2013.

9 ASIO Report 'BARNETT, June Hyett', 20 April 1950, NAA: A6119 733 BARNETT, June Hyett, Volume 1, 13.

10 Ibid.

11 ASIO Director Melbourne to Director Canberra, 2 May 1950, NAA: A6119 733 BARNETT, June Hyett, Vol. 1, 14.

12 Ibid.

13 'Subject: BARNETT, June Hyett. Case Summary', NAA: A6119 734, BARNETT, June Hyett, Volume 2, 29.

14 Report to ASIO Director Canberra, 'Persons who attended Canberra University College Review', 2 August 1950, NAA: A6119 733, BARNETT, June Hyett, Volume 1, 15.

15   Memorandum for Record Purposes 'June Hyett Barnett', 10 April 1951, NAA: A6119 733 BARNETT, June Hyett, Volume 1, 24.
16   ASIO Headquarters. Security Checking. Adverse Record 'June Hyett Barnett', NAA: A6119 733, BARNETT, June Hyett, Volume 1, 32.
17   Director General ASIO, memorandum to Officer in Charge ACT, 2 August 1951, NAA: A6119 733, BARNETT, June Hyett, Volume 1, 34.
18   Memorandum for Secretary Department of External Affairs from Officer-in-Charge ACT, 'June Hyett Barnett', 8 August 1951, NAA: A6119 733, BARNETT, June Hyett, Volume 1, 36.
19   Director-General ASIO to R.G. Casey, Minister for External Affairs, 1 April 1953, NAA: A6119 733, BARNETT, June Hyett, Volume 1, 79.
20   Memorandum for Director-General, 'June Hyett BARNETT', NAA: A6119 733, BARNETT, June Hyett, Volume 1, 92.
21   Ibid., 84–92.
22   Ibid.
23   Ibid.
24   Ibid., 84–87.
25   'Fred Rose (politician)' en.wikipedia.org/wiki/Fred_Rose_(politician), accessed 3 December 2012.
26   Memorandum for Director-General, 'June Hyett BARNETT', NAA: A6119 733, BARNETT, June Hyett, Volume 1, 87.
27   Ibid. 87.
28   Ibid. 86.
29   Ball and Horner, *Breaking the Codes*, 27.
30   Memorandum for Director-General, 'June Hyett BARNETT', NAA: A6119 733 BARNETT, June Hyett, Volume 1, 86.
31   Ibid.
32   Top Secret Minute. Director-General. SUBJECT: Miss June Hyett BARNETT, May 1953, NAA: A6119 733, BARNETT, June Hyett, Volume 1, 80.
33   Director-General ASIO to R.G. Casey, Minister for External Affairs, 1 April 1953, NAA: A6119 733, BARNETT, June Hyett, Volume 1, 79.
34   Minute to Director-General ASIO, 18 June 1953, NAA: A6119 1007, ROSE, Frederick George Godfrey Rose, Volume 1, 203.
35   Minute to Director-General, 18 June 1953, 'SUBJECT: Miss June Hyett BARNETT', NAA: A6119 733, BARNETT, June Hyett, Volume 1, 100.
36   Ibid., 101.
37   'June Hyett BARNETT', NAA: A6119 733, Barnett, June Hyett, Vol. 2, 2.
38   'Frederick George Godfrey ROSE' (undated), NAA: A6119 1010, ROSE, Frederick George Godfrey, Volume 4, 103.
39   David McKnight, 'Bialoguski, Michael (1917–1984)', *Australian Dictionary of Biography*, National Centre of Biography, Australian National University, adb.anu.edu.au/biography/bialoguski-michael-12207/text21887, accessed 3 December 2012.
40   Whitlam and Stubbs, *Nest of Traitors*, 1.

41 Ilene Philipson, *Ethel Rosenberg: Beyond the myths*, New Brunswick: Rutgers University Press 1993, 351–52.

42 David McKnight, *Australia's Spies and Their Secrets*, St Leonards NSW: Allen & Unwin, 1974, 78.

43 G.R. Richards, 'The Royal Commission Section. June Barnett', 29 June 1954, NAA: A6119 733, BARNETT, June Hyett, Volume 1, 165.

44 J.M. Gilmour to Deputy Director General (Op), 23 June 1954, NAA: A6119 733, BARNETT, June Hyett, Volume 1, 121.

45 Jenny McNaughton and Tony Stephens, 'Crusader for politics of good. Obituary for Keith Dowding, 1911–2008', *Sydney Morning Herald*, 7 October 2008, www.smh.com.au/news/obituaries/crusader-for-politics-of-good/2008/10/06/1223145260054.html, accessed 10 December 2012.

46 David Horner, *The Spy Catchers. Volume I. The Official History of ASIO 1949–1963*, Sydney: Allen & Unwin, 2014, 299.

47 Interview with Miss June Hyett BARNETT, on 24 June, 1954, at 2.15 p.m., NAA: A6119 733, BARNETT, June Hyett, Volume 1, 146.

48 'June Hyett BARNETT states', 25 June 1954, NAA: A6119 733, BARNETT, June Hyett, Volume 1, 125–32; 'Interview with Miss June Hyett BARNETT and Mrs Betty Blunden', NAA: A6119 733, BARNETT, June Hyett, Volume 1, 162–63.

49 Leo Carter and J.M. Gilmour to Deputy Director-General (Operations) 28 June 1954, NAA: A6119 733 BARNETT, June Hyett, Volume 1, 133.

16 | The Petrov Commission

1 David McKnight, *Australia's Spies and Their Secrets*, Sydney: Allen & Unwin, 1994, 63; Nicholas Whitlam and Stubbs, *Nest of Traitors: The Petrov affair*, Brisbane: Jacaranda, 1974, 68; Robert Manne, *The Petrov Affair*, revised ed., Melbourne: Text, 2004, 62.

2 Cited in Manne, *The Petrov Affair*, 90.

3 Whitlam and Stubbs, *Nest of Traitors*, 107.

4 *Report of the Royal Commission on Espionage*, Sydney: Commonwealth of Australia, 1956, 348.

5 Manne, *The Petrov Affair*, 93.

6 Ibid., 95–96.

7 David Horner, *The Spy Catchers. Volume I. The Official History of ASIO 1949–1963*, Sydney: Allen & Unwin 2014, 89, 91.

8 Manne, *The Petrov Affair*, 158–60.

9 Ibid., 163.

10 John McGuire, 'Julius, Max Nordau (1916–1963)', *Australian Dictionary of Biography*, National Centre of Biography, Australian National University, adb.anu.edu.au/biography/julius-max-nordau-10652/text18929, accessed 6 December 2012.

11 Ibid.

12 Frederick Rose, *Australia Revisited: The Aborigine story from stone age to space age*, Berlin: Seven Seas, 1968, 84.

13 Ibid.

14 Commonwealth of Australia, *Royal Commission on Espionage: Official transcript of proceedings*, Canberra: Government Printers, 1954–55, 21 July 1954, 321–22.

15 Commonwealth of Australia, *Royal Commission on Espionage*, 322–23.

16 Rose, *Australia Revisited*, 85.

17 Ibid., 86; also in W.J. Brown (ed.), *The Petrov Conspiracy Unmasked*, Sydney: Current Books, n.d., 301–302.

18 ASIO report 'Subject: Frederick George Godfrey ROSE', 22 July 1955, NAA: A6119 1011, ROSE, Frederick George Godfrey, Volume 5, 9.

19 Manne, *The Petrov Affair*, 179.

20 Commonwealth of Australia, *Royal Commission on Espionage*, 25 October 1954, 1354.

21 Ibid.

22 Ibid., 1358.

23 ASIO report, 'Walter Seddon CLAYTON', 29 July 1952, NAA: A6119 53, Walter Seddon CLAYTON, Volume 3, Part 1, 73.

24 Commonwealth of Australia, *Royal Commission on Espionage*, 1361.

25 Ibid., 1364.

26 Ibid., 1368.

27 Ibid., 1370.

28 Ibid., 1372.

29 Ibid., 1374.

30 Ibid., 1377.

31 Ibid., 1379.

32 Ibid., 1380–81.

33 Ibid., 1381.

34 David Horner, *The Spy Catchers. Volume I. The Official History of ASIO 1949–1963*, Sydney: Allen & Unwin 2014, 237.

35 Memorandum for Deputy/Director-General, Operations, Royal Commission Section, Sydney, Royal Commission on Espionage. Department of Territories – Frederick George Godfrey ROSE. U.S. Embassy, 27 October 1954, NAA: A6119 1010, ROSE, Frederick George Godfrey, Volume 4, 111.

36 Ibid.

37 *Sydney Morning Herald*, 26 October 1954, 1.

38 Commonwealth of Australia, *Royal Commission on Espionage*, 26 October 1954, 1391.

39 Commonwealth of Australia, *Royal Commission on Espionage*, 27 October 1954, 1432–33.

40 ASIO report 'Subject: Frederick George Godfrey ROSE', 3 November 1954, NAA: A6119 1011, ROSE, Frederick George Godfrey, Volume 5, 32.

41 ASIO secret report, 'Fred ROSE', 27 October 1954, NAA: A6119 1010, ROSE, Frederick George Godfrey, Volume 4, 106–107.

42 Commonwealth of Australia, *Royal Commission on Espionage*, 5 November 1954, 1545.

43 Commonwealth of Australia, *Royal Commission on Espionage*, 24 February 1955, 2405.

44 Commonwealth of Australia, *Royal Commission on Espionage*, 27 January 1955, 1971.

45 Commonwealth of Australia, *Royal Commission on Espionage*, 2 February 1955, 2016.

46 Commonwealth of Australia, *Royal Commission on Espionage*, 4 February 1955, 2075.

47 Commonwealth of Australia, *Royal Commission on Espionage*, 4 February 1955, 2058–59.

48 Commonwealth of Australia, *Royal Commission on Espionage*, 15 March 1955, 2455.

49 Commonwealth of Australia, *Royal Commission on Espionage*, 18 March 1955, 2538–39.

50 Ibid., 2544.

51 ASIO report, 'June Hyett BARNETT', 24 March 1955, NAA: A6119 734, BARNETT, June Hyett, Volume 2, 89.

52 Australian Women's History Forum, 'Heather Sutherland 1903–1953', womenshistory.net.au/2012/02/20/heather-sutherland-1903–1953/ accessed 7 August 2013.

53 ASIO report 'Subject: Frederick George Godfrey ROSE', 23 August 1955, NAA: A6119 1011, ROSE, Frederick George Godfrey, Volume 5, 43.

54 *Report of the Royal Commission on Espionage*, 156.

55 Ibid., 154.

56 Ibid., 157.

17 | On the Hook

1 'Frederick George Godfrey Rose', Memo from ASIO Director-General, 8 March 1956, NAA: A6119 1011, ROSE, Frederick George Godfrey, Volume 5, 134. Cited in Desmond Ball and David Horner, *Breaking the Codes: Australia's KGB network, 1944–1950*, Sydney: Allen & Unwin, 1998, 230.

2 ASIO report 'Extracted from Interview with Leslie ("Tim") WHITE 1957, 1958, 1959', NAA: A6119 1012, ROSE, Frederick George Godfrey, Volume 6, 98.

3 Ibid., 97–98.

4 Victorian Office ASIO, report on 'Mabel Roma LINCOLN', 28 June 1960, NAA: A6119 1012, ROSE, Frederick George Godfrey ROSE, Volume 6, 106–108.

5 Extracts from interview of Robert Rodon Michell, September to November 1960, NAA: A6119 1012, ROSE, Frederick George Godfrey, Volume 6, 120.

6 'Questions To Be Put To "C" about Persons Selected for Future Work', 2nd reissue, 16 May 1948, National National Security Agency official website, www.nsa.gov/public_info/_files/venona/1948/16may_questions_for_c.pdf, accessed 12 August 2013.

7 Ibid.

8 Ibid.

9 We are grateful to David McKnight for supplying this version of the decrypt dated 31 May 1974. Why the official NSA website currently uses the older version of the decrypt is not clear; it could reflect an uncertainty that 'Professor' was Rose.

10 'Questions To Be Put To "C"'.

11 Michele Meeks, CIA Information and Privacy Coordinator, email communication to the authors, 27 June 2013.

12 The Enquiries Team, The Security Service, email communication to the authors, 4 December 2012.

13 Desmond Ball, 'The Spy Who Came Out as Klod', *Weekend Australian*, 24 September 2011, www.theaustralian.com.au/news/opinion/the-spy-who-came-out-as-klod/story-e6frg6zo-1226144286825, accessed 27 March 2012.

14 Ball and Horner, *Breaking the Codes*, 186–88.

15 Ibid., 229.

16 Ibid., 238.

17 Ball, 'The Spy Who Came Out as Klod'.

18 David Horner, *The Spy Catchers. Volume I. The Official History of ASIO 1949–1963*, Sydney: Allen & Unwin, 2014, 298.

19 ASIO report 'Edith Hildegard Ruth ROSE nee LINDE', NAA: A6119 1009, ROSE, Frederick George Godfrey, Volume 3, 21.

20 Ball, 'The Spy Who Came Out as Klod'. The authors are grateful also to Des Ball for a discussion held in Canberra on 22 April 2013.

21 Commonwealth of Australia, *Royal Commission on Espionage: Official transcript of proceedings*, Canberra: Government Printers, 1954–55, 1374. Cited in Ball and Horner, *Breaking the Codes*, 230.

22 Files for the relevant time-frame are NAA: A6119 53, CLAYTON, Walter Seddon, Volume 1, Part 1; and NAA: A6119 53, CLAYTON, Walter Seddon, Volume 3, Part 1.

23 'Persons known to have been friends or associates of Frederick George Godfrey ROSE', NAA: A6119 1009, ROSE, Frederick George Godfrey, Volume 3, 28–30.

24 Horner, *The Spy Catchers*, 87.

25 Ball and Horner, *Breaking the Codes*, 253.

26 Ibid., 308–309. With the help of Rupert Lockwood, who happened to be in London at the time, word soon got to Australia that the security services were onto the spy network. See Horner, *The Spy Catchers*, 143.

27 Ball and Horner, *Breaking the Codes*, 266.

28 Ibid., 273.

29 Coral Bell, 'A Preoccupation with Armageddon', unpublished manuscript provided courtesy Desmond Ball, 5; Desmond Ball, 'Soviet Spies Had Protection In Very High Places', *Weekend Australian*, 14–15 January 2012, Inquirer 14.

30 Coral Bell, telephone conversation with Peter Monteath, 19 March 2012.

31 Bell, 'A Preoccupation with Armageddon', 5.

32 Ibid.

33 Desmond Ball, 'Soviet Spies Had Protection in Very High Places', *Weekend Australian*, 14–15 January 2012, Inquirer 14.

34 Bell, 'A Preoccupation with Armageddon', 5; Ball, 'Soviet Spies Had Protection in Very High Places', 14.

35 Coral Bell, telephone conversation,19 March 2012.

36 Bell, 'A Preoccupation with Armageddon', 5–6; Ball, 'Soviet Spies Had Protection in Very High Places', 14.

37 Linde to Department Head Köhler, Staatssekretariat für Hochschulwesen, 9 October 1953, Rose family collection.

38 Auskunft. Betr.: Hinweis 'Frieden', vorgesehen als Werber, 28 August 1963, BStU, AIM 5163/91 Bd. I/1, 148.

39 ASIO Regional Director Tasmania, 'Mrs Kathleen PHILLIPS', 2 August 1955, NAA: A6119 1904, PHILLIPS, Kathleen, 42.

40 Memorandum from Regional Director Victoria to Regional Director NSW, John Williamson LEGGE, 9 January 1956, NAA: A6119, 1012, ROSE, Frederick George Godfrey, Volume 6, 38; Faith Bandler, *Turning the Tide: A personal history of the Federal Council for the Advancement of Aborigines and Torres Strait Islanders*, Canberra: Aboriginal Studies Press, 1989, 63.

41 Marilyn Lake, *Faith: Faith Bandler, gentle activist*, Sydney: Allen & Unwin, 2002, 70.

42 'Emil and Hannah Witton', National Museum of Australia, 'Collaborating for Indigenous Rights', indigenousrights.net.au/person.asp?pID=1044. Irene McIlwraith was another of such background who took on the cause of Aboriginal rights. See Philip Mendes, 'The Australian Jewish Left and Indigenous Rights', *Australian Jewish Historical Society Journal*, 20, 3 (November 2011), 430–43.

43 Frederick G.G. Rose, 'Memoirs', 100, SLNSW, Frederick Rose Papers, Box 1.

44 Frederick Rose, *Australia Revisited: The Aborigine story from stone age to space age*, Berlin: Seven Seas, 1968, 91.

45 Ibid., 92. Here Rose gives November 1954 as the starting point for his membership of the WWF; later in his memoirs he corrects this to March 1955. See Rose, 'Memoirs', 100.

46 Rose, *Australia Revisited*, 93–94.

47 Ibid., 95.

48 Tom Sheridan, *Australia's Own Cold War: The waterfront under Menzies*, Carlton, Vic.: Melbourne University Press, 2006, 4.

49 Ibid., 92.

50 *Sydney Morning Herald*, 7 June 1951, cited in Sheridan, *Australia's Own Cold War*, 77.

51 Sheridan, *Australia's Own Cold War*, 62.

52 Ray Markey, 'Healy, James (Jim) (1898–1961)', *Australian Dictionary of Biography*, National Centre of Biography, Australian National University, adb.anu.edu.au/biography/healy-james-jim-10470/text18571, accessed 24 November 2011.

53 Ibid.

54 Rose, *Australia Revisited*, 95–96.

55 Rose, 'Memoirs', 100.

56 Rose, *Australia Revisited*, 97.

18 | Germany

1 Cited in Peter Grieder, *The East German Leadership: Conflict and crisis 1946–73*, Manchester: Manchester University Press, 1999, 13.

2 As reported by his then comrade Wolfgang Leonhard in Leonhard, *Die Revolution entlässt ihre Kinder*, Cologne: Kiepenheuer & Witsch, 1981, 317.

3 Recollections of Esther Linde, 25 July 2005, Rose family collection.

4 Ibid.

5 Frederick G.G. Rose, 'Memoirs', 111, SLNSW, Frederick Rose Papers, Box 1.

6   Rose to Edith, 14 May 1954, Rose family collection.

7   Rose, 'Memoirs', 112.

8   Sonja Lenz interview with Valerie Munt, Canberra, 24 August 2012.

9   Ruth Struwe email to Valerie Munt, 22 February 2013.

10   Ruth to Rose, 9 October 1953, SLNSW, Frederick Rose Papers, MLMSS, Box 20.

11   Richard Linde to Rose, 26 March 1947. Rose family collection.

12   Nadel to Firth, 24 Feb 1950, Archive of Sir Raymond Firth, British Archive of Political and Economic Science, London School of Economics FIRTH 7/5/9. This quote was generously supplied to the authors from an unpublished paper by Geoffrey Gray).

13   Richard Linde to Rose, 28 November 1947. Rose family collection.

14   Richard Linde to Anton Ackermann, 8 June 1948, Rose family collection.

15   C. Halle, Hauptabteilungsleiter Ministerium für Volksbildung to Richard Linde, 11 August 1950, Rose family collection.

16   Richard Linde to Rose, 13 March 1951, Rose family collection.

17   Richard Linde to Politbüro, 27 July 1953, Rose family collection.

18   Edith Rose to Ministerium für Auswärtige Angelegenheiten, Abteilung für konsularische Angelegenheiten, 20 June 1955, Rose family collection.

19   Rose, 'Memoirs', 113.

20   Richard Linde to Fred Rose, 16 May 1955, SLNSW, Frederick Rose Papers, Box 34.

21   See SLNSW, Frederick Rose Papers, Box 20, containing articles from *The Times* July 1954, including: 'New Witness Refuses to Answer Questions: Crown Law Office to be Informed' and 'Cambridge Master of Arts'.

22   Frances Rose to Fred Rose, undated, SLNSW, Frederick Rose Papers, Box 20.

23   Senior Field Officer E.O. Redford, Minute for Regional Director, Victoria, ASIO Victorian Office, 10 February 1956. NAA: A6119 1011, ROSE, Frederick George Godfrey, Volume 5, 93–94.

24   Travel Officer 'C' Section, 'Kim Donald ROSE', ASIO Sydney Office, 7 February 1956. NAA: A6119 1011, ROSE, Frederick George Godfrey, Volume 5, 83.

25   Minute for Senior Field Officer, 'Kim Donald Rose. Subject: Reverend Brother N.K. Phelan', ASIO Victorian Office, 9 Feb. 1956, NAA: A6119 1011, ROSE, Frederick George Godfrey, Volume 5, 89.

26   Spry to F.C. Scharenguivel, Director of Public Security, Ceylon, 2 March 1956, NAA: A6119 1011, ROSE, Frederick George Godfrey, Volume 5, 126.

27   Rose to Laurie Aarons, 5 May 1955. See also Rose to Secretariat ACP, 14 May 1955, with a 33-page typed document re Rose's 'errors' in using Engels' theories in *Origin of the Family*. SLNSW, Frederick Rose Papers, Box 20.

28   L.L. Sharkey, General Secretary CPA to Socialist Unity Party, 16 January 1956, Rose family collection.

29   Cited in Rose, 'Memoirs', 114.

30   Rose, 'Memoirs', 114.

31   See especially their 1957 correspondence in SLNSW, Frederick Rose Papers, Box 34.

32   Kim to Fred Rose, undated, SLNSW, Frederick Rose Papers, Box 26.

33   Rose letter to the *Tribune*, 6 September 1956, SLNSW, Frederick Rose Papers, Box 26.

34 Rose to Günter Harig, Staatssekretariat für Hochschulwesen, 12 May 1956, Rose family collection.

35 Rose, 'Memoirs', 115.

36 'Ergänzungen zum Lebenslauf', 28 April 1961, Rose family collection.

37 Bericht 'Miller', 17 October 1962, BStU, AIM 11120/70, Band I /1, 215.

19 | Professor

1 Andre Gingrich, 'The German Speaking Countries', in Fredrik Barth, Andre Gingrich, Robert Parkin and Sydel Silverman, *One Discipline, Four Ways: British, German, French and American anthropology*, Chicago, London: University of Chicago Press, 2005, 69.

2 Lewis Henry Morgan, 'Preface', in Lorimer Fison and A.W. Howitt, *Kamilaroi and Kurnai*, Melbourne: Angus and Robertson, 1880, 2.

3 Gingrich, 'The German Speaking Countries', 113.

4 On the emergence of an anti-humanist paradigm in German anthropology, see especially Andrew Zimmerman, *Anthropology and Anti-Humanism in Imperial Germany*, Chicago and London: University of Chicago Press, 2001.

5 Viola König (ed.), *Ethnologisches Museum Berlin*, Munich: Prestel, 2003, 19.

6 On the development of anthropology at the Karl-Marx University see especially Dietrich Treide, 'Anthropology at the University of Leipzig, 1950–1968', in Chris Hann, Mihály Sárkány and Peter Skalníky (eds.), *Studying Peoples in the People's Democracies: Socialist era anthropology in East-Central Europe*, Münster: Lit Verlag, 2005, 133–58.

7 Ute Mohrmann and Walter Rusch, 'Vier Jahrzehnte Ethnographie an der Humboldt-Universität zu Berlin', *Beiträge zur Geschichte der Humboldt-Universität zu Berlin. Nr. 28. Geschichte der Völkerkunde und Volkskunde an der Berliner Universität*, Berlin: Humboldt-Universität, 1991, 61. The initial title *Institut für Völkerkunde* was changed to *Institut für Völkerkunde und Deutsche Volkskunde* in 1953. See Wolfgang Kaschuba and Leonore Scholze-Irrlitz, 'Von der Ethnographie zur Europäischen Ethnologie', in Heinz-Elmar Tenorth (ed.), *Geschichte der Universität Unter den Linden 1810–2010. Selbstbehauptung einer Vision*, Berlin: Akademie-Verlag, 2010, 423.

8 Karoline Noack and Martina Krause, '*Ethnographie* as a Unified Anthropological Science in the German Democratic Republic', in Chris Hann, Mihály Sárkány and Peter Skalníky (eds.), *Studying Peoples in the People's Democracies: Socialist era anthropology in East-Central Europe*, Münster: Lit Verlag, 2005, 28 – 31.

9 This according to the plaque placed by GDR authorities on the front of the building.

10 'Auszug aus dem Protokoll der Fakulätssitzung vo. 19.9.1956', Archiv der Humboldt-Universität zu Berlin, Habilitation Frederick G.G. Rose, 1 October 1958.

11 Mohrmann and Rusch, 'Vier Jahrzehnte Ethnographie', 61. See also 'Interviews with German Anthropologists. Vincenz Kokot, Short Portrait: Sigrid Westphal-Hellbusch', www.germananthropology.com/short-portrait/sigrid-westphal-hellbusch/290, accessed 2 January 2013.

12 Sigrid Westphal-Hellbusch, 'Beurteilung der Arbeit: The Relationship System of the Groote Eylandt Aborigines, by F.G.G. Rose, M.A. (Cantab.)', Archiv der Humboldt-Universität zu Berlin. Habilitation Frederick G.G. Rose. 17 January 1957.

13 Prof. Dr. Otto, 'Gutachten über die Habilitationsschrift. F.G.G. Rose, M.A., Classification of kin, age structure and marriage amongst the Groote Eylandt aborigines. A study in method and a theory of Australian kinship', Archiv der Humboldt-Universität zu Berlin. 'Habilitation Frederick G.G. Rose', 28 January 1958, 8; Gertrud Pätsch, 'Gutachten über die Habilitationsschrift', Archiv der Humboldt-Universität zu Berlin. 'Habilitation Frederick G.G. Rose', 9 January 1958.

14 'You will find plenty of "warts" and you may suggest some excisions ... but for God's sake, don't suggest re-writing – I have just about had typing!! If you do adjudicate on it and I hope you do, you might add a rider to the effect that you recommend it be published as early as possible.' Rose to Worsley, 18 October 1957, Frederick Rose Papers, SLNSW, Box 34.

15 Peter Worsley, Report on 'Classification of Kin, Age Structure and Marriage amongst the Groote Eylandt Aborigines (Habilitationsschrift) by F.G.G.Rose', Archiv der Humboldt-Universität zu Berlin. 'Habilitation Frederick G.G. Rose', 3–4.

16 Archiv der Humboldt-Universität Berlin. Habilitation Frederick G.G. Rose, 1 October 1958. After the qualification was achieved Rose received a formal appointment as 'Professor mit Lehrauftrag' (Professor with teaching duties) in September 1961, then five years later as 'Professor mit vollem Lehrauftrag' (Professor with full teaching duties).

17 Frederick G.G. Rose, *The Classification of Kin, Age Structure and Marriage Amongst the Groote Eylandt Aborigines: A study in method and a theory of Australian kinship*, Berlin: Akademie-Verlag, 1960, dedication.

18 For this information we are indebted to Geoff Gray.

19 Rose to L.A. White, 7 February 1950, SLNSW, Frederick Rose Papers, Box 20.

20 Rose, *The Classification of Kin*, 23, 2.

21 Meyer Fortes, Review of *The Classification of Kin, Age Structure and Marriage Amongst the Groote Eylandt Aborigines: A study in method and a theory of Australian kinship*, by F.G.G. Rose, *British Journal of Sociology* 13,1 (1962), 81–82.

22 Jane C. Goodale, 'Review of *Classification of Kin*', *American Anthropologist* 64, 3 (1962), 663–67.

23 Levi-Strauss to Rose, 31 Mach 1958. SLNSW, Frederick Rose Papers, Box 34.

24 Patrick de Josselin de Jong, 'A New Approach to Kinship Studies', *Bijdragen tot de Taal-, Land- en Volkenkunde* 118, 1 (1962), 66.

25 Rodney Needham, 'Review of *Classification of Kin*', *Nature*, 191, (1 July 1961), 6–7.

26 Frances Rose to Fred Rose, 21 November 1960, SLNSW, Frederick Rose Papers, Box 26.

27 Fred Rose to Auntie Edie, 23 December 1956, SLNSW, Frederick Rose Papers, Box 26.

28 Cited in Frederick G.G. Rose, *The Wind of Change in Central Australia*, Berlin: Akademie-Verlag, 1965, 3.

29 Thanks to Rose's former colleagues and students Ute Mohrmann, Stefan Kurella, Hans-Horst Bethge, Monika Wolf, Erika Karasek and Ursula Thiemer-Sachse for their recollections of his teaching practices.

30 Rose, untitled manuscript, SLNSW, Frederick Rose Papers, Box 5.

20 | Angas Downs

1 Rose to Fred Gray, 31 December 1956, SLNSW, Frederick Rose Papers, Box 26.

2 Fred Gray to Fred and Edith Rose, 1 February 1968. SLNSW, Frederick Rose Papers, Box 34.

3 R.B. Dent to H.C. Giese, 26 September 1962, NAA: F423 S43 R.B. Dent – Alleged Communist activity among Aborigines – Groote Eylandt Mission, 11–12.

4 H.C. Giese to R.B. Dent, 21 October 1963, NAA: F423 S43 R.B. Dent – Alleged Communist activity among Aborigines – Groote Eylandt Mission, 13.

5 F. Lancaster Jones, *Demographic Survey of the Aboriginal population of the Northern Territory*, Canberra: Australian Institute of Aboriginal Studies, 1963, cited in Frederick Rose, *The Wind of Change in Central Australia: The Aborigines at Angas Downs, 1962*, Berlin: Akademie, 1965, 5.

6 Paul Hasluck as cited in Stephen Gray, *The Protectors: A journey through whitefella past*, Sydney: Allen and Unwin, 2011, 282.

7 Telegram, ASIO Regional Director ACT to ASIO Headquarters, 28 February 1962, NAA: A6119 1012 ROSE, Frederick George Godfrey, Volume 6, 131–32.

8 ASIO Minute Paper by A/Director B2, 'Frederick George Godfrey ROSE', 1 March 1962, NAA: A6119 1012, ROSE, Frederick George Godfrey, Volume 6, 133.

9 Rose, *Australia Revisited: The Aborigine story from stone age to space age*, East Berlin: Seven Seas, 1968, 99–100.

10 Ibid., 100.

11 Ibid., 101.

12 ASIO Q Report No. 4475, 'Frederick George Godfrey ROSE, Eric Charles FRY, 4 April 1962', NAA: A6119 1012, ROSE, Frederick George Godfrey, Volume 6, 157.

13 Rose, *Australia Revisited*, 99.

14 Paul Hasluck to Rose, 21 February 1961, SLNSW, Frederick Rose Papers, Box 31.

15 Rose to Paul Hasluck, 10 July 1962. SLNSW, Frederick Rose Papers, Box 21.

16 Rose, *Australia Revisited*, 182.

17 Rose to A.P. Elkin, 24 March 1962, SLNSW, Frederick Rose Papers, Box 34.

18 A.P.Elkin to Rose, 13 March 1962, SLNSW, Frederick Rose Papers, Box 34.

19 Rose to Jessie Street, 26 March 1962, SLNSW Frederick Rose Papers, Box 34.

20 Ibid.

21 ASIO Minute Paper by A/Director B2, 'Frederick George Godfrey ROSE', 1 March 1962, NAA: A6119 1012, ROSE, Frederick George Godfrey, Volume 6, 132–33.

22 Paul Hasluck to Jessie Street, 6 March 1962, NAA: A6119 1012, ROSE, Frederick George Godfrey, Volume 6, 148.

23 John Mulvaney, *Digging Up a Past*, Sydney: UNSW Press, 2011, 170.

24 Ibid.

25 See John Mulvaney, 'Reflections', *Antiquity* 80, 308 (June 2006), 425–34.

26 Telephone message received from Regional Director ACT on 5 April 1962, 'Frederick George Godfrey ROSE', NAA: A6119 1012, ROSE, Frederick George Godfrey, Volume 6, 158.

27 Ibid.

28 Regional Director ACT to Director-General ASIO, 'Frederick George Godfrey ROSE. AUSTRALIAN ABORIGINES', 5 April 1962, NAA: A6119 1012, ROSE, Frederick George Godfrey, Volume 6, 159.

29 NAA: A9626 281, ROSE Frederick George.

30 Regional Director ACT to Director-General ASIO, 'Frederick George Godfrey ROSE. AUSTRALIAN ABORIGINES', 5 April 1962, NAA: A6119 1012, ROSE, Frederick George Godfrey, Volume 6, 161.

31 Memorandum to Prime Minister by E.J.B. Foxcroft, 'Application by F.G.G. Rose for a Grant from the Australian Institute of Aboriginal Studies', 30 April 1962, NAA: A6119 1012, ROSE, Frederick George Godfrey, Volume 6, 173.

32 Ibid.

33 Among the anthropologists pressing Rose's case was Patrick de Josselin de Jong, an admirer of *Classification of Kin*. Addressing Hasluck as 'Your Excellency', the Leiden Professor concluded his petition persuasively by stating emphatically: 'I may add that I do not share Dr Rose's political convictions – to the contrary – but in his case too I have not the slightest doubt that in wishing to carry out his field studies he is actuated entirely by scholarly motives.' Patrick Josselin de Jong to Paul Hasluck, 18 June 1962, SLNSW, Frederick Rose Papers, Box 34.

34 Cited in Rose, *The Wind of Change*, 5.

35 Rose, *The Wind of Change*, 2.

36 Ibid., 6.

37 Paul Hasluck to Rose 1 August 1962, SLNSW, Frederick Rose Papers, Box 21.

38 Rose, *The Wind of Change*, 6.

39 Ibid.

40 Rose, *Australia Revisited*, 188–92.

41 Regional Director Victoria to Headquarters ASIO, 'Frederick George Godfrey ROSE', 2 August 1962, NAA: A6119 1012, ROSE, Frederick George Godfrey, Volume 6, 189.

42 Telephone Message from Regional Director NT to ASIO Headquarters, 'Frederick George Godfrey ROSE', 9 August 1962, NAA: A6119 1012, ROSE, Frederick George Godfrey, Volume 6, 190.

43 Rose, *The Wind of Change*, 21.

44 Ibid., 18–21.

45 PL 584, Department of Lands, Land Administration Branch, Correspondence files with 'PL' prefix (pastoral lease), 1915–1994. NTRS, 246/P1, Box 22; Rose, *The Wind of Change*, 196.

46 R.C. Oliver, Pastoral Inspector, 'Angas Downs – General Inspection', 30 August 1962, PL 584, Department of Lands, Land Administration Branch, Correspondence files with 'PL' prefix (pastoral lease), 1915–1994. NTRS, 246/P1, Box 22.

47 Rose, *The Wind of Change*, 202.

48 Rose, *Australia Revisited*, 191–92.

49 Ibid., 204.

50 Ibid., 203.

51 Ibid., 210–11.

52 Ibid., 196.

53 Rose, *The Wind of Change*, 125.
54 Ibid., 73.
55 Ibid., 42–43.
56 Ibid., 46.
57 Ibid., 99.
58 Ibid., 99.
59 Mervyn Meggitt, 'Review of *The Wind of Change in Central Australia*', *Bijdragen tot de Taal-, Land- en Volkenkunde*, 123, 1 (1967), 161.
60 Rose, *The Wind of Change*, 125–184.
61 Elkin, A.P. '*The Wind of Change*: A Review Article', *Oceania*, 40, 2 (December 1969), 148–152.

21 | By Any Other Name

1 Frederick Rose 'Memoirs', 117, SLNSW, Frederick Rose Papers, Box 1.
2 Ibid., 34.
3 The commonly used abbreviation in GDR times was the acronym 'MfS'.
4 Mike Dennis, *The Stasi: Myth and reality*, Harlow: Pearson, 2003, 21.
5 Gabriele Camphausen et al., *Stasi: die Ausstellung zur DDR-Staatssicherheit*, Berlin: Der Bundesbeauftragte für die Unterlagen des Staatssicherheitsdienstes der ehemaligen Deutschen Demokratischen Republick, 2011, 13.
6 Ibid., 6.
7 Jens Gieseke, *The GDR State Security: Shield and sword of the party*, 2nd ed. Berlin: Bundeszentrale für politische Bildung, 2006, 7.
8 Ibid., 7.
9 Kaderakte, 29 May 1963, BStU, AIM 5163/91, Teil I/1, 96.
10 Kaderakte, 29 May 1963, BStU, AIM 5163/91 Teil I/1, 95.
11 Einschätzung einer Ausländerin. Volkspolizeikreisamt Potsdam. Potsdam, 26 October 1961, BStU, AIM 5163/91 Teil I/ 1, 22.
12 Gesprächsplan zur ersten Kontaktaufnahme, 16 May 1963, BStU, AIM 5163/91 Teil I/1, 160–61.
13 Ibid.
14 Kontaktgespräch, 20 May 1963, BStU, AIM 5163/91 Teil I/1, 162.
15 Werbevorlage 1.6.1964, BStU, AIM 5163/91 Teil I/1, 195.
16 Ibid., 194.
17 Vermerk über eine Aussprache mit Gen. Kepernick, HA V/2, und Gen. Wunderlich, BV Potsdam, am 04.01.64, BStU, AIM 5163/91 Teil I/1, 212.
18 Bericht über den Stand der Zusammenarbeit, 30 December 1964, BStU, Frederick Rose, Personalakte, Bln. AIM 5163/91 Teil I/ 1, 280.
19 Treffbericht, 29 January 1964, BStU, AIM 5163/91 Teil I/ 1, 216–20.
20 Treffauswertung, Potsdam, 17 January 1964, BStU, MfS AIM 11120/70 Teil I/1 Miller, 171.
21 Kontaktgespräch, Berlin, 13 December 1963, BStU, 5163/91 Bd. I,1, 204.
22 Werbevorlage, 1 June 1964, BStU, AIM 5163/91 Teil I/1, 195.

23   It was noted that neither the Soviet security organs nor military intelligence knew of any connection between Rose and Petrov: Auskunft. Hinweis 'Frieden', vorgesehen als Werber, 28 August 1963, BStU, AIM 5163/91 Teil I/1, 190.

24   Bericht, 2 March 64, BStU, AIM 5163/91 Teil I/ 1; Frederick Rose, Personalakte, AIM 5136/91 Teil I/1, 224.

25   Kontaktgespräch, 19 December 1963, BStU, AIM 5163/91 Teil I/.1, 208.

26   Bericht betr. Hirsch, 29 January 1964, BStU, AIM 5163/91Teil I/ 1, 254.

27   Treffbericht, 26 January 1965, BStU, AIM 5163/91 Teil I/1, 293.

28   Kontaktgespräch, 12 December 1963, BStU, AIM 5163/91 Teil I/1, 207.

29   Bericht, 17 November 1964, BStU, AIM 5163/91 Teil I/1, 271.

30   Treffbericht 26 January 1965, BStU, AIM 5163/91 Teil I/1, 291.

31   Here and elsewhere the use of pseudonyms to protect identities is indicated with quotation marks.

32   Hinweis Abteilung I/SR Berlin, 6 June 1967, BStU, Frederick Rose, Personalakte, Bln. AIM 5163/91 Teil I/1, 410–11.

33   Treffbericht, 27 March 1965, BStU, AIM 5163/91 Teil I/1, 302–306.

34   Abschlussbericht zur Zusammenarbeit mit dem IMF 'Aust', 10 August 1977, BStU, AIM 5163/91 Teil I/3, 234.

35   Hauptverwaltung A Sonderreferat, Abschlussbericht, 8 May 1968, BstU, AIM 5163/91 Teil I/1, 431.

22 | A Modest Proposal

1   Ermittlungsbericht, 6 September 1962, BStU, AGMS 2924/89, Bd I, 14–16.

2   Betr.: Kontaktaufnahme zum Kandidaten – Rose, Edith, Potsdam 7.9.62, BStU, AIM 11120/70 Teil I/1 Miller, 199–202.

3   Ibid.

4   Bericht über durchgeführte Werbung der Rose, geb. Linde, Edith, 21 September 1962, BStU, AIM 11120/70 I/1 Miller, 212.

5   Ibid.

6   Verpflichtung, Potsdam, 19 September 1962, BStU, AIM 11120/70 Teil I/1 Miller, 211.

7   'Wander, Fred (Fritz Rosenblatt)', in *Wer war wer in der DDR*, online databank, www.bundesstiftung-aufarbeitung.de/wer-war-wer-in-der-ddr-%2363%3B-1424.html?ID=3688, accessed 21 March 2013.

8   Bericht über durchgeführte Werbung der Rose, geb. Linde, Edith, 21 September 1962, BStU, AIM 11120/70 Teil I/1 Miller, 213.

9   Steve Gibson, *The Last Mission Behind the Iron Curtain*, Phoenix Mill: Sutton, 1997, xiii – xiv.

10   For an overview of the history and functions of BRIXMIS, see Peter G. Williams, 'BRIXMIS in the 1980s: The Cold War's "Great Game". Memories of liaising with the Soviet army in East Germany', Canberra, 2006, archive.org/details/BrixmisInThe1980sTheColdWarsGreatGame, accessed 10 October 2012.

11   Tony Geraghty, *Beyond the Frontline: The untold exploits of Britain's most daring Cold War spy mission*, London: HarperCollins, 1996, 17.

12 Gibson, *The Last Mission*, 5.

13 Australian Military Mission to Allied Control Council for Germany and Austria/ Allied High Commission/Federal Republic of Germany [West Berlin], recordsearch. naa.gov.au/SearchNRetrieve/Interface/DetailsReports/AgencyDetail.aspx?reg_ no=CA%208069, accessed 10 October 2012.

14 Einschätzung von IM Miller, Potsdam 22 September 1969, BStU, AIM 11120/70 Teil I/1 Miller, 258–61.

15 Vorschlag für Einsatz des GI 'Miller' in Westberlin, Potsdam den. 18.9.1963, BStU, AIM 11120/70 Teil I/1 Miller, 115.

16 Abschlussbericht über die IMK 'Miller', Potsdam 17.5.1978, Einschätzung der Zusammenarbeit (Zeitraum 1975/76) Potsdam, 2 November 1976, BStU, AIM 11120/70 Teil I/1 Miller, 393.

17 Bericht, Potsdam 18 February 1963, BStU, MfS AIM 11120/70 Teil I/1 Miller, 224.

18 Bericht Teltow, 9 June 1971, BStU, AIM 11120/70 I/1 Miller, Bd. II, 191; Aktenvermerk, Potsdam, 23 July 1971, BStU, AIM 11120/70 Bd. II, 194.

19 'Conferring of Degrees', *Canberra Times*, 15 March 1951, 4.

20 Hoyle had a diplomatic posting to Wellington in 1956. NAA: A1838 1500/2/34/3 Australian Diplomatic Representatives Abroad – New Zealand – J H A Hoyle.

21 Einschätzung des IMV 'Miller', Potsdam, 11 September 1968, BStU, AIM 11120/70 Bd. I/1 Miller, 259.

22 Ibid.

23 Überprüfung von Ausländern, 18 March 1966, BStU, AP 5153/73 Rose, Kim, 24.

24 Bericht, Kontaktaufnahme zu Rose Kim 14.10.1966, BStU, AP 5153/73 Rose, Kim, 146.

25 Ibid.

26 Ibid.

27 Ibid., 147.

28 Kontaktgespräch mit Rose Kim, 11 November 1966, BStU, AP 5153/73 Rose, Kim, 151.

29 Britischer Staatsbürger Rose Kim, 19 January 1972. BStU, AP 5153/73 Rose, Kim, 64.

30 Ibid.

31 Abverfügung zur Archivierung. Die Akte über Rose, Kim, 20 April 1973, BStU, AP 5153/73 Rose, Kim, 183.

32 ASIO Regional Director SA to ASIO Headquarters ASIO, 'ROSE, Kim Donald', 24 October 1974, NAA: A6119, ROSE, Frederick George Godfrey, Volume 8, 178.

23 | Australia Revisited

1 National Museum of Australia, 'Brian Manning', www.indigenousrights.net.au/ person.asp?pID=1028, accessed 28 November 2011.

2 On the Freedom Ride and its politics see especially Ann Curthoys, *Freedom Ride: A freedom rider remembers*, Sydney: Allen Unwin, 2002.

3 Peter Sekuless, *Jessie Street: A rewarding but unrewarded life*, Brisbane: UQP, 1978, chapter 8; Marilyn Lake, *Faith: Faith Bandler, gentle activist*, Sydney: Allen & Unwin, 2002, 72–73.

4   Terry Townsend, *The Aboriginal Struggle and the Left*, Sydney: Resistance Books, 2008, 49.

5   Bain Attwood and Andrew Markus (eds.), *The Struggle for Aboriginal Rights: A documentary history*, Sydney: Allen & Unwin, 1999, 171; Townsend, *The Aboriginal Struggle and the Left*, 50.

6   Joe McGinness, *Son of Alyandabu: My fight for Aboriginal rights*, Brisbane: University of Queensland Press, 1991, 1–51.

7   'Faith Bandler', en.wikipedia.org/wiki/Faith_Bandler; Tony Stephens, 'Escapee from Nazis fought for Aborigines', Obituary for Hans Bandler, www.smh.com.au/national/obituaries/escapee-from-nazis-fought-for-aborigines-20090913-fmad.html, accessed 30 November 2012.

8   Faith Bandler, *Turning the Tide: A personal history of the Federal Council for the Advancement of Aborigines and Torres Strait Islanders*, Canberra: Aboriginal Studies Press, 1989, 3.

9   Bob Boughton, 'The Communist Party of Australia's involvement in the Struggle for Aboriginal and Torres Strait Islander People's Rights 1930–1970', in Ray Markey (ed.), *Labour and Community: historical essays*, Wollongong: University of Wollongong Press, 2001, 286.

10 Townsend, *The Aboriginal Struggle and the Left*, 49–50.

11 Sue Taffe, *Black and White Together: The Federal Council for the Advancement of Aborigines and Torres Strait Islanders 1958–1973*, Brisbane: University of Queensland Press, 2005, 98; Townsend, *The Aboriginal Struggle and the Left*, 51.

12 Townsend, *The Aboriginal Struggle and the Left*, 9, 45–46.

13 Lake, *Faith*, 96–97; Lachlan Clohesy, 'Fighting the Enemy Within: Anti-communism and Aboriginal Affairs', *History Australia*, 8, 2 (August 2011), 139.

14 Lake, *Faith*, 98.

15 Cited in Bain Attwood, 'The articulation of "land rights" in Australia: the case of Wave Hill', *Social Analysis*, 44, 1 (April 2000), 3–39; also Jenny Hocking, *Frank Hardy: Politics, literature, life*, South Melbourne, Vic.: Lothian Books, 2005, 172.

16 Clohessy, 'Fighting the Enemy Within', 140.

17 ASIO report on FCAATSI, 1 November 1967, NAA: A6119, 3661, cited in Clohessy, 'Fighting the Enemy Within', 139.

18 Rose, *Australia Revisited: The Aborigine story from stone age to space age*, Berlin: Seven Seas, 257.

19 *Herald*, 5 April 1965.

20 *Sun*, 7 April 1965.

21 The ASIO file covering Jolly's postwar life is NAA: A6119 4879 JOLLY, Alexander Thomas Hicks Volume 1.

22 'Aborigines' treatment "slur on reputation"', *Australian*, 14 April 1965.

23 'Extract from "People" (TV) – 20 April, 1965. Interview by Bob Sanders with Professor Rose', NAA: A6119 5025, ROSE, Frederick George Godfrey, Volume 7, 21.

24 Ibid. 20.

25 'Advice received from Deputy Director General (New South Wales) p.m. on 14th April, 1965', 14 April 1965, NAA: A6119 5025, ROSE, Frederick George Godfrey, Volume 7, 10.

26 Secret report, Non Gratis 'Professor Frederick Godfrey George ROSE', 17 April 1965, NAA: A6119 5025, ROSE, Frederick George Godfrey, Volume 7, 16.

27 ASIO report '8th Annual Conference and Annual General Meeting Federal Council for Advancement of Aborigines & Torres Strait Islanders', 22 April 1965, 'Extract from "People" (TV) – 20 April, 1965. Interview by Bob Sanders with Professor Rose', NAA: A6119 5025, ROSE, Frederick George Godfrey, Volume 7, 22.

28 See 'Operation Shiver' images collected in NAA: A9626 281, ROSE, Frederick George.

29 'Non Gratis' report on Rose 29 April 1965, NAA: A6119 5025 5025, ROSE, Frederick George Godfrey, Volume 7, 14.

30 ASIO report 'Walter Seddon CLAYTON', Non Gratis, 29 April 1965, NAA: A6119 5025, ROSE, Frederick George Godfrey, Volume 7, 37.

31 Ibid.

32 ASIO Regional Director NT to Headquarters ASIO, 7 July 1965, NAA: A6119 5025, ROSE, Frederick George Godfrey, Volume 7, 59.

33 Rose, *Australia Revisited*, 115–16.

34 Ibid., 154.

35 ASIO Regional Director NT to Headquarters ASIO 26 July 1965, NAA: A6119 5025, ROSE, Frederick George Godfrey, Volume 7, 73.

36 ASIO Regional Director NT to Headquarters ASIO 26 July 1965, NAA: A6119 5025, ROSE, Frederick George Godfrey, Volume 7, 72.

37 ASIO report 'Dr. Frederick George Godfrey ROSE', (undated), NAA: A6119 5025 ROSE, Frederick George Godfrey, Volume 7, 102.

38 Frederick Rose, *Ureinwohner, Känguruhs und Düsenclipper. Fünfundzwanzig Jahre unter Australiern*, transl. Anneliese Dangel, Leipzig: Brockhaus, 1966.

39 Leipzig: Koehler & Amelang, 1969.

40 Frederick Rose, 'Paintings of the Groote Eylandt Aborigines', *Oceania* 13 (1942), 170–76.

41 Egon Erwin Kisch, *Australian Landfall*, transl. John Fischer et al., London: Secker, 1937.

42 May Davis, 'Red Professor. Australia Revisited', *Age*, 28 December 1968, NAA: A3753 1972/79 Commonwealth Literary Fund.

24 |1968

1 Terry Townsend, *The Aboriginal Struggle and the Left*, Sydney: Resistance Books, 2008, 64.

2 Ibid., 66.

3 Lachlan Clohesy, 'Fighting the Enemy Within: Anti-Communism and Aboriginal Affairs', *History Australia*, 8, 2 (August 2011), 146.

4 Hansard, House of Representatives, 13 August 1968, 19. Cited in Jenny Hocking, *Frank Hardy: Politics, literature, life*, Melbourne: Lothian Books, 2005, 173.

5 Peter Howson and Don Aitken, *The Howson Diaries: The life of politics*, Melbourne: Viking, 1984, 433–34, cited in Clohessy, 'Fighting the Enemy Within', 147.

6 Clohessy, 'Fighting the Enemy Within', 142.

7   The iterations of the application are available in AIATSIS File No. 65/85, Rose, Professor F.G.G.

8   AIAS to Rose 3.4.1968, AIATSIS File No. 65/85, Rose, Professor F.G.G.

9   ASIO, Minute Paper, 'Frederick George Godfrey ROSE', 21 March 1968, NAA: A6119 5025, ROSE, Frederick George Godfrey, Volume 7, 153.

10   Snedden to Wentworth, Confidential text of letter as dictated to Minister's office', NAA: A6119 5025, ROSE, Frederick George Godfrey, Volume 7, 163.

11   Ibid., 162.

12   AIAS to Rose, 3 April 1968, NAA: A6119 5025, ROSE, Frederick George Godfrey, Volume 7, 161.

13   Secretary, Department of the Interior to ASIO, 29 April 1968, NAA: A6119 5025, ROSE, Frederick George Godfrey, Volume 7, 173.

14   Spry to Secretary, Department of the Interior, 3 May 1968, NAA: A6119 5025, ROSE, Frederick George Godfrey, Volume 7, 178–80.

15   Rose to Bryant, 12 April 1968, BStU, AIM 5163/91 Teil I/2, 29.

16   Calwell to Rose 29 April 1968, BStU, AIM 5163/91 Teil I/2, 27.

17   Cabinet Minute, Canberra, 9 May 1968, Decision No. 204, NAA: A6119 5025, ROSE, Frederick George Godfrey, Volume 7, 181.

18   Copy of cablegram Giese to Rose 10 May 1968, BStU, AIM 5163/91 Teil I/2, 26.

19   W.C. Wentworth, Cabinet submission no. 92. 15 May 1968. Cited in Bob Boughton, 'The Communist Party of Australia's involvement in the Struggle for Aboriginal and Torres Strait Islander People's Rights 1930–1970', in Ray Markey (ed.), *Labour and Community: historical essays*, Wollongong: University of Wollongong Press, 2001, 284.

20   'Paternalism, Says Barred Prof.', *Sun*, 1 June 1968.

21   'Open Entry Sought to Aboriginal Reserves', *Age*, 1 June 1968.

22   'Island Ban Ridiculous: Communist', *Sydney Morning Herald*, 1 June 1968.

23   'Banned Expert is Friend of Natives', *Australian*, 1 June 1968.

24   'Frederick George Godfrey ROSE', 4 June 1968, NAA: A6119 5027, ROSE, Frederick George Godfrey, Volume 9, 51.

25   J.A Barnes, 'Politics, Permits, and Professional Interests: The Rose Case', *Australian Quarterly* 41, 1 (March 1969), 17.

26   Les Hiatt, letter to the editor, *Australian*, 1 June 1968.

27   Barnes, 'Politics, Permits, and Professional Interests', 30.

28   Senate. Official Hansard. No. 23, 1968, Tuesday 4 June 1968, 1352.

29   Minute Paper by ASIO Deputy Director-General (Operations) to Director-General ASIO 16 May 1968, NAA: A6119 5025 ROSE, Frederick George Godfrey, Volume 7, 211.

30   Gordon Bryant MP had been communicating with Rose in Berlin since 1966. In that year he indicated he would support Rose's AIAS application, while also advising Rose of Bryant's upcoming visit to Southeast Asia, in relation to which he wondered if Rose could 'find a line of communication to the North Vietnam authorities, so that I can obtain permission to visit the country somewhere along the route'. Bryant to Rose, 9 July 1966, SLNSW, Frederick Rose papers, Box 31.

31 House of Representatives. Official Hansard, No. 23, 1968, Tuesday, 4 June 1968, 1886.

32 Ibid., 1887.

33 Frederick Rose to editor, *Australian*, 7 June 1968.

34 Rose to Hannah Middleton, 17 July 1968, SLNSW. Frederick Rose Papers, Box 21.

35 ASIO Report Queensland, 'Professor Frederick ROSE; 5 September 1968, NAA: A6119 5027, ROSE, Frederick George Godfrey, Volume 9, 175–85.

36 ASIO report 'Professor Frederick George Godfrey ROSE, 23 August 1968, NAA: A6119 5027, ROSE, Frederick George Godfrey, Volume 9, 144.

37 Ibid.

38 ASIO QLD report 'Townsville Inter-Racial Citizen's [sic] Committee', 31 July 1968, NAA: A6119 5027, ROSE, Frederick George Godfrey, Volume 9, 135.

39 Regional Director Northern Territory to Headquarters ASIO, 9 August 1968, NAA: A6119 5027, ROSE, Frederick George Godfrey, Volume 9, 128.

40 ASIO Outward Message Headquarters to Canberra for passing to Payne, Dept. of Interior, NAA: A6119 5027, ROSE, Frederick George Godfrey, Volume 9, 139.

41 ASIO Regional Director to Headquarters 22 August 1968, NAA: A6119 5027, ROSE, Frederick George Godfrey, Volume 9, 141.

42 ASIO NT Report, 'Professor Frederick George Godfrey ROSE' 18 August 1968. NAA: A6119 5027 ROSE, Frederick George Godfrey, Volume 9, 188.

43 Rose to Birch, 21 September 1968, BStU AIM 5163/91 Teil I/2, 32–33.

44 NTRS 1942, CD 569, Interview with Christopher Crellin, 14 April 2003.

45 'Trouble forecast on N.T. island', *Sydney Morning Herald*, 3 September 1968.

46 M. Mark Stolarik, *The Prague Spring and the Warsaw Pact Invasion of Czechoslovakia 1968: Forty Years Later*, Mundelein ILL: Bolchazi-Carducci, 2010, xxvii.

47 ASIO NT report 'Frederick George Godfrey ROSE', 27 August 1968, NAA: A6119 5027, ROSE, Frederick George Godfrey, Volume 9, 142.

48 '"No comment" on Czechs: Violence Forecast by Red Professor', *NT News*, 2 September 1968.

49 Richard Crossman (ed.), *The God That Failed: Six studies in communism*, London: Hamish Hamilton, 1950, 207.

50 Peter Worsley to Fred Rose, 18 July 1957, SLNSW, Frederick Rose Papers, Box 34.

25 | Double Lives

1 Martin Thomas, *The Many Worlds of R.H. Mathews: In search of an Australian anthropologist*, Sydney: Allen and Unwin, 2011, 352.

2 Signed Statement by Frederick Rose, 19 August 1988, Rose family collection.

3 Hannah Middleton, interview with Valerie Munt, 3 February 2010.

4 Ibid.

5 Rose to Ernst Hoffmann, 8 April 1967, SLNSW, Frederick Rose Papers, Box 16.

6 Hannah Middleton, interview.

7 Rose to Hannah Middleton, 15 June 1968, SLNSW, Frederick Rose Papers, Box 21.

8 Rose to Middleton undated (1969), Rose family collection.

9 Ibid.

10 Middleton, *But Now We Want the Land Back: A history of the Australian Aboriginal people*, Sydney: New Age Publishers, 1977, 13.

11 Material relating to her thesis and other papers are deposited in a collection in the State Library of New South Wales. See SLNSW, Hannah Middleton Collection – research papers relating to Aboriginal issues, 1918–1985, MLMSS 5866.

12 Hannah Middleton, interview.

13 Vorschlag zur Verpflichtung als IMF, Berlin 20. Oktober 1969, BStU, AIM 5163/91 Bd. I/3, 22–38.

14 Verwaltung für Staatssicherheit Gross-Berlin Abteilng XX/3. O. Information Nr. 252/69, 10.4.1969. BStU, AIM 5163/91 Bd. I/2, 88–91.

15 Robert Loest, Susanne Oehlschläger, 'Die "Münchener Bibliothek". Neuerschliessung einer historischen Sammlung durch das Bundesinstitut für Ostwissenschaftliche und Internationale Studien (BIOst) in Köln', *Bibliotheksdienst*, 31, 3 (1997) 419–20.

16 Verwaltung für Staatssicherheit Gross-Berlin Abteilung XX/3. Vorschlag, Berlin 29.5.1969. BStU, AIM 5163/91 Bd. I/2, 106–108.

17 Arch Puddington, *Broadcasting Freedom: The Cold War triumph of Radio Free Europe and Radio Liberty*, Lexington: University Press of Kentucky, 2000, 13.

18 Puddington, *Broadcasting Freedom*, 187–213.

19 Ian Johnson, *A Mosque in Munich: Nazis, the CIA, and the rise of the Muslim Brotherhood in the West*, New York: Houghton, Mifflin, Harcourt, 2010, 49–64; Gene Sosin, *Sparks of Liberty: An insider's memoir of Radio Liberty*, Pennsylvania: Pennsylvania State University Press, 1999, 1–11.

20 Puddington, *Broadcasting Freedom*, 176–79.

21 Ibid., 235–36.

22 Verwaltung für Staatssicherheit Gross-Berlin Abteilng XX/3. Vorschlag, Berlin 29.5.1969. BStU, AIM 5163/91 Bd. I/2, 106–108.

23 Ibid.

24 'Zusammenfassender Bericht über den operativen Einsatz des IMF-Kandidaten "Aust" zur Aufklärung des indsichen Staatsbürgers XXXXXX und des "Instituts zur Erforschung der UdSSR e.V." in München, 22 October 1969, BStU, AIM 5163/91 Bd. I/3, 52–58.

25 Vorschlag zur Verpflichtung als IM, 20.10, BStU, AIM 5163/91 Bd. I/3, 23.

26 Bericht zur Anwerbung des IMF 'Aust', BStU, AIM 5163/91 Bd. I/3, 40.

27 Begründung des Antrages zur Ausstellung von Visa nach WB und WD für das Jahr 1969 für den IMF 'Aust'; Bericht zur Anwerbung des IMF 'Aust', BStU, AIM 5163/91 Bd. I/3, 40, 95.

28 Abschlussbericht zur Zusammenarbeit mit dem IMF 'Aust'. Reg. Nr. XV/4229/64. 10.8.1977, BStU, AIM 5163/ 91 Bd. 1/ 3, 234.

29 Verwaltung für Staatssicherheit Gross-Berlin Abteilung XX/3, Antrag auf Visa für den IMF-Kandidaten 'Aust', Berlin, 8 July 1969, BStU, AIM 5163/91 Teil I/2, 190–91.

30 Pilling was the co-author, with C.W.M.Hart, of *The Tiwi of North Australia*, New York: Holt, Rinehard and Winston, 1960.

31 Bericht über die Reise nach den USA und nach Kanada von Prof. Dr. F. Rose, BStU, AIM 11120/70 I/1 Miller Bd. II, 148–52.

32 Ibid.

33 Ibid.

34 Ibid.

26 | Anthropologist

1   Karl Marx, 'Theses on Feuerbach', 1845, www.marxists.org/archive/marx/
    works/1845/theses/theses.htm, accessed 19 August 2013.

2   Frederick Rose, 'Die Bedeutung der ethnographischen und historischen Erforschung
    der Völker Afrikas und Lateinamerikas für die Gegenwart', conference presentation,
    Berlin 19 December 1962. SLNSW, Frederick Rose Papers, Box 21.

3   'Kurt Hager', in *Wer war wer in der DDR*. Online database, www.bundesstiftung-
    aufarbeitung.de/wer-war-wer-in-der-ddr-%2363%3B-1424.html?ID=1207,
    accessed 19 August 2013.

4   Politische und wissenschaftliche Einschätzung des Gen. Prof. Dr. Frederick Rose und
    seiner Lage in der DDR seit 1956, Berlin, 11 April 1973, BStU, AIM 5163/91 Bd. I/3,
    186.

5   Rose to Kurt Hager (undated, 1971), BStU, AIM 5163/91 Bd. I/3, 100–101.

6   Bericht, Berlin, 25 February 1971, BStU, AIM 5163/91 Bd. I/3, 96.

7   Rose to Kurt Hager (undated, 1971), BStU, AIM 5163/91 Bd. I/3, 99–100.

8   Ibid., 99–105.

9   Rose, Memorandum, September 1972, BStU, AIM 5163/91 Bd. II/2, 204–209.

10 Daniel Tumarkin to Rose, 11 February 1966, SLNSW, Frederick Rose Papers, Box 21.

11 Rose, Memorandum, September 1972, BStU, AIM 5163/91 Bd. II/2, 208.

12 Frederik Rouz, *Aborigeny, kenguru i reaktivnye lainery*. Afterword by V.R. Kabo.
    Translation from Russian by S.D. Komarova of *Ureinwohner, Känguruhs und
    Düsenklipper*, Moscow: Progress, 1972.

13 Rose, Memorandum, September 1972, BStU, AIM 5163/91 Bd. II/2, 209.

14 Ibid., 218–20.

15 Rose to Ernst Hoffmann, 25 May 1973, BStU, AIM 5163/91 Bd. II/2, 237.

16 Ibid., 241.

17 Ibid., 244.

18 Martin Thomas, *The Many Worlds of R.H. Mathews: In search of an Australian
    anthropologist*, Sydney: Allen and Unwin, 2011, 348.

19 Rose's thinking in this area inspired studies by others. See especially David H.
    Turner, *Tradition and Transformation: A study of the Groote Eylandt area Aborigines
    of Northern Australia*, Canberra: Australian Institute of Aboriginal Studies,
    1974; Woodrow Denham, 'Kinship, Marriage and Age in Aboriginal Australia',
    Mathematical Anthropology and Cultural Theory: An International Journal, 4, 1 (May
    2012), mathematicalanthropology.org/Pdf/MACT_Denham_0512.pdf, accessed
    18 Nov. 2013.

20 Rose to Ernst Hoffmann, 11 June 1978, quoting his own 1968 article, SLNSW,
    Frederick Rose Papers, Box 30.

21 Frederick G.G. Rose, *Australia Revisited: The Aborigine story from stone age to space age*,
    Berlin: Seven Seas, 1968, 169.

22 Frederick G.G. Rose, *The Traditional Mode of Production of the Australian Aborigines*, Sydney: Angus and Robertson, 1987, 114.

23 Frederick G.G. Rose, 'Australian Marriage, Land-Owning Groups, and Initiations', in Richard B. Lee and Irven de Vere (eds.), *Man the Hunter*, Chicago: Aldine Publishing Company, 1963, 201.

24 Frederick G.G. Rose, *The Classification of Kin, Age Structure and Marriage Amongst the Groote Eylandt Aborigines: A study in method and a theory of Australian kinship*, Berlin: Akademie-Verlag, 1960, 491.

25 Mervyn J. Meggitt, *Desert People: A study of the Walbiri Aborigines of Central Australia*. Chicago: University of Chicago Press, 1965.

26 Rose, *The Traditional Mode of Production*, xi.

27 Rose, *Classification of Kin*, 90.

28 Ibid., 133.

29 Rose, *Australia Revisited*, 63–64.

30 Despite critiques such as Les Hiatt's, which revealed the disjunction between Radcliffe-Brown's 'horde' model of local organisation and the evidence of actual behaviour from a wide variety of Aboriginal case studies. See L.R. Hiatt, 'Local organization amongst the Australian Aborigines', *Oceania*, 32 (1962), 267–86.

31 See Rose to Sally Green (Gordon V. Childe's biographer), 9 May 1990, SLNSW, Frederick Rose Papers, Box 25.

32 See Amir Weiner, 'Nature and Nurture in a Socialist Utopia: Delineating the Soviet Socio-Ethnic Body in the Age of Socialism', in David L. Hoffman (ed.), *Stalinism*, Oxford: Blackwell, 2003.

33 Rose, 'Australian Marriage', 201.

34 Ibid.

35 Rose, *The Traditional Mode of Production*, 153.

36 Rose, *Australia Revisited*, 16.

37 Rose, *The Traditional Mode of Production*, xi.

27 | The Whitlam Years

1 On the events and processes leading to mutual recognition see Peter Monteath, 'The German Democratic Republic and Australia', *Debatte: Journal of Contemporary Central and Eastern Europe*, 16, 2 (August 2008), 213–36; Peter Monteath, 'Die DDR und Australien', *Zeitschrift für Geschichtswissenschaft*, 60, 2 (2012), 146–68.

2 Brief Parsche, 22 October 1971, Politisches Archiv des Auswärtigen Amtes (hereafter PAAA), C 1534/75, 17.

3 Rose to Whitlam, 2 December 1972, BStU, AIM 5163/91 Bd. II/2, 49–50.

4 Treffen im Ministry for Trade and Industry, Canberra, 6 December 1972, PAAA C 1531/75, Entwicklung der Beziehungen DDR-Australien, 86.

5 Abschlussbericht von Opitz und Andres, Cairo, 19 December 1972, PAAA, C 1531/75, Entwicklung der Beziehungen DDR-Australien, 75.

6 Monteath, 'Die DDR und Australien', 165.

7 Mark Aarons, *The Family File*, Melbourne: Black Inc., 2010, 191–92.

8 Ibid., 231–32.

9   Ibid., 233.

10 Bericht über den Australien-Besuch von Prof. Dr. Frederick Rose von 10. Juni bis 18. November 1973, BStU, AIM 5163/91 Bd. II/2, 267.

11 Rose to Director of Welfare Northern Territory, AIATSIS File No. 65/85, Rose, Professor F.G.G.,unpag.

12 Chairman Combined Aboriginal Communities Groote Eylandt to Rose, 13 April 1973. AIATSIS File No. 65/85, Rose, Professor F.G.G., unpag.

13 Gordon Bryant to Rose, 14 April 1973, SLNSW, Frederick Rose Papers, Box 31.

14 Rose to Fred Gray, 20 April 1973, SLNSW, Frederick Rose Papers, Box 31.

15 Bericht über den Australien-Besuch von Prof. Dr. Frederick Rose von 10. Juni bis 18. November 1973, BStU, AIM 5163/91 Bd. II/2, 264.

16 Rose, Report on Visit to Australia 1973, SLNSW, Frederick Rose Papers, Box 38.

17 Bericht über den Australien-Besuch von Prof. Dr. Frederick Rose von 10. Juni bis 18. November 1973, BStU, 5163/91 Bd. II/2, 270.

18 Ibid., 272.

19 Cited in Jenny Hocking, *Gough Whitlam. His Time: The biography volume II*, Melbourne: Miegunyah Press, 2012, 107.

20 Bericht über den Australien-Besuch von Prof. Dr. Frederick Rose von 10. Juni bis 18. November 1973, BStU, AIM 5163/91 Bd. II/2, 273.

21 Ibid., 279.

22 Frederick G.G. Rose, 'Class Differentiation and Present Struggles of the Aborigines', *Australian Marxist Review*, 4, 1 (1975), 29–33.

23 Jenny Hocking, *Frank Hardy: Politics, literature, life*, Melbourne: Lothian Books, 2005, 179–80.

24 The file containing material relating to Rose's application is: NAA: A3753 1972/79, Com Lit Fund.

25 Bericht über den Australien-Aufenthalt von Prof. Dr. F. Rose 11. Dez. 1974 – 21. Mai 1975', BStU, AIM 5163/91 Bd. II/2, 336.

26 Report on 1973 visit, discussion with Gen. Sec. Peter Symons, SLNSW, Frederick Rose Papers, Box 38.

27 Hannah Middleton, *But Now We Want Our Land Back: a history of the Australian Aboriginal people*, Sydney: New Age Publishers, 1977, cover.

28 Frederick Rose, *Australien und seine Ureinwohner. Ihre Geschichte und Gegenwart*, Berlin: Akademie Verlag, 1976. The similarities between Rose's book and Middleton's were obvious to the Soviet publisher as it prepared a translation of Rose's book. See Rose to 'Chips', 27 July 1988, SLNSW, Frederick Rose Papers, Box 23.

29 Bericht über den Australien-Aufenthalt von Prof. Dr. F. Rose 11. Dez. 1974 – 21. Mai 1975', BStU, AIM 5163/91 Bd. II/2, 344.

30 Hocking, *Gough Whitlam*, 186.

31 National Museum of Australia, 'Collaborating for Indigenous Rights. The hand back', indigenousrights.net.au/subsection.asp?ssID=37; Hocking, *Gough Whitlam*, 186.

32 Jon Altman and Nicolas Peterson, 'A Case for Retaining Aboriginal Mining Veto and Royalty Rights in the Northern Territory', *Australian Aboriginal Studies*, 2 (1984), 45.

33 Middleton, *But Now We Want Our Land Back*, 166–67.

34 Rose, *Australien und seine Ureinwohner*, 137.

28 | Leipzig

1   L.A. Gilbert, 'Dietrich, Amalie (1821–1891)', *Australian Dictionary of Biography*, National Centre of Biography, Australian National University, adb.anu.edu.au/biography/dietrich-amalie-3412/text5189, accessed 26 March 2013.

2   Fred to Edith, 17 November 1974, BStU, AIM 5163/91 Bd. II/2, 324.

3   Ibid., 327–28.

4   Ibid., 327.

5   Ibid., 327–328.

6   Ibid., 328.

7   Vermerk zum Bericht des IMF 'Aust' vom 24.10.1974, BStU, AIM 5163/91 Bd. I/3, 208.

8   Ibid., 210.

9   Rose to Middleton, 22 December 1976, SLNSW, Hannah Middleton papers, MLMSS 5866/15/2.

10   Rose to Middleton, 14 June 1976, SLNSW, Hannah Middleton papers, MLMSS 5866/15/2.

11   Josie McClellan, *Love in the Time of Communism: Intimacy and sexuality in the GDR*, Cambridge: Cambridge University Press, 2011, 3.

12   Auszug aus dem Befehl Nr. K 161/74 Berlin, 7 October 1974, BStU, AIM 5163/91 Bd. I/3, 207.

13   Äusserungen des Geschäftsträgers der australischen Botschaft in der DDR, Peters, 8 January 1976, BStU, HA XX, 10075.

14   Rose's reports on and diagrams of the Australian and British embassies are in BStU, AIM 5163/91 Bd. II/3, 89–129.

15   Information, Berlin, 9 October 1974, BStU, AIM 5163/91 Bd. II/2, 352.

16   E. Feller to Secretary, Department of Foreign Affairs, Canberra, 18 September 1974, NAA: A 6119 5026, Rose, Frederick George Godfrey, Volume 8, 180.

17   Abschlussbericht zur Zusammenarbeit mit dem IM 'Aust', 10 August 1977, BStU, AIM 5163/91 Bd. I/3, 234–35.

18   Ibid., 235.

19   Ibid.

20   Ibid., 236.

21   Aktenvermerk, 3 June 1976, BStU, MfS AGMS 2924/89 Bd. I, 19–20.

22   Bericht, Berlin, 10 July 1974, BStU, MfS AIM 11120/70 Bd. I/1, 290.

23   Informationen zur Aufarbeitung der SED-Diktatur. Abkürzungen des MfS. stasiopfer.de/content/view/141/77/, accessed 28 June 2013.

24   Bericht, Potsdam, 30 August 1976, BStU, AIM 11120/70 Bd. II/2, 330–32.

25   Communication Ruth Struwe to authors, 26 May 2013.

26   Empfehlungen in der Arbeitsrechtssache Dr. Kim Rose, SLNSW, Frederick Rose Papers, Box 23.

27   Einschätzung der Zusammenarbeit IMK 'Miller', BStU, MfS AGMS2924/89 Bd. I, 21.

28   Aktenvermerk, 29 May 1976, BStU, AIM 11120/70 Bd. I/1, 317–18.

29   Operativinformation Nr. 132/80, 13 May 1980, BStU, AIM 5163/91 Bd. I/3, 278–79.

30 Abschlussbericht über die IMK 'Miller', 17 May 1978, BStU, AIM 11120/70 Bd. I/1 Miller, 393–96.
31 Abschlussbericht zu GMS-Akte 20 February 1989, BStU, MfS AGMS2924/89 Bd. I, 12.
32 Rose to Dymphna Clark, April 1985, SLNSW, Frederick Rose Papers, Box 13.
33 Rechnung/Quittung, 16 July 1987, SLNSW, Frederick Rose Papers, Box 23.
34 Vermerk IM 'Aust', BStU, AIM 5163/91 Bd. I/4, 38.

29 | The Unravelling

1   David Turner and Ken Maddock, 'Essays on the Anthropology of Frederick Rose', for prospective contributors to a *Festschrift* in honour of Rose, 23 April 1980, SLNSW, Frederick Rose Papers, Box 17.
2   David Turner, correspondence to Valerie Munt, 26 February 2013.
3   Peter Worsley et al., *Introducing Sociology*, Harmondsworth: Penguin, 1970, and multiple subsequent editions. In total more than half a million copies were sold.
4   A version of Peter Worsley's essay was published as 'The Practice of Politics and the Study of Australian Kinship', in Christine Ward Gailey (ed.), *Dialectical Anthropology: Essays in honor of Stanley Diamond. Volume 2. The politics of culture and creativity*, Gainesville: University of Florida Press, 1992, 25–66.
5   Rose draft letter to Peter Worsley, marked 'Not sent', undated, SLNSW, Frederick Rose Papers, Box 17.
6   Frederick Rose, 'The Question of tactics and some unresolved questions', unpublished and undated paper, SLNSW, Frederick Rose Papers, Box 17.
7   Rose to Ernst Hoffmann, 17 June 1980, SLNSW, Frederick Rose Papers, Box 17.
8   Rose draft letter to Peter Worsley, marked 'Not Sent', undated, SLNSW, Frederick Rose Papers, Box 17.
9   Peter Worsley to Rose, 6 May 1980, SLNSW, Frederick Rose Papers, Box 17.
10 Rose draft letter to Peter Worsley, marked 'Not Sent', SLNSW, Frederick Rose Papers, Box 17.
11 See Rose, 'Discussion with David Turner on train in Holland', 27 May 1980, SLNSW, Frederick Rose Papers, Box 17.
12 Rose 'COMMENT' on the *Festschrift* issue, 21 October 1980, SLNSW, Frederick Rose Papers, Box 17.
13 Transcript of interview of Fred Rose by Robyn Williams, ABC Science show, recorded 9 July 1983, SLNSW, Frederick Rose Papers, Box 13.
14 Ibid.
15 Rose to Lothar Stein, 29 July 1983, BStU, AIM 5163/91 Bd. I/4, 45.
16 Rose, 'Comments on the 4 pages of notes submitted to Ms Netta Burns of the Minister for Social Security's Parliament House Office on 19 Jan 1987', BStU, AIM 5163/91 Bd. I/4, Rose 205.
17 Sonja Lenz communication to the authors, 21 October 2013.
18 National Archives of Australia communication to authors 16 May 2013, headed 'Access Application – Notification Title: ROSE, Frederick George Godfrey Volume 10, Application number: 2013/222766'.

Notes

19 'Einige Bemerkungen zur politischen Situation in Australien: Ende 1986/Anfang 1987. Übersetzung aus dem Englischen', 40–44, BStU, MfS HA II, Nr 28983.

20 John Mulvaney to Rose, 20 February 1984, SLNSW, Frederick Rose Papers, Box 13.

21 Rose to Dymphna Clark, 'written April 1985, posted May 1985', SLNSW, Frederick Rose Papers, Box 13.

22 Anthony Reid to 'Anna Wittmann', 26 March 1986, SLNSW, Frederick Rose Papers, Box 13.

23 Rose, 'Dialogue 2', 3, SLNSW, Frederick Rose Papers, Box 23.

24 Ibid.

25 Rose to Sonja Lenz, 8 November 1987, SLNSW, Frederick Rose Papers, Box 23.

26 For the details of Kabo's life story see especially his autobiography, *The Road to Australia: Memoirs*, Canberra: Aboriginal Studies Press, 1998.

27 See especially Yuri Slezkine, 'The Fall of Soviet Ethnography', *Current Anthropology*, 32, 4 (August to Oct. 1991), 476–84.

28 Anne Summers and Elena Govor, 'Survived Stalin's Gulag to shed more light on Australia's indigenous people. Vladimir Rafailovich Kabo, Ethnographer 7.2.1925 – 4.6.2009', *Age*, 26 June 2009, www.theage.com.au/world/survived-stalins-gulag-to-shed-more-light-on-australias-indigenous-people-20090625-cy7p.html, accessed 5 November 2013.

29 Vladimir Kabo, letter to his mother 3 November 1963, in Vladimir Kabo, 'Letters from Afar', aboriginals.narod.ru/LettersfromAfar.htm, accessed 5 November 2013.

30 Frederik Rouz, *Aborigeny, kenguru i reaktivnye lainery*. Afterword by V.R. Kabo. Translation from Russian by S.D. Komarova of *Ureinwohner, Känguruhs und Düsenclipper*, Moscow: Progress,1972.

31 Elena Govor, interview with authors, Canberra, 22 April 2013.

32 Kabo, *The Road to Australia*, 224.

33 See especially Rhys Jones, 'Afterword', in Kabo, *The Road to* Australia, 293–94.

34 The notion that 'group marriage' existed in Aboriginal society was 'one of the most notable fantasies in the history of anthropology'. See Les Hiatt, *Arguments about Aborigines: Australia and the evolution of social anthropology*, Cambridge: Cambridge University Press, 1996, 56.

35 Under Stalin 'both applied and theoretical ethnography was ruthlessly repressed, many practitioners were killed'. T. Hylland Eriksen and F. Sivert Nielsen, *A History of Anthropology*, London; Ann Arbor: Pluto Press, 2001, 159.

36 Vladimir Kabo email to the authors, 18 February 2008.

37 Kabo, *The Road to Australia*, 260.

38 Rose to V. Gordon Childe, 24 September 1956, SLNSW, Frederick Rose Papers, Box 34.

39 See letters from Maurice Godlier of the *Maison des Sciences de L'Homme* to Rose re International Conference on Hunters & Gatherers, 2 February 1978 and 23 March 1978, SLNSW, Frederick Rose Papers, Box 30.

40 Rose to Wolfgang König, 7 November 1978, SLNSW, Frederick Rose Papers, Box 30.

41 Lewis Henry Morgan, *Ancient Society*, New York: Henry Holt and Co., 1877.

42 Rose to Ernst Hoffman, 17 June 1980, SLNSW, Frederick Rose Papers, Box 30.

43 Rose to Hannah Middleton, 13 November 1971. Courtesy Hannah Middleton.

44 Ibid.

45 Rose to Vladimir Kabo, 9 September 1980. Courtesy Elena Govor.

46 Rose to Peter Worsley, 15 May 1989, SLNSW, Frederick Rose Papers, Box 24.

47 Rose to Ernst Hoffmann, 4 April 1978, SLNSW, Frederick Rose Papers, Box 30.

48 Frederick G.G. Rose, *The Traditional Mode of Production of the Australian Aborigines*, Sydney: Angus and Robertson, 1987; Frederick Rose, 'The Australian Aborigines and the last stage of hominization', unpublished manuscript, SLNSW, Frederick Rose Papers, Box 30.

49 Rose to Worsley 15 May 89, SLNSW, Frederick Rose Papers, Box 24.

50 Abschlussbericht zu GMS-Akte, 20 February 1989, 12, BStU, AGMS2924/89 Bd I.

51 Agency note, Australian Embassy East Berlin, NAA, recordsearch.naa.gov.au/SearchNRetrieve/Interface/DetailsReports/AgencyDetail.aspx?reg_no=CA%20 4407, accessed 2 December 2013.

52 Rose to Eric Bogle (undated), BStU, AIM 5163/91 Bd. II/4, 170.

53 Operativinformation 167/85, 5 March 1985, AIM 5163/91 Bd. II/4, 172.

54 Eric Bogle, email to Peter Monteath, 16 May 2012.

30 | Annus Horribilis

1 Information provided to the authors courtesy Anke Bornschein, 8 April 2013.

2 Rose to Anke Bornschein, 30 April 1989. SLNSW, Frederick Rose Papers, Box 23.

3 Rose to Anke Bornschein, 21 August 1989, SLNSW, Frederick Rose Papers, Box 23.

4 Rose to Anke Bornschein. 27 May 1989, SLNSW, Frederick Rose Papers, Box 23.

5 Transcript of Humphrey McQueen, review of Frederick G.G. Rose, *The Traditional Mode of Production of the Australian Aborigines*, ABC Science Bookshop, 17 October 1987.

6 Rose, 'Report on the Australian Situation: Mid 1989', BStU, AIM 5163/91 Teil II/4, 317.

7 Ibid., 319.

8 Ibid., 322.

9 Untited report, PdVP Berlin, 19 June 1989, BStU, AIM 5153/73, Kim Rose, 184.

10 Rose to Connie Healy, 13 August 1989, SLNSW, Frederick Rose Papers, Box 18.

11 Rose, Funeral Oration for Kim, Third and Final Draft 28 July 1989, SLNSW, Frederick Rose Papers, Box 4.

12 Ibid.

13 Ibid.

14 Cited in Ulrich Mählert, *Kleine Geschichte der DDR*, Munich: Beck, 1998, 162.

15 Ibid., 163–68.

16 See Konrad Jarausch, *The Rush to German Unity*, Oxford, New York: Oxford University Press, 1994, 3.

17 Mike Dennis, *The Stasi: Myth and reality*, Harlow: Pearson, 2003, 236–38.

18 Rose interviewed by Richard Carlton, *60 Minutes*, Nine Network, episode broadcast 30 September 1990.

19 Ibid.

20 Ibid.

21 Frederick Rose, 'Memoirs of an Unapologetic Anthropologist', SLNSW, Frederick Rose Papers, Box 1.

22 Ibid., 11.

23 Ibid., 9.

Epilogue

1 Worsley, 'Iconoclast of the Outback: Obituary for Professor Rose', *Guardian*, 18 February 1991, 35.

2 Peter Worsley, 'Barriers to Ethnographic Fieldwork', *RAIN*, 53 (1982), 12–14.

3 Matthew Condon, 'Petrov Spy Dies in Germany', *Sun Herald*, 24 February 1991. February 24, 1991.

4 'Fred Rose Commemoration', *Guardian*, 1 May 1991.

5 Kenneth Maddock, 'Frederick Rose, 1915–1991. An Appreciation', *Oceania* 62, 1 (Sept. 1991), 66–69.

6 Cited in Rupert Lockwood, 'Wilfred Burchett's Retreat from Moscow', in Radical Sydney/Radical History blog, located at radicalsydney.blogspot.com.au/p/wilred-burchetts-tretreat-from-moscow.html, accessed 2 August 2013.

7 Cited in Maddock, 'Frederick Rose', 68.

8 Humphrey McQueen, Review of *The Traditional Mode of Production of the Australian Aborigines*, ABC Science Bookshop, broadcast 17 October 1987.

Bibliography

PRIMARY SOURCES

Archiv der Humboldt-Universität zu Berlin
Habilitation Frederick G.G. Rose 1.10.1958
Philosophische Fakultät, Fakultätsratssitzungen 1961–1964. Signatur 7
Sektion Geschichte. Konferenzen, Tagungen, Kolloquien 1958–1976. Signatur 123
Sektion Geschichte. Erziehung und Ausbildung 1969–1976. Signatur 120
Sektion Geschichte. Bereich Ethnographie. Protokolle der Arbeitsbesprechungen,
   Berichte 1960–73. Signatur 117

Australian Institute of Aboriginal and Torres Strait Islander Studies (AIATSIS)
Correspondence of Professor F.G.G. Rose, File No. 65/85
Groote. 1.BW N6254 – N6265
Rose.F2.BW 9943 – 10072
Rose.F3.N394 N396
Rose.F4.BW N430-N439
Rose.F5.BW N467

Bundesarchiv (Berlin-Lichterfelde) (BArchiv)
DR 1/2341 Verlag Volk und Welt, Verlag für internationale Literatur
DR 1/2231a Verlag Rütten & Loening

Bundesbeauftragter für die Stasi-Unterlagen, Berlin (BStU)
AIM 5136/91 Frederick Rose (2 parts of 4 volumes)
AIM 5153/73 Kim Rose
AIM 11120/70 Edith Rose, ('Miller') (2 parts of 2 volumes)
AGMS 2924/89 Edith Rose, ('Miller') (2 volumes)
HA II, 28983. Reports from Abteilung USA/AV Canberra

J.S. Battye Library of West Australian History. Private Archives
Katharine Susanne Prichard Papers, 1935–1969, MN 1465

Bibliography

Landesarchiv Berlin

C Rep. 903-01-12 Nr. 100. SED Kreisleitung Humboldt-Universität. Berichte und Protokolle der GO Biologen, Minerologen, Geologen, Psychologen, Völkerkunde, Urgeschichte und Altertumskunde, May 1958–February 1960

Mitchell Library, State Library of New South Wales (SLNSW)

Frederick Rose Papers, MLMSS (uncatalogued)

Frederick Rose papers relating to Groote Eylandt, Northern Territory, 1938–1939, MLMSS 2076

Hannah Middleton, 'Papers concerning Professor Frederick Rose, 1965–1979', MLMSS 5866/15

National Archives of Australia (Canberra Office) (NAA)

A5619 C135 Application by Professor F G G Rose for permit to enter Aboriginal Reserve

A659 1944/1/4313, Rose, F G – Anthropological research at Groote Eylandt

A5882 CO148 Professor F G G Rose

A659 1944/1/4313 Rose, F G – Anthropological research at Groote Eylandt

A6119 ASIO Personal files, alpha-numeric series (numerous items in this series)

A9300, RAAF Officers Personnel files, 1921–1948

A9626, 234 JOLLY, Alexander Thomas Hicks

A9626, 281 ROSE, Frederick George

A12508 21/2581 LINDE, Edith

B883 Second Australian Imperial Force Personnel Dossiers, 1939–1947 (numerous items in this series)

C123 World War II security investigation dossiers

CP 216 Professor Frederick George Godfrey ROSE

National Archives of Australia (Darwin Office) (NAA)

F133 1963/466 Angas Downs Station

F1 38/557 Flying Boat Base in Gulf of Carpentaria 'Little Lagoon' at Groote Eylandt

F1 1949/468 Review Report Umbakumba Native Settlement

National Library of Australia (NLA)

484250 Biographical cuttings on Frederick Rose, anthropologist, containing one or more cuttings from newspapers or journal

MS 2481 Letters and diary written by Frederick Rose when he was a meteorologist on Groote Eylandt in 1938

Northern Territory Archives Service (NTRS)

226, TS 224, Typed transcript of oral history interview with Fred Gray 1976

246/P2, Box 2, item PL 216. Dept of Lands, Land Administration Branch, Correspondence files with 'PL' prefix (pastoral lease), 1915–1994

246/P1, Box 22, PL 584, Department of Lands, Land Administration Branch, Correspondence files with 'PL' prefix (pastoral lease), 1915–1994

1942, CD 569 Interview with Christopher Crellin 14 April 2003

1195 Box PB 215. Mackey, George William, Memoirs including as merchant marine and with the Bureau of Meteorology, 1927–1940

Politisches Archiv des Auswärtigen Amtes (Berlin) (PAAA)

C 1531/75, Entwicklung der Beziehungen DDR-Australien

South Australian Museum Archive

AA270 Frederick George Godfrey Rose

State Records Office of Western Australia

1940/0617 Public Health Department Personal File Dr A.T.H. Jolly

Published primary sources

Commonwealth of Australia, *Royal Commission on Espionage: Official transcript of proceedings*, Canberra: Government Printers, 1954–1955

House of Representatives. Official Hansard. No. 23, 1968

Report of the Royal Commission on Espionage, Sydney: Commonwealth of Australia, 1956

Senate. Official Hansard. No. 23, 1968

Unpublished manuscripts

Bell, Coral, 'A Preoccupation with Armageddon', unpublished manuscript, undated

Works by Frederick Rose

[For an extensive bibliography of Rose's works see 'Veröffentlichungen von Frederick G.G.Rose. Zusammengestellt von Günter Guhr', *Ethnographisch-Archäologische Zeitschrift*, 32 (1991), 820–27.]

'Jagara' (nom de plume of Frederick Rose), *Frederick Engels, Lewis Morgan and the Australian Aborigine*, Sydney: Current Books, 1946.

Jolly, A.T.H., and F.G.G. Rose, 'The Place of the Australian Aboriginal in the Evolution of Society', *Annals of Eugenics*, 12, 1 (1943), 44–87.

Rose, F.G.G. and A.T.H. Jolly, 'An Interpretation of the Taboo between Mother and Son in Law', *Man* 42, 5 (1942), 15–16.

Rose, Frederick, 'To Jim Healy', *Tribune*, 9 August 1961.

Rose, Frederick, 'Tribal Custom: Marriage Law Infringed. Story behind mission murder. To the editor', *West Australian*, 23 April 1941, 11.

Rose, Frederick George Godfrey, *Australia Revisited: The Aboriginal story from stone age to space age*, Berlin: Seven Seas, 1968.

Bibliography

Rose, Frederick G.G., 'The Australian Aboriginal Family: Some theoretical considerations', *Forschen und Wirken*, 111 (1960), 415–37.

Rose, Frederick G.G., 'Australian Marriage, Land-Owning Groups, and Initiations', in Richard B. Lee and Irven de Vore (eds.), *Man the Hunter*, Chicago: Aldine Publishing Company, 1963, 200–208.

Rose, Frederick G.G., *Australien und seine Einwohner. Ihre Geschichte und Gegenwart*, East Berlin: Akademie Verlag, 1976.

Rose, Frederick G.G., 'Bedenken am Quellenwert der ethnographischen Angaben über die australischen Ureinwohner in dem Buch von Jens Bjerre *Die letzten Kannibalen*', *Ethnographisch-Archäologische Zeitschrift*, 1 (1960), 174–75.

Rose, Frederick G.G., 'Class Differentiation and Present Struggles of the Aborigines', *Australian Marxist Review*, 4, 1 (1975), 29–33.

Rose, Frederick G.G., *Classification of Kin, Age Structure and Marriage amongst the Groote Eylandt Aborigines: A study in method and a theory of Australian kinship*, Berlin: Akademie-Verlag, 1960.

Rose, Frederick G.G., 'Die Familie und die Periodisierung der Urgeschichte. Im Anschluss an Irgmard Sellnow, Grundprinzipien einer Periodisierung der Urgeschichte', *Ethnographisch-Archäologische Zeitschrift*, 9 (1968) 148–155.

Rose, Frederick.G.G., 'Die unilaterale Heirat auf der Grundlage der Altersstruktur auf Groote Eylandt (Nordaustralien)', *Ethnographisch-Archäologische Zeitschrift*, 1 (1960), 18–24.

Rose, Frederick G.G., *Die Ureinwohner Australiens: Gesellschaft und Kunst*, Leipzig: Koehler & Amelang, 1969.

Rose, Frederick G.G., 'Grundlage und Entstehung der "Northern Territory Welfare (Native) Ordinance" von 1953', *Ethnographisch-Archäologische Zeitschrift*, 3 (1962), 59–71.

Rose, Frederick G.G., 'The Indonesians and the Genesis of the Groote Eylandt Society, Northern Australia', in *Beiträge zur Völkerforschung. Veröffentlichungen des Museums für Völkerkunde Leipzig* 11 (1961), 524–31.

Rose, Frederick G.G., 'Memoirs', SLNSW, Frederick Rose Papers, Box 1.

Rose, Frederick, 'Paintings of the Groote Eylandt Aborigines', *Oceania* 13 (1942), 170–76.

Rose, F.G.G., 'The Pastoral Industry in the Northern Territory during the Period of Commonwealth Administration 1911–1953', *Historical Studies*, 6, 22 (1954), 150–72.

Rose, 'Ripples in the Gulf', unpublished manuscript, National Library of Australia, MS 248, Frederick G.G. Rose, 1938/39 Papers: Groote Eylandt.

Rose, Frederick G.G., *The Traditional Mode of Production of the Australian Aborigines*, Sydney: Angus & Robertson, 1987.

Rose, Frederick, *Ureinwohner, Känguruhs und Düsenclipper. Fünfundzwanzig Jahre unter Australiern*, transl. Anneliese Dangel, Leipzig: Brockhaus, 1966.

Rose, Frederick G.G., *The Wind of Change in Central Australia*, East Berlin: Akademie, 1965.

Rouz, Frederik, *Aborigeny, kenguru i reaktivnye lainery*. Afterword by V.R. Kabo. Translation from Russian by S.D. Komarova of *Ureinwohner, Känguruhs und Düsenklipper*, Moscow: Progress, 1972.

SECONDARY SOURCES

Aarons, Mark, *The Family File*, Melbourne: Black Inc., 2010.

Altman, Jon and Nicolas Peterson, 'A case for retaining Aboriginal mining veto and royalty rights in the Northern Territory', *Australian Aboriginal Studies*, 2 (1984), 47–53.

Alumna profile: Ms Erika Feller – UNHCR Assistant High Commissioner, http://blogs. unimelb.edu.au/futurestudents/2010/06/28/alumna-profile-ms-erika-feller/, accessed 25 November 2012.

Andrew, Christopher, *The Defence of the Realm: The authorized history of MI5*, London: Penguin, 2010.

Andrew, Christopher and Oleg Gordievsky , *KGB: The inside story of its foreign operations from Lenin to Gorbachev*, London: Hodder & Stoughton, 1990.

Andrew, Christopher and Vasili Mitrokhin, *The Mitrokhin Archive 11: The KGB and the world*, London: Penguin, 2006.

Attwood, Bain, 'The articulation of "land rights" in Australia: The case of Wave Hill', *Social Analysis* 44, 1 (April 2000), 3–39.

Attwood, Bain, *Rights for Aborigines*, Sydney: Allen & Unwin, 2003.

Attwood, Bain and Andrew Markus (eds.), *The Struggle for Aboriginal Rights: A documentary history*, Sydney: Allen & Unwin, 1999.

Australian Dictionary of Biography, accessible online at http://adb.anu.edu.au/

Australian Women's History Forum, 'Heather Sutherland 1903–1953', http:// womenshistory.net.au/2012/02/20/heather-sutherland-1903–1953/ accessed 7 August 2013.

Ball, Desmond and David Horner, *Breaking the Codes: Australia's KGB network, 1944–1950*, Sydney: Allen & Unwin, 1998.

Ball, Desmond, 'Soviet spies had protection in very high places', *Weekend Australian* 14–15 January 2012, Inquirer 14.

Ball, Desmond, 'The moles at the very heart of government', *Weekend Australian*, 17–18 April 2011, Inquirer 4.

Ball, Desmond, 'The Spy Who Came Out as Klod', *Australian*, 24 September 2011, 5.

Bandler, Faith, *Turning the Tide: A personal history of the Federal Council for the Advancement of Aborigines and Torres Strait Islanders*, Canberra: Aboriginal Studies Press, 1989.

Barnes, J.A., 'Politics, Permits, and Professional Interests: The Rose case', *Australian Quarterly* 41, 1 (March 1969), 17–31.

Barth, Fredrik, Andre Gingrich, Robert Parkin, and Sydel Silverman, *One Discipline Four Ways: British, German, French, and American anthropology*, Chicago: University of Chicago Press, 2005.

Beazley, Kim E., *Father of the House: The memoirs of Kim E. Beazley*, Perth: Fremantle Press, 2009.

Bodrogi, Tibor, 'Review of *Classification of Kin*', *Acta Ethnographica*, 3 (1961).

Boughton, Bob, 'The Communist Party of Australia's involvement in the Struggle for Aboriginal and Torres Strait Islander People's Rights 1930–1970', in Ray Markey (ed.),

Labour and Community: Historical essays, Wollongong: University of Wollongong Press, 2001, 37–46.

Bracegirdle, Simon, *My Lucky Life*, Brisbane: Simon Bracegirdle, 1997.

Brown, Wilton John (ed.), *The Petrov Conspiracy Unmasked*, Sydney: Current Books, 1956.

Cain, Frank, *The Australian Security Intelligence Organisation: An unofficial history*, Melbourne: Spectrum Publications, 1994.

Camphausen, Gabriele, et al., *Stasi: Die Ausstellung zur DDR-Staatssicherheit*, Berlin: Der Bundesbeauftragte für die Unterlagen des Staatssicherheitsdienstes der ehemaligen Deutschen Demokratischen Republik, 2011.

Capp, Fiona, *Writers Defiled: Security surveillance of Australian authors and intellectuals 1920–1960*, Melbourne: McPhee Gribble, 1993.

Carment, David et al (eds.), *Northern Territory Dictionary of Biography*, revised edition, Darwin: Charles Darwin University Press, 2008.

Carter, Miranda, *Anthony Blunt: His lives*, London: Macmillan, 2001.

'Charles P. Mountford, SA Memory, South Australia: Past and present for the future, Arnhem Land, 1948 – The Expedition', State Library of SA. www.samememory. sa.gov.au/site/pagesfor?u=1298 , accessed 10 November 2012.

Clohesy, Lachlan, 'Fighting the Enemy Within: Anti-Communism and Aboriginal Affairs', *History Australia*, 8, 2 (August 2011), 128–52.

Cole, Keith, *Arnhem Land: Places and People*, Adelaide: Rigby, 1980.

Cole, Keith, *Fred Gray of Umbakumba: The story of Frederick Harold Gray, the founder of the Umbakumba Aboriginal settlement on Groote Eylandt*, Bendigo: Keith Cole, 1984.

Cole, Keith, *Groote-Eylandt Mission: A short history of the CMS Groote-Eylandt mission 1921–1971*, Melbourne: Church Mission Historical Publications, 1971.

Cole, Keith, *A History of the Church Missionary Society of Australia*, Melbourne: Church Missionary Historical Publications, 1971.

Crossman, Richard (ed.), *The God That Failed: Six studies in communism*, London: Hamish Hamilton, 1950.

Curthoys, Ann, *Freedom Ride: A freedom rider remembers*, Sydney: Allen Unwin, 2002.

Davidson, Alistair, *The Communist Party of Australia: A short history*, Stanford CA: Hoover Institution Press, 1969.

Davis, May, 'Red Professor. Australia Revisited', *Age*, 28 December 1968.

De Groen, Frances, *Xavier Herbert: A biography*, Brisbane: UQP, 1998.

Deery, Phillip, 'Cold War Victim or Rhodes Scholar Spy? Revisiting the Case of Ian Milner', *Overland*, 147 (1997), 9–12.

Denham, Woodrow, 'Kinship, Marriage and Age in Aboriginal Australia', *Mathematical Anthropology and Cultural Theory: An international journal*, 4, 1 (May 2012), http://mathematicalanthropology.org/Pdf/MACT_Denham_0512.pdf, accessed 18 November 2013.

Dennis, Mike, *The Stasi: Myth and reality*, Harlow: Pearson, 2003.

Dewar, Mickey, 'Fred Gray and Umbakumba: The 1930s and 1940s', presentation at 'Picturing relations: Groote Eylandt barks symposium', University of Melbourne, 23 September 2006, http://www.artmuseum.unimelb.edu.au/resources. ashx/events.transcripts/18/PDF/2FF7660C7E20663DE38EF97593485986/ Fred%2BGray%2Band%, accessed 9 May 2012.

Edmonds, Penelope, 'Making Indigenous Place in the Australian City, Unofficial Apartheid, Convention and Country Towns: Reflections on Australian history and the New South Wales Freedom Rides of 1965', *Postcolonial Studies*, 15, 2 (2012), 167–190.

Edwards, Elizabeth, 'Performing Science', in A. Herle and S. Rouse (eds.), *Cambridge and the Torres Strait: Centenary essays on the 1898 anthropological expedition*, Cambridge: Cambridge University Press, 1998.

Edwards, Hugh, *Port of Pearls: A history of Broome*, Adelaide: Rigby, 1983.

Eildermann, Heinrich, *Urkommunismus und Urreligion*, Berlin: A. Seehof & Co., 1921.

Elder, Peter, 'The Winds of Change: E.W.P. Chinnery (1887–1972) and F.G.G. Rose (1915–1991) in the Australian territories', *South Pacific. Journal of Philosophy and Culture*, 5 (2001), 50–93.

Elkin, A.P. *The Australian Aborigines: How to understand them*, Sydney: Angus & Robertson, 1938.

Elkin, A.P. '*The Wind of Change*: A review article', *Oceania*, 40, 2 (December 1969) 148–152.

'Emil and Hannah Witton', National Museum of Australia, 'Collaborating for Indigenous Rights', http://indigenousrights.net.au/person.asp?pID=1044, accessed 25 May 2012.

Engels, Friedrich, *The Origin of the Family, Private Property and the State*, Middlesex: Penguin, 1972.

Eriksen, T. Hylland and F. Sivert Nielsen, *A History of Anthropology*, London; Ann Arbor, MI: Pluto Press, 2001.

Ferrier, Carole, *Jean Devanny: Romantic revolutionary*, Melbourne: MUP, 1999.

Flinders, Matthew, *A Voyage to Terra Australis*, volume II, London: G. and W. Nicol, 1814.

Fortes, Meyer, *Kinship and the Social Order: The legacy of Lewis Henry Morgan*, Chicago: Aldine Publishing, 1969.

Fortes, Meyer, 'Review of *The Classification of Kin, Age Structure and Marriage amongst the Groote Eylandt Aborigines: A study in method and a theory of Australian kinship*, by F.G.G. Rose', *British Journal of Sociology* 13, 1 (1962), 81–82.

Foucault, Michel, *The Order of Things: An archaeology of the human sciences*, London and New York: Routledge, 2000.

Fox, Robin, *Kinship and Marriage: An anthropological perspective*, Harmondsworth: Penguin, 1967.

Frazer, James, *The Golden Bough: A study in magic and religion*, 2 vols., London: Macmillan, 1890.

Ganter, Regina, Julia Martinez and Gary Lee, *Mixed Relations: Asian/Aboriginal contact in north Australia*, Perth: University of Western Australia Press, 2006.

Bibliography

Gellately, Robert, *Lenin, Stalin and Hitler: The age of social catastrophe*, New York: Vintage, 2008.

Geraghty, Tony, *Beyond the Frontline: The untold exploits of Britain's most daring Cold War spy mission*, London: HarperCollins, 1996.

Gibson, Steve, *The Last Mission Behind the Iron Curtain*, Phoenix Mill: Sutton, 1997.

Gieseke, Jens, *The GDR State Security: Shield and sword of the party*, 2nd ed. Berlin: Bundeszentrale für politische Bildung, 2006.

Goodale, Jane C., 'Review of *Classification of Kin*', *American Anthropologist*, 64, 3 (1962), 663–67.

Gray, Geoffrey, *A Cautious Silence: The politics of Australian anthropology*, Canberra: Aboriginal Studies Press, 2007.

Gray, Geoffrey (ed.), *Before It's Too Late: Anthropological reflections, 1950–1970*, Sydney: Oceania Monographs, 2001.

Gray, Stephen, *The Protectors: A journey through whitefella past*, Sydney: Allen & Unwin, 2011.

Grieder, Peter, *The East German Leadership: Conflict and crisis 1946–73*, Manchester: Manchester University Press, 1999.

Grimshaw, Anna, *The Ethnographer's Eye: Ways of seeing in anthropology*, Cambridge: Cambridge University Press, 2001.

Guhr, Günter, 'Frederick G.G. Rose (1915–1991) zum Gedenken. Biographisches und Werk', *Ethnographisch-Archäologische Zeitschrift*, 32 (1991), 811–19.

Guhr, Günter, 'Rezension, *Classification of Kin*', *Ethnographisch-Archäologische Zeitschrift*, 6 (1965), 91.

Hann, Chris, Mihály Sárkány and Peter Skalníky (eds.), *Studying Peoples in the People's Democracies: Socialist era anthropology in east-central Europe*, Münster: Lit-Verlag, 2005.

Harney, Bill, *North of 23: Ramblings in northern Australia*, Sydney: Australasian Publishing, 1946.

Hewett, Dorothy, *Wild Card: An autobiography 1923–1958*, Melbourne: McPhee Gribble, 1990.

Hiatt, L.R. 'Maidens, Males and Marx: Some contrasts in the work of Frederick Rose and Claude Meillassoux', *Oceania* 56, 1 (September 1985), 34–36.

Hiatt, Les, *Arguments about Aborigines: Australia and the evolution of social anthropology*, Cambridge: Cambridge University Press, 1996.

Hobsbawm, Eric, *Interesting Times: A twentieth-century life*, London: Allen Lane, 2002.

Hocking, Jenny, *Frank Hardy: Politics, literature, life*, Melbourne: Lothian Books, 2005.

Hocking, *Gough Whitlam. His Time: The biography volume II*, Melbourne: Miegunyah Press, 2012.

Hogbin, Ian, 'Radcliffe-Brown, Alfred Reginald (1881–1955)', *Australian Dictionary of Biography*, National Centre of Biography, Australian National University, http://adb. anu.edu.au/biography/radcliffe-brown-alfred-reginald-8146/text14233, accessed 1 November 2012.

Holt, Stephen, *A Short History of Manning Clark*, Sydney: Allen & Unwin, 1999.

Horner, Jack, *Seeking Racial Justice: An insider's memoir of the movement for Aboriginal advancement 1938–1978*, Canberra: Aboriginal Studies Press, 2004.

Horner, David, *The Spy Catchers. Vol. 1: The official history of ASIO, 1949–1963*, Sydney: Allen & Unwin, 2014.

Hruby, Peter, *Dangerous Dreamers: The Australian anti-democratic left and Czechoslovak agents*, New York, Bloomington: iUniverse, Inc., 2010.

Hunt, Tristram, *The Frock-Coated Communist: The revolutionary life of Friedrich Engels*, London: Penguin, 2009.

Huxley, Julian, A.C. Haddon, and A.M. Saunders, *We Europeans: A survey of racial problems*, London: J. Cape, 1935.

'Interviews with German Anthropologists. Vincenz Kokot, Short Portrait: Sigrid Westphal-Hellbusch', http://www.germananthropology.com/short-portrait/sigrid-westphal-hellbusch/290, accessed 2 January 2013.

Jarausch, Konrad, *The Rush to German Unity*, Oxford, New York: Oxford University Press, 1994.

Johnson, Ian, *A Mosque in Munich: Nazis, the CIA, and the rise of the muslim brotherhood in the west*, New York: Houghton, Mifflin, Harcourt, 2010.

Jones, G.A., 'Constructing an Air Base at Groote', *Shell House Journal*, 10, 2 (February 1939), 10–13.

Jones, Philip, Obituary for Norman B. Tindale, at http://www.anu.edu.au/linguistics/nash/aust/nbt/obituary.html, accessed 24 July 2013.

Josselin de Jong, P. de, 'A new approach to kinship studies', *Bijdragen tot de Taal-, Land- en Volkenkunde*, 118, 1 (1962), 42–67.

Joyce, John, 'The Story of the RAAF Meteorological Service', http://www.austehc.unimelb.edu.au/fam/0317.html, accessed 12 March 2012.

Kabo, Vladimir, 'Letters from Afar', http://aboriginals.narod.ru/LettersfromAfar.htm, accessed 5 December 2013.

Kabo, Vladimir, *The Road to Australia: Memoirs*, Canberra, Aboriginal Studies Press, 1998.

Kaschuba, Wolfgang and Leonore Scholze-Irrlitz, 'Von der Ethnographie zur europäischen Ethnologie', in Heinz-Elmar Tenorth (ed.), *Geschichte der Universität Unter den Linden 1810–2010. Selbstbehauptung einer Vision*, Berlin: Akademie-Verlag, 2010, 423–38.

Kisch, Egon Erwin, *Australian Landfall*, transl. John Fischer et al., London: Secker, 1937.

Klepner, Frank, *Yosl Bergner: Art as a meeting of cultures*, Melbourne: Macmillan, 2004.

König, Viola (ed.), *Ethnologisches Museum Berlin*, Munich: Prestel, 2003.

Lake, Marilyn, *Faith: Faith Bandler, gentle activist*, Sydney: Allen & Unwin, 2002.

Langham, Ian, *The Building of British Social Anthropology: W.H.R. Rivers and his Cambridge disciples in the development of kinship studies, 1898–1931*, Dordrecht: Holland/Boston: USA; London, England: D. Reidel Publishing Company, 1981.

Bibliography

Leach, E.R., 'Concerning Trobriand Clans and the Kinship Category "Tabu"', in Jack Goody (ed.), *The Developmental Cycle in Domestic Groups*, Cambridge: Cambridge University Press, 1966.

Lenihan, Denis, 'Was Ian Milner a Spy? A Review of the Evidence', *Kotare* (2008), 1–18, *http://ojs.victoria.ac.nz/kotare/article/view/785/594*, accessed 29 November 2013.

Leonhard, Wolfgang, *Die Revolution entlässt ihre Kinder*, Cologne: Kiepenheuer und Witsch, 1981.

Leontiev, L.A., 'Political Economy in the Soviet Union', *Communist Review*, (December 1944/January 1945), 381–82, 410–12.

Lillywhite, J.W., 'My Early Years in the Bureau of Meteorology', 177. http://www.austehc.unimelb.edu.au/fam/0169.html, accessed 23 July 2013.

Lindquist, Sven, *Terra Nullius: A journey through No One's Land*, London: Granta Books, 2007.

Lockwood, Rupert, 'Wilfred Burchett's Retreat from Moscow', in Radical Sydney/Radical History blog, located at http://radicalsydney.blogspot.com.au/p/wilred-burchetts-tretreat-from-moscow.html, accessed 2 August 2013.

Loest, Robert and Susanne Oehlschläger, 'Die "Münchener Bibliothek". Neuerschliessung einer historischen Sammlung durch das Bundesinstitut für Ostwissenschaftliche und International Studien (BIOst) in Köln', *Bibliotheksdienst*, 31, 3 (1997), 419–25.

Lowe, David, *Australian Between Empires: The life of Percy Spender*, London: Pickering and Chatto, 2010.

Lowie, Robert H., 'Richard Thurnwald 1869–1954. Obituary', *American Anthropologist*, 56 (October 1954), 863–67.

Macintyre, Stuart, *A Concise History of Australia*, 3rd ed., Cambridge: Cambridge University Press, 2009.

Maddock, Ken, 'Frederick Rose 1915–1991. An appreciation', *Oceania*, 62 (1991), 66–69.

Mählert, Ulrich, *Kleine Geschichte der DDR*, Munich: Beck, 1998.

Malinowski, Bronisław, *Argonauts of the Western Pacific: An account of native enterprise and adventure in the archipelagoes of Melanesian New Guinea*, London: Routledge, 1922.

Malinowski, Bronisław, *The Family Amongst the Australian Aborigines: A sociological study*, London: University of London Press, 1913.

Malinowski, Bronisław, 'Must Kinship Studies be Dehumanised by Mock Algebra?', *Man*, 30 (1930), 256–57.

Manne, Robert, *The Petrov Affair*, rev. ed. Melbourne: Text, 2004.

Marcus, Julie, *The Indomitable Miss Pink: A life in anthropology*, Sydney: UNSW Press, 2001.

Martínez, Julia, 'The End of Indenture? Asian Workers in the Australian Pearling Industry, 1901–1972', *International Labour and Working Class History*, 67 (Spring 2005), 125–47.

Marx, Karl and Friedrich Engels, *Marx/Engels Collected Works*, London: Lawrence and Wishart, 1975–2004.

Matthews, Brian, *Manning Clark: A life*, Sydney: Allen & Unwin, 2008.

McClellan, Josie, *Love in the Time of Communism: Intimacy and sexuality in the GDR*, Cambridge: Cambridge University Press, 2011.

McGinness, Joe, *Son of Alyandabu: My fight for Aboriginal rights*, Brisbane: University of Queensland Press, 1991.

McKenna, Mark, *An Eye for Eternity: The life of Manning Clark*, 2011, Melbourne: The Miegunyah Press, 2011.

McKnight, David, *Australia's Spies and Their Secrets*, Sydney: Allen & Unwin, 1994.

David McKnight, D.C. 1998, 'The Moscow-Canberra Cables: How Soviet intelligence obtained British secrets through the back door', *Intelligence and National Security*, 13, 2 (1998), 159–170.

McMillan, Andrew, *An Intruder's Guide to East Arnhem Land*, Sydney: Duffy & Snellgrove, 2001.

McNaughton, Jenny and Tony Stephens, 'Crusader for politics of good. Obituary for Keith Dowding, 1911–2008', *Sydney Morning Herald*, 7 October 2008, http://www.smh.com.au/news/obituaries/crusader-for-politics-of-good/2008/10/06/1223145260054.html, accessed 10 December 2012.

Meggitt, Mervyn J., *Desert People: A study of the Walbiri Aborigines of central Australia*. Chicago: University of Chicago Press, 1965.

Megitt, Mervyn, 'Review of *The Wind of Change in Central Australia*', *Bijdragen tot de Taal-, Land- en Volkenkunde*, 123, 1 (1967), 161.

Mendes, Philip, 'The Australian Jewish Left and Indigenous Rights', *Australian Jewish Historical Society Journal*, 20, 3 (November 2011), 430–43.

Middleton, Hannah, *But Now We Want the Land Back: A history of the Australian Aboriginal people*, Sydney: New Age Publishers, 1977.

Mohrmann, Ute and Walter Rusch, 'Vier Jahrzehnte Ethnographie an der Humboldt-Universität zu Berlin', *Beiträge zur Geschichte der Humboldt-Universität zu Berlin. Nr. 28. Geschichte der Völkerkunde und Volkskunde an der Berliner Universität*, Berlin: Humboldt-Universität, 1991, 61–72.

Monteath, Peter, 'The Anthropologist as Cold Warrior: The interesting times of Frederick Rose', in Evan Smith (ed.), *Europe's Expansions and Contractions*, Adelaide: Australian Humanities Press, 2010, 259–280.

Monteath, Peter, 'Die DDR und Australien', *Zeitschrift für Geschichtswissenschaft*, 60, 2 (2012), 146–68.

Monteath, Peter, 'The German Democratic Republic and Australia', *Debatte: Journal of Contemporary Central and Eastern Europe*, 16, 2 (August 2008), 213–36.

Morgan, Lewis Henry, *Ancient Society*, New York: Henry Holt and Co., 1877.

Morgan, Lewis Henry, 'Preface', in Lorimer Fison and A.W. Howitt, *Kamilaroi and Kurnai*, Melbourne: Angus and Robertson, 1880.

Morphy, Howard, 'Thomson, Donald Finlay Fergusson (1901–1970)', *Australian Dictionary of Biography*, National Centre of Biography, Australian National University, http://adb.anu.edu.au/biography/thomson-donald-finlay-fergusson-11851/text21213, accessed 1 November 2012.

Mountford, Charles Pearcy (ed.), *Records of the American-Australian Scientific Expedition to Arnhem Land. Volume 1: Art, myth and symbolism*, Melbourne: Melbourne University Press, 1956.

Mulvaney, Derek John, *Digging Up a Past*, Sydney: UNSW Press, 2011.

Mulvaney, Derek John, 'Reflections', *Antiquity*, 80, 308 (June 2006), 425–34.

Mulvaney, Derek John, and John Henry Calaby, *'So Much That is New': Baldwin Spencer 1860–1929, a biography*, Melbourne: Melbourne University Press, 1985.

Munt, Valerie, 'Australian Anthropology, Ideology and Political Repression: The Cold War experience of Frederick G.G. Rose', *Anthropological Forum*, 21, 2 (July 2011), 109–29.

Munt, Valerie, ' "Back to the USSR": Frederick Rose, the "Stalin Criticism" and anthropological theory during the Cold War', in Evan Smith (ed.), *Europe's Expansions and Contractions*, Adelaide: Australian Humanities Press, 2010, 281–300.

National Museum of Australia (NMA), 'The 1948 expedition. Barks, Birds & Billabongs: Exploring the legacy of the 1948 American-Australian scientific expedition to Arnhem Land. 16–20 November 2009', http://www.nma.gov.au/history/research/conferences_and_seminars/barks_birds_billabongs/the_1948_expedition, accessed 5 November 2012.

National Museum of Australia, 'Brian Manning', http://www.indigenousrights.net.au/person.asp?pID=1028, accessed 28 November 2011.

National Museum of Australia, 'Collaborating for Indigenous Rights. The hand back', http://indigenousrights.net.au/subsection.asp?ssID=37, accessed 23 May 2012.

Needham, Rodney, 'Review of *Classification of Kin*', *Nature*, 191, (1 July 1961), 6–7.

Payne, Joseph, 'The "Spy Who Never Was" Comes Back', *Australian*, 13 April 1965.

Peet, John, *The Long Engagement: Memoirs of a Cold War legend*, London: Fourth Estate, 1989.

Pescott, Roger, 'Why Kerr never told Whitlam of his intention to dismiss him', *Sydney Morning Herald*, 6 September 2012, http://www.smh.com.au/opinion/politics/why-kerr-never-told-whitlam-of-his-intention-to-dismiss-him-20120905-25env.html#ixzz2TntWGFzT, accessed 12 September 2013.

Peterson, Nicolas, *Donald Thomson in Arnhem Land*, compiled and introduced by Nicolas Peterson, Melbourne: Currey O'Neil, 1983.

Philipson, Ilene, *Ethel Rosenberg: Beyond the myths*, New Brunswick: Rutgers University Press, 1993.

Pilling, Arnold and C.W.M. Hart, *The Tiwi of North Australia*, New York: Holt, Rinehard and Winston, 1960.

Puddington, Arch, *Broadcasting Freedom: The Cold War triumph of Radio Free Europe and Radio Liberty*, Lexington: University Press of Kentucky, 2000.

Pybus, Cassandra, *The Devil and James McAuley*, Brisbane: University of Queensland Press, 1999.

Radcliffe-Brown, A.R., 'The Social Organization of Australian Tribes', *Oceania*, 1 (1931), 206–246.

Resolutions of the 14th Congress of the Australian Communist Party, Sydney: Central Committee of the Australian Communist Party, 1945.

Rivers, W.H.R., 'A Genealogical Method of Collecting Social and Vital Statistics', *Journal of the Anthropological Institute of Great Britain and Ireland*, 30 (1900), 74–82.

Royal Anthropological Institute of Great Britain and Ireland; British Association for the Advancement of Science *Notes and Queries on Anthropology*, fifth edition, London: The Royal Anthropological Institute, 1929 (1874).

Rowse, Tim, *Nugget Coombs: A reforming life*, Cambridge: Cambridge University Press, 2002.

Alan Rusbridger, 'Hedi Stadlen: From political activism in Colombo to new insights on Beethoven', *Guardian*, 29 January 2004, http://www.guardian.co.uk/news/2004/jan/29/guardianobituaries.alanrusbridger , accessed 25 September 2013.

Sekuless, Peter, *Jessie Street: A rewarding but unrewarded life*, Brisbane: University of Queensland Press, 1978.

Sheridan, Tom, *Australia's Own Cold War: The waterfront under Menzies*, Melbourne: Melbourne University Press, 2006.

Simkin, John, 'Kenneth Sinclair Loutit', http://www.spartacus.schoolnet.co.uk/TUloutit.htm, accessed 8 September 2010.

Simkin, John, 'Margot Heinemann', http://www. schoolnet.co.uk/SPheinemann.htm, accessed 6 September 2010.

Slezkine, Yuri, 'The Fall of Soviet Ethnography', *Current Anthropology*, 32, 4 (August to Oct. 1991), 476–84.

Slobodin, Richard, *W. H .R. Rivers: Pioneer anthropologist and psychiatrist of the 'Ghost Road'*, Stroud: Sutton Publishing, 1997.

Smith, Bernard, *Noel Counihan: Artist and revolutionary*, Melbourne: Oxford University Press, 1993.

Sosin, Gene, *Sparks of Liberty: An insider's memoir of Radio Liberty*, Pennsylvania: Pennsylvania State University Press, 1999.

Stephens, Tony, 'Escapee from Nazis fought for Aborigines', Obituary for Hans Bandler, http://www.smh.com.au/national/obituaries/escapee-from-nazis-fought-for-aborigines-20090913-fmad.html, accessed 30 November 2012.

Stocking Jr., George, *The Ethnographer's Magic and Other Essays in the History of Anthropology*, Wisconsin: University of Wisconsin Press, 1992.

Stolarik, M. Mark, *The Prague Spring and the Warsaw Pact Invasion of Czechoslovakia 1968: Forty years later*, Mundelein ILL: Bolchazi-Carducci, 2010.

Strehlow, Carl, *Die Aranda- und Loritja-Stämme in Zentral-Australien*, Frankfurt a.M.: Städtisches Völker-Museum, Frankfurt, 1907–20.

Summers, Anne and Elena Govor, 'Survived Stalin's Gulag to shed more light on Australia's indigenous people. Vladimir Rafailovich Kabo, Ethnographer 7.2.1925 – 4.6.2009', *Sydney Morning Herald*, 26 June 2009.

Taffe, Sue, *Black and White Together: The Federal Council for the Advancement of Aborigines and Torres Strait Islander 1958–1973*, St Lucia QLD: UQP, 2005.

Thomas, Martin, *The Many Worlds of R.H. Mathews: In search of an Australian anthropologist*, Sydney: Allen and Unwin, 2011.

Thomas, Martin and Margo Neale (eds.), *Exploring the legacy of the 1948 Arnhem Land expedition*, Acton, A.C.T. ANU E Press, 2011, http://epress.anu.edu.au?p=116081

Throssell, Ric (ed.), *Wild Weeds and Wind Flowers: The life and letters of Katharine Susannah Prichard*, London: Angus & Robertson, 1975.

Townsend, Terry, *The Aboriginal Struggle and the Left*, Sydney: Resistance Books, 2008.

Trautmann, Thomas, *Lewis Henry Morgan and the Invention of Kinship*, Lincoln NE: University of Nebraska Press, 2008 (1987).

Tuchel, Johannes (ed.), *Gedenkstätte Stille Helden: Ausstellungskatalog*, Berlin: Allprint Media, 2008.

Turner, David H., *Tradition and transformation: A study of the Groote Eylandt area Aborigines of northern Australia*, Canberra: Australian Institute of Aboriginal Studies, 1974.

Wax, Dustin (ed.), *Anthropology at the Dawn of the Cold War: The influence of foundations, McCarthyism, and the CIA*, London; Ann Arbor, MI: Pluto Press, 2008.

Weiner, Amir, 'Nature and Nurture in a Socialist Utopia: Delineating the Soviet socio-ethnic body in the age of socialism', in David L. Hoffman (ed.), *Stalinism*, Oxford: Blackwell, 2003, 243–74.

Wer war wer in der DDR, online databank, http://www.bundesstiftung-aufarbeitung.de/wer-war-wer-in-der-ddr-%2363%3B-1424.html?ID=3688

Whitlam, Nicholas and John Stubbs, *Nest of Traitors: The Petrov affair*, Brisbane: Jacaranda, 1974.

Wilcken, Patrick, *Claude Lévi-Strauss, the poet in the laboratory*, New York: Penguin, 2010.

Williams, Peter G., 'BRIXMIS in the 1980s: The Cold War's "Great Game". Memories of liaising with the Soviet army in East Germany', Canberra, 2006. http://archive.org/details/BrixmisInThe1980sTheColdWarsGreatGame, accessed 10 October 2012.

Wise, Tigger, 'Elkin, Adolphus Peter (1891–1979)', *Australian Dictionary of Biography*, National Centre of Biography, Australian National University, http://adb.anu.edu.au/biography/elkin-adolphus-peter-10109/text17845, accessed 1 November 2012.

Wise, Tigger, *The Self-Made Anthropologist: A life of A.P. Elkin*, Sydney: George Allen & Unwin, 1985.

Wiseman, Judith, *Thomson Time: Arnhem Land in the 1930s. A photographic essay*, Melbourne: Museum of Victoria, 1996.

Worsley, Peter, *An Academic Skating on Thin Ice*, New York: Berghahn, 2008.

Worsley, Peter M., 'The Changing Social Structure of the Wanindiljaugwa', Doctoral Dissertation, ANU, June 1954.

Worsley, Peter et al., *Introducing Sociology*, Harmondsworth: Penguin, 1970.

Worsley, Peter, 'The Practice of Politics and the Study of Australian Kinship', in Christine Ward Gailey (ed.), *Dialectical Anthropology: Essays in Honor of Stanley Diamond. Volume 2. The Politics of Culture and Creativity*, Gainesville: University of Florida Press, 1992, 25–66.

Wright, Tom, *A New Deal for Aborigines*, Sydney: Labour Council of NSW, 1939.

Writer, Larry, *Razor: A true story of slashers, gangsters, prostitutes and sly grog*, Sydney: Macmillan, 2001.

Zimmerman, Andrew, *Anthropology and Anti-Humanism in Imperial Germany*, Chicago and London: University of Chicago Press, 2001.

Index

Index

Wakefield Press is an independent publishing and
distribution company based in Adelaide, South Australia.
We love good stories and publish beautiful books.
To see our full range of books, please visit our website at
www.wakefieldpress.com.au
where all titles are available for purchase.

Find us!

Twitter: www.twitter.com/wakefieldpress
Facebook: www.facebook.com/wakefield.press
Instagram: instagram.com/wakefieldpress

www.ingramcontent.com/pod-product-compliance
Lightning Source LLC
Chambersburg PA
CBHW060134280326
41932CB00012B/1512